ASP.NET jQuery Cookbook
Second Edition

Over 60 recipes for writing client script in ASP.NET 4.6 applications using jQuery

Sonal Aneel Allana

[PACKT]
PUBLISHING

BIRMINGHAM - MUMBAI

ASP.NET jQuery Cookbook
Second Edition

First published: April 2011

Second edition: February 2016

Production reference: 1220216

Published by Packt Publishing Ltd.
Livery Place
35 Livery Street
Birmingham B3 2PB, UK.

ISBN 978-1-78217-311-3

www.packtpub.com

Credits

Author
Sonal Aneel Allana

Reviewer
Ayad Boudiab

Commissioning Editor
Dipika Gaonkar

Acquisition Editor
Divya Poojari

Content Development Editor
Priyanka Mehta

Technical Editors
Dhiraj Chandanshive

Devesh Chugh

Copy Editor
Rashmi Sawant

Project Coordinator
Izzat Contractor

Proofreader
Safis Editing

Indexer
Priya Sane

Graphics
Jason Monteiro

Production Coordinator
Shantanu N. Zagade

Cover Work
Shantanu N. Zagade

About the Author

Sonal Aneel Allana works as a sessional lecturer at the Singapore campus of the *University of Newcastle* and the *University of Hertfordshire*. Her teaching areas include degree level courses in e-learning, intelligent systems, robotics, operating systems, and programming in C/C++, .NET, Java, and Android. She is keenly interested in JavaScript frameworks, such as Bootstrap, Node.js, and AngularJS. She has worked in the IT industry for over 10 years in various positions, such as an application developer, project leader, and trainer. She holds a master's degree in computing from the *National University of Singapore* and a bachelor's degree in computer engineering from the *University of Mumbai*. She is certified in security technology and computational neuroscience. She is also the author of the first edition of *ASP.NET jQuery Cookbook*.

I have enjoyed the journey of writing this book. The process of discovering the magic of jQuery has been enlightening and enthralling. I would like to thank my readers for their valuable feedback that I have incorporated in this edition.

This journey would not be possible without the support of my lovely family. Heartfelt thanks to everyone, especially to my parents, my husband, Aneel, and little, Abraham.

Thanks to the excellent team at Packt and to Priyanka for keeping me going. Special thanks to my reviewer, Ayad Boudiab, for his critical analysis of the material and for providing me valuable insights.

About the Reviewer

Ayad Boudiab is a senior software engineer. He has more than 17 years of experience in application development on Windows platforms. He works across multiple technologies in the .NET stack. In addition to his corporate experience, he has more than 20 years of experience in technical training and teaching. He has taught multiple courses in colleges and online. He has most recently worked with C#, JavaScript, jQuery, ASP.NET, Knockout JS, Angular JS, Kendo UI, HTML5, and SQL Server. You can contact him at ayad.boudiab@gmail.com.

Ayad is currently a contractor for a healthcare company in Atlanta. He has reviewed many IT books and written supplements for Wiley, Pearson, nSight, Prentice Hall, among other publishers.

www.PacktPub.com

eBooks, discount offers, and more

Did you know that Packt offers eBook versions of every book published, with PDF and ePub files available? You can upgrade to the eBook version at www.PacktPub.com and as a print book customer, you are entitled to a discount on the eBook copy. Get in touch with us at customercare@packtpub.com for more details.

At www.PacktPub.com, you can also read a collection of free technical articles, sign up for a range of free newsletters and receive exclusive discounts and offers on Packt books and eBooks.

PACKT LiB™

https://www2.packtpub.com/books/subscription/packtlib

Do you need instant solutions to your IT questions? PacktLib is Packt's online digital book library. Here, you can search, access, and read Packt's entire library of books.

Why subscribe?

- ▶ Fully searchable across every book published by Packt
- ▶ Copy and paste, print, and bookmark content
- ▶ On demand and accessible via a web browser

Table of Contents

Preface   **v**

Chapter 1: Getting Started with jQuery in ASP.NET   **1**

Introduction   2

Downloading jQuery from jQuery.com   2

Understanding CDN for jQuery   5

Using NuGet Package Manager to download jQuery   8

Adding jQuery to an empty ASP.NET web project using a script block   10

Adding jQuery to an empty ASP.NET web project using ScriptManager control   17

Adding jQuery to an ASP.NET Master Page   22

Adding jQuery programmatically to a web form   27

Understanding jQuery reference in the default web application template   28

Hello World in a web project using jQuery   32

Bundling jQuery in ASP.NET MVC   34

Using CDN to load jQuery in MVC   42

Hello World in ASP.NET MVC using jQuery   43

Debugging jQuery code in Visual Studio   45

Chapter 2: Using jQuery Selectors with ASP.NET Controls   **49**

Introduction   49

Selecting a control using ID and displaying its value   54

Selecting a control using the CSS class   63

Selecting a control using HTML tag   69

Selecting a control by its attribute   83

Selecting an element by its position in the DOM   88

Enabling/disabling controls on a web form   102

Using selectors in MVC applications   110

Chapter 3: Event Handling Using jQuery — 125

Introduction	125
Responding to mouse events	128
Responding to keyboard events	133
Responding to form events	138
Using event delegation to attach events to future controls	145
Running an event only once	151
Triggering an event programmatically	158
Passing data with events and using event namespacing	167
Detaching events	172

Chapter 4: DOM Traversal and Manipulation in ASP.NET — 179

Introduction	179
Adding/removing DOM elements	180
Accessing parent and child controls	188
Accessing sibling controls	198
Refining selection using a filter	205
Adding items to controls at runtime	215

Chapter 5: Visual Effects in ASP.NET Sites — 221

Introduction	221
Animating the Menu control	223
Animating a Label control to create a digital clock	229
Animating the alt text of the AdRotator control	234
Animating images in the TreeView control	243
Creating scrolling text in a Panel control	250
Creating a vertical accordion menu using Panel controls	254
Showing/hiding the GridView control with the explode effect	259

Chapter 6: Working with Graphics in ASP.NET Sites — 269

Introduction	269
Creating a spotlight effect on images	270
Zooming images on mouseover	274
Creating an image scroller	281
Building a photo gallery using z-index property	290
Building a photo gallery using ImageMap control	296
Using images to create effects in the Menu control	304
Creating a 5 star rating control	309
Previewing image uploads in MVC	316

Chapter 7: Ajax Using jQuery — 325

Introduction	325
Setting up Ajax with ASP.NET using jQuery	327
Consuming page methods	336
Consuming Web services	349
Consuming WCF services	361
Retrieving data from a Web API	371
Making Ajax calls to a controller action	382
Making Ajax calls to a HTTP handler	391

Chapter 8: Creating and Using jQuery Plugins — 403

Introduction	403
Creating and using a simple plugin	404
Using the $ alias in the plugin	406
Calling methods on DOM elements	409
Providing default values	415
Providing method chaining	420
Adding actions to plugins	424
Using the form validation plugin	431
Downloading plugins using the NPM	447

Index — 451

Preface

jQuery is a lightweight JavaScript library that has changed the landscape of client scripting in web applications. Developed by John Resig in 2006, it has taken the Web by storm because of its cross-browser compatibility and its ability to get more done with less code. The library is supported by an active community of developers and has grown significantly over the years. Using jQuery eases many client scripting tasks, such as event handling, embedding animations, writing Ajax enabled pages, among many more, and adds to the interactive experience of the end user. Its extensible plugin architecture enables developers to build additional functionalities on top of the core library.

Learning jQuery and using it in ASP.NET applications is an indispensable skill for ASP.NET developers. This book attempts to impart this skill by exploring diverse recipes for fast and easy solutions to some of the commonly encountered problems in ASP.NET 4.6 applications.

What this book covers

Chapter 1, Getting Started with jQuery in ASP.NET, describes recipes to download and include jQuery in ASP.NET 4.6 Web and MVC applications. It discusses the CDN, NuGet Package Manager, as well as debugging the jQuery code in Visual Studio.

Chapter 2, Using jQuery Selectors with ASP.NET Controls, describes various jQuery selectors that can be used to manipulate ASP.NET controls. These selectors can select controls based on the ID, CSS class, HTML tag, attribute, or position in the document.

Chapter 3, Event Handling Using jQuery, describes recipes to handle different types of events, such as mouse, keyboard, and form events. It also explains event delegation and detaching of events.

Chapter 4, DOM Traversal and Manipulation in ASP.NET, describes techniques to traverse the document, such as accessing parent, child, or sibling elements. It also teaches manipulation strategies to add and remove elements at runtime.

Chapter 5, Visual Effects in ASP.NET Sites, discusses recipes to create different types of animation effects on ASP.NET controls, such as Panel, AdRotator, TreeView, Menu, and GridView. Effects such as enlarging, sliding, and fading are covered in this chapter.

Chapter 6, Working with Graphics in ASP.NET Sites, discusses recipes to work with images and explains effects, such as zooming, scrolling, and fading on images. Utilities such as image gallery, image preview, and 5-star rating control are also explored in this chapter.

Chapter 7, Ajax Using jQuery, explains how Ajax calls can be made to page methods, web services, WCF services, Web API, MVC controllers, and HTTP handlers.

Chapter 8, Creating and Using jQuery Plugins, demonstrates how plugins can be created and included in projects. It also describes how to use the Node Package Manager (NPM) and Bower to download and manage third-party plugins.

Chapter 9, Useful jQuery Recipes for ASP.NET Sites, summarizes the book with diverse recipes to solve common real-world problems. You can find this chapter at: `https://www.packtpub.com/sites/default/files/downloads/4836OT_Chapter_09`.

What you need for this book

To work with the examples of this book, you will need the following:

- ▶ Visual Studio 2015
- ▶ MS SQL Server 2014
- ▶ The Northwind database
- ▶ The jQuery library
- ▶ The jQuery UI library
- ▶ A web browser
- ▶ The Node Package Manager (NPM)
- ▶ Bower

Some recipes also require the use of third-party jQuery plugins, such as validation and cycle plugins.

Who this book is for

This book is for ASP.NET developers who want to use jQuery to write client scripts for cross-browser compatibility. No prior knowledge of ASP.NET or jQuery is expected, and every recipe is self-contained and explained in an easy-to-follow manner. The code samples in this book are provided in both C# and VB. Familiarity with Visual Studio and MS SQL Server is preferred, but not compulsory.

Sections

In this book, you will find several headings that appear frequently (Getting ready, How to do it..., How it works..., There's more..., and See also).

To give clear instructions on how to complete a recipe, we use these sections as follows:

Getting ready

This section tells you what to expect in the recipe, and describes how to set up any software or any preliminary settings required for the recipe.

How to do it...

This section contains the steps required to follow the recipe.

How it works...

This section usually consists of a detailed explanation of what happened in the previous section.

There's more...

This section consists of additional information about the recipe in order to make the reader more knowledgeable about the recipe.

See also

This section provides helpful links to other useful information for the recipe.

Conventions

In this book, you will find a number of text styles that distinguish between different kinds of information. Here are some examples of these styles and an explanation of their meaning.

Code words in text, database table names, folder names, filenames, file extensions, pathnames, dummy URLs, user input, and Twitter handles are shown as follows: "On the download page, there is also a map file available with the `.min.map` extension. Sometimes, when bugs appear in the production environment necessitating troubleshooting, the use of the minified file for debugging can be difficult."

A block of code is set as follows:

```
Sub Application_Start(ByVal sender As Object, ByVal e As EventArgs)
   ScriptManager.ScriptResourceMapping.AddDefinition("jquery", New
ScriptResourceDefinition() With {
   .Path = "~/Scripts/jquery-2.1.4.min.js",
   .DebugPath = "~/Scripts/jquery-2.1.4.js",
   .CdnPath =
"https://ajax.googleapis.com/ajax/libs/jquery/2.1.4/jquery.min.js",
   .CdnDebugPath =
"https://ajax.googleapis.com/ajax/libs/jquery/2.1.4/jquery.js",
   .CdnSupportsSecureConnection = True,
   .LoadSuccessExpression = "window.jQuery"})
End Sub
```

When we wish to draw your attention to a particular part of a code block, the relevant lines or items are set in bold:

```
<asp:ScriptManager ID="ScriptManager1" runat="server"
EnableCdn="true">
   <Scripts>
     <asp:ScriptReference Name="jquery"  />
     </Scripts>
</asp:ScriptManager>
```

Any command-line input or output is written as follows:

```
bower install jquery-validation
```

New terms and **important words** are shown in bold. Words that you see on the screen, for example, in menus or dialog boxes, appear in the text like this: "Click on the **Download jQuery** button (highlighted in the preceding screenshot) on the right-hand side of the page. This opens up the download page with the list of available files."

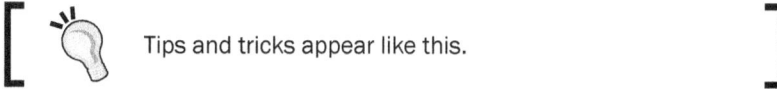

> Warnings or important notes appear in a box like this.

> Tips and tricks appear like this.

Reader feedback

Feedback from our readers is always welcome. Let us know what you think about this book—what you liked or disliked. Reader feedback is important for us as it helps us develop titles that you will really get the most out of.

To send us general feedback, simply e-mail feedback@packtpub.com, and mention the book's title in the subject of your message.

If there is a topic that you have expertise in and you are interested in either writing or contributing to a book, see our author guide at www.packtpub.com/authors.

Customer support

Now that you are the proud owner of a Packt book, we have a number of things to help you to get the most from your purchase.

Downloading the example code

You can download the example code files for this book from your account at http://www.packtpub.com. If you purchased this book elsewhere, you can visit http://www.packtpub.com/support and register to have the files e-mailed directly to you.

You can download the code files by following these steps:

1. Log in or register to our website using your e-mail address and password.
2. Hover the mouse pointer on the **SUPPORT** tab at the top.
3. Click on **Code Downloads & Errata**.
4. Enter the name of the book in the **Search** box.
5. Select the book for which you're looking to download the code files.
6. Choose from the drop-down menu where you purchased this book from.
7. Click on **Code Download**.

Once the file is downloaded, please make sure that you unzip or extract the folder using the latest version of:

- WinRAR / 7-Zip for Windows
- Zipeg / iZip / UnRarX for Mac
- 7-Zip / PeaZip for Linux

Downloading the color images of this book

We also provide you with a PDF file that has color images of the screenshots/diagrams used in this book. The color images will help you better understand the changes in the output. You can download this file from `https://www.packtpub.com/sites/default/files/downloads/ASPNET_jQuery_Cookbook_Second_Edition_ColorImages.pdf`.

Errata

Although we have taken every care to ensure the accuracy of our content, mistakes do happen. If you find a mistake in one of our books – maybe a mistake in the text or the code—we would be grateful if you could report this to us. By doing so, you can save other readers from frustration and help us improve subsequent versions of this book. If you find any errata, please report them by visiting `http://www.packtpub.com/submit-errata`, selecting your book, clicking on the **Errata Submission Form** link, and entering the details of your errata. Once your errata are verified, your submission will be accepted and the errata will be uploaded to our website or added to any list of existing errata under the Errata section of that title.

To view the previously submitted errata, go to `https://www.packtpub.com/books/content/support` and enter the name of the book in the search field. The required information will appear under the **Errata** section.

Piracy

Piracy of copyrighted material on the Internet is an ongoing problem across all media. At Packt, we take the protection of our copyright and licenses very seriously. If you come across any illegal copies of our works in any form on the Internet, please provide us with the location address or website name immediately so that we can pursue a remedy.

Please contact us at copyright@packtpub.com with a link to the suspected pirated material.

We appreciate your help in protecting our authors and our ability to bring you valuable content.

Questions

If you have a problem with any aspect of this book, you can contact us at questions@ packtpub.com, and we will do our best to address the problem.

1
Getting Started with jQuery in ASP.NET

In this chapter, we will cover the following recipes:

- ▶ Downloading jQuery from `jQuery.com`
- ▶ Understanding CDN for jQuery
- ▶ Using the NuGet Package Manager to download jQuery
- ▶ Adding jQuery to an empty ASP.NET web project using a script block
- ▶ Adding jQuery to an empty ASP.NET web project using the ScriptManager control
- ▶ Adding jQuery to an ASP.NET Master Page
- ▶ Adding jQuery programmatically to a web form
- ▶ Understanding the jQuery reference in the default Web Application template
- ▶ Hello World in a web project using jQuery
- ▶ Bundling jQuery in ASP.NET MVC
- ▶ Using a CDN to load jQuery in MVC
- ▶ Hello World in ASP.NET MVC using jQuery
- ▶ Debugging jQuery code in Visual Studio

Introduction

As a web developer, you often require to include functionalities in your websites that make writing a client script in JavaScript inevitable. Getting the client script to produce the same response for all browsers has always been a challenge. jQuery helps you overcome this difficulty. In essence, jQuery is a powerful JavaScript library that works across all browsers, such as Internet Explorer (IE), Firefox, Safari, Chrome, Opera, iOS, and Android. It takes away the agony that developers face in order to maintain their client scripts across different platforms.

jQuery is popular not only because of its cross-browser support, but also because it is packed with features that developers can plug and play. It has changed the way developers write a client script. In addition to reducing the amount of code that needs to be written, it provides features for traversing the DOM, event handling, building animations, and AJAX, among many more.

This chapter deals with acquiring the library and other supporting files. It aims to cover different aspects of including and using jQuery in ASP.NET 4.6 web application projects, such as web forms and MVCs.

> This book is based on Visual Studio 2015 and jQuery 2.1.4. The scripts have been tested in Internet Explorer 11.0.96, Mozilla Firefox 38.0.1, and Google Chrome 47.0.2526.
>
> If you are familiar with downloading and including jQuery in your ASP. NET applications, you can skip this chapter and move on to recipes for manipulating controls in *Chapter 2, Using jQuery Selectors with ASP. NET Controls*.

Downloading jQuery from jQuery.com

This recipe explains how to download jQuery on your system along with the version/build to use and the supporting files that are required.

Getting ready

Following are the steps to download jQuery:

1. Launch any web browser and enter the URL `http://www.jquery.com` to access the **jQuery** home page:

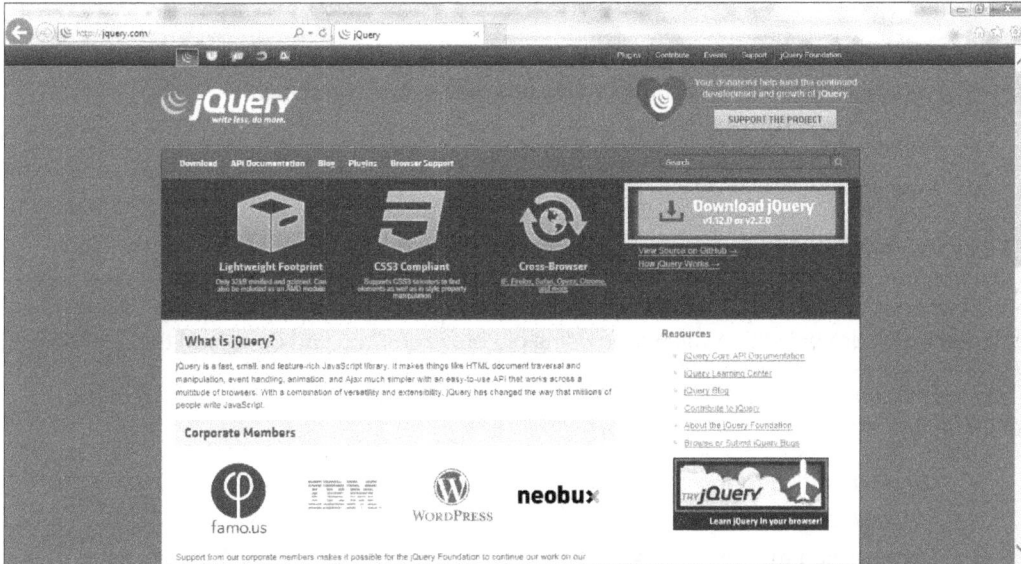

2. Click on the **Download jQuery** button (highlighted in the preceding screenshot) on the right-hand side of the page. This opens up the download page with a list of available files, as shown in the following screenshot:

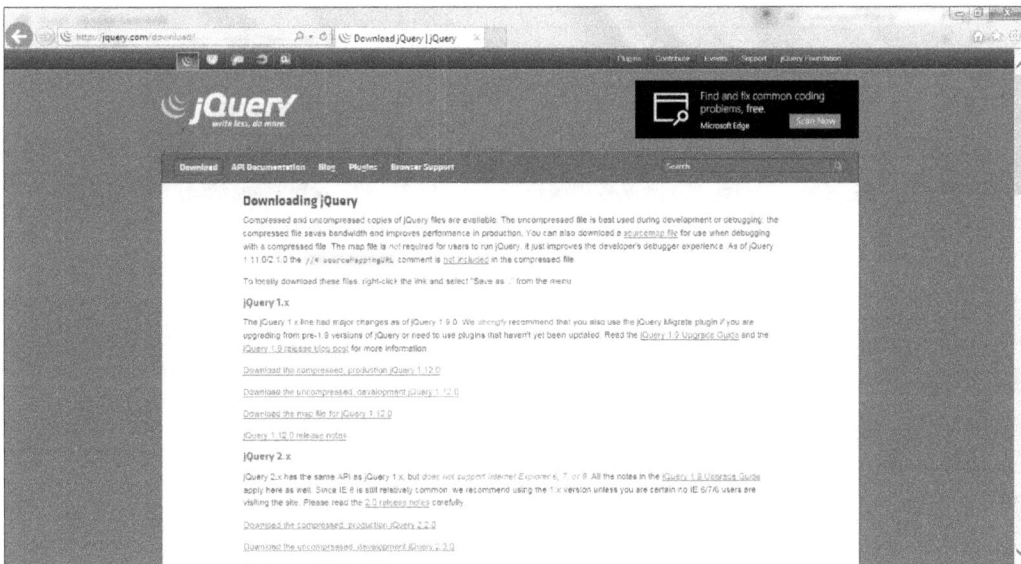

How to do it...

jQuery is available in two different major versions at the time of writing:

- ▸ Version 1.x
- ▸ Version 2.x

Though the **Application Programming Interface** (**API**) is the same for both major versions, the difference lies in the support offered for certain browsers. The 2.x line does not support old browsers, such as IE 6, 7, and 8, while the 1.x line continues with this support. So, if the end users of your application will not be using old browsers, you can download the 2.x version.

The jQuery library consists of a single JavaScript (.js) file and can be downloaded in the following formats:

- ▸ **Uncompressed format**: This is used in a development environment or when debugging the code.
- ▸ **Compressed format**: This is used in a production (that is, release) environment. It is compact and uses low bandwidth. It is commonly referred to as the **minified** version.

To download the file, simply right-click on the required version, 1.x or 2.x, and the required format: uncompressed or compressed. Save the file in a location of your choice as shown in the following screenshot:

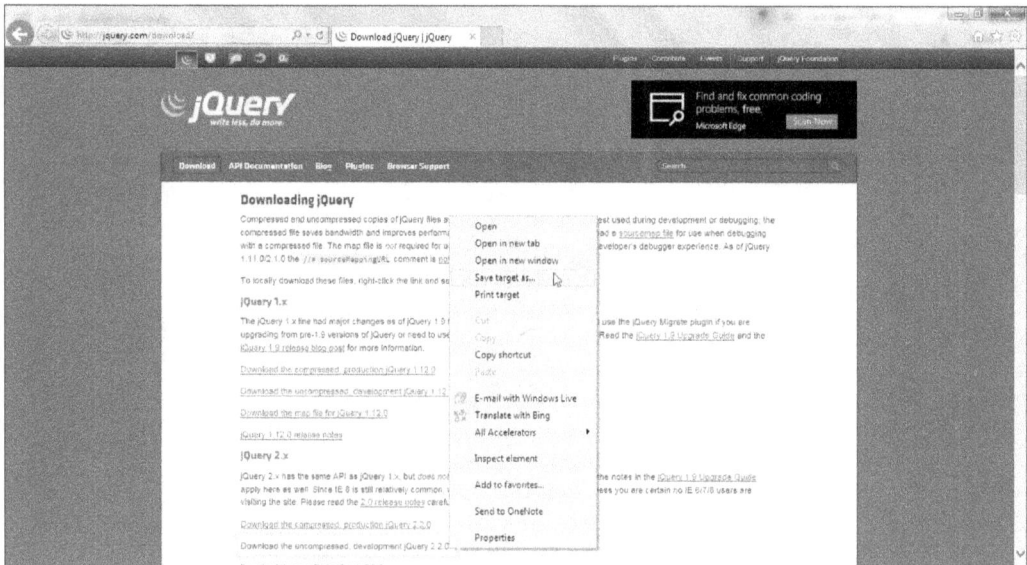

Note the following naming convention for the jQuery library:

	Uncompressed	**Compressed**
Version 1.x	jquery-1.x.x.js	jquery-1.x.x.min.js
Version 2.x	jquery-2.x.x.js	jquery-2.x.x.min.js

The compressed (minified) version is clearly distinct from the uncompressed version because of the `.min.js` extension. The minified file uses code optimization techniques, such as removing whitespaces and comments as well as reducing variable names to one character. This version is difficult to read, so the uncompressed version is preferred when debugging.

On the download page, there is also a map file available with the `.min.map` extension. Sometimes, when bugs appear in the production environment necessitating troubleshooting, the use of the minified file for debugging can be difficult. The map file simplifies this process. It maps the compressed file back to its unbuilt state so that during debugging, the experience becomes similar to using the uncompressed version.

See also...

The *Understanding CDN for jQuery* recipe.

Understanding CDN for jQuery

A **Content Delivery Network** (**CDN**) hosts content for users through large distributed systems. The advantage of using a CDN is to improve the performance. When using a CDN to retrieve the jQuery library, if the files have been downloaded earlier, they will not be re-downloaded. This can help you improve the response time.

How to do it...

The following CDNs are available for jQuery files:

- jQuery's CDN provided by MaxCDN
- The Google CDN
- The Microsoft CDN
- The CDNJS CDN
- The jsDelivr CDN

To include jQuery on a web page, the URL of the respective CDN can be used so that files can be directly served from the CDN instead of using the local copies. The following table summarizes the respective CDN URLs for jQuery files:

CDN	URL

jQuery's CDN	Version 2.x:
	
	`http://code.jquery.com/jquery-2.x.x.js`
	
	`http://code.jquery.com/jquery-2.x.x.min.js`
	
	Version 1.x:
	
	`http://code.jquery.com/jquery-1.x.x.js`
	
	`http://code.jquery.com/jquery-1.x.x.min.js`

The Google CDN	Version 2.x:
	
	`https://ajax.googleapis.com/ajax/libs/jquery/2.x.x/jquery.js`
	
	`https://ajax.googleapis.com/ajax/libs/jquery/2.x.x/jquery.min.js`
	
	Version 1.x:
	
	`https://ajax.googleapis.com/ajax/libs/jquery/1.x.x/jquery.js`
	
	`https://ajax.googleapis.com/ajax/libs/jquery/1.x.x/jquery.min.js`

The Microsoft CDN	Version 2.x:
	
	`http://ajax.aspnetcdn.com/ajax/jQuery/jquery-2.x.x.js`
	
	`http://ajax.aspnetcdn.com/ajax/jQuery/jquery-2.x.x.min.js`
	
	`http://ajax.aspnetcdn.com/ajax/jQuery/jquery-2.x.x.min.map`
	
	Version 1.x:
	
	`http://ajax.aspnetcdn.com/ajax/jQuery/jquery-1.x.x.js`
	
	`http://ajax.aspnetcdn.com/ajax/jQuery/jquery-1.x.x.min.js`
	
	`http://ajax.aspnetcdn.com/ajax/jQuery/jquery-1.x.x.min.map`

CDN	URL
The CDNJS CDN	Version 2.x:
	`https://cdnjs.cloudflare.com/ajax/libs/jquery/2.x.x/jquery.js`
	`https://cdnjs.cloudflare.com/ajax/libs/jquery/2.x.x/jquery.min.js`
	`https://cdnjs.cloudflare.com/ajax/libs/jquery/2.x.x/jquery.min.map`
	Version 1.x:
	`https://cdnjs.cloudflare.com/ajax/libs/jquery/1.x.x/jquery.js`
	`https://cdnjs.cloudflare.com/ajax/libs/jquery/1.x.x/jquery.min.js`
	`https://cdnjs.cloudflare.com/ajax/libs/jquery/1.x.x/jquery.min.map`
The jsDelivr CDN	Version 2.x:
	`https://cdn.jsdelivr.net/jquery/2.x.x/jquery.js`
	`https://cdn.jsdelivr.net/jquery/2.x.x/jquery.min.js`
	`https://cdn.jsdelivr.net/jquery/2.x.x/jquery.min.map`
	Version 1.x:
	`https://cdn.jsdelivr.net/jquery/1.x.x/jquery.js`
	`https://cdn.jsdelivr.net/jquery/1.x.x/jquery.min.js`
	`https://cdn.jsdelivr.net/jquery/1.x.x/jquery.min.map`

Using CDNs for new releases

Note that CDNs may not have the latest files when new versions of the jQuery library are launched since it usually takes a couple of days for third-parties to update their files. In the case of new releases, always check the available version before downloading them.

How it works...

CDNs consist of servers situated in data centers in strategic locations across the globe. When a client requests a resource from a CDN, the server that is geographically closest to the client processes the request. These servers are also known as **edge servers**. In addition to this, edge servers have a caching mechanism to serve various assets. All this helps you improve the client's response time.

See also

The *Using NuGet Package Manager to download jQuery* recipe

Using NuGet Package Manager to download jQuery

NuGet is a package manager available with Visual Studio. It simplifies the process of installing and upgrading packages. This recipe demonstrates the use of NuGet to download the jQuery library.

Getting ready

To launch NuGet for a particular project, go to **Tools** | **NuGet Package Manager** | **Manage NuGet Packages for Solution...** as shown in the following screenshot:

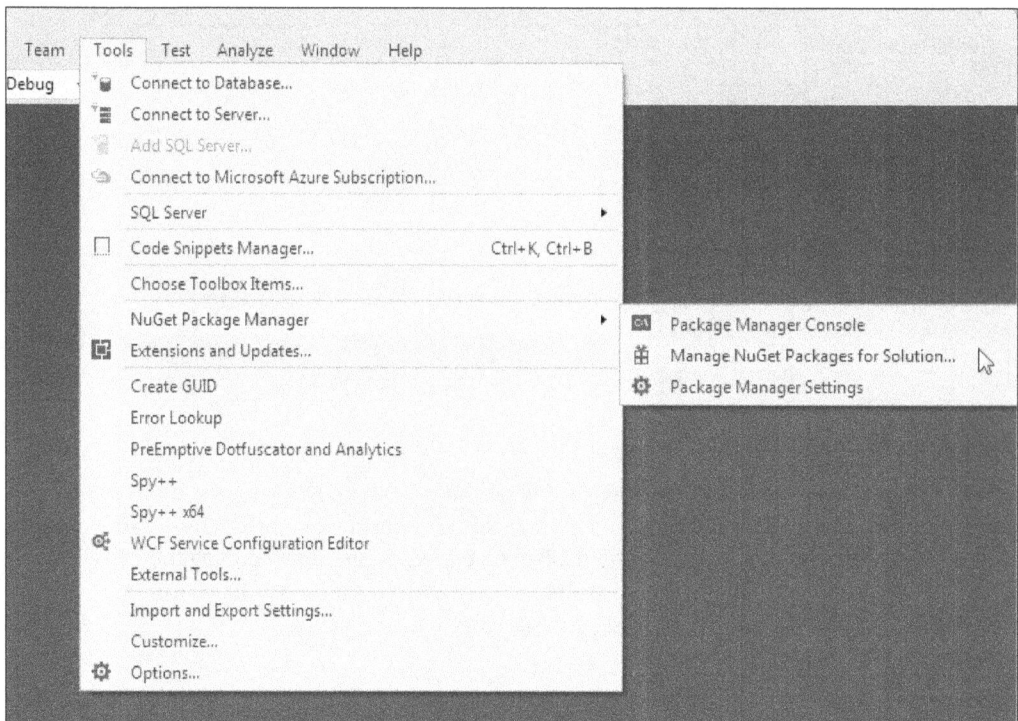

Alternatively, right-click on the project in the **Solution Explorer** tab, and select **Manage NuGet Packages**.

How to do it...

Perform the following steps to download jQuery using NuGet Manager:

1. In the **NuGet Package Manager**, as shown in the following screenshot, select the **jQuery** package from the left-hand side panel. In the right-hand side panel, select the **Version** that you would like to use in your web project from the drop-down menu. Click on the **Install** button:

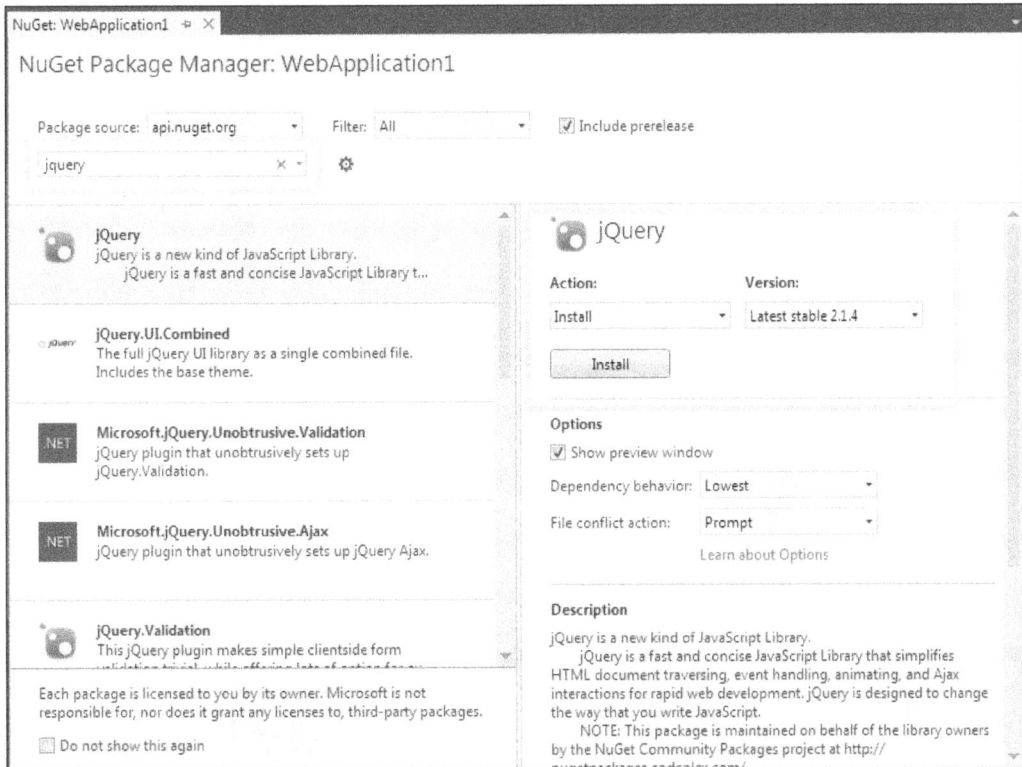

> **Searching for packages in NuGet**
>
> If jQuery is not visible in the left-hand side panel, you need to search for it by keying in `jQuery` in the search box in the top left corner of the NuGet Manager screen.

2. Click on **OK** when prompted for confirmation in order to make the required changes to the solution.

How it works...

The NuGet Package Manager downloads the selected version of jQuery in the **Scripts** folder. Any other version existing in the **Scripts** folder is deleted. The **Scripts** folder will look like the following screenshot:

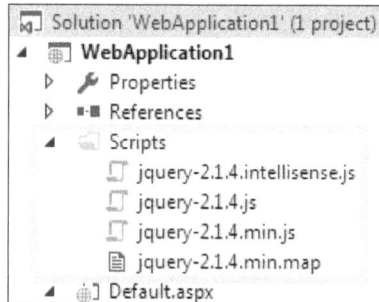

```
Solution 'WebApplication1' (1 project)
    WebApplication1
        Properties
        References
        Scripts
            jquery-2.1.4.intellisense.js
            jquery-2.1.4.js
            jquery-2.1.4.min.js
            jquery-2.1.4.min.map
        Default.aspx
```

The files downloaded by NuGet are as follows (the version numbers may change in the future):

- The Intellisense file: **jquery-2.1.4.intellisense.js**
- The debug version : **jquery-2.1.4.js**
- The release version: **jquery-2.1.4.min.js**
- The map file: **jquery-2.1.4.min.map**

See also

The *Downloading jQuery from jQuery.com* recipe

Adding jQuery to an empty ASP.NET web project using a script block

To create ASP.NET 4 .6 Web Applications, Visual Studio provides various ready templates such as Empty, Web Forms, MVC, Web API, and so on. This recipe will use the Empty template, which provides the developer with an empty project structure that consists of only the web.config file.

Getting ready

Following are the steps to create a project by using Empty template:

1. Create a new project in Visual Studio by going to **File | New | Project...**, as shown in the following screenshot:

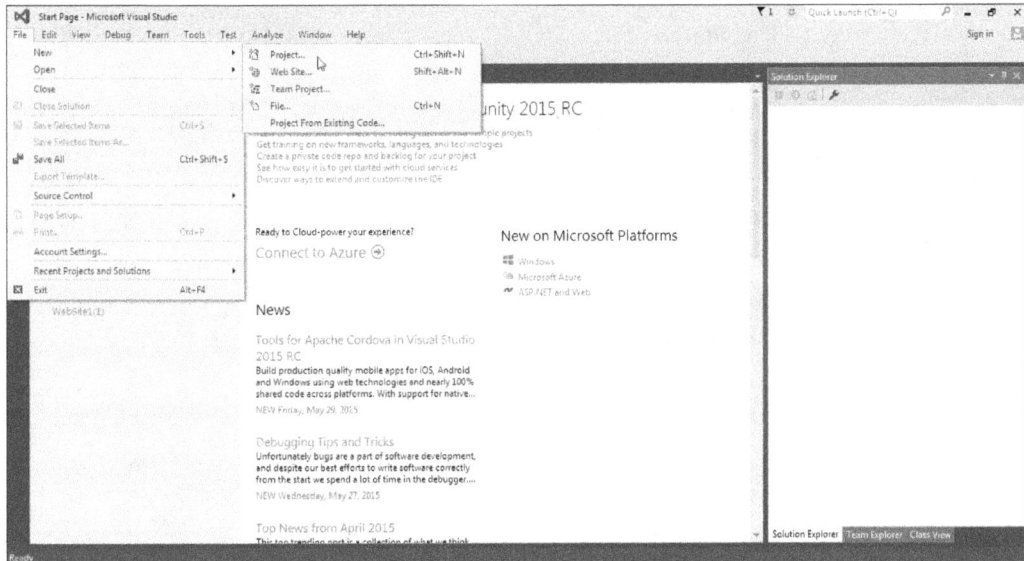

> **Website or web project?**
>
> Instead of creating a new project, you can also create a new website. Unlike a project, a website does not contain a collective project file to track individual files in the application. To create a website, go to **File | New | Web Site....** This will launch the **New Website** dialog box with the list of available templates. Select the **ASP.NET Empty WebSite** template.

2. This will launch the **New Project** dialog box, as shown in the following screenshot. From the left-hand side panel, select your desired programming language, **Visual C#** or **Visual Basic**, and then, select **ASP.NET Web Application** from the middle panel:

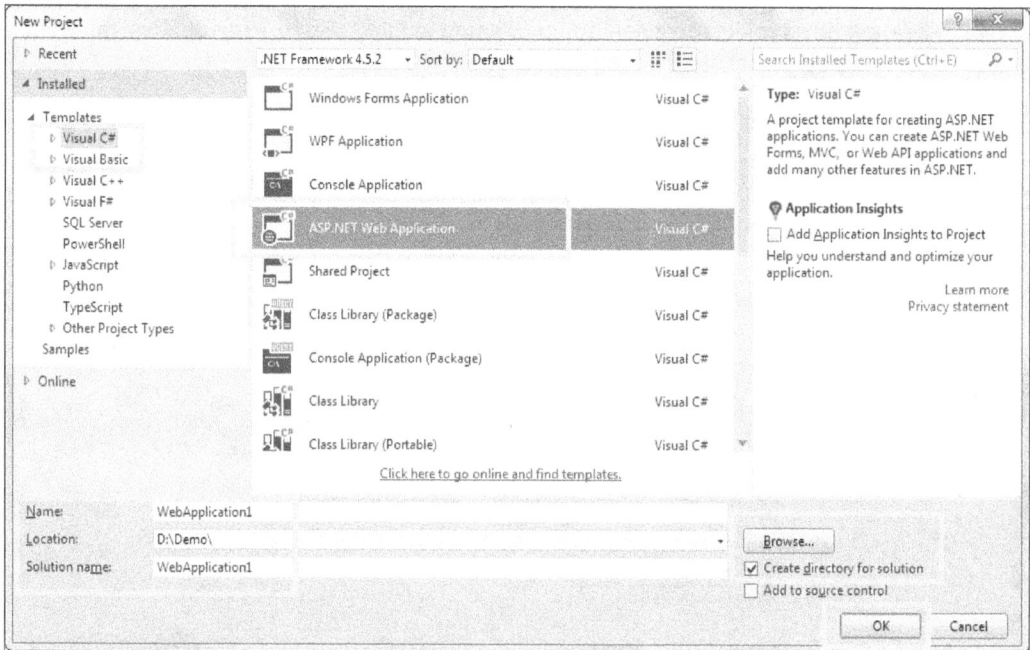

3. Enter WebApplication1 (or any suitable name) in the **Name** field. Click on the **Browse** button to go to the desired **Location** where you would like to save the application. Click on **OK**.

4. This will launch the **Select a template** dialog box, as shown in the following screenshot:

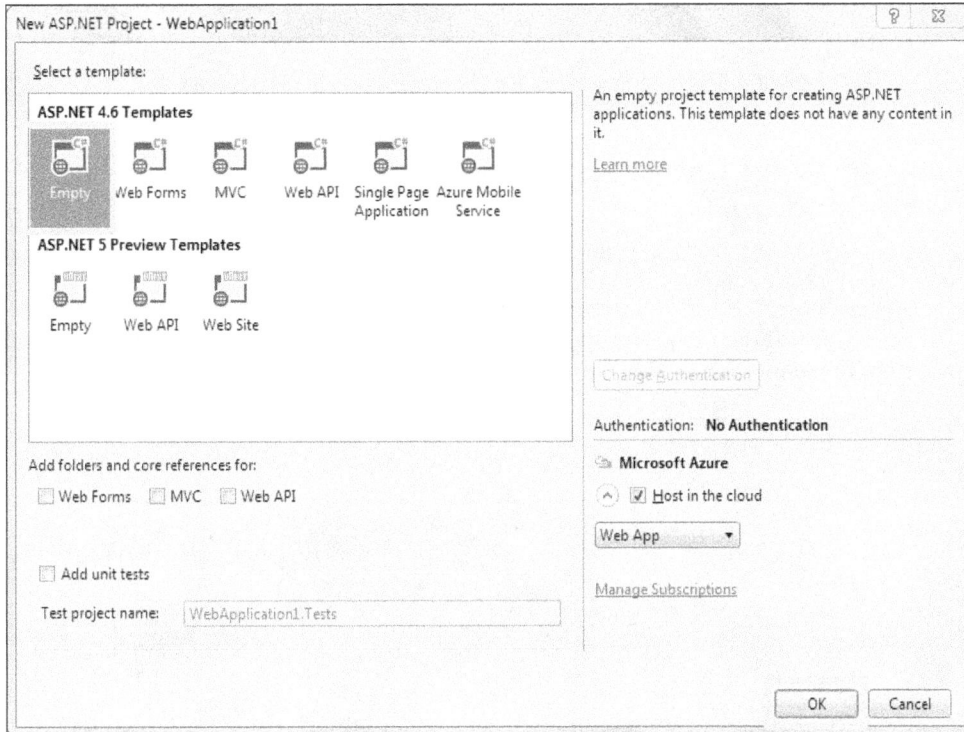

5. From **ASP.NET 4.6 Templates**, select **Empty**, and click on **OK**. Visual Studio will create an empty project in the **Solution Explorer** tab, as shown in the following screenshot:

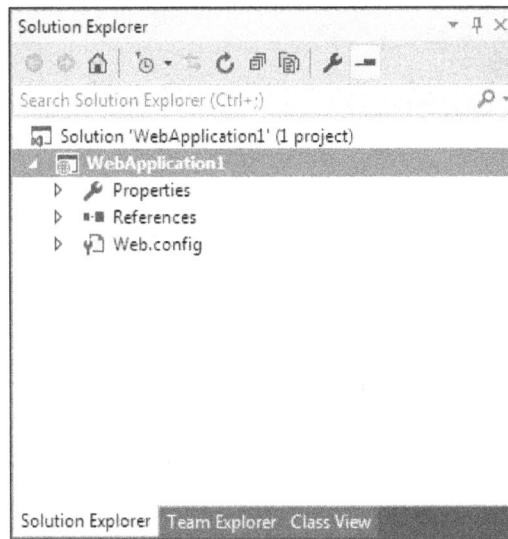

> In the remaining recipes, when asked to create a Web Application project using the Empty template, follow the steps listed in this section.

How to do it...

Following are the steps to include jQuery using script block:

1. JavaScript files are usually placed in a folder named **Scripts** in the web application. So, in the **Solution Explorer** tab, right-click on the project and go to **Add | New Folder** from the menu:

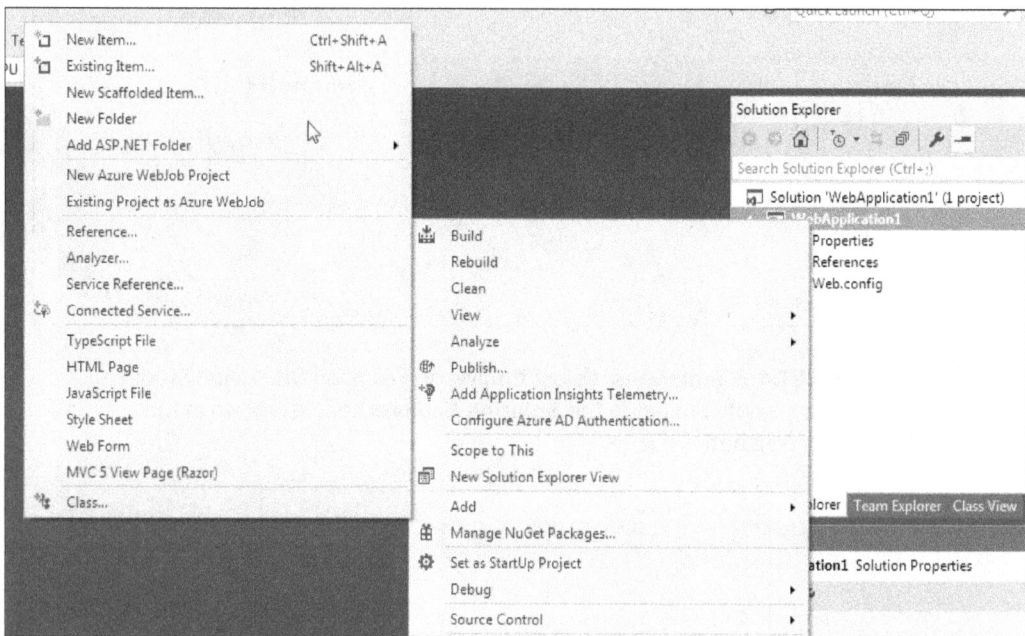

2. Rename the folder to Scripts. Now, right-click on the **Scripts** folder, and go to **Add | Existing Item...** as shown in the following screenshot:

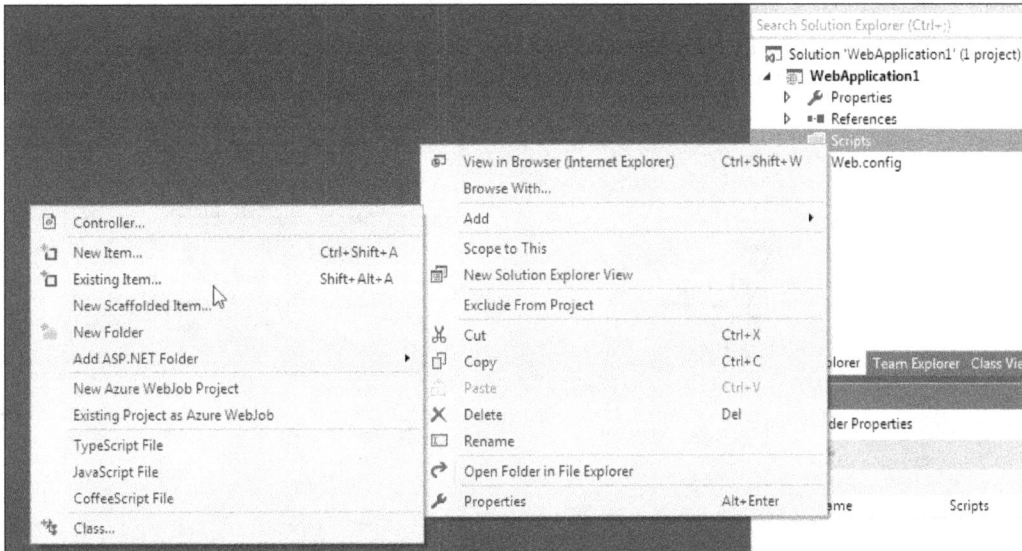

3. Now, browse to the location where you have saved the downloaded copy of the jQuery files (refer to the *Downloading jQuery from jQuery.com* recipe), and click on **OK**. It is recommended that you add both the uncompressed and compressed versions. The **Scripts** folder will be updated, as shown in the following screenshot:

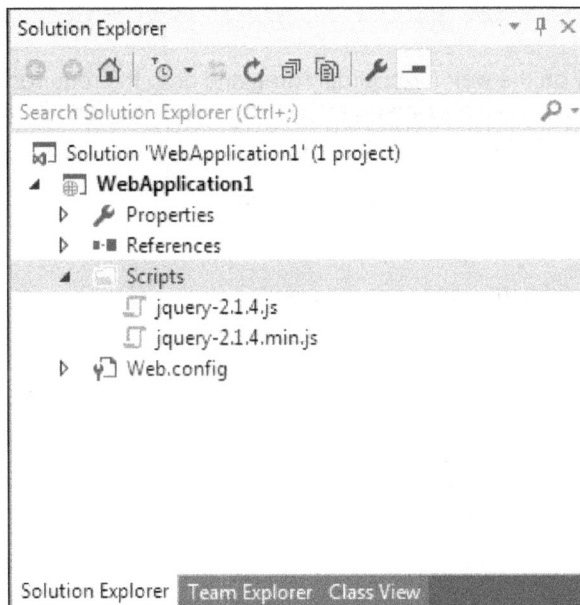

4. Next, create a new web form in the project by right-clicking on the project and navigating to **Add** | **New Item....** From the dialog box, select **Web Form**, and enter a suitable name for the web form, such as `Default.aspx`:

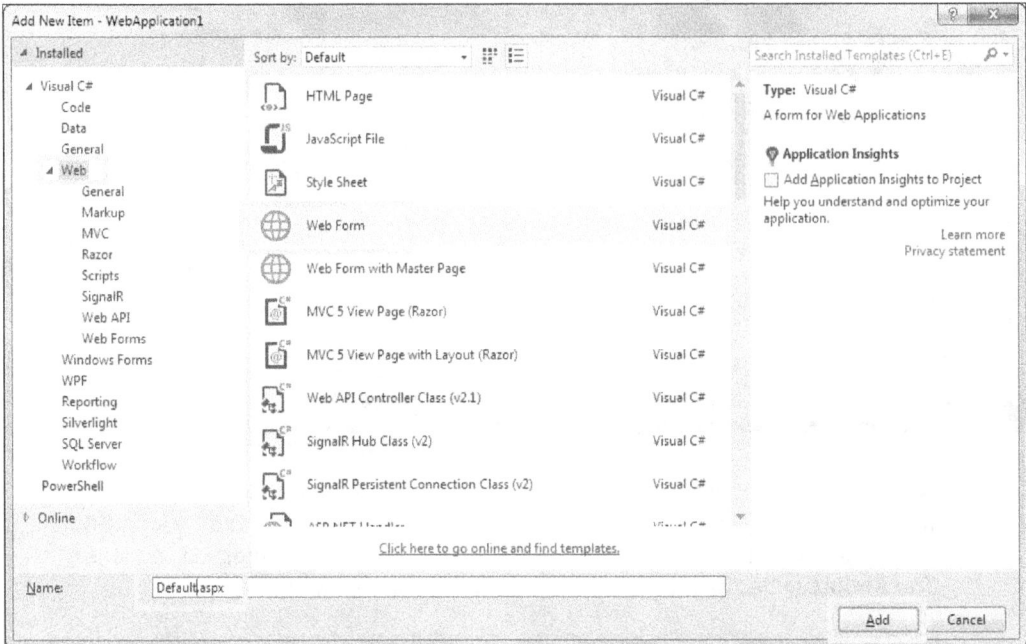

5. To use jQuery on the web form, simply drag and drop the required jQuery file, that is, uncompressed or compressed on the web form. Or alternatively, include the following `<script>` tag in the `<head>` element:

For development mode, the code is as follows:

```
<script src="Scripts/jquery-2.1.4.js"></script>
```

For release mode, the code is as follows:

```
<script src="Scripts/jquery-2.1.4.min.js"></script>
```

```
Default.aspx  ⊕ ✕
     <%@ Page Language="C#" AutoEventWireup="true" CodeBehind="Default.aspx.cs" Inherits="WebApplication1.Default" %>

    <!DOCTYPE html>

⊟ <html xmlns="http://www.w3.org/1999/xhtml">
⊟ <head runat="server">
        <title></title>
        <script src="Scripts/jquery-2.1.4.js"></script>
    </head>
⊟ <body>
⊟       <form id="form1" runat="server">
⊟       <div>

        </div>
        </form>
    </body>
    </html>
```

See also

The *Downloading jQuery from jQuery.com* recipe

Adding jQuery to an empty ASP.NET web project using ScriptManager control

Adding jQuery to a web form using the script block has some disadvantages. If the application is upgraded to use the latest version of jQuery, all the web forms with the `<script>` tag require to be changed. Secondly, switching from the uncompressed version in the development environment to the compressed version in the release environment should be handled manually and is hence error-prone. Using the ASP.NET `ScriptManager` control helps you overcome this problem. It can also load jQuery directly from CDN instead of using the local copy.

Getting ready

1. Create a new **ASP.NET Web Application** project using the **Empty** template by following the steps listed in the *Adding jQuery to an empty ASP.NET web project using a script block* recipe. Name the project `WebApplication2` (or any other suitable name).

2. Follow the steps in the preceding recipe to add the jQuery library (the uncompressed and compressed formats) to the **Scripts** folder.

3. Follow the steps to add a new web form to the project.

How to do it...

Following are the steps to add jQuery to ASP.NET web project using the
`ScriptManager` control:

1. Open the web form in the **Design** mode.

2. Launch the Toolbox. This can be done in two ways. From the **File** menu at the top of
    the page, go to **View | Toolbox**. Alternatively, use the shortcut keys, *Ctrl + Alt + X*.

3. Go to **Toolbox | AJAX Extensions**, and drag and drop the **ScriptManager** control onto
    the form:

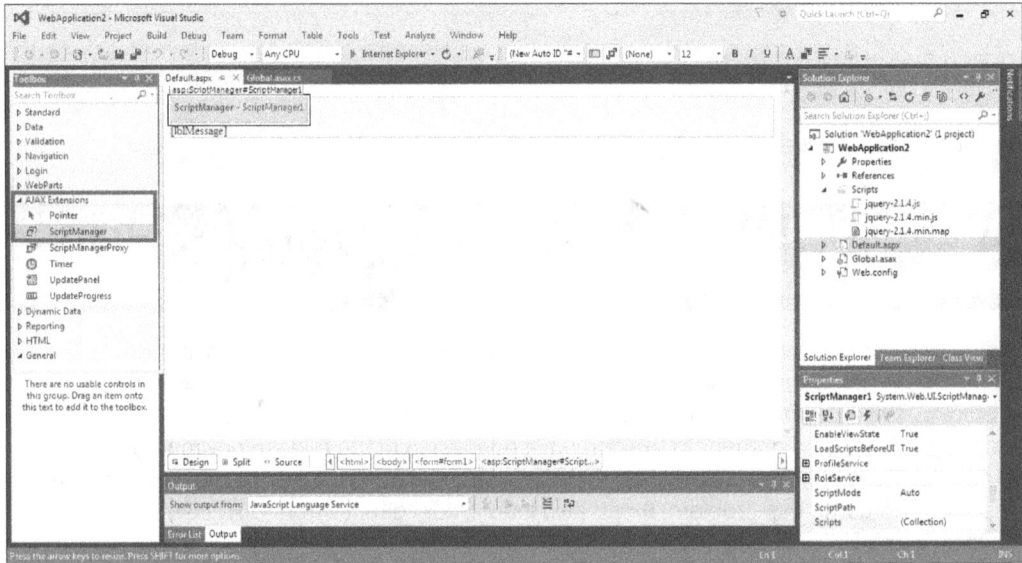

4. Right-click on the project in the **Solution Explorer** tab, and go to **Add | New Item....**
    From the dialog box, select **Global Application Class**. This will add the **Global.asax**
    file to the project:

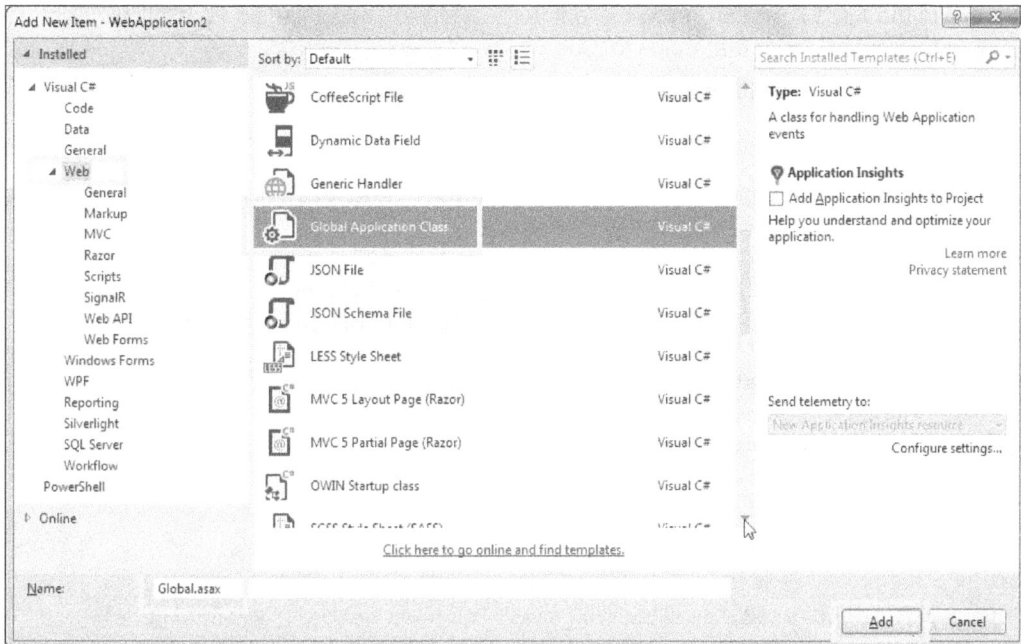

The `Global.asax` file is an optional file that resides in the root directory of the application and responds to events at the application and session levels, such as the starting and ending an application or session.

5. Open the `Global.asax` file and include the following namespace at the top of the page:

For VB, the code is as follows:

```
Imports System.Web.UI
```

For C#, the code is as follows:

```
using System.Web.UI;
```

6. In the `Application_Start` event in the `Global.asax` file, add the following code to create a script that maps to jQuery:

For VB, the code is as follows:

```
Sub Application_Start(ByVal sender As Object, ByVal e As
EventArgs)
    ScriptManager.ScriptResourceMapping.AddDefinition("jquery", New
ScriptResourceDefinition() With {
    .Path = "~/Scripts/jquery-2.1.4.min.js",
    .DebugPath = "~/Scripts/jquery-2.1.4.js",
    .CdnPath = "https://ajax.googleapis.com/ajax/libs/jquery/2.1.4/
jquery.min.js",
    .CdnDebugPath = "https://ajax.googleapis.com/ajax/libs/
jquery/2.1.4/jquery.js",
    .CdnSupportsSecureConnection = True,
    .LoadSuccessExpression = "window.jQuery"})
End Sub
```

For C#, the code is as follows:

```
protected void Application_Start(object sender, EventArgs e)
{
    ScriptManager.ScriptResourceMapping.AddDefinition("jquery", new
ScriptResourceDefinition
    {
        Path = "~/Scripts/jquery-2.1.4.min.js",
        DebugPath = "~/Scripts/jquery-2.1.4.js",
        CdnPath = "https://ajax.googleapis.com/ajax/libs/
jquery/2.1.4/jquery.min.js",
        CdnDebugPath = "https://ajax.googleapis.com/ajax/libs/
jquery/2.1.4/jquery.js",
        CdnSupportsSecureConnection = true,
        LoadSuccessExpression = "window.jQuery"
    });
}
```

7. Open the `Default.aspx` web form in the **Source** mode. Add the following `ScriptReference` to the `ScriptManager` control:

```
<asp:ScriptManager ID="ScriptManager1" runat="server">
    <Scripts>
        <asp:ScriptReference Name="jquery"  />
    </Scripts>
</asp:ScriptManager>
```

> When using the `ScriptManager` control to add a reference to the jQuery library, the jQuery code should be placed after the `ScriptManager` control, that is, after the jQuery reference has been declared; otherwise, the page will throw an error. It is also important to note that the `ScriptManager` control should reside inside the `<form>` element.

8. To retrieve the jQuery files from CDN, set the `EnableCdn` property of the `ScriptManager` control to `true`, as follows:

```
<asp:ScriptManager ID="ScriptManager1" runat="server"
EnableCdn="true">
    <Scripts>
        <asp:ScriptReference Name="jquery"  />
    </Scripts>
</asp:ScriptManager>
```

How it works...

This is how the ScriptManager control works:

1. The `ScriptManager` control can be used to load JavaScript files, such as the jQuery library. This can be done by adding the `ScriptReference` to jQuery in the `ScriptManager` control, as follows:

```
<asp:ScriptReference Name="jquery"  />
```

2. However, we require to define this mapping. This can be done in the `Global.asax` file using a `ScriptResourceDefinition` object, which exposes the following properties:

Property	Description
Path	This is the release path of the script resource
DebugPath	This is the development/debug path of the script resource
CdnPath	This is the release path of the script resource served from a CDN
CdnDebugPath	This is the development/debug path of the script resource served from a CDN
CdnSupportsSecureConnection	This indicates whether the HTTPS mode needs to be used to retrieve the resource when the page is accessed using a secure connection
LoadSuccessExpression	This is the JavaScript expression that detects whether a JavaScript file has been loaded successfully

3. The `ScriptResourceDefinition` object defined in `Global.asax` is named `jquery`. The `ScriptManager` control uses the same name to load the reference on the web form.

4. In the development/debug mode, the script is served from `DebugPath` while in the release mode, it is served from `Path`.

> **Running in development/debug and release modes**
>
> To run the application in the development/debug mode, set the `debug` attribute of the `<compilation>` element in the `web.config` to `true` as follows:
>
> ```
>     <system.web>
>         <compilation debug="true"/>
>         ….
>     </system.web>
> ```
>
> When the `debug` attribute is set to `false`, the application will run in the release mode.

5. If `EnableCdn` is set to `true`, the script is served from the CDN path, that is, from `CdnDebugPath` in the development/debug mode and `CdnPath` in the release mode.

6. The `LoadSuccessExpression` property renders an inline script to load the library from the local path in the event of a CDN failure. By right-clicking on the web page and viewing the source, note that the `ScriptManager` control adds a fall back mechanism when the CDN is unavailable and files are served locally instead:

```
60  <script src="https://ajax.googleapis.com/ajax/libs/jquery/2.1.4/jquery.js" type="text/javascript"></script>
61  <script type="text/javascript">
62  //<![CDATA[
63  (window.jQuery)||document.write('<script type="text/javascript" src="Scripts/jquery-2.1.4.js"><\/script>'); /]]>
64  </script>
```

See also

The *Adding jQuery to an empty ASP.NET web project using a script block* recipe

Adding jQuery to an ASP.NET Master Page

Master Pages are used to achieve a uniform look and feel in the website. They maintain a consistent layout across all the content pages. Including jQuery in the Master Page ensures that all the content pages using that Master Page will also have the library included by default. This recipe will demonstrate how this can be done.

> A Master Page is an ASP.NET file with the `.Master` extension. It has a `@Master` directive at the top of the layout instead of the `@Page` directive in an ordinary `.aspx` page.

Getting ready

1. Create a new **ASP.NET Web Application** project using the **Empty** template by following the steps listed in the *Adding jQuery to an empty ASP.NET web project using a script block* recipe. Name the project `WebApplicationWithMaster` (or any other suitable name).

2. Follow the steps in the previous recipe to add the jQuery library (the uncompressed and compressed formats) to the **Scripts** folder.

3. In the **Solution Explorer** tab, right-click on the project, and go to **Add** | **New Item...**. This will launch a dialog box, as shown in the following screenshot. From the dialog box, select **Web Forms Master Page**. Name the Master Page `Default.Master`, and click on **Add**:

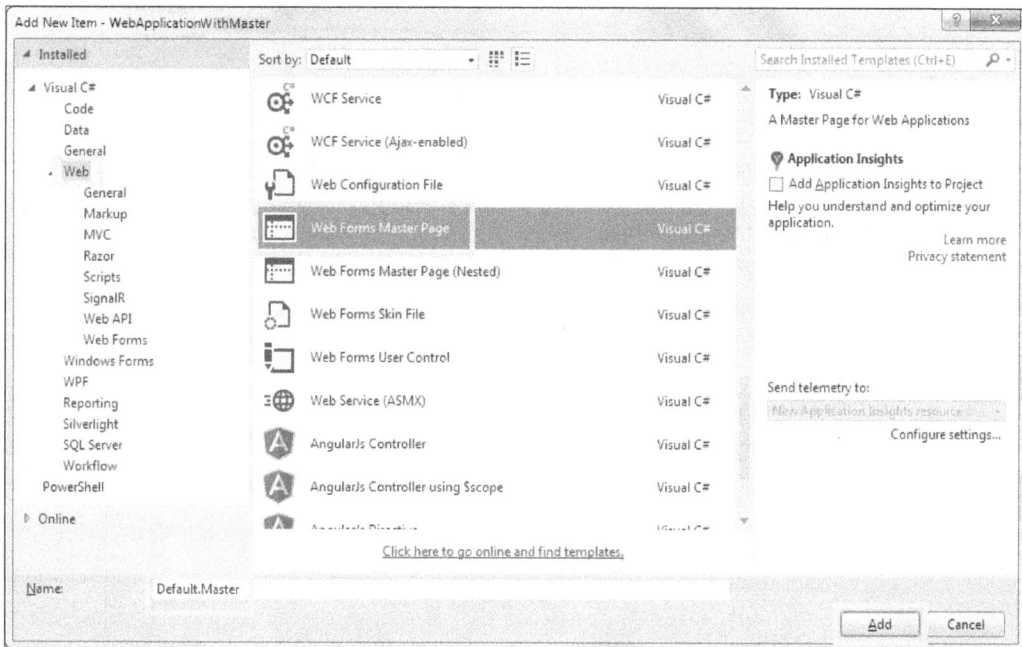

4. To add a web form—that is, a content page—to the project, right-click on the project in the **Solution Explorer** tab again, and navigate to **Add | New Item...**. From the dialog box, this time select **Web Form with Master Page**, as shown in the following screenshot. Name the web form `Default.aspx`, and click on **Add**:

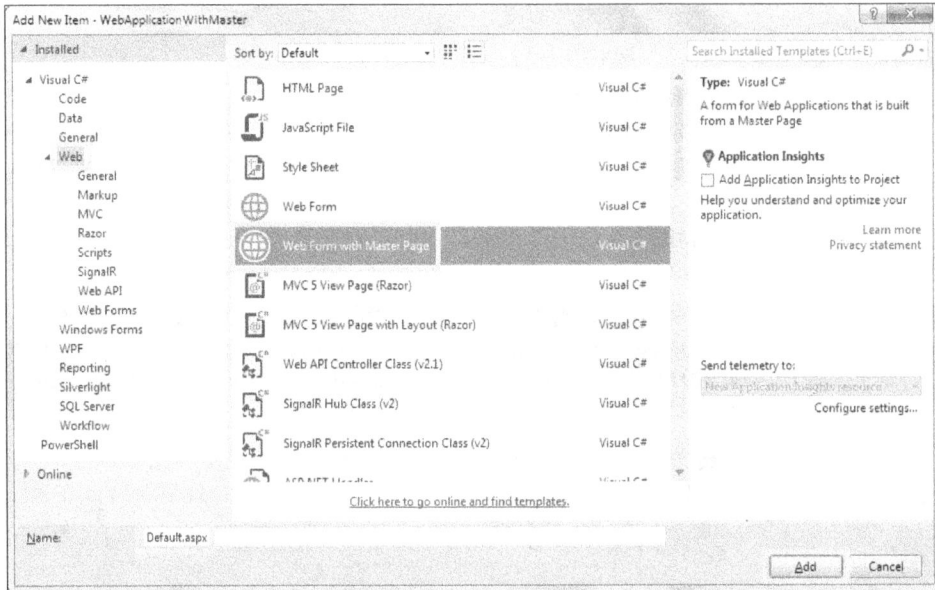

5. This will launch a dialog box so that you can select the Master Page. From the dialog box, as shown in the following screenshot, select the Master Page to be associated with the content page, and click on **OK**:

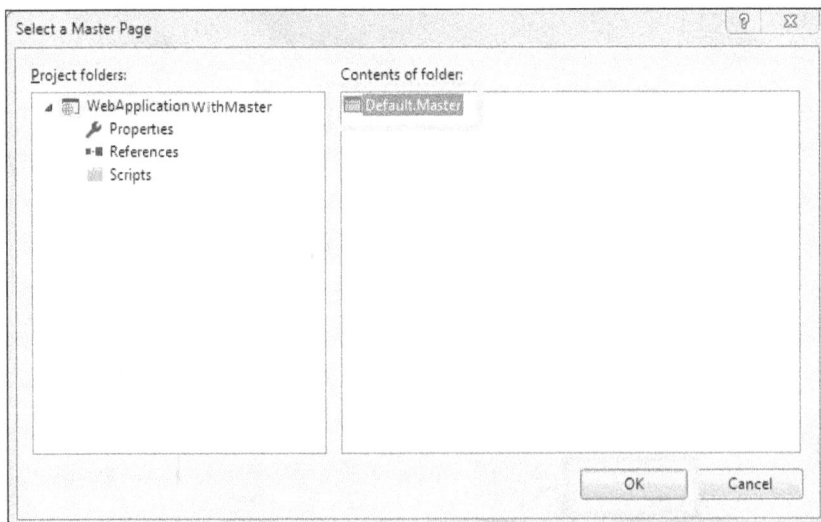

How to do it...

To incorporate jQuery in an ASP.NET Master Page, follow these steps:

1. Open the `Default.Master` Master Page in the Source mode, and add a reference to the jQuery library using either the `<script>` block (refer to the *Adding jQuery to an empty ASP.NET web project using a script block* recipe) or the `ScriptManager` control (refer to the *Adding jQuery to an empty ASP.NET web project using the ScriptManager control* recipe), as shown in the following screenshot:

```
Default.Master  ⊕ ×
    <%@ Master Language="C#" AutoEventWireup="true" CodeBehind="Default.master.cs"

    <!DOCTYPE html>

    <html xmlns="http://www.w3.org/1999/xhtml">
    <head runat="server">
        <title></title>
        <script src="Scripts/jquery-2.1.4.js"></script>
        <asp:ContentPlaceHolder ID="head" runat="server">
        </asp:ContentPlaceHolder>
    </head>
    <body>
        <form id="form1" runat="server">
        <div>
            <asp:ContentPlaceHolder ID="ContentPlaceHolder1" runat="server">
            </asp:ContentPlaceHolder>
        </div>
        </form>
    </body>
    </html>
```

```
Default.Master  ⊕ ×
    <%@ Master Language="C#" AutoEventWireup="true" CodeBehind="Default.master.cs"

    <!DOCTYPE html>

    <html xmlns="http://www.w3.org/1999/xhtml">
    <head runat="server">
        <title></title>
        <asp:ContentPlaceHolder ID="head" runat="server">
        </asp:ContentPlaceHolder>
    </head>
    <body>
        <form id="form1" runat="server">
            <asp:ScriptManager ID="ScriptManager1" runat="server">
                <Scripts>
                    <asp:ScriptReference Name="jquery" />
                </Scripts>
            </asp:ScriptManager>
        <div>
            <asp:ContentPlaceHolder ID="ContentPlaceHolder1" runat="server">
            </asp:ContentPlaceHolder>
        </div>
        </form>
    </body>
    </html>
```

> When using the `<script>` block, the jQuery reference should preferably be placed in the `<head>` element.
>
> When using the `ScriptManager` control, the control should preferably be placed in the `<form>` element before the `ContentPlaceHolder` in which the jQuery code will be added later to the content pages. The `Global.asax` file should also be updated in order to add the required `ScriptResourceDefinition`, as described in the *Adding jQuery to an empty ASP.NET web project using the ScriptManager control* recipe.

2. The required jQuery code can now be added to the `ContentPlaceHolder` (with `ID = "ContentPlaceHolder1"`) in the `Default.aspx` web form.

How it works...

On running the application, when the `Default.aspx` content page is loaded, the HTML markup from the Master page adds the reference to the jQuery library. This makes the content page jQuery-ready so that any jQuery code can be executed.

To check whether the jQuery reference has been added to the page, run the project and launch `Default.aspx` in the browser. Right-click on the page in the browser window and select **View Source**. The jQuery reference will be seen on the page, as shown in the following screenshot:

```
47  <script src="/ScriptResource.axd?d=JnUc-
    DEDOM5KzzVKtsL1tWQXgDXznDSNNISjzAByW3drmtadyDwn22DpnoivCLvgS6CzoVY7dYC3walQJKE6aW1Zclo_
    6yPYvjEG5QqgOFFLhkfTLCEj1jxPSSUWwsFV5bV1NYyzwfaajkgqSWoqa7KdhV5zseD3mySnEudsbag83BrohiUsPTc_UWJzv7Av0
    &amp;t=ffffffffa1161f9a" type="text/javascript"></script>
48  <script src="Scripts/jquery-2.1.4.js" type="text/javascript"></script>
49      <script type="text/javascript">
50  //<![CDATA[
51  Sys.WebForms.PageRequestManager._initialize('ctl00$ctl02', 'form1', [], [], [], 90, 'ctl00');
52  //]]>
53  </script>
54
55      <div>
56
57      <span id="ContentPlaceHolder1_lblMessage">Label</span>
```

See also

The *Adding jQuery to an empty ASP.NET web project using the ScriptManager control* recipe

Adding jQuery programmatically to a web form

In addition to adding jQuery to web forms using the script block and the `ScriptManager` control, the code-behind file can also emit the required script code. This recipe will demonstrate how this can be done.

Getting ready

1. Create an ASP.NET Web Application project by navigating to **File | New | Project | ASP.NET Web Application**. Select the **Empty** template. Name the project `WebApplicationWithPageLoad` (or any other suitable name).

2. Add a new **Web Form** to the project and name it `Default.aspx`.

3. Add the jQuery library files to the **Scripts** folder.

4. From the **Solution Explorer** tab, navigate to **Default.aspx.vb** (VB) or **Default.aspx.cs** (C#), which is the code-behind file for the web form. Open this file.

How to do it...

In the `Page_Load` event handler of `Default.aspx.vb`, use the `RegisterClientScriptInclude` method to generate a script block on the page, as follows:

For VB, the code is as follows:

```
Protected Sub Page_Load(ByVal sender As Object, ByVal e As System.
EventArgs) Handles Me.Load
    Page.ClientScript.RegisterClientScriptInclude("jquery",    Page.
ResolveUrl("~/Scripts/jquery-2.1.4.js"))
End Sub
```

For C#, the code is as follows:

```
protected void Page_Load(object sender, EventArgs e)
{
    Page.ClientScript.RegisterClientScriptInclude("jquery",    Page.
ResolveUrl("~/Scripts/jquery-2.1.4.js"));
}
```

How it works...

The `RegisterClientScriptInclude` method requires two parameters: the key and URL. It adds the script block with the path to the jQuery library in the `<form>` element, as shown in the following screenshot. The `Page.ResolveUrl` method is used to return a URL relative to the site root:

```
 9  <body>
10      <form method="post" action="Default.aspx" id="form1">
11  <div class="aspNetHidden">
12  <input type="hidden" name="__VIEWSTATE" id="__VIEWSTATE"
    value="izrmZujHjwYbcnI3hW8PheF062FHsi0Sjmb3mW3HH8rlXD2c4NHk7hA9ArlPuYZLe5Dg4Mu9BcLi/zmD8r4ntHC4xCnZIHgUyEu
    Sg+74g5k=" />
13  </div>
14
15
16  <script src="/Scripts/jquery-2.1.4.js" type="text/javascript"></script>
```

Since the jQuery library is added to the `<form>` element, all the jQuery code should be written in the `<form>` element instead of the `<head>` element, preferably toward the end of the page before closing the `<form>` element.

See also

The *Adding jQuery to an empty ASP.NET web project using a script block* recipe

Understanding jQuery reference in the default web application template

So far, all examples have used the **Empty** template for the ASP.NET Web Application project. When using a non-empty built-in web application template, ASP.NET adds a reference to the jQuery library in the Master Page using the `ScriptManager` control. This recipe walks you through the important details of this mapping.

How to do it...

Here are the steps to create an ASP.NET web application using the default web application template:

1. Create a new project by navigating to **File | New | Project...**. From the dialog box, select **ASP.NET Web Application**. Name the project `DemoWebApplication` (or any other suitable name), and click on **OK**.

2. A new dialog box will be launched. Select **Web Forms** from the available templates. Note that the **Web Forms** checkbox is checked by selecting the **Web Forms** template (refer to the following screenshot) and click on **OK** as shown in the following screenshot:

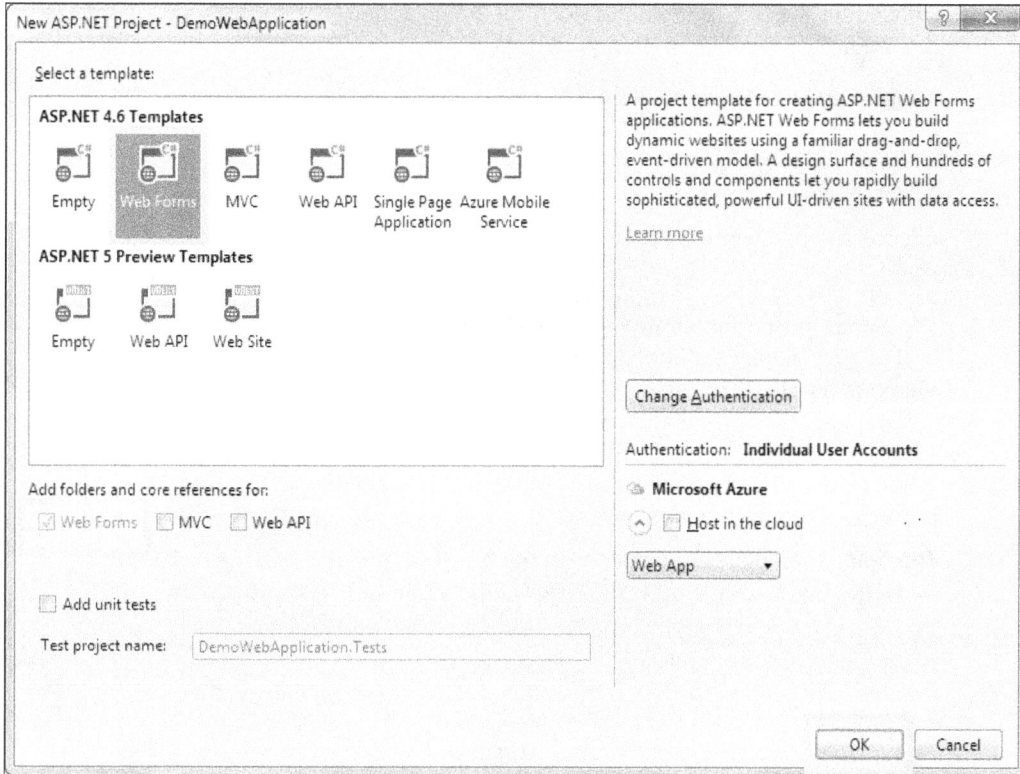

3. Open the `Site.Master` Master Page in the Source mode, as shown in the following screenshot:

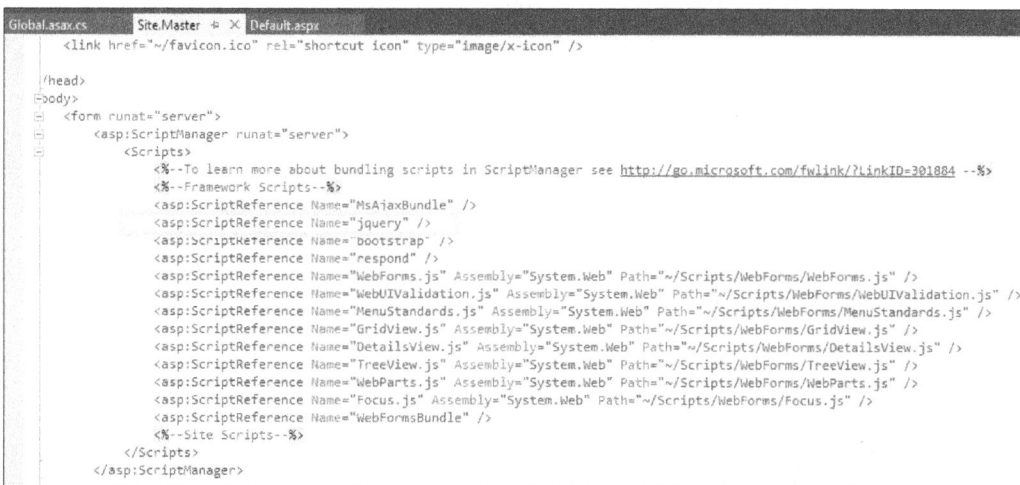

4. Notice that the `ScriptManager` control that is added to the `<form>` element has the following reference to jQuery:

```
<asp:ScriptReference Name="jquery" />
```

How it works...

When you follow the preceding steps, this is how the web application is mapped to the jQuery library:

1. The `ScriptManager` control switches the jQuery library between the development and release versions, depending on the `debug` attribute of the `<compilation>` element in `web.config`:

    ```
    <compilation debug="true"/>
    ```

2. When the `debug` attribute is `true`, the uncompressed version is used. When `debug` is `false`, the minified version is used.

3. The default template is shipped with the `AspNet.ScriptManager.jQuery` package. This package adds the following `ScriptMappings` to jQuery in the `PreApplicationStart` method of the application as follows:

    For C#, the code is as follows:

    ```
    string str = "2.4.1";
    ScriptManager.ScriptResourceMapping.AddDefinition("jquery", new
    ScriptResourceDefinition
    {
        Path = "~/Scripts/jquery-" + str + ".min.js",
        DebugPath = "~/Scripts/jquery-" + str + ".js",
        CdnPath = "http://ajax.aspnetcdn.com/ajax/jQuery/jquery-" +
    str + ".min.js",
        CdnDebugPath = "http://ajax.aspnetcdn.com/ajax/jQuery/jquery-"
    + str + ".js",
        CdnSupportsSecureConnection = true,
        LoadSuccessExpression = "window.jQuery"
    });
    ```

    > The default Web Forms template adds the Microsoft CDN URL, as shown in the preceding code.

4. When the `EnableCdn` property of the `ScriptManager` control is set to `true`, `CdnPath` and `CdnDebugPath` are used in release and development modes, respectively, to serve scripts from the Microsoft CDN:

    ```
    <asp:ScriptManager runat="server" EnableCdn="true">
    ```

5. However, if the CDN is down or if the application is offline, the `ScriptManager` control will include a fallback mechanism to serve the local copy of jQuery, as shown in the following screenshot:

```
50  <script src="http://ajax.aspnetcdn.com/ajax/jQuery/jquery-2.1.4.js" type="text/javascript"></script>
51  <script type="text/javascript">
52  //<![CDATA[
53  (window.jQuery)||document.write('<script type="text/javascript" src="Scripts/jquery-2.1.4.js"><\/script>');//]]>
54  </script>
```

6. To change the CDN to another, for example Google CDN, we need to change `ScriptResourceMapping` in the `RegisterBundles` method in `BundleConfig`, as shown in the following code. This module/class is located in the `App_Start` folder:

For VB, the code is as follows:

```
ScriptManager.ScriptResourceMapping.AddDefinition("jquery", New
ScriptResourceDefinition() With {
    .Path = "~/Scripts/jquery-2.1.4.min.js",
    .DebugPath = "~/Scripts/jquery-2.1.4.js",
    .CdnPath = "https://ajax.googleapis.com/ajax/libs/jquery/2.1.4/
jquery.min.js",
    .CdnDebugPath = "https://ajax.googleapis.com/ajax/libs/
jquery/2.1.4/jquery.js",
    .CdnSupportsSecureConnection = True,
    .LoadSuccessExpression = "window.jQuery"})
```

For C#, the code is as follows:

```
ScriptManager.ScriptResourceMapping.AddDefinition("jquery", new
ScriptResourceDefinition
{
    Path = "~/Scripts/jquery-2.1.4.min.js",
    DebugPath = "~/Scripts/jquery-2.1.4.js",
    CdnPath = "https://ajax.googleapis.com/ajax/libs/jquery/2.1.4/
jquery.min.js",
    CdnDebugPath = "https://ajax.googleapis.com/ajax/libs/
jquery/2.1.4/jquery.js",
    CdnSupportsSecureConnection = true,
    LoadSuccessExpression = "window.jQuery"
});
```

7. By running the page and viewing the source in the browser window, note that Microsoft CDN is replaced with Google CDN as required:

```
50  <script src="https://ajax.googleapis.com/ajax/libs/jquery/2.1.4/jquery.js" type="text/javascript"></script>
51  <script type="text/javascript">
52  //<![CDATA[
53  (window.jQuery)||document.write('<script type="text/javascript" src="Scripts/jquery-2.1.4.js"><\/script>');//]]>
54  </script>
55
```

8. Open the `Global.asax` page to view the registration of bundles in the `Application_Start` event handler as follows:

For VB, the code is as follows:

```
BundleConfig.RegisterBundles(BundleTable.Bundles)
```

For C#, the code is as follows:

```
BundleConfig.RegisterBundles(BundleTable.Bundles);
```

See also

The *Adding jQuery to an empty ASP.NET web project using the ScriptManager control* recipe

Hello World in a web project using jQuery

Until now, all recipes have demonstrated different ways to add the jQuery library to web pages. This is the first step in making the page jQuery-ready. In this recipe, let's move on to the next step: writing the jQuery code inside a script block to manipulate controls in a web form. We will display a simple Hello World message on the web page by manipulating a `Label` control on a web form.

Getting ready

1. Create a Web Application project by going to **File | New | Project | ASP.NET Web Application**. Select the **Empty** template. Name the project `HelloWorld` (or any other suitable name).

2. Add a new **Web Form** to the project.

3. Add the jQuery library files to the **Scripts** folder.

4. Add a reference to the jQuery library on the web form using any method of your choice.

5. Open the web form in the **Design** mode and drag and drop a **Label** control by navigating to the **Toolbox | Standard** controls. Change the properties of the `Label` control as follows:

```
<asp:Label ID="lblMessage" runat="server" Text=""></asp:Label>
```

How to do it...

If a jQuery reference is added to the `<head>` element, then include the following `<script>` block in the `<head>` element. Otherwise, include the `<form>` element, preferably before the `<form>` tag is closed:

```
<script type="text/javascript">
    $(document).ready(function () {
        var fontStyle = "Arial";
        var fontSize = 28;
        $("#<%=lblMessage.ClientID%>").css("font-family", fontStyle);
        $("#<%=lblMessage.ClientID%>").css("font-size", fontSize);
        $("#<%=lblMessage.ClientID%>").text("Hello World!!");
    });
</script>
```

How it works...

Following are the steps to print Hello World!! in a web project using jQuery:

1. In the preceding jQuery code, the `$` symbol is used to instantiate the `jQuery` object.

2. The `.ready()` function is triggered when the DOM is ready. It is commonly used to execute the required jQuery code on the page.

3. The `Label` control can be accessed from the jQuery code using ASP.NET's `ClientID` property and jQuery's `#identifier` selector.

4. Using the `.css()` property of the `jQuery` object, the font style, size, and text of the `Label` control are manipulated so that the following output is displayed on running the application:

See also

The *Hello World in ASP.NET MVC using jQuery* recipe

Bundling jQuery in ASP.NET MVC

Model View Controller (**MVC**) is a design pattern that separates design (Model), presentation (View), and action (Controller). Because of its popularity with developers, Visual Studio provides ready templates that are used to create MVC projects.

Similar to web forms, jQuery can be included in MVC views using the `<script>` tag. In this example, however, let's take a look at the use of bundling for this purpose.

Bundling helps you reduce the number of HTTP requests made by the browser. It is a feature that allows style sheets, JavaScript, or other files to be combined together in a single file called a bundle. This combined file can be downloaded as one unit using a single HTTP request.

Getting ready

1. Launch a new ASP.NET Web Application project in Visual Studio using the **Empty** template. Ensure that the **MVC** checkbox is checked, as shown in the following screenshot:

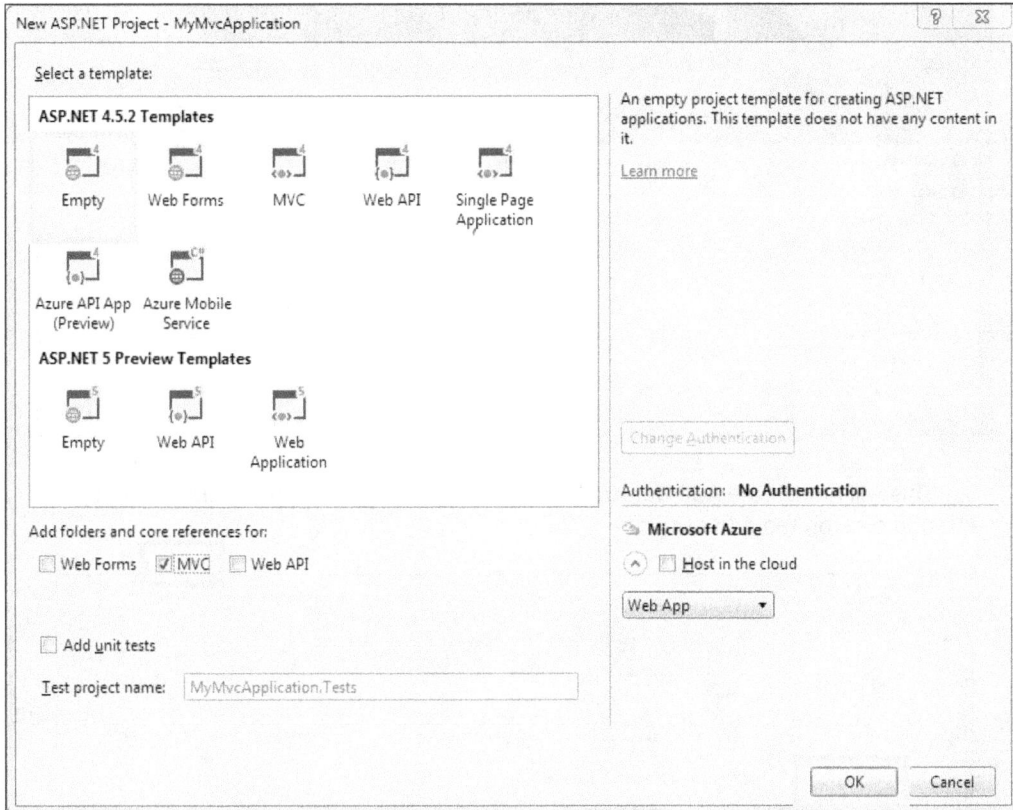

2. This will create a project with MVC folders. Right-click on the **Controllers** folder in the **Solution Explorer** tab, and go to **Add | Controller...** as shown in the following screenshot:

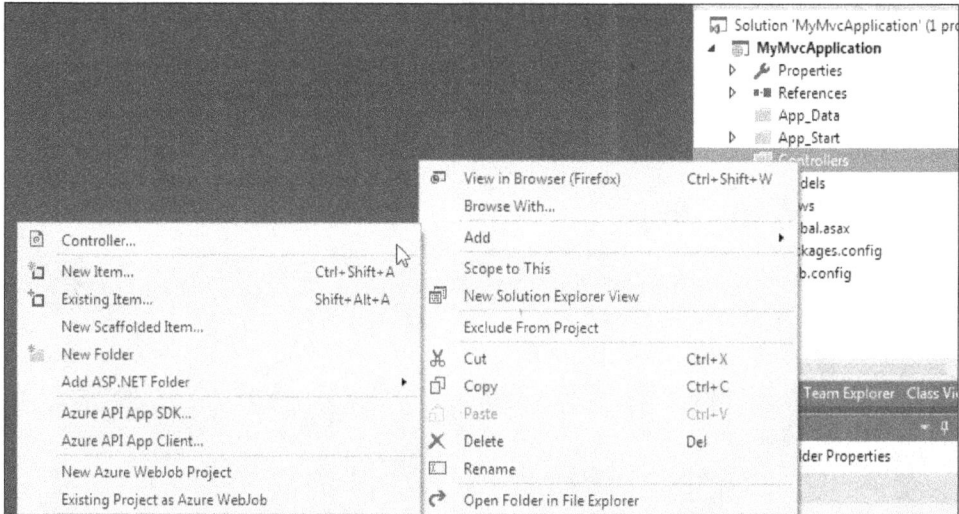

3. This will launch the **Add Scaffold** dialog box. Select **MVC 5 Controller – Empty**, and click on the **Add** button:

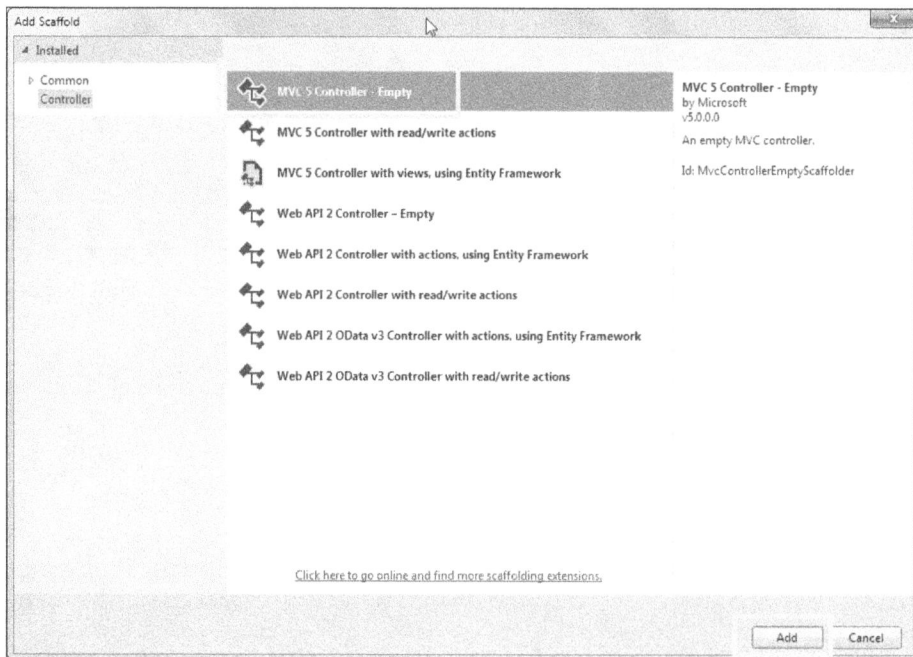

4. On being prompted to add a name for the controller, type `HomeController` and click on the **Add** button:

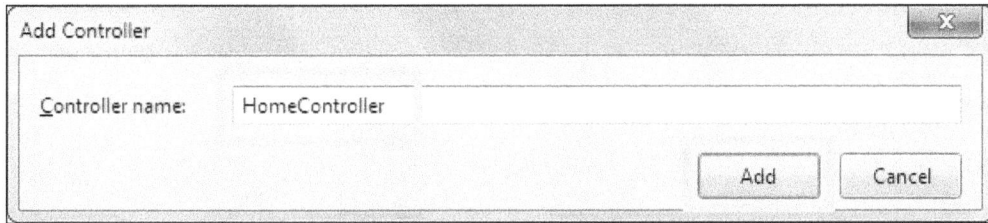

Add Controller			X
Controller name:	HomeController		
		Add	Cancel

5. Next, open the **HomeController** in the source mode, and right-click on the `Index` action method, as shown in the following screenshot. Click on **Add View...** as shown in the following screenshot:

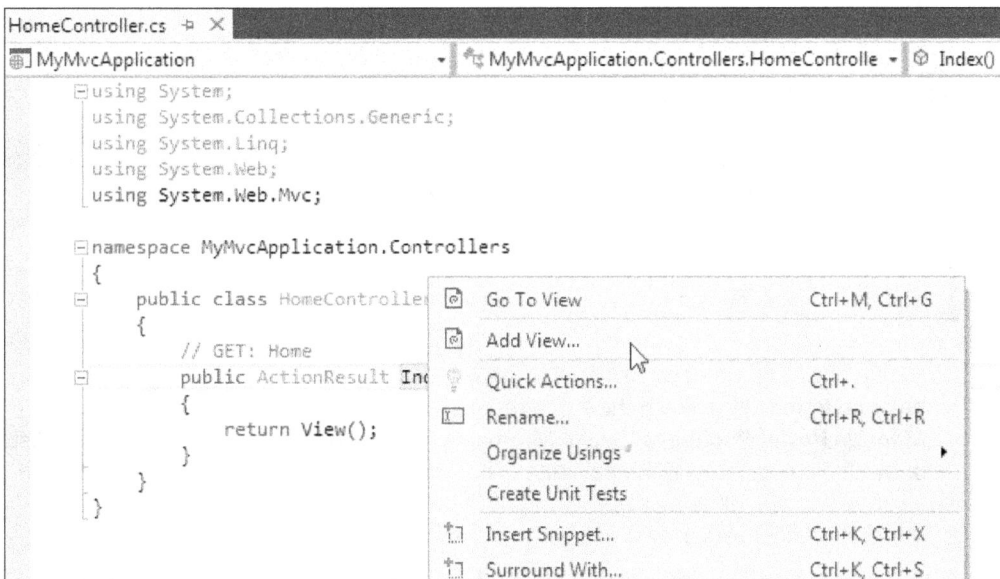

```
HomeController.cs  ⌐  X

MyMvcApplication                          ▾  MyMvcApplication.Controllers.HomeControlle  ▾  Index()

using System;
using System.Collections.Generic;
using System.Linq;
using System.Web;
using System.Web.Mvc;

namespace MyMvcApplication.Controllers
{
    public class HomeControlle         Go To View              Ctrl+M, Ctrl+G
    {
        // GET: Home                    Add View...
        public ActionResult Ind         Quick Actions...        Ctrl+.
        {
            return View();              Rename...               Ctrl+R, Ctrl+R
        }
    }                                   Organize Usings                   ▶
}
                                        Create Unit Tests

                                        Insert Snippet...       Ctrl+K, Ctrl+X
                                        Surround With...        Ctrl+K, Ctrl+S
```

6. This will launch the **Add View** dialog box. From the **Template** field, select **Empty (without model)**. Uncheck the **Use a layout page** option and click the **Add** button to continue:

Add View	
View name:	Index
Template:	Empty (without model) ▼
Model class:	

Options:

☐ Create as a partial view

☑ Reference script libraries

☐ Use a layout page:

(Leave empty if it is set in a Razor _viewstart file)

Add   Cancel

[In the remaining recipes, when asked to create a MVC application, follow steps 1 to 6 as mentioned earlier.]

7. To use bundling, we need to install the ASP.NET Web Optimization package. This can be done from NuGet. From the `File` menu, launch NuGet by navigating to **Project | Manage NuGet Packages**. Select **Microsoft.AspNet.Web.Optimization** from the list of available packages. If the package is not visible, search for `web.optimization`, as shown in the following screenshot. Click on the **Install** button to download and install the latest version:

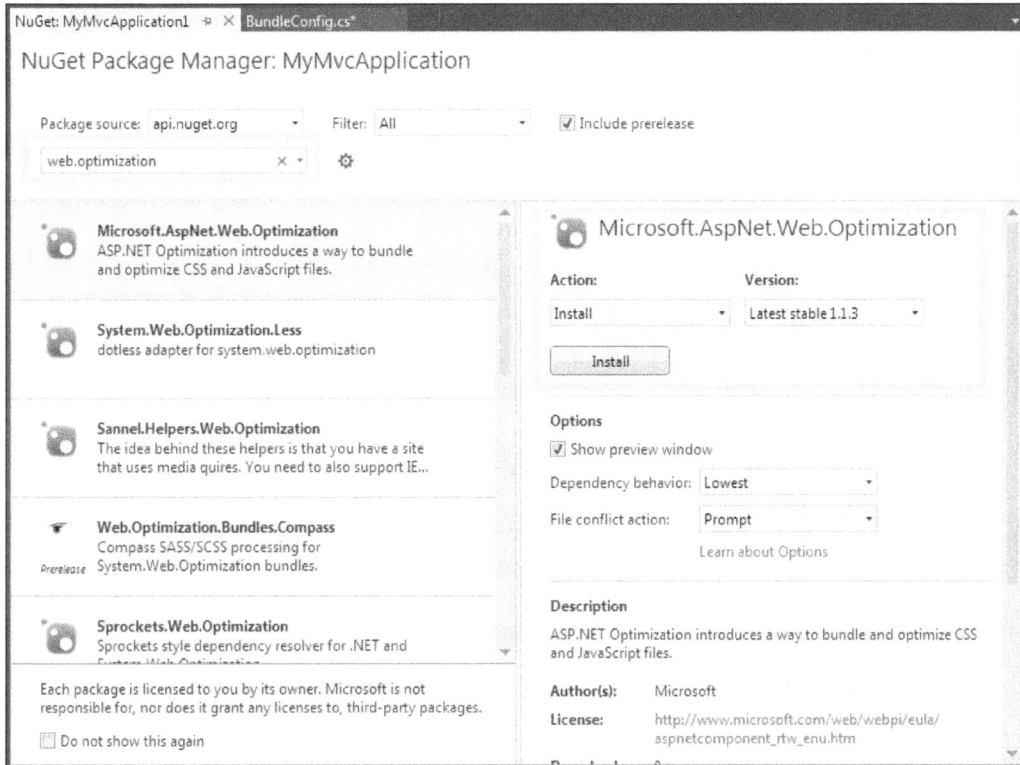

8. Lastly, create a `Scripts` folder in the project and include the jQuery library files in the folder.

How to do it...

Follow these steps to bundle jQuery in ASP.NET MVC:

1. Open the `BundleConfig` class in the `App_Start` folder in the MVC project. If the file does not exist, create a new `module` (VB)/`class` (C#) in the `App_Start` folder, and name it `BundleConfig.vb/BundleConfig.cs`.

2. In `BundleConfig.vb/BundleConfig.cs`, add a namespace to `System.Web.Optimization` at the top of the file:

   For VB, the code is as follows:

   ```
   Imports System.Web.Optimization
   ```

   For C#, the code is as follows:

   ```
   using System.Web.Optimization;
   ```

3. Register and configure a bundle for jQuery in the `RegisterBundles` method in `BundleConfig` as follows:

   For VB, the code is as follows:

   ```
   Public Module BundleConfig
       Public Sub RegisterBundles(ByVal bundles As BundleCollection)
           bundles.Add(New ScriptBundle("~/Scripts/jquery").Include(
                   "~/Scripts/jquery-{version}.js"))
       End Sub
   End Module
   ```

   For C#, the code is as follows:

   ```
   public class BundleConfig
   {
       public static void RegisterBundles(BundleCollection bundles)
       {
           bundles.Add(new ScriptBundle("~/Scripts/jquery").Include(
                   "~/Scripts/jquery-{version}.js"));
       }
   }
   ```

4. To enable bundling in the development mode (optional), add the following code to the `RegisterBundles` method:

   For VB, the code is as follows:

   ```
   BundleTable.EnableOptimizations = True
   ```

   For C#, the code is as follows:

   ```
   BundleTable.EnableOptimizations = true;
   ```

5. In the `Global.asax file`, include the namespace for `System.Web. Optimization`, as shown in step 2 mentioned previously. Then, register the bundle in the `Application_Start` method as follows:

   For VB, the code is as follows:

   ```
   BundleConfig.RegisterBundles(BundleTable.Bundles)
   ```

   For C#, the code is as follows:

   ```
   BundleConfig.RegisterBundles(BundleTable.Bundles);
   ```

6. Now, open the Index view and include the namespace for `System.Web.Optimization`, as shown in the following code:

    For VB, the code is as follows:

    ```
    @Imports System.Web.Optimization
    ```

    For C#, the code is as follows:

    ```
    @using System.Web.Optimization
    ```

7. Next, add the script reference for jQuery to the view in the `<head>` element as follows:

    ```
    @Scripts.Render("~/Scripts/jquery")
    ```

> Bundling is disabled in the debug mode by setting the `debug` attribute to `true` in the `<compilation>` element in the `web.config` file. To override this setting and enable bundling in the debug mode, set the `EnableOptimizations` property of the `BundleTable` class to `true` in the `RegisterBundles` method.
>
> Unless `EnableOptimizations` is set to `true`, or the `debug` attribute is set to `false`, the files will not be bundled and the debug versions of the files will be used instead of the minified versions.

How it works...

Bundling jQuery in ASP.NET MVC can be done by following these steps:

1. The wildcard string used for bundling jQuery `~/Scripts/jquery-{version}.js` includes the development as well as the minified versions. The `.vsdoc` file, which is used by IntelliSense, is not included in the bundle.

2. When the debug mode is on, the corresponding debug version is used. In the release mode, the minified version is bundled.

3. On running the view in a browser, the bundled file can be seen on viewing the source in the browser window, as shown in the following HTML markup:

```
<html>
<head>
    <meta name="viewport" content="width=device-width" />
    <title>Index</title>
    <script src="/Scripts/jquery?v=gGGRI7xCOnEK-4qvkXXwhmbyGmA8S3tmz-Wto5bGsIc1"></script>

</head>
<body>
```

See also

The *Using a CDN to load jQuery in MVC* recipe

Using CDN to load jQuery in MVC

Because of the advantages of using CDN in web applications, bundling also supports the loading of files directly from CDN. This recipe will explain how a MVC project can be configured to use CDN.

Getting ready

This recipe is a continuation of the previous recipe, *Bundling jQuery in ASP.NET MVC*. So, follow all the steps described in the previous recipe.

How to do it...

Following are the steps to load jQuery in MVC:

1. In the `BundleConfig` module/class, modify the `RegisterBundles` method in order to set the `UseCdn` property to `true`, as shown in the code snippet in step 2.

2. Declare the required CDN path, and add a `ScriptBundle` with two parameters: the virtual path of the bundle and the CDN path, as follows:

For VB, the code is as follows:

```
Public Module BundleConfig
    Public Sub RegisterBundles(ByVal bundles As BundleCollection)
        bundles.UseCdn = True
        Dim cdnPath As String =  "http://ajax.aspnetcdn.com/ajax/
jQuery/jquery-2.1.4.min.js"
bundles.Add(New ScriptBundle("~/Scripts/jquery", cdnPath).
Include("~/Scripts/jquery-{version}.js"))
    End Sub
End Module
```

For C#, the code is as follows:

```
public class BundleConfig
{
    public static void RegisterBundles(BundleCollection bundles)
    {
```

```
        bundles.UseCdn = true;
        string cdnPath = "http://ajax.aspnetcdn.com/ajax/jQuery/
jquery-2.1.4.min.js";
        bundles.Add(new ScriptBundle("~/Scripts/jquery", cdnPath).
Include("~/Scripts/jquery-{version}.js"));
    }
}
```

How it works...

Following are the steps to load jQuery in MVC using CDN:

1. By setting the `UseCdn` property, serving of bundled scripts from the CDN is enabled.

2. In the development mode, the application retrieves files from the local **Scripts** folder. In the release mode, the CDN path is used to serve the bundled scripts.

3. However, there is a possibility that the CDN is down. Hence, a fallback mechanism is required so that the scripts are served locally in such a scenario. This can be done by adding the following `<script>` block in the required view:

```
@Scripts.Render("~/Scripts/jquery")
<script type="text/javascript">
    if (typeof jQuery == 'undefined') {
        var e = document.createElement('script');
        e.src = '@Url.Content("~/Scripts/jquery-2.4.1.js")';
        e.type = 'text/javascript';
        document.getElementsByTagName("head")[0].appendChild(e);
    }
</script>
```

See also

The *Hello World in ASP.NET MVC using jQuery* recipe

Hello World in ASP.NET MVC using jQuery

This recipe demonstrates how to write a simple jQuery code to display Hello World in the ASP.NET MVC project.

Getting ready

Use the `MyMvcApplication` project created in the *Bundling jQuery in ASP.NET MVC* recipe.

How to do it...

Following are the steps to write simple jQuery code:

1. Open the Index view, and add the following markup to the `<body>` element:

   ```
   <div id="divMessage">
   </div>
   ```

2. In the `<head>` element, include the following jQuery code:

   ```
   <script type="text/javascript">
       $(document).ready(function () {
           var fontStyle = "Arial";
           var fontSize = 28;
           $("#divMessage").css("font-family", fontStyle);
           $("#divMessage").css("font-size", fontSize);
           $("#divMessage").text("Hello World!!");
       });
   </script>
   ```

3. Right-click on the Index view, and select **View in Browser (Internet Explorer)**.

How it works...

Following are the steps to print Hello World in ASP.NET MVC using jQuery:

1. The `$` symbol is used to instantiate the `jQuery` object.

2. The `.ready()` function is triggered when the DOM is ready. It is commonly used to execute the required jQuery code on the page.

3. The HTML `<div>` element with `id = "divMessage"`, which is used to display the Hello World message, can be accessed using its ID with jQuery's `#identifier` selector—that is, using the `#divMessage` selector.

4. Using the `.css()` property of the `jQuery` object, the font style, size, and text of the `<div>` element are manipulated so that the following output is displayed on running the application:

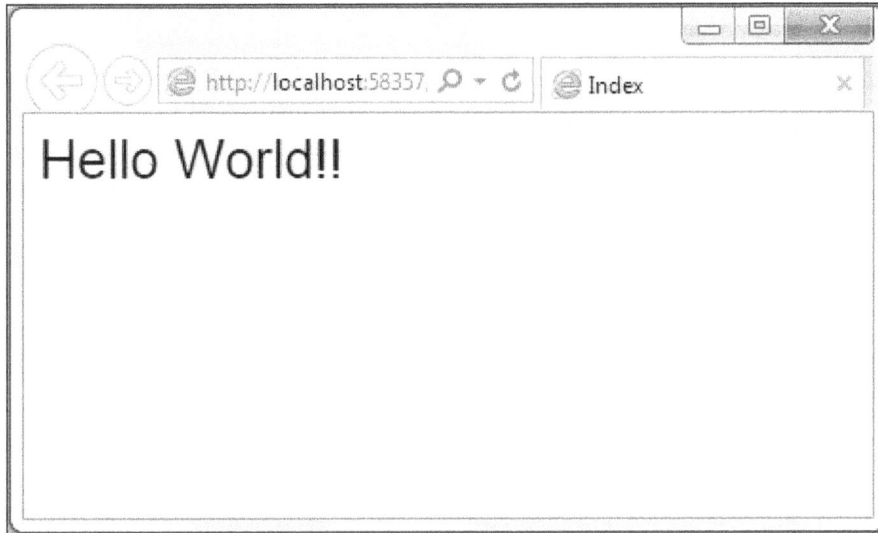

See also

The *Bundling jQuery in ASP.NET MVC* recipe

Debugging jQuery code in Visual Studio

Debugging is inevitable for resolving bugs in the code during the development phase. Sometimes, bugs also slip into production. Visual Studio provides support for developers to debug the JavaScript code in the same manner as the server-side code. However, there is a limitation and debugging in Visual Studio can only be done using the Internet Explorer browser at present.

Getting ready

1. To enable debugging for a particular project, both the project properties and `web.config` must be updated. To update the project properties, right-click on the project in the **Solution Explorer** tab, and select **Properties**. Go to the **Web** tab, and select the **ASP.NET** checkbox in the **Debuggers** section, as shown in the following screenshot:

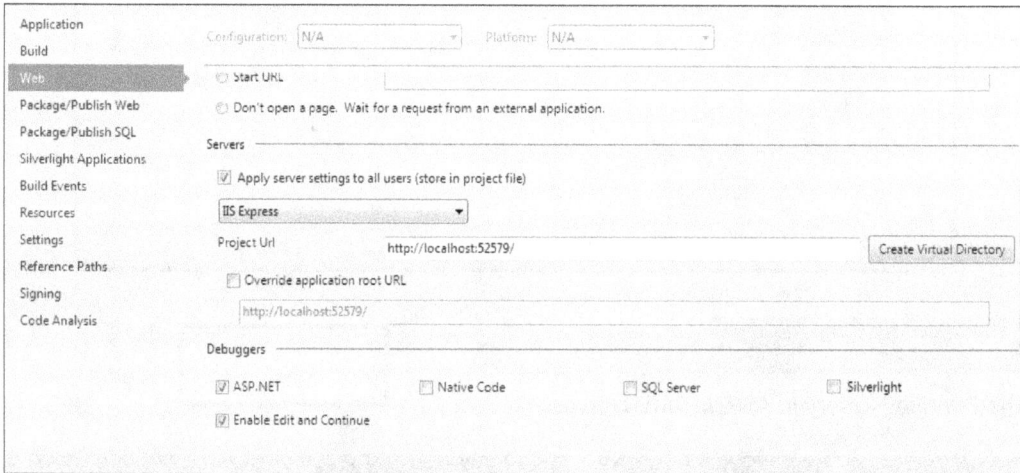

2. In the `web.config` file, go to the `configuration/system.web/compilation` element. If the element does not exist, add a new node. To enable debugging, the `debug` property of the `<compilation>` node should be set to `true`, as follows:

```
<compilation debug="true" … />
```

How to do it...

Debugging jQuery code in Visual Studio can be done by performing the following steps:

1. The first step in debugging is to define breakpoints in the JavaScript code, where the execution will be halted so that variables, program flow, and so on can be inspected. To define breakpoints, just click on the left-hand side gray margin in the source code. Each breakpoint is represented by a small red circle, as shown in the following figure:

```
Default.aspx  ⊕ ✕
  Client Objects & Events                              ▾    (No Events)
    <%@ Page Language="C#" AutoEventWireup="true" CodeBehind="Default.aspx.cs" Inherits="HelloWorld.Default" %>

    <!DOCTYPE html>

    <html xmlns="http://www.w3.org/1999/xhtml">
    <head runat="server">
        <title></title>
        <script src="Scripts/jquery-2.1.4.js"></script>
        <script type="text/javascript">
            $(document).ready(function () {          CLICK HERE TO SET BREAKPOINTS
                var fontStyle = "Arial";
                var fontSize = 28;
                $("#<%=lblMessage.ClientID%>").css("font-family", fontStyle);
                $("#<%=lblMessage.ClientID%>").css("font-size", fontSize);
                $("#<%=lblMessage.ClientID%>").text("Hello World!!");
            });
        </script>
    </head>
```

2. Press *F5,* or navigate to **Debug** | **Start Debugging**, to start running the application in the debug mode. The execution will stop at the first breakpoint that it comes across, as shown in the following screenshot:

```
Default.aspx
    <html xmlns="http://www.w3.org/1999/xhtml">
    <head><title>

    </title>
        <script src="Scripts/jquery-2.1.4.js"></script>
        <script type="text/javascript">
            $(document).ready(function () {
                var fontStyle = "Arial";
                var fontSize = 28;
                $("#lblMessage").css("font-family", fontStyle);
                $("#lblMessage").css("font-size", fontSize);
                $("#lblMessage").text("Hello World!!");
            });
        </script>
    </head>

100 %  ▾
  ‹› Source     ◀ <html> <head> <script>
```

| Watch 1 | | | ▾ ⋤ ✕ |
Name	Value		Type
🔗 fontStyle	"Arial"	🔍 ▾	String
🔗 fontSize	28		Number

Watch 1 Autos Locals

3. To launch the Watch window in order to observe the values of variables during runtime, go to **Debug | Windows | Watch**. This will display the window, as shown in the preceding screenshot.

4. You will also be able to see a window showing the breakpoints by navigating to **Debug | Windows | Breakpoints**. The result is shown in the following screenshot:

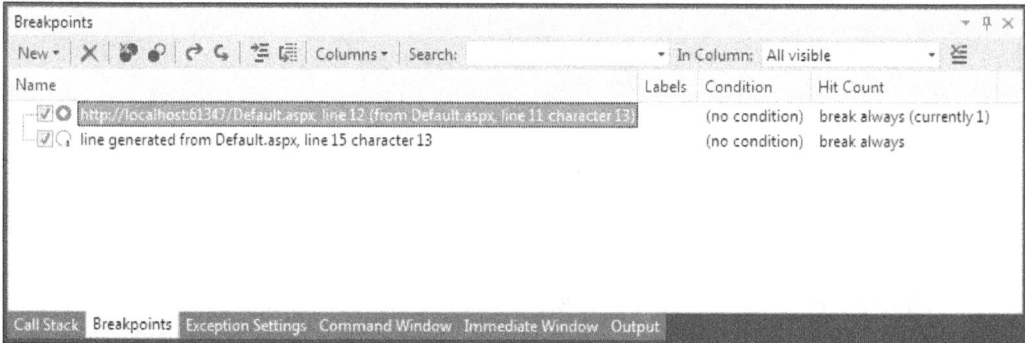

5. To trace the code line by line, press *F11* or navigate to **Debug | Step Into** at each line. To skip to the next breakpoint, press *F5*.

6. Press *Shift + F5* to stop debugging.

> Make sure that you turn off debugging before launching the application in the production environment. An application that has debugging enabled has a slower performance since debugging generates additional information to enable the debugger to display the contents of variables. It also outputs more information to the call stack, which can become a security issue in the production environment.

See also

The *Hello World in a web project using jQuery* recipe

2

Using jQuery Selectors
with ASP.NET Controls

This chapter will introduce you to the various types of selectors that can be used to work with ASP.NET controls. We will cover the following recipes in this chapter:

- ▶ Selecting a control using an ID and displaying its value
- ▶ Selecting a control using the CSS class
- ▶ Selecting a control using HTML tag
- ▶ Selecting a control by its attribute
- ▶ Selecting an element by its position in the DOM
- ▶ Enabling/disabling controls on a web form
- ▶ Using selectors in MVC applications

> The source code provided with the book has each recipe written as an independent project and named as `Recipe1, Recipe2, Recipe3,` and so on.

Introduction

A web page is composed of a variety of HTML elements, such as form, div, span, paragraph, hyperlink, table, input, select, and so on. When writing a client script, there is often a need to manipulate these elements. In JavaScript, it is possible to access these elements using their unique IDs with the help of the `document.getElementById()` statement.

However, in real-world applications, there might be a requirement to retrieve elements based on attributes other than their IDs. Or some applications may require retrieval and manipulation of more than one element. This is made possible by the use of selectors in jQuery.

A **selector** is a jQuery construct that retrieves elements on a page based on a specified condition. It can be used to return single or multiple elements. Using jQuery selectors, it is possible to match elements using their **ID**, **CSS class**, **tag name**, and **position** in the Document Object Model (DOM) or other attributes.

When an ASP.NET page is viewed in the browser, the controls are rendered as HTML elements. This makes it possible to select ASP.NET controls using standard jQuery selectors. The following table summarizes the mapping of some common ASP.NET controls to their rendered HTML equivalents:

ASP.NET Control	Rendered HTML Element	Rendered HTML Tag
BulletedList	ul, li	`<ul><li></li>` `<li></li></ul>`
Button	input	`<input type= "submit"/>`
CheckBox	input	`<input type= "checkbox"/>`
CheckBoxList	input	`<input type= "checkbox" name="CheckBoxList1"/>` `<input type= "checkbox" name="CheckBoxList1"/>`
DropDownList	select, option	`<select><option></option>` `<option></option></select>`
Hyperlink	a	`<a>`
Image	img	`<img>`
ImageButton	input	`<input type= "image"/>`
Label	span	`<span>`
LinkButton	a	`<a>`
ListBox	select, option	`<select><option></option>` `<option></option></select>`
Panel	div	`<div>`
RadioButton	input	`<input type= "radio"/>`
RadioButtonList	input	`<input type= "radio" name="RadioButtonList1"/>` `<input type= "radio" name="RadioButtonList1"/>`

ASP.NET Control	Rendered HTML Element	Rendered HTML Tag
TextBox	input	`<input type="text">`
GridView	table	`<table>`

Standard jQuery selectors can also be used with ASP.NET MVC since MVC applications use raw HTML markups or built-in extension methods of the HTML class to render the content.

jQuery selectors can be broadly classified into the following types:

- **Basic selectors**: These selectors are similar to CSS selectors that are used in style sheets to apply styles to selected elements. Basic selectors can be used to retrieve elements based on the HTML tag, CSS class, element ID, or a combination of all these. The examples of basic selectors are as follows:

Example	Description
`$("*")`	This selects all elements on the page
`$("div")`	This selects all `<div>` elements on the page
`$(".highlight")`	This selects all elements on the page with the CSS class `highlight`
`$("#footer")`	This selects an element with an ID equal to `footer`
`$("div, p, .highlight, #footer")`	This selects all `<div>` and `<p>` elements, all elements with the CSS class `highlight`, and the element with an ID equal to `footer`

- **Hierarchy selectors**: These selectors are also similar to CSS selectors and are used to select child elements in the DOM tree. The examples of hierarchy selectors are listed as follows:

Example	Description
`$("div p")`	This selects all `<p>` elements inside `<div>` elements
`$("#footer p")`	This selects all `<p>` elements that are descendants of the element with ID equal to footer
`$("div > p")`	This selects all `<p>` elements that are immediate children of `<div>` elements
`$("div ~ p")`	This selects all `<p>` elements that follow a `<div>` element and have the same parent as the `<div>` element
`$("div + p")`	This selects all `<p>` elements that are immediately preceded by `<div>` elements

► **Attribute selectors**: These selectors retrieve elements based on the attributes they have. The examples of attribute selectors are listed as follows:

Example	Description
`$("a[href]")`	This selects all `<a>` elements that have the `href` attribute
`$("a[href= 'http://www.google.com']")`	This selects all `<a>` elements whose `href` is exactly equal to `'http://www.google.com'`
`$("a[href*= 'google.com']")`	This selects all `<a>` elements whose `href` contains `'google.com'`
`$("a[href^= 'https']")`	This selects all `<a>` elements whose `href` starts with `'https'`
`$("a[href$= '.org']")`	This selects all `<a>` elements whose `href` ends with `'.org'`
`$("a[hreflang|= 'en']")`	This selects all `<a>` elements whose `hreflang` is equal to `'en'` or starts with `'en-'`

► **Form selectors**: These selectors are used to work with various form elements, such as an `input`, `checkbox`, `radio`, and so on. The examples of form selectors are as follows:

Example	Description
`$(":button")`, `$(":submit")`, `$(":reset")`, `$(":text")`, `$(":radio")`, `$(":checkbox")`, `$(":password")`, `$(":image")`, `$(":file")`	This selects the `input` element of the specific type
`$(":input")`	This selects all `form` elements
`$(":checked")`	This selects all checked checkboxes and radio buttons
`$(":selected")`	This returns all selected `<option>` elements
`$(":enabled")`	This returns all enabled `form` elements
`$(":disabled")`	This returns all disabled `form` elements

▶ **Position filters**: These selectors retrieve elements based on their position in a collection. The examples of position selectors are listed as follows:

Example	Description
`$(".highlight :first")`	This selects the first element with the CSS class `highlight`
`$(".highlight :last")`	This selects the last element with the CSS class `highlight`
`$(".highlight :odd")`	This selects the odd elements from all elements with the CSS class `highlight` when the index is zero-based
`$(".highlight :even")`	This selects the even elements from all elements with the CSS class `highlight` when the index is zero-based
`$(".highlight :eq(3)")`	This selects the element with an index equal to 3 from all elements with the CSS class `highlight` when the index is zero-based
`$(".highlight :lt(3)")`	This selects elements with an index less than 3 from all elements with the CSS class `highlight` when the index is zero-based
`$(".highlight :gt(3)")`	This selects elements with an index greater than 3 from all elements with the CSS class `highlight` when the index is zero-based

> Find out more about the different types of jQuery selectors at `http://api.jquery.com/category/selectors`.

When writing the jQuery code, often **anonymous** functions are used. An **anonymous** function is a function without a named identifier. It is usually used as an argument to other functions.

Let's say we have an `onDocumentReady()` function. This function is passed to the `$(document).ready()` function as an argument, as follows:

```
function onDocumentReady() {…}

$(document).ready(onDocumentReady);
```

Instead of working in this way, an anonymous function can be directly passed to `$(document).ready()` as an argument, as follows:

```
$(document).ready(function(){ …} );
```

However, note that anonymous functions are not accessible once they have been created.

Selecting a control using ID and displaying its value

This recipe demonstrates how to access basic ASP.NET controls, such as `CheckBoxList`, `TextBox`, and `RadioButtonList` on a web form using jQuery's `#identifier` selector. The constructs used in this example are as follows:

Construct	Type	Description
`$(#identifier)`	jQuery selector	This selects an element based on its `ID`
`$(this)`	jQuery object	This refers to the current jQuery object
`:checked`	jQuery selector	This selects checked input elements
`.click()`	jQuery event binder	This binds a handler to the `click` event of an element
`.each()`	jQuery method	This iterates over the matched elements and executes a function for each element
`.find()`	jQuery method	This finds all elements that match the filter
`.html()`	jQuery method	This returns the HTML content of the first matched element or sets the HTML content of every matched element
`.is()`	jQuery method	This returns a Boolean value if the matched element satisfies a given condition
`.next()`	jQuery method	This gets the immediate sibling of an element
`:selected`	jQuery selector	This retrieves selected input elements
`.text()`	jQuery method	This returns the combined text content of each of the matched elements or sets the text content of every matched element
`.val()`	jQuery method	This returns the value of the first matched element or sets the value of every matched element

Getting ready

Following are the steps to create a form using basic ASP.NET controls:

1. In this example, we will create a simple **User Registration** form, as shown in the following screenshot:

User Registration

Name

Gender
- Male
- Female

Highest Education --Select--

Interest Areas
- ASP.NET
- Java
- Android
- HTML5
- XML

- Subscribe to newsletter

Submit

2. Create an **ASP.NET Web Application** project using the **Empty** template and **name** the project Recipe1 (or any other suitable name).

3. Add a **Web Form** to the project and **name** it Default.aspx.

4. Create a Scripts folder and add jQuery files (debug and release versions of a library) to it.

5. Include the jQuery library in the form using either the `<script>` block or the ScriptManager control, as described in *Chapter 1, Getting Started with jQuery in ASP.NET*.

6. Now, drag and drop ASP.NET controls by navigating to the **Toolbox | Standard** controls to create the form, as shown in the preceding screenshot.

7. The HTML markup for the form is as follows:

```
<table>
  <tr>
    <td>
      <asp:Label ID="lblName" runat="server"
Text="Name"></asp:Label>
    </td>
    <td>
```

2. Create an **ASP.NET Web Application** project using the **Empty** template and **name** the project Recipe1 (or any other suitable name).

3. Add a **Web Form** to the project and **name** it Default.aspx.

4. Create a Scripts folder and add jQuery files (debug and release versions of a library) to it.

5. Include the jQuery library in the form using either the `<script>` block or the ScriptManager control, as described in *Chapter 1, Getting Started with jQuery in ASP.NET*.

6. Now, drag and drop ASP.NET controls by navigating to the **Toolbox | Standard** controls to create the form, as shown in the preceding screenshot.

7. The HTML markup for the form is as follows:

```
<table>
  <tr>
    <td>
      <asp:Label ID="lblName" runat="server"
Text="Name"></asp:Label>
    </td>
    <td>
```

```
      <asp:TextBox ID="txtName" runat="server"
Width="223px"></asp:TextBox>
    </td>
  </tr>
  <tr>
    <td>
      <asp:Label ID="lblGender" runat="server"
Text="Gender"></asp:Label>
    </td>
    <td>
      <asp:RadioButtonList ID="rblGender" runat="server">
        <asp:ListItem Text="Male"
Value="Male"></asp:ListItem>
        <asp:ListItem Text="Female"
Value="Female"></asp:ListItem>
      </asp:RadioButtonList>
    </td>
  </tr>
  <tr>
    <td>
      <asp:Label ID="lblEducation" runat="server"
Text="Highest Education"></asp:Label>
    </td>
    <td>
      <asp:DropDownList ID="ddlEducation" runat="server"
Height="16px" Width="231px">
        <asp:ListItem Text="--Select--"
Value=""></asp:ListItem>
        <asp:ListItem Text="Post Graduate"
Value="PG"></asp:ListItem>
        <asp:ListItem Text="Degree"
Value="DG"></asp:ListItem>
        <asp:ListItem Text="Diploma"
Value="DP"></asp:ListItem>
        <asp:ListItem Text="A-Levels"
Value="AL"></asp:ListItem>
        <asp:ListItem Text="O-Levels"
Value="OL"></asp:ListItem>
      </asp:DropDownList>
    </td>
  </tr>
  <tr>
    <td>
      <asp:Label ID="lblInterest" runat="server"
Text="Interest Areas"></asp:Label>
    </td>
```

```
        <td>
           <asp:CheckBoxList ID="chkInterest" runat="server">
              <asp:ListItem Text="ASP.NET"
    Value="ASP.NET"></asp:ListItem>
              <asp:ListItem Text="Java"
    Value="Java"></asp:ListItem>
              <asp:ListItem Text="Android"
    Value="Android"></asp:ListItem>
              <asp:ListItem Text="HTML5"
    Value="HTML5"></asp:ListItem>
              <asp:ListItem Text="XML"
    Value="XML"></asp:ListItem>
           </asp:CheckBoxList>
        </td>
     </tr>
     <tr>
        <td colspan="2">
            
           <asp:CheckBox ID="chkSubscribe" runat="server"
    Text="Subscribe to newsletter" />
        </td>
     </tr>
     <tr>
        <td> </td>
        <td> </td>
     </tr>
     <tr>
        <td> </td>
        <td>
           <asp:Button ID="btnSubmit" runat="server"
    Text="Submit" />
        </td>
     </tr>
  </table>
```

How to do it...

Include the following jQuery code in a `<script>` block after the jQuery library has been included in the form:

```
<script type="text/javascript">
  $(document).ready(function() {
    $("#<%=btnSubmit.ClientID%>").click(function() {
      var strName = $("#<%=txtName.ClientID%>").val();
      var strGender =
```

```
        $("#<%=rblGender.ClientID%> input:checked").val();
      var strEducation =
$("#<%=ddlEducation.ClientID%>").find(":selected").text();
      var strInterest = "";
      $("#<%=chkInterest.ClientID%> input:checked").each(
        function() {
          strInterest += " " + $(this).val();
        });
      var strSubscribe = "";
      if ($("#<%=chkSubscribe.ClientID%>").is(":checked")) {
        strSubscribe =
$("#<%=chkSubscribe.ClientID%>").next().html();
      }
      var strDisplayMsg = "You are about to submit the following
data: \r\n\r\n" +
        "Name: " + strName + "\r\n" +
        "Gender: " + strGender + "\r\n" +
        "Highest Education: " + strEducation + "\r\n" +
        "Interest Areas: " + strInterest + "\r\n" +
        strSubscribe + "\r\n\r\n" +
        "Click OK to proceed"
      window.confirm(strDisplayMsg);
    });
  });
</script>
```

> The preceding `<script>` block can be included in the `<head>` or `<form>` element, depending on how the jQuery library has been included in the page.

How it works...

Let's look at how the form works:

1. Save the application using *Ctrl + S*, and run it by pressing *F5*. This will launch the **User Registration** page. Enter some test values in the controls, and click on the **Submit** button. A confirmation prompt is displayed that summarizes the values of the controls as follows:

User Registration

Name Abraham A.

Gender ● Male ○ Female

Highest Education Post Graduate

Interest Areas ☑ ASP.NET ☐ Java ☑ Android ☐ HTML5 ☑ XML

☑ Subscribe to newsletter

[Submit]

Message from webpage

You are about to submit the following data:

Name: Abraham A.
Gender: Male
Highest Education: Post Graduate
Interest Areas: ASP.NET Android XML
Subscribe to newsletter

Click OK to proceed

[OK] [Cancel]

> Note that no validation has been done on the controls, and the page allows you to submit a blank form as well. Validation will be described in subsequent chapters.

2. In the jQuery `<script>` block, every ASP.NET control is retrieved using the `#identifier` selector on the equivalent rendered HTML tag. The code is executed when the `click` event of the `Submit` button is raised, as shown in the following code:

```
$("#<%=btnSubmit.ClientID%>").click(function () {…});
```

> `ClientID` is the value assigned by ASP.NET to the ID of the equivalent HTML tag generated by a server control at runtime. ASP.NET provides various algorithms for the generation of ClientIDs such as AutoID, Static, Predictable, and Inherit.

3. At runtime, the `TextBox` control is rendered as the following HTML `input` element (right-click on the page in the browser, and click on **View Source** to see the rendered HTML):

```
<input name="txtName" type="text" id="txtName"
style="width:223px; " />
```

4. So, in the jQuery code, the value of the `TextBox` control with an `ID` equal to `txtName` can be accessed using the following code:

```
var strName = $("#<%=txtName.ClientID%>").val();
```

5. The `RadioButtonList` control is rendered as the following HTML code:

```
<table id="rblGender">
  <tr>
    <td><input id="rblGender_0" type="radio"
name="rblGender" value="Male" /><label
for="rblGender_0">Male</label></td>
  </tr>
  <tr>
    <td><input id="rblGender_1" type="radio"
name="rblGender" value="Female" /><label
for="rblGender_1">Female</label></td>
  </tr>
</table>
```

In the jQuery code, the selected radio button from the list can be accessed using the checked filter, as follows:

```
var strGender = $("#<%=rblGender.ClientID%> input:checked").val();
```

6. The `DropDownList` control is rendered as the following HTML code:

```
<select name="ddlEducation" id="ddlEducation" style="height:16px;width:231px;">
<option value="">--Select--</option>
<option value="PG">Post Graduate</option>
<option value="DG">Degree</option>
<option value="DP">Diploma</option>
<option value="AL">A-Levels</option>
<option value="OL">O-Levels</option>
</select>
```

The jQuery code finds the selected item from the `DropDownList` control using the `selected` filter and returns its `text` value as follows:

```
 var strEducation = $("#<%=ddlEducation.ClientID%>").
find(":selected").text();
```

7. The `CheckBoxList` control is rendered as the following HTML code:

```
<table id="chkInterest">
<tr>
   <td><input id="chkInterest_0" type="checkbox"
name="chkInterest$0" value="ASP.NET" /><label
for="chkInterest_0">ASP.NET</label></td>
</tr>
<tr>
   <td><input id="chkInterest_1" type="checkbox"
name="chkInterest$1" value="Java" /><label
for="chkInterest_1">Java</label></td>
</tr>
<tr>
   <td><input id="chkInterest_2" type="checkbox"
name="chkInterest$2" value="Android" /><label
for="chkInterest_2">Android</label></td>
</tr>
<tr>
   <td><input id="chkInterest_3" type="checkbox"
name="chkInterest$3" value="HTML5" /><label
for="chkInterest_3">HTML5</label></td>
</tr>
<tr>
   <td><input id="chkInterest_4" type="checkbox"
name="chkInterest$4" value="XML" /><label
for="chkInterest_4">XML</label></td>
</tr>
<table>
```

The jQuery code loops through each `checked` element using the `.each()` method, and appends its value to a `strInterest` string as follows:

```
var strInterest = "";
$("#<%=chkInterest.ClientID%> input:checked").each(function
() {
   strInterest += " " + $(this).val();
});
```

8. The subscribe `CheckBox` control renders two sibling HTML tags: `<input>` and `<label>`, as follows:

```
<input id="chkSubscribe" type="checkbox"
name="chkSubscribe" /><label for="chkSubscribe">Subscribe
to newsletter</label>
```

Hence, the jQuery code uses `.next().html()` to determine the text value of the `CheckBox` control as follows:

```
var strSubscribe = "";
if ($("#<%=chkSubscribe.ClientID%>").is(":checked")) {
    strSubscribe =
$("#<%=chkSubscribe.ClientID%>").next().html();
}
```

If the checkbox is unchecked, `strSubscribe` is an empty string.

9. Finally, all the retrieved values of the controls are appended to the `strDisplayMsg` string, and the script uses JavaScript's `window.confirm()` command to display the confirmation dialog box to the user. If the user clicks on **OK**, the form is submitted. Clicking on **Cancel** prevents the form from being submitted:

```
var strDisplayMsg = "You are about to submit the following data:
\r\n\r\n" +
"Name: " + strName + "\r\n" +
"Gender: " + strGender + "\r\n" +
"Highest Education: " + strEducation + "\r\n" +
"Interest Areas: " + strInterest + "\r\n" +
strSubscribe + "\r\n\r\n" +
"Click OK to proceed"
window.confirm(strDisplayMsg);
```

See also

▶ The *Selecting a control using the CSS class* recipe

Selecting a control using the CSS class

This recipe will demonstrate how to access ASP.NET controls, such as `Image`, `Panel`, and `BulletedList` based on the `CSSClass` assigned to them. The constructs used in this example are as follows:

Construct	Type	Description
`$(".class")`	jQuery selector	This matches all elements with the specified CSS class.
`.attr("name")` OR `.attr("name", "value")`	jQuery method	This returns a string with the required attribute value of the first matched element. It can also be used to set the attribute to the required value.
`.click()`	jQuery event binder	This binds a handler to the `click` event of an element.
`event. preventDefault()`	jQuery method	This prevents the default action of the event from being triggered.
`.hide()`	jQuery method	This hides the matched elements.
`.is()`	jQuery method	This returns a Boolean value if the matched element satisfies a given condition.
`.next()`	jQuery method	This gets the immediate sibling of an element.
`.show()`	jQuery method	This displays the matched elements.
`.toggle()`	jQuery method	This displays or hides the matched elements.

Getting ready

Let's access the ASP.NET controls using `CssClass`:

1. To demonstrate the CSS selector in jQuery, we will build a simple application that displays a **List of Questions**. The answers can be seen by clicking on the respective plus **+** icon next to the question:

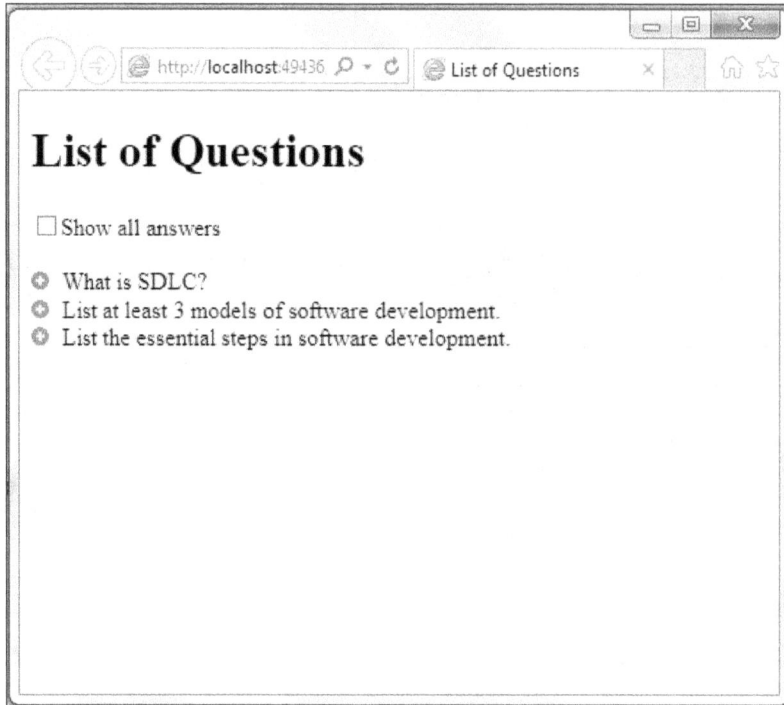

The page also has a checkbox on top. By clicking on this checkbox, all the answers will be displayed, as shown in the following screenshot:

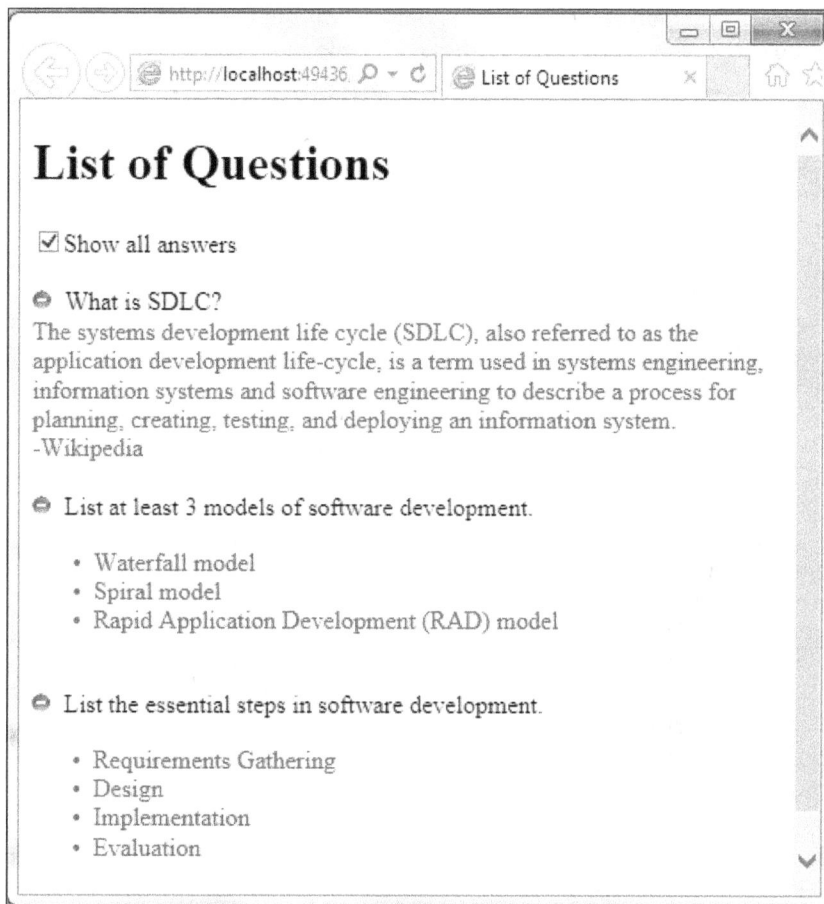

2. By clicking on the minus - icon, the corresponding answer can be collapsed.

3. To get started, create an **ASP.NET Web Application** project using the **Empty** template, and **name** the project Recipe2 (or any other suitable name).

4. Add a **Web Form** to the project and **name** it Default.aspx.

5. Create a Scripts folder and add jQuery files (debug and release versions of a library) to it.

6. Include the jQuery library in the form using either the <script> block or the ScriptManager control, as described in *Chapter 1, Getting Started with jQuery in ASP.NET*.

7. Create an images folder in the project and include images for the plus and minus icons.

8. Now, drag and drop ASP.NET controls by navigating to the **Toolbox** | **Standard** controls to create the required form, as shown in the preceding screenshot.

9. The HTML markup for the form is as follows:

```
<asp:CheckBox ID="chkShowAll" runat="server" Text="Show all
answers" />
<br /><br />
<asp:ImageButton ID="imgExpand1" runat="server"
CssClass="image" ImageUrl="~/images/plus.png"/>
<asp:Literal ID="litQuestion1" runat="server">What is
SDLC?</asp:Literal>
<asp:Panel ID="pnlAnswer1" CssClass="answer"
runat="server">
   The systems development life cycle …</asp:Panel>
<br />
<asp:ImageButton ID="imgExpand2" runat="server"
CssClass="image" ImageUrl="~/images/plus.png"/>
<asp:Literal ID="litQuestion2" runat="server">List at least
3 models of software development.</asp:Literal>
<asp:BulletedList ID="bltAnswer2" CssClass="answer"
runat="server">
   <asp:ListItem>Waterfall model</asp:ListItem>
   <asp:ListItem>Spiral model</asp:ListItem>
   <asp:ListItem>Rapid Application Development (RAD)
model</asp:ListItem>
</asp:BulletedList>
<br />
<asp:ImageButton ID="imgExpand3" runat="server"
CssClass="image" ImageUrl="~/images/plus.png"/>
<asp:Literal ID="litQuestion3" runat="server">List the
essential steps in software development.</asp:Literal>
<asp:BulletedList ID="bltAnswer3" CssClass="answer"
runat="server">
   <asp:ListItem>Requirements Gathering</asp:ListItem>
   <asp:ListItem>Design</asp:ListItem>
   <asp:ListItem>Implementation</asp:ListItem>
   <asp:ListItem>Evaluation</asp:ListItem>
</asp:BulletedList>
```

10. Add the following CSS styles to the page:

```
.answer {
  color: blue;
}
.image {
  height: 12 px;
```

```
    width: 12 px;
    margin - right: 5 px;
  }
```

How to do it...

Create a `<script>` block after the reference to the jQuery library has been added, and add the following code:

```
<script type="text/javascript">
$(document).ready(function() {
  $(".answer").hide();
  $("#<%=chkShowAll.ClientID%>").click(function() {
    if ($("#<%=chkShowAll.ClientID%>").is(":checked")) {
      $(".answer").show();
      $(".image").attr("src", "images/minus.png");
    } else {
      $(".answer").hide();
      $(".image").attr("src", "images/plus.png");
    }
  });
  $(".image").click(function(evt) {
    $(this).next(".answer").toggle();
    var src = ($(this).attr("src") === "images/plus.png") ?
"images/minus.png" : "images/plus.png";
    $(this).("src", src);
    evt.preventDefault();
  });
});
</script>
```

How it works...

Using the `CssClass` to select ASP.NET controls can be done in the following steps:

1. On running the application by pressing *F5*, all page elements with the `answer` CssClass are hidden by executing the following statement:

   ```
   $(".answer").hide();
   ```

   > Note: Because of this, once the page loads, only questions are visible.

2. When you click on the checkbox on the top of the page, its `click` event is triggered. An event handler is tied to the `click` event as follows:

```
$("#<%=chkShowAll.ClientID%>").click(function () {…});
```

3. In the preceding `click` event handler, firstly, the status of the checkbox is determined using the `checked` filter. If the checkbox is checked, then the answers are shown and the plus icons are changed to minus icons:

```
if ($("#<%=chkShowAll.ClientID%>").is(":checked")) {
    $(".answer").show();
    $(".image").attr("src", "images/minus.png");
}
```

If the checkbox is unchecked, the answers are hidden and the minus icons are updated to plus icons:

```
else {
    $(".answer").hide();
    $(".image").attr("src", "images/plus.png");
}
```

Thus, using the CSS selector on the `answer` and the `image` elements, the required contents can be shown or hidden.

4. In addition to this, the user can click on the plus and minus icons to expand or collapse the answers, respectively. Hence, a `click` event is tied to the `image` elements using the CSS selector for the images, as follows:

```
$(".image").click(function (evt) {…});
```

In the preceding event handler, the `answer` element following the image is toggled to show or hide, as follows:

```
$(this).next(".answer").toggle();
```

Lastly, the image is also toggled—that is, plus to minus or minus to plus, using the `.attr()` method:

```
var src = ($(this).attr("src") === "images/plus.png") ?
"images/minus.png" : "images/plus.png";
$(this).attr("src", src);
```

Lastly, to prevent the image `click` event from submitting the form, `evt.preventDefault()` is executed.

See also

▶   The *Selecting an element by its position in the DOM* recipe

Selecting a control using HTML tag

This recipe demonstrates how to access ASP.NET controls using the corresponding HTML tag generated at runtime. We will demonstrate how to use the `GridView` control, which generates the `table` HTML tag. Each row of the `GridView` renders the `tr` HTML tag. This example uses the following constructs:

Construct	Type	Description
`$("html_tag")`	jQuery selector	This selects all elements with the specified HTML tag
`$(this)`	jQuery object	This refers to the current jQuery object
`.addClass()`	jQuery method	This adds the specified CSS class to each matched element
`[attribute$="value"]`	jQuery selector	This selects an element with the specified attribute, ending with the string `"value"`
`:checkbox`	jQuery selector	This selects only checkbox elements from the matched elements
`.click()`	jQuery event binder	This binds a handler to the `click` event of an element
`.find()`	jQuery method	This finds all elements matching the filter
`.is()`	jQuery method	This returns a Boolean value if the matched element satisfies a given condition
`.parents()`	jQuery method	This selects the ancestors of the matched elements in the DOM tree
`.removeClass()`	jQuery method	This removes the specified CSS class from each matched element

Getting ready

Let's select ASP.NET controls using HTML tag:

1. In this example, we will create a web page to display a **List of Suppliers** from the Northwind database in a `GridView` control, as shown in the following screenshot:

2. Each row in the `GridView` has a `CheckBox` control in the first column. By selecting the checkbox, the respective row is highlighted, as shown in the following screenshot:

List of Suppliers

SupplierID	CompanyName	Address	City	Region	PostalCode	Country
☐ 18	Aux joyeux ecclésiastiques	203, Rue des Francs-Bourgeois	Paris		75004	France
☐ 16	Bigfoot Breweries	3400 - 8th Avenue Suite 210	Bend	OR	97101	USA
☐ 5	Cooperativa de Quesos 'Las Cabras'	Calle del Rosal 4	Oviedo	Asturias	33007	Spain
☑ 27	Escargots Nouveaux	22, rue H. Voiron	Montceau		71300	France
☐ 1	Exotic Liquids	49 Gilbert St.	London		EC1 4SD	UK
☐ 29	Forêts d'érables	148 rue Chasseur	Ste-Hyacinthe	Québec	J2S 7S8	Canada
☑ 14	Formaggi Fortini s.r.l.	Viale Dante, 75	Ravenna		48100	Italy
☐ 28	Gai pâturage	Bat. B 3, rue des Alpes	Annecy		74000	France
☐ 24	G'day, Mate	170 Prince Edward Parade Hunter's Hill	Sydney	NSW	2042	Australia
☑ 3	Grandma Kelly's Homestead	707 Oxford Rd.	Ann Arbor	MI	48104	USA

1 2 3

> Likewise, by unchecking the checkbox, the highlighting is removed.

3. To get started, create an **ASP.NET Web Application** project using the **Empty** template, and **name** the project `Recipe3` (or any other suitable name).

4. Add a **Web Form** to the project and **name** it `Default.aspx`.

5. Create a `Scripts` folder and add jQuery files (debug and release versions of a library) to it.

6. Include the jQuery library in the form using either the `<script>` block or the `ScriptManager` control, as described in *Chapter 1, Getting Started with jQuery in ASP.NET*.

7. Open `Default.aspx` in the **Design** mode, and drag and drop a **GridView** control by navigating to **Toolbox | Data**.

8. Populate the gridview with the Suppliers data from the Northwind database using LINQ by following Steps 9 to 15. If you are familiar with using LINQ, proceed to Step 16 to add the checkbox field and required columns to the gridview markup.

Installing the Northwind database

Northwind is an open source database that can be downloaded from: `https://northwinddatabase.codeplex.com`.

Read more about: How to install sample databases from the MSDN page at: `https://msdn.microsoft.com/en-us/library/8b6y4c7s.aspx`.

9. Add the **App_Code** folder to the project by right-clicking on the project and navigating to **Add** | **Add ASP.NET Folder** | **App_Code**.

10. Right-click on the **App_Code** folder, and go to **Add** | **Add New Item**. From the dialog box, select **LINQ to SQL Classes**, and **name** the file `Northwind.dbml`, as shown in the following screenshot. Click on the **Add** button to proceed:

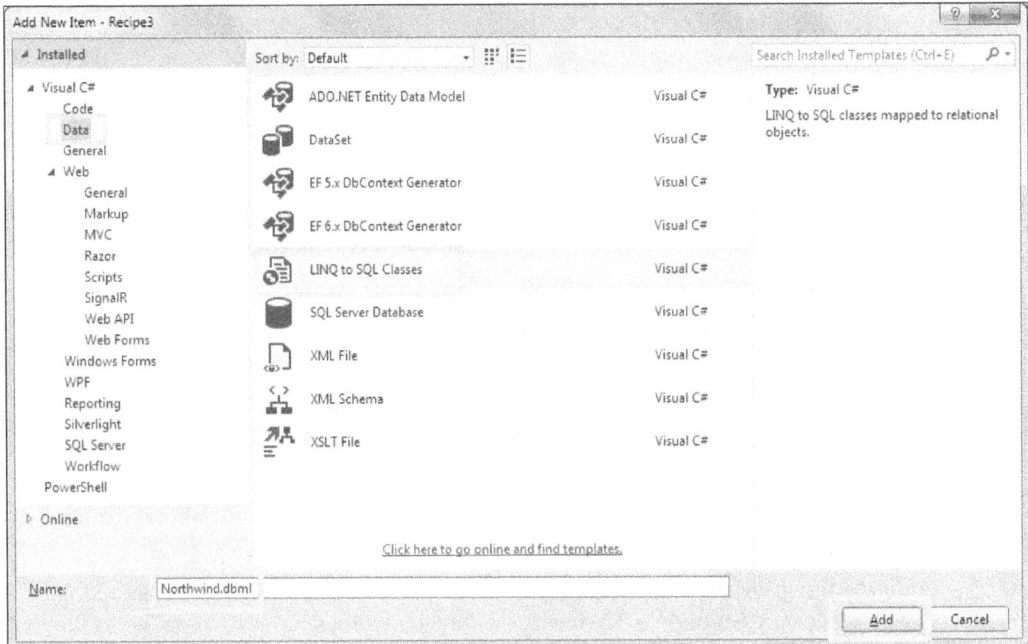

11. Open `Northwind.dbml` in the designer. Connect to the Northwind database, running on MS SQL Server using **Server Explorer**. Drag and drop the **Suppliers** table onto the designer, as shown in the following screenshot:

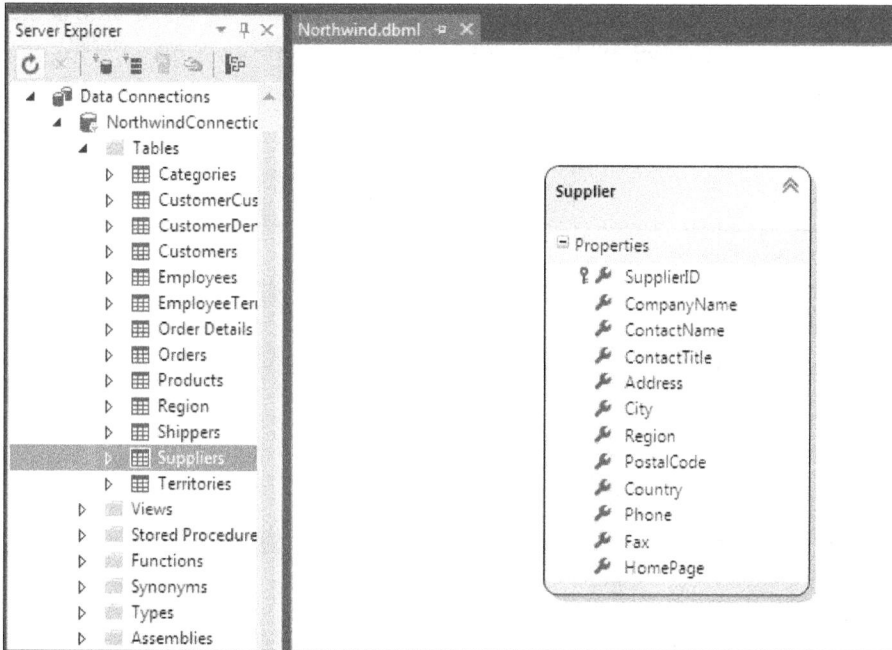

12. Now, open the `Default.aspx` web form in the **Design** mode, and click on the **GridView** control. A small arrow icon appears in the top-right corner of the **GridView** control, and when you click on it, the **GridView Tasks** submenu opens up, as shown in the following screenshot:

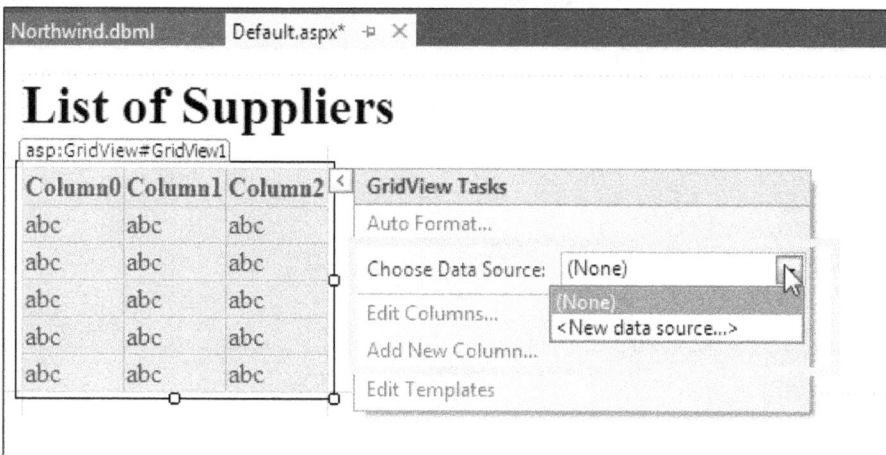

13. In the **GridView Tasks** submenu, go to **Choose Data Source** | **<New data source...>**. From the **Data Source Configuration Wizard**, select **LINQ**, and click on **OK**.

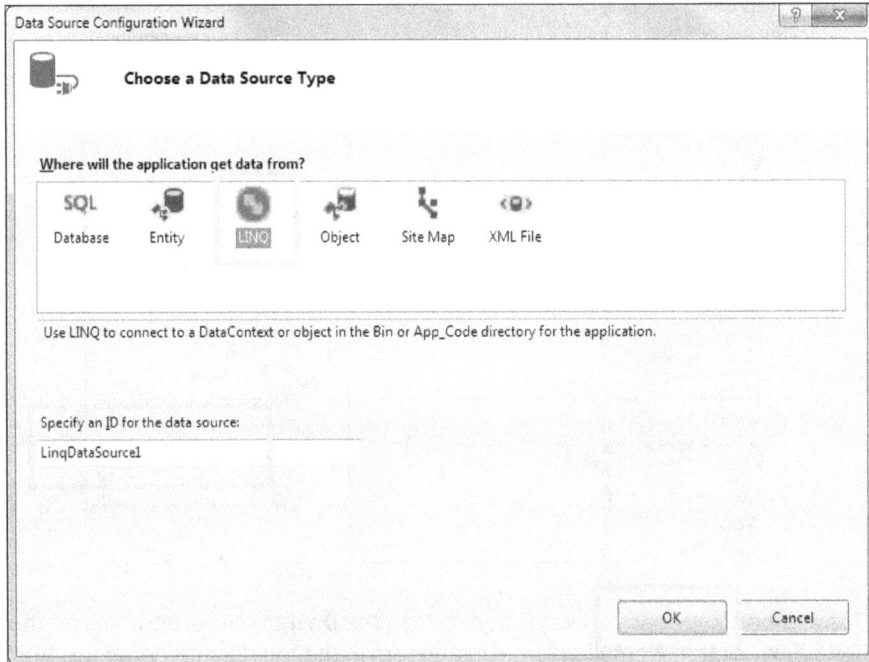

14. This will launch the **Configure Data Source** dialog box. From the drop-down menu, select the **Recipe3.App_Code.NorthwindDataContext** option, and click on **Next**.

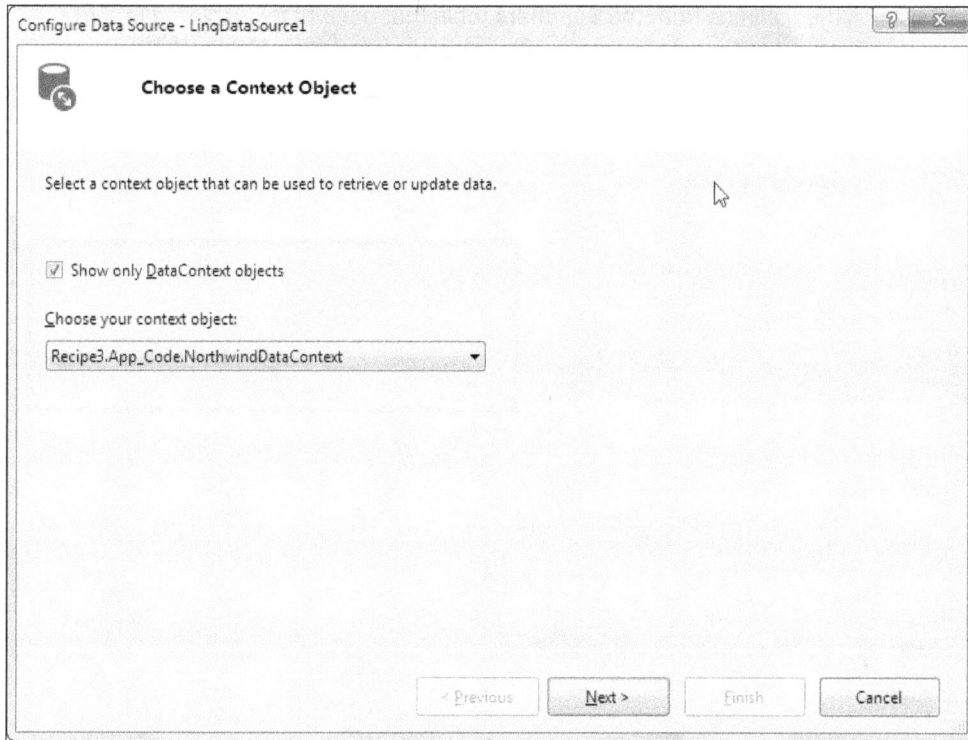

Note that, if the **NorthwindDataContext** does not appear in the drop-down menu, then add `System.Data.Linq` to the `system.web/compilation/assemblies` element in `web.config`, as follows:

```
<system.web>
  <compilation debug="true">
    <assemblies>
      <add assembly="System.Data.Linq,
Version=4.0.30319.17929, Culture=neutral,
PublicKeyToken=b77a5c561934e089" />
    </assemblies>
  </compilation>
</system.web>
```

15. Check the columns from the **Suppliers** table that need to be displayed in the `GridView`, or select ***** to retrieve all columns, and click on **Finish**:

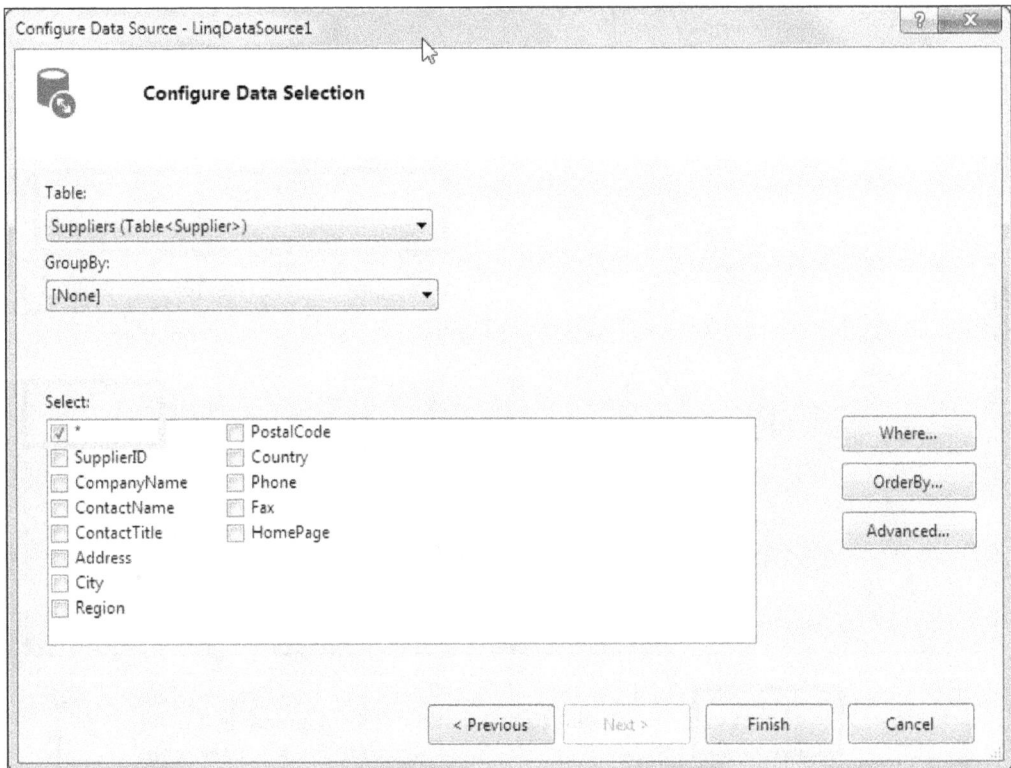

16. Open `Default.aspx` in the **Source** mode, and update the markup of the gridview, as follows, to add a **CheckBox** control as a **TemplateField** in the first column. We will also limit the display to a few important columns. Also, change the ID of the `GridView` to gvSupplierList:

```
<asp:GridView ID="gvSupplierList" runat="server"
AutoGenerateColumns="False" DataKeyNames="SupplierID"
DataSourceID="LinqDataSource1">
  <Columns>
    <asp:TemplateField>
      <ItemTemplate>
        <asp:CheckBox ID="chkSelect" runat="server" />
      </ItemTemplate>
    </asp:TemplateField>
    <asp:BoundField DataField="SupplierID"
HeaderText="SupplierID" InsertVisible="False"
ReadOnly="True" SortExpression="SupplierID" />
```

```
    <asp:BoundField DataField="CompanyName"
HeaderText="CompanyName" SortExpression="CompanyName" />
    <asp:BoundField DataField="Address"
HeaderText="Address" SortExpression="Address" />
    <asp:BoundField DataField="City" HeaderText="City"
SortExpression="City" />
    <asp:BoundField DataField="Region" HeaderText="Region"
SortExpression="Region" />
    <asp:BoundField DataField="PostalCode"
HeaderText="PostalCode" SortExpression="PostalCode" />
    <asp:BoundField DataField="Country"
HeaderText="Country" SortExpression="Country" />
  </Columns>
</asp:GridView>
```

17. To enable paging and sorting on the **GridView** (optional), from the **GridView Tasks** submenu, check the **Enable Paging** and **Enable Sorting** options as shown in the following screenshot:

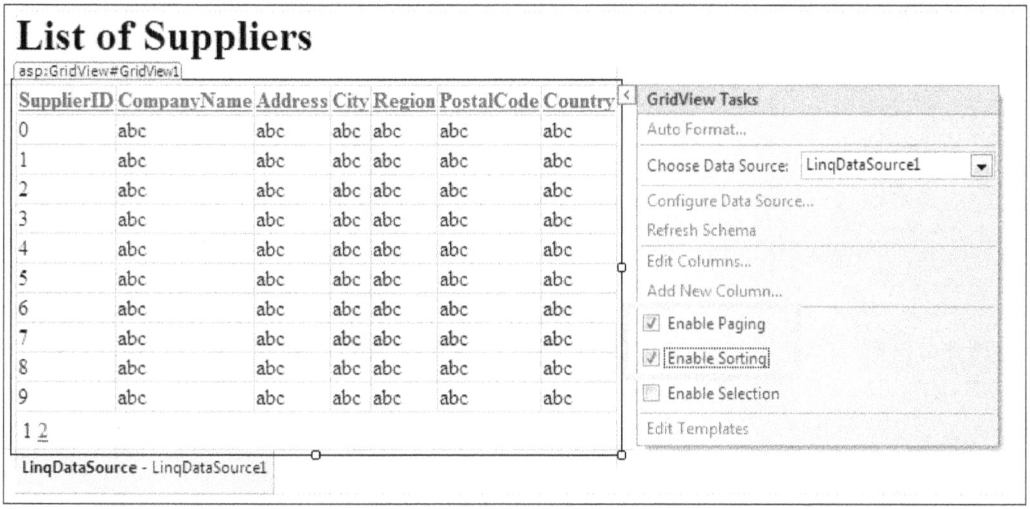

18. Add the following `<style>` to the `<head>` element of the web form:

```
<style>
  .highlight{
    background-color:darkgrey;
  }
</style>
```

Since we are using Integrated Security, the windows account should be given permission to access the Northwind database, as shown in the following steps:

1. In the SQL Server **Object Explorer** dialog box, go to **Databases** | **Northwind** | **Security** | **Users**. Right-click on **Users** and click on **New User**, as shown in the following screenshot:

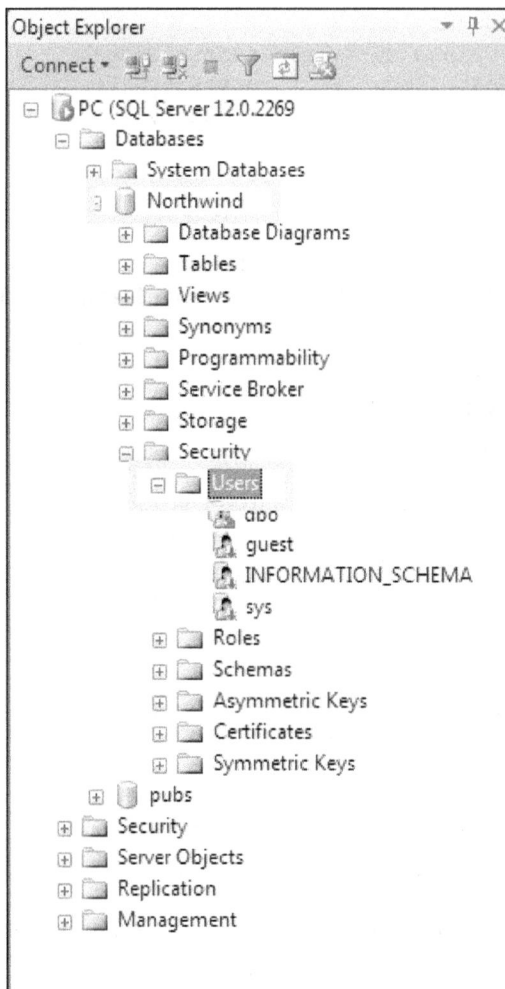

2. This will launch the **User-New** dialog box. From the drop-down menu, change **User type** to **Windows user**. Go the **User name** option, and select the windows account that you have used to log in to the system, as shown in the following screenshot:

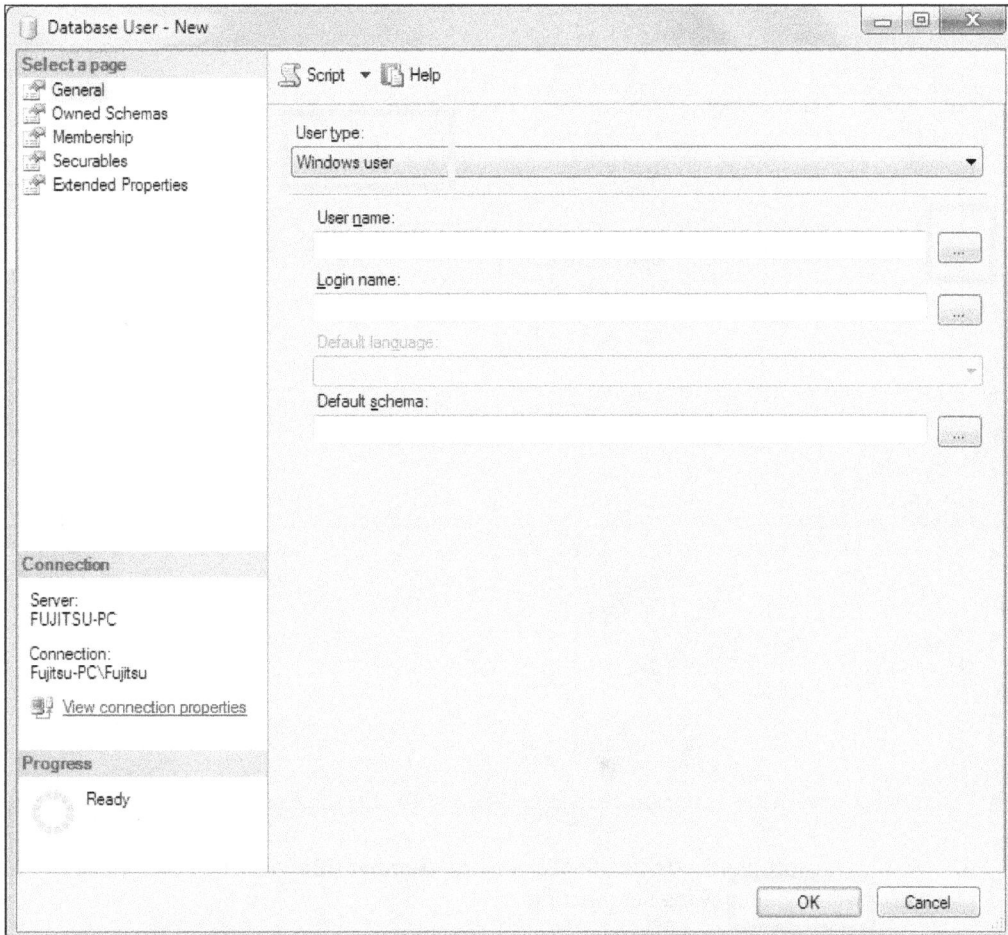

3. In the same dialog box, in the left-hand side panel, click on the **Owned Schemas** tab. Check **db_owner**, as shown in the following screenshot:

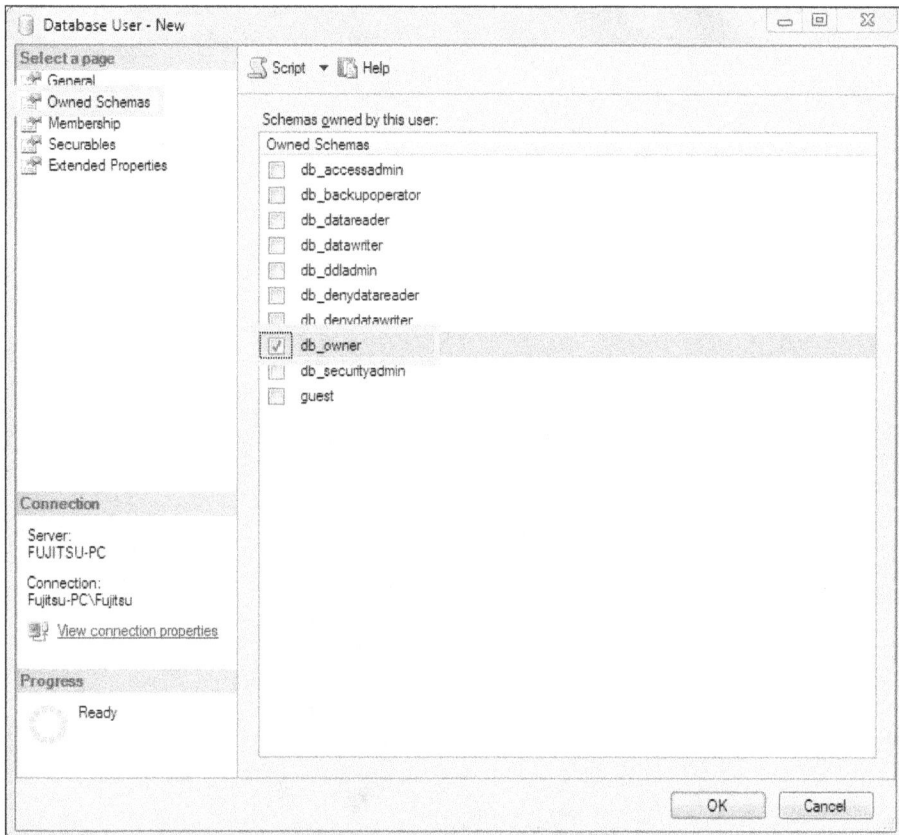

4. Next, in the left-hand side panel, click on the **Membership** tab. Check **db_owner**, as shown in the following screenshot:

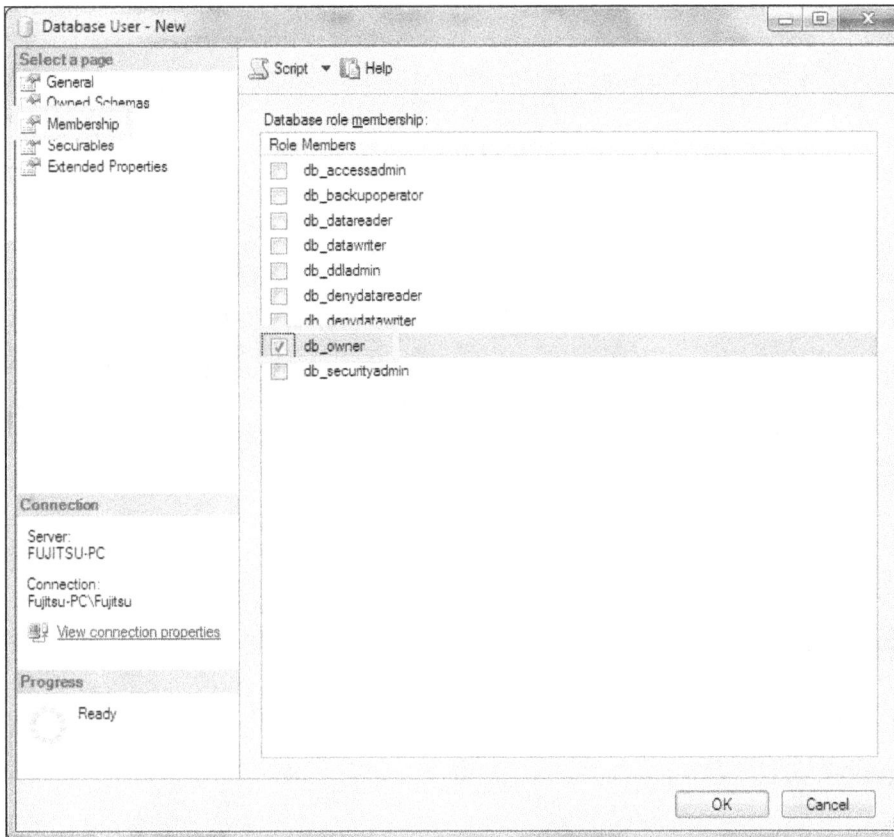

5.   Click on **OK** to save.

How to do it...

Add the following jQuery code to a `<script>` block after the jQuery library is included in the page:

```
<script type="text/javascript">
$(document).ready(function() {
  $("table[id$=<%=gvSupplierList.ClientID%>").find("input:checkbox").
click(
    function() {
      if ($(this).is(":checked"))
```

```
            $(this).parents("tr").addClass("highlight");
        else
            $(this).parents("tr").removeClass("highlight");
    });
});
</script>
```

How it works...

Selecting ASP.NET controls using HTML tag can be done in the following steps:

1. In this example, the gridview is selected using the `<table>` HTML tag that it generates at runtime. Each row of the `GridView` control is rendered as a `tr` HTML tag. This can be seen by viewing the source at runtime:

```
52        <h1>List of Suppliers</h1>
53          ...
54        <table cellspacing="0" rules="all" border="1" id="gvSupplierList" style="border-collapse:collapse;">
55          ...
56                <th scope="col"> </th><th scope="col"><a href="javascript:__doPostBack(&#39;gvSupplierList&#39;,&#39;Sort
    $SupplierID&#39;)">SupplierID</a></th><th scope="col"><a href="javascript:__doPostBack(&#39;gvSupplierList&#39;,&#39;Sort$CompanyName&#
    39;)">CompanyName</a></th><th scope="col"><a href="javascript:__doPostBack(&#39;gvSupplierList&#39;,&#39;Sort$Address&#39;)">Address
    </a></th><th scope="col"><a href="javascript:__doPostBack(&#39;gvSupplierList&#39;,&#39;Sort$City&#39;)">City</a></th><th scope="col">
    <a href="javascript:__doPostBack(&#39;gvSupplierList&#39;,&#39;Sort$Region&#39;)">Region</a></th><th scope="col"><a href="javascript:
    __doPostBack(&#39;gvSupplierList&#39;,&#39;Sort$PostalCode&#39;)">PostalCode</a></th><th scope="col"><a href="javascript:__doPostBack
    (&#39;gvSupplierList&#39;,&#39;Sort$Country&#39;)">Country</a></th>
57            </tr><tr>
58                <td>
59                    <input id="gvSupplierList_chkSelect_0" type="checkbox" name="gvSupplierList$ctl02$chkSelect" />
60                </td><td>1</td><td>Exotic Liquids</td><td>49 Gilbert St.</td><td>London</td><td> </td><td>EC1 4SD</td><td>UK
    </td>
61            </tr><tr>
62                <td>
63                    <input id="gvSupplierList_chkSelect_1" type="checkbox" name="gvSupplierList$ctl03$chkSelect" />
64                </td><td>2</td><td>New Orleans Cajun Delights</td><td>P.O. Box 78934</td><td>New Orleans</td><td>LA</td><td>70117
    </td><td>USA</td>
65            </tr><tr>
66                <td>
67                    <input id="gvSupplierList_chkSelect_2" type="checkbox" name="gvSupplierList$ctl04$chkSelect" />
68                </td><td>3</td><td>Grandma Kelly&#39;s Homestead</td><td>707 Oxford Rd.</td><td>Ann Arbor</td><td>MI</td><td>48104
    </td><td>USA</td>
69            </tr><tr>
```

2. Since there can be more than one `<table>` element on the page, the table elements are filtered using `id`. Once the required `<table>` element—that is, the `GridView` control is selected, the `CheckBox` control in the first column is matched using the `.find("input:checkbox")` selector. A `click` event handler is tied to the `CheckBox` control as follows:

    ```
    $("table[id$=<%=gvSupplierList.ClientID%>]").find("input:ch
    eckbox").click(function(){...});
    ```

3. After the `click` event handler is tied to the `CheckBox` elements, the next task is to determine whether the checkbox has been checked or unchecked using the `:checked` selector as follows:

    ```
    if ($(this).is(":checked"))
    ```

4. If the checkbox is checked, then its parent table row is selected using the
   `.parents("tr")` selector. Next, the `highlight` CSS class is tied to this
   table row as follows:

   ```
   $(this).parents("tr").addClass("highlight");
   ```

5. However, if the checkbox is unchecked, the highlight needs to be removed. This can
   be done using the `.removeClass()` method on the respective table row, as follows:

   ```
   $(this).parents("tr").removeClass("highlight");
   ```

See also

▶ The *Selecting a control using an ID and displaying its value* recipe

Selecting a control by its attribute

In this recipe, we will select ASP.NET controls based on a particular attribute they have.
The demonstration uses the `NavigateUrl` property of ASP.NET Hyperlink controls,
which is rendered as an `href` attribute of the `anchor` tag. The constructs used are
summarized as follows:

Construct	Type	Description
`$("#identifier")`	jQuery selector	This selects an element based on its `ID`
`.addClass()`	jQuery selector	This adds the specified CSS class to each matched element
`[attribute*="value"]`	jQuery selector	This selects an element with the specified attribute containing the string `"value"`
`.click()`	jQuery event binder	This binds a handler to the `click` event of an element
`event.preventDefault()`	jQuery method	This prevents the default action of the event from being triggered
`.focus()`	jQuery event binder	This triggers the `focus` event of an element or binds an event handler to the `focus` JavaScript event
`.removeClass()`	jQuery method	This removes the specified CSS class from each matched element
`.toLowerCase()`	JavaScript function	This converts a string to lowercase characters

Construct	Type	Description
`.val()`	jQuery method	This returns the value of the first matched element or sets the value of every matched element

Getting ready

Let's create a web page where we will retrieve controls using their attributes:

1. Consider the web page in the following screenshot:

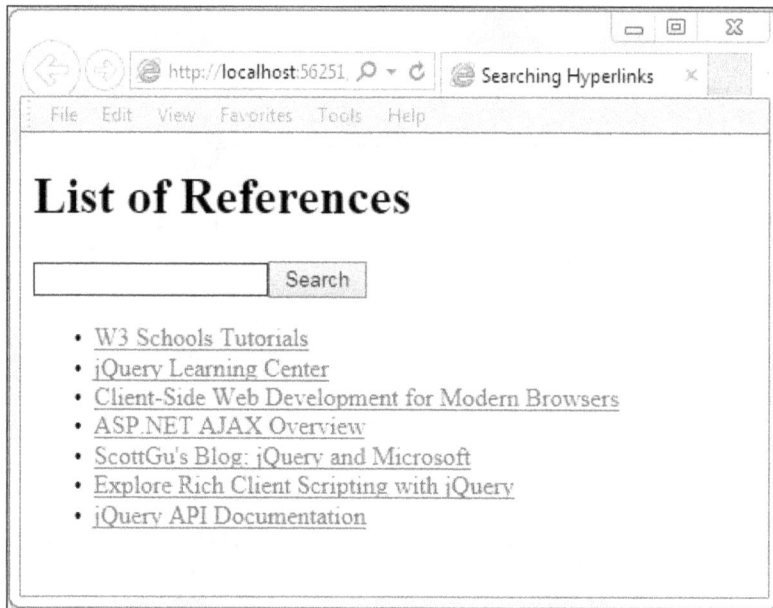

2. The web page consists of a list of Hyperlink controls. The **Search** textbox on the top of the page allows you to search the URLs set in the `NavigateUrl` property of the `Hyperlink` controls by a keyword. If a particular keyword is present in the URL link, the corresponding link is highlighted, as shown in the following screenshot:

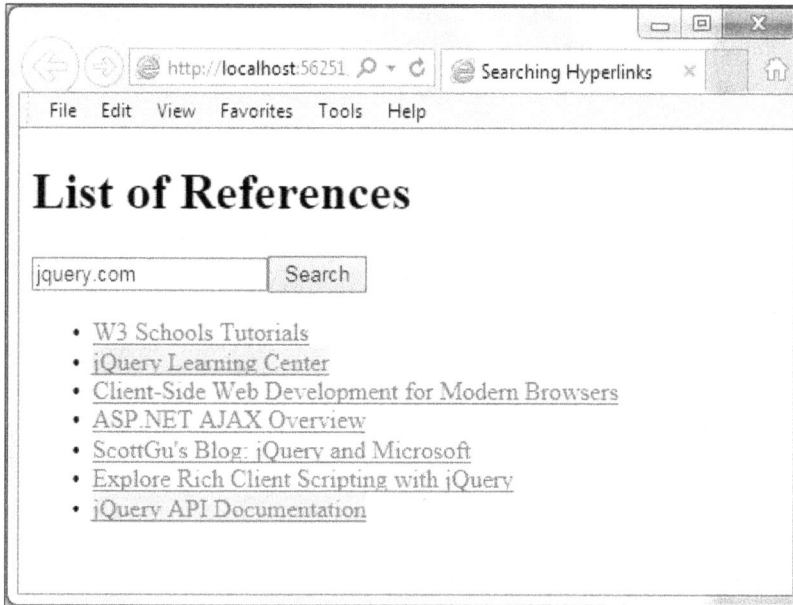

3. If another keyword is searched, a new set of links matching the new search keyword are highlighted, as follows:

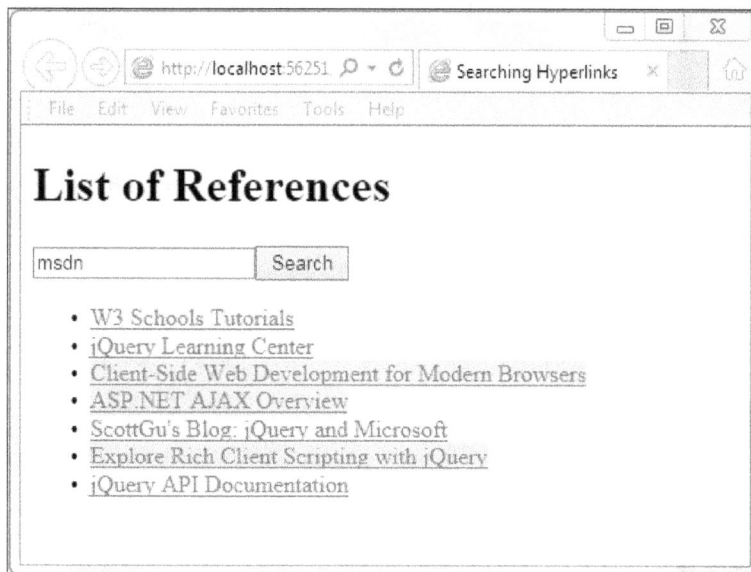

4. To get started, create an **ASP.NET Web Application** project using the **Empty** template, and **name** the project `Recipe4` (or any other suitable name).

5. Add a **Web Form** to the project and **name** it `Default.aspx`.

6. Create a `Scripts` folder and add jQuery files (debug and release versions of a library) to it.

7. Include the jQuery library in the form using either the `<script>` block or the `ScriptManager` control, as described in *Chapter 1, Getting Started with jQuery in ASP.NET*.

8. Open `Default.aspx` in the **Design** mode, and drag and drop the required controls by navigating to **Toolbox | Standard** to create the form with the following markup:

```
<asp:TextBox ID="txtKeyword" runat="server"></asp:TextBox>
<asp:Button ID="btnSearch" runat="server" Text="Search" />
<br />
<ul>
  <li>
    <asp:HyperLink runat="server"
NavigateUrl="http://www.w3schools.com/jquery/"
Target="_blank">W3 Schools Tutorials</asp:HyperLink>
  </li>
  <li>
    <asp:HyperLink runat="server"
NavigateUrl="https://learn.jquery.com/"
Target="_blank">jQuery Learning Center</asp:HyperLink>
  </li>
  <li>
    <asp:HyperLink runat="server"
NavigateUrl="https://msdn.microsoft.com/en-
us/library/hh396380.aspx" Target="_blank">Client-Side Web
Development for Modern Browsers</asp:HyperLink>
  </li>
  <li>
    <asp:HyperLink runat="server"
NavigateUrl="https://msdn.microsoft.com/en-
us/library/bb398874(VS.100).aspx" Target="_blank">ASP.NET
AJAX Overview</asp:HyperLink>
  </li>
  <li>
    <asp:HyperLink runat="server"
NavigateUrl="http://weblogs.asp.net/scottgu/jquery-and-
microsoft" Target="_blank">ScottGu's Blog: jQuery and
Microsoft</asp:HyperLink>
  </li>
  <li>
```

```
    <asp:HyperLink runat="server"
NavigateUrl="https://msdn.microsoft.com/en-
us/magazine/dd453033.aspx" Target="_blank">Explore Rich
Client Scripting with jQuery</asp:HyperLink>
  </li>
  <li>
    <asp:HyperLink runat="server"
NavigateUrl="http://api.jquery.com/" Target="_blank">jQuery
API Documentation</asp:HyperLink>
  </li>
</ul>
```

9. In the `<head>` element of the page, add the following style:

```
<style type="text/css">
  .highlight{
    background-color:yellow;
  }
</style>
```

How to do it...

Include the following jQuery code in the page in a `<script>` block after including the jQuery library:

```
<script type="text/javascript">
  $(document).ready(function() {
    $("table[id$=<%=gvSupplierList.ClientID%>").
find("input:checkbox").click(
      function() {
        if ($(this).is(":checked"))
          $(this).parents("tr").addClass("highlight");
        else
          $(this).parents("tr").removeClass("highlight");
      });
  });
</script>
```

How it works...

The selection of controls by attribute works as follows:

1. When the page is launched, the search textbox receives focus by calling its `focus` event using the following code:

   ```
   $("#<%=txtKeyword.ClientID%>").focus();
   ```

2. Simultaneously, an event handler is attached to the `click` event of the **Search** button:

```
$("#<%=btnSearch.ClientID %>").click(function (evt) {…}
```

3. The event handler reads the searched keyword from the textbox and converts it to a lowercase string:

```
var strKeyword = $("#<%=txtKeyword.ClientID%>").val().
toLowerCase();
```

4. Before we begin with highlighting the matched `anchor` tags, the CSS class of all `anchor` tags on the page is reset using the `$("a")` selector:

```
$("a").removeClass("highlight");
```

5. A search by its attribute is done on all `anchor` tags using their `href` attributes. If the `href` attribute contains the search keyword, the link is highlighted by attaching the respective CSS class:

```
$('a[href*= "' + strKeyword + '"]').addClass("highlight");
```

Lastly, `evt.preventDefault()` prevents the page from submitting because of the button `click` event.

See also

▶ The *Selecting a control using HTML tag* recipe

Selecting an element by its position in the DOM

This recipe demonstrates how to use an element's position with respect to its parent when you access it in the DOM tree. We will use the ASP.NET `ListBox` control for this purpose. The constructs used in this example are as follows:

Construct	Type	Description
`$("#id > *")`	jQuery selector	This selects all descendant elements of the control with the specified ID.
`$("#id :first-child")`	jQuery selector	This selects the first child element of the control with the specified ID.
`$("#id :last-child")`	jQuery selector	This selects the last child element of the control with the specified ID.

Construct	Type	Description
`$("#id :lt(i)")`	jQuery selector	This selects all child elements of the control with the specified ID that have an index less than `i`. Note that the index starts at zero.
`$("#id :gt(i)")`	jQuery selector	This selects all child elements of the control with the specified ID that have an index greater than `i`. Note that the index starts at zero.
`$("#id :nth-child(i)")`	jQuery selector	This selects the child element of the control with the specified ID that has an index `i`. Note that the index for the nth child starts at 1.
`$("#id :nth-child(even)")`	jQuery selector	This selects all the child elements of the control with the specified ID that have even indices.
`$("#id :nth-child(odd)")`	jQuery selector	This selects all the child elements of the control with the specified ID that have odd indices.
`.addClass()`	jQuery method	This adds the specified CSS class to each matched element.
`.click()`	jQuery event binder	This binds a handler to the `click` event of an element.
`event.preventDefault()`	jQuery method	This prevents the default action of the event from being triggered.
`.removeClass()`	jQuery method	This removes the specified CSS class from each matched element.
`.val()`	jQuery method	This returns the value of the first matched element or sets the value of every matched element.

Getting ready

Let's create a webpage that selects elements based on their position:

1. Consider the following web page that consists of a list box populated with data from the Suppliers table from the Northwind database, as follows:

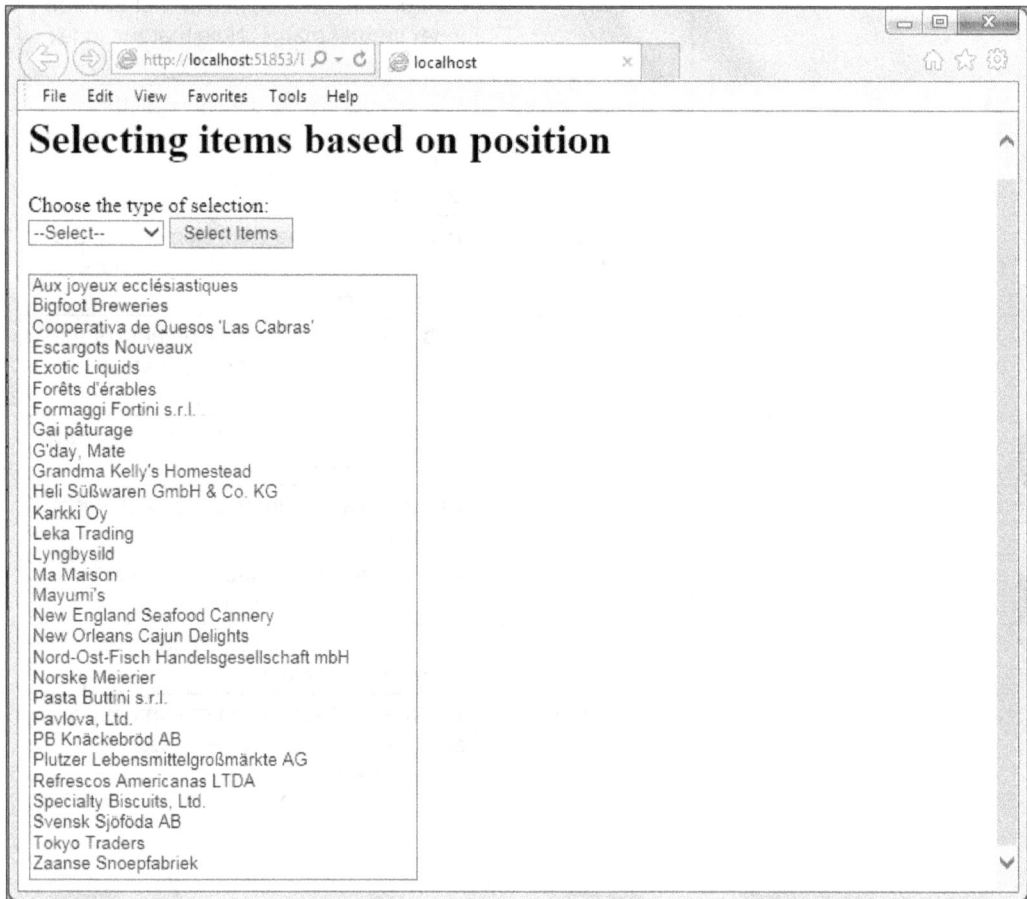

2. There is a dropdown list at the top of the page that allows you to select items in the list box, depending on their position in the DOM tree. The dropdown list has options to select the first, last, items less than or greater than a particular index, the nth item, as well as odd or even items, as shown in the following screenshot:

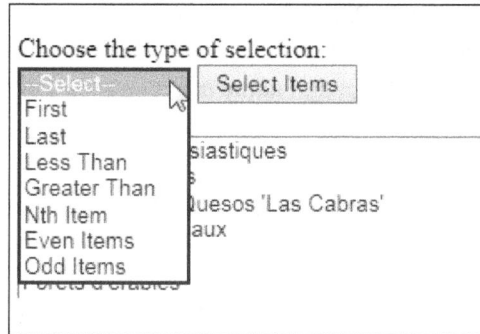

Note that we will be using hardcoded indices in this recipe. In a practical scenario, it is preferable to provide a textbox or a dropdown list to enable the user to enter or select the required index.

3. To demonstrate the working of the form, consider the scenario in which **Odd Items** is selected from the dropdown list. In this case, only odd indexed items from the list box are highlighted, as shown here:

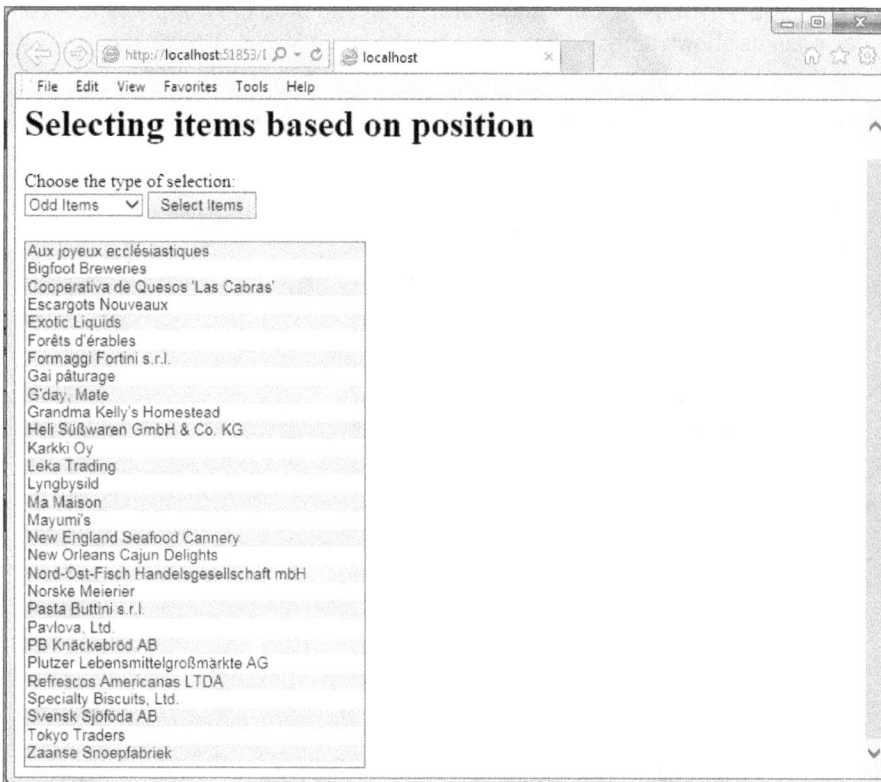

4. To get started, create an **ASP.NET Web Application** project using the **Empty** template, and **name** the project Recipe5 (or any other suitable name).

5. Add a **Web Form** to the project and **name** it Default.aspx.

6. Create a Scripts folder and add jQuery files (debug and release versions of a library) to it.

7. Include the jQuery library in the form using either the <script> block or the ScriptManager control, as described in *Chapter 1, Getting Started with jQuery in ASP.NET*.

8. Open the Default.aspx web form in the **Design** mode and drag and drop a **ListBox** control by navigating to **Toolbox | Standard**.

9. Populate the listbox with the Suppliers data from the Northwind database using LINQ by following Steps 10 to 18. If you are familiar with using LINQ, proceed to step 19.

10. Add the **App_Code** folder to the project by right-clicking on the project and navigating to **Add | Add ASP.NET Folder | App_Code**.

11. Right-click on the **App_Code** folder, and go to **Add | Add New Item**. From the dialog box, select **LINQ to SQL Classes**, and **name** the file Northwind.dbml.

12. Open Northwind.dbml in the designer. Connect to the Northwind database running on MS SQL Server using **Server Explorer**. Drag and drop the **Suppliers** table on the designer, as shown here:

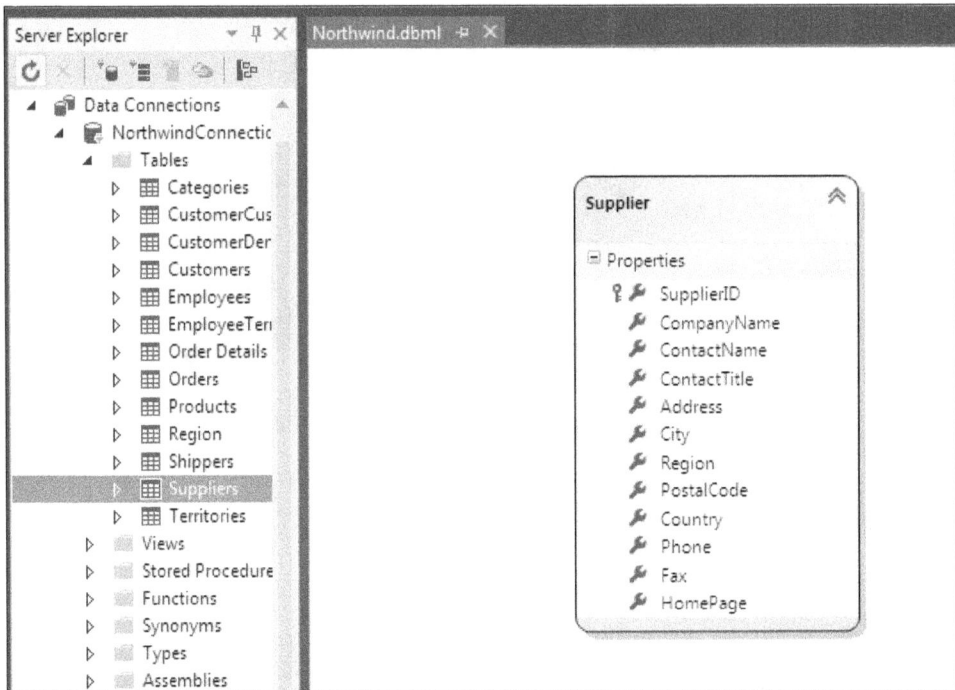

13. Now, open the `Default.aspx` web form in the **Design** mode, and click on the **ListBox** control. A small arrow icon appears in the top-right corner of the **ListBox** control, and when you click on it, the **ListBox Tasks** submenu opens up, as shown in the following screenshot:

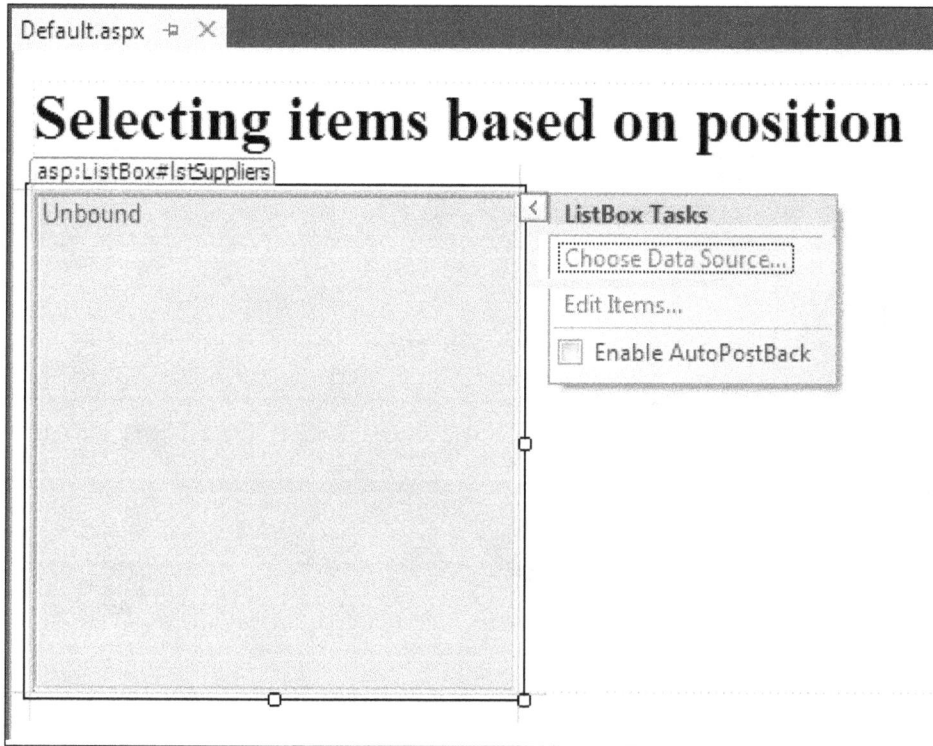

14. From the **ListBox Tasks** submenu, select **Choose Data Source**. This launches the **Data Source Configuration Wizard**, as shown in the following screenshot. Select **<New data source...>** from the first drop-down menu:

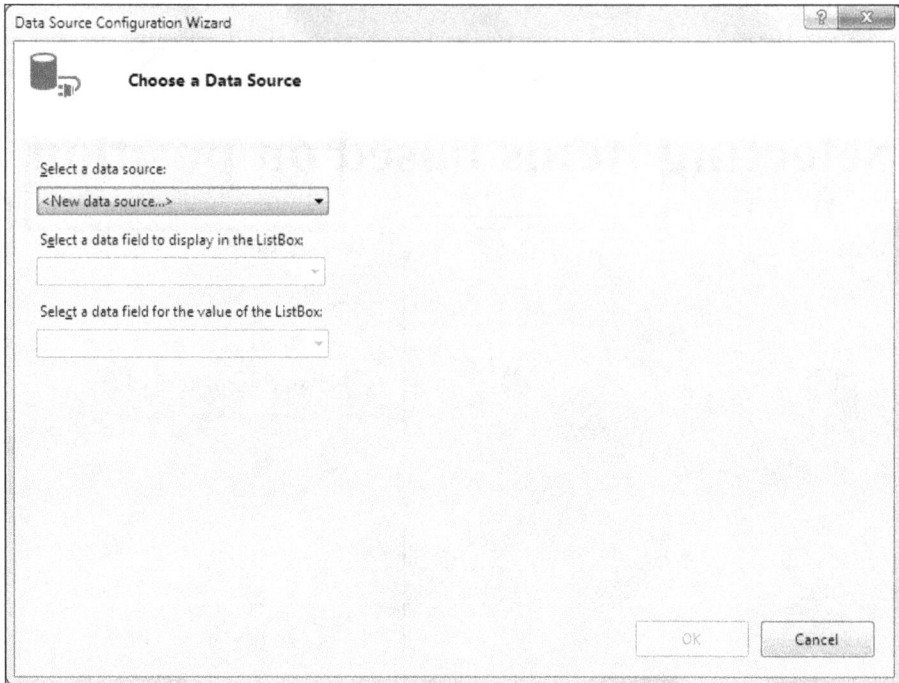

15. This will prompt you to select **Choose a Data Source Type**. Select **LINQ**, and click on **OK**:

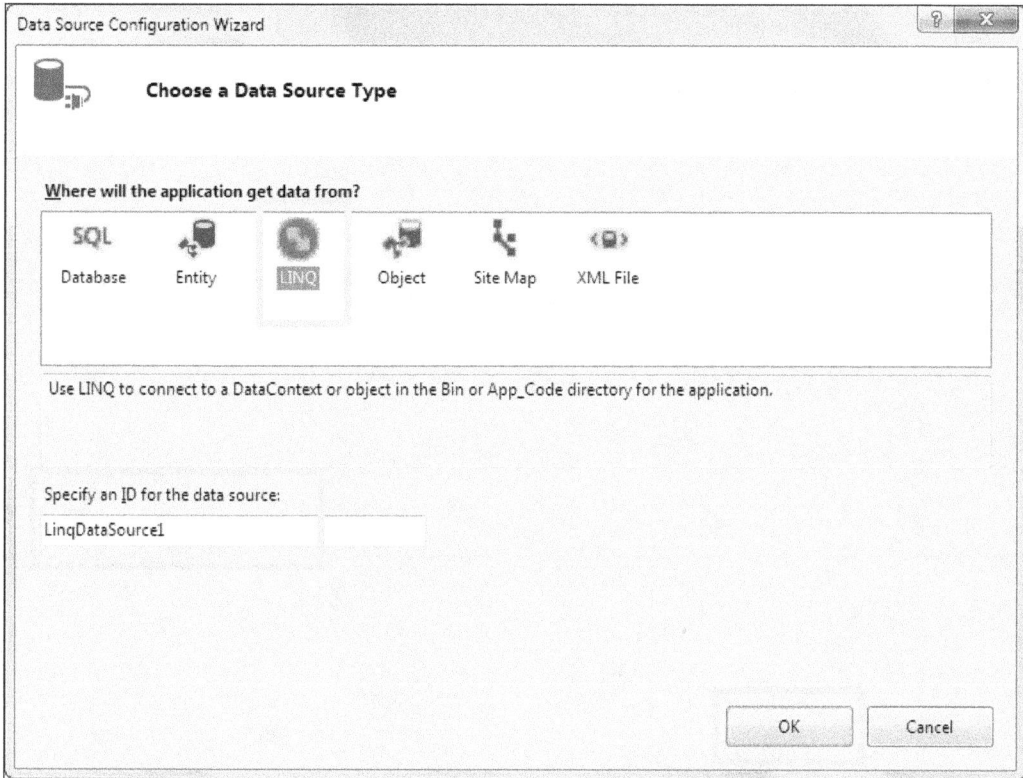

16. On being prompted to select **Choose a Context Object**, choose **Recipe5.App_Code. NorthwindDataContext** from the drop-down menu, and click on **Next**:

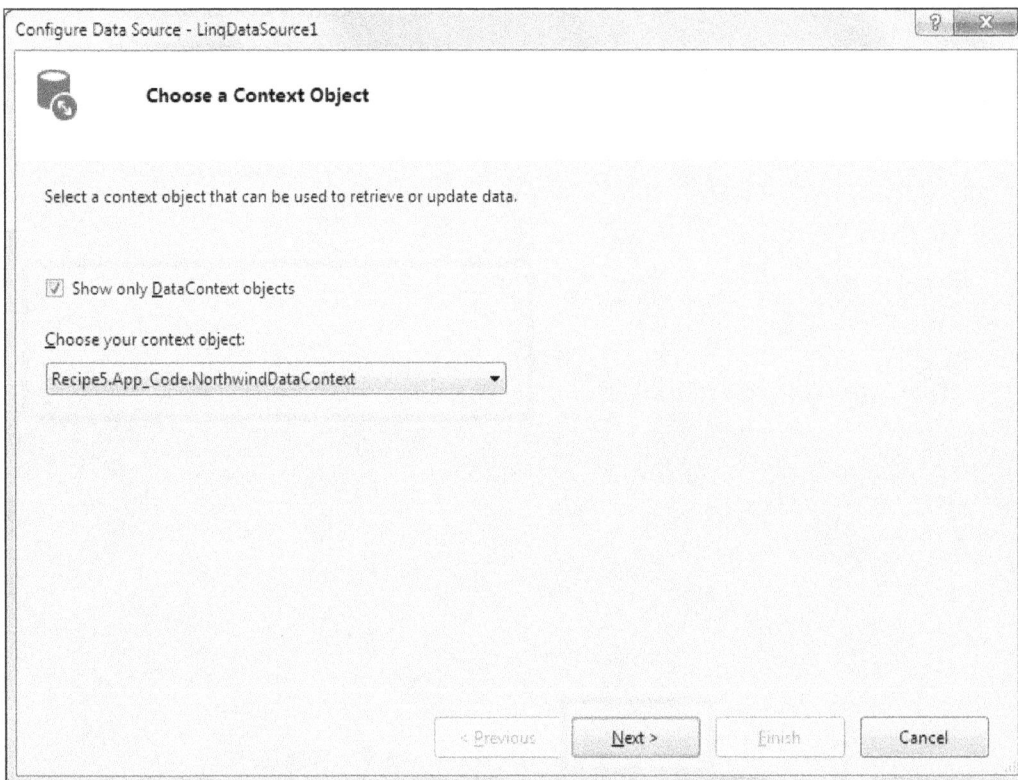

```
Configure Data Source - LinqDataSource1                              ? X

         Choose a Context Object

Select a context object that can be used to retrieve or update data.


☑ Show only DataContext objects

Choose your context object:

Recipe5.App_Code.NorthwindDataContext          ▼



                        < Previous    Next >     Finish       Cancel
```

Note that if the **NorthwindDataContext** does not appear in the drop-down menu, add `System.Data.Linq` to the `system.web/compilation/assemblies` element in `web.config`, as follows:

```
<system.web>
  <compilation debug="true">
    <assemblies>
      <add assembly="System.Data.Linq,
Version=4.0.30319.17929, Culture=neutral,
PublicKeyToken=b77a5c561934e089" />
    </assemblies>
  </compilation>
</system.web>
```

17. Check the **SupplierID** and **CompanyName** columns from the **Suppliers** table, and click on **Finish**:

18. Set the display field of the list box to `CompanyName` and the value field to `SupplierID`, as shown in the following screenshot, and click on **OK**:

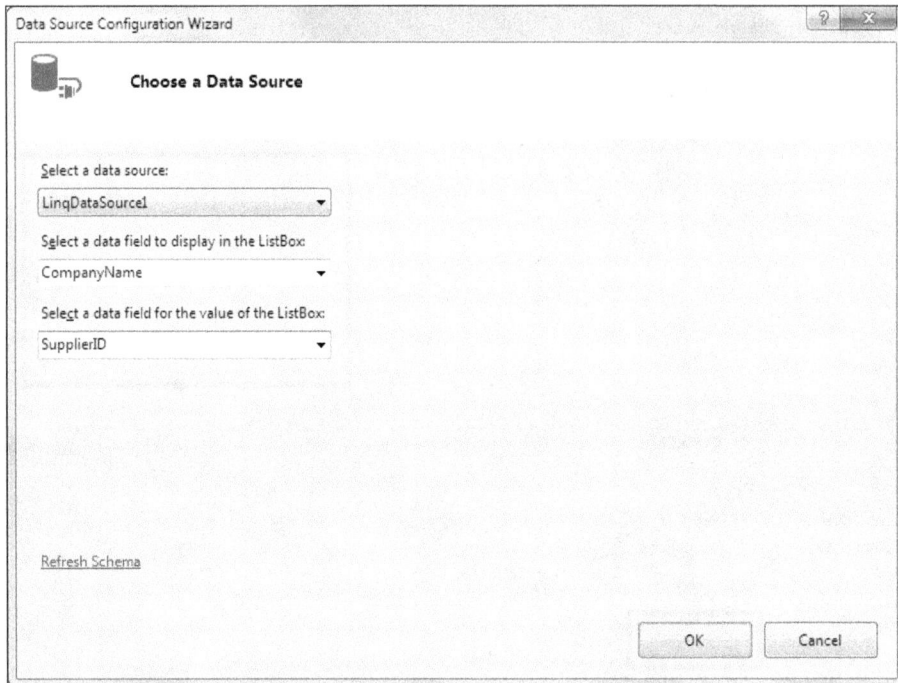

19. The following code is the complete markup of the page after completing the preceding steps:

```
<asp:Label ID="lblSelectItems" runat="server" Text="Choose the
type of selection:"></asp:Label>
<br />
<asp:DropDownList ID="ddlType" runat="server">
  <asp:ListItem Text="--Select--" Value="0"></asp:ListItem>
  <asp:ListItem Text="First" Value="1"></asp:ListItem>
  <asp:ListItem Text="Last" Value="2"></asp:ListItem>
  <asp:ListItem Text="Less Than" Value="3"></asp:ListItem>
  <asp:ListItem Text="Greater Than"
Value="4"></asp:ListItem>
  <asp:ListItem Text="Nth Item" Value="5"></asp:ListItem>
  <asp:ListItem Text="Even Items" Value="6"></asp:ListItem>
  <asp:ListItem Text="Odd Items" Value="7"></asp:ListItem>
</asp:DropDownList>
<asp:Button ID="btnSelect" runat="server" Text="Select
Items" />
<br /><br />
```

```
<asp:ListBox ID="lstSuppliers" runat="server" Width="300px"
Height="450px" DataSourceID="LinqDataSource1"
DataTextField="CompanyName"
DataValueField="SupplierID"></asp:ListBox>
<asp:LinqDataSource ID="LinqDataSource1" runat="server"
ContextTypeName="Recipe5.App_Code.NorthwindDataContext"
EntityTypeName="" Select="new (SupplierID, CompanyName)"
TableName="Suppliers"></asp:LinqDataSource>
```

20. In the `<head>` element of the page, include the following style to highlight the selected child items:

```css
<style type="text/css">
  .highlight{
    background-color:yellow;
  }
</style>
```

How to do it...

Add the following jQuery code to a `<script>` block after the library is included in the page:

```javascript
<script type="text/javascript">
$(document).ready(function() {
  $("#<%=btnSelect.ClientID%>").click(function(evt) {
    $("#<%=lstSuppliers.ClientID%> > *").removeClass("highlight");
    var iType = $("#<%=ddlType.ClientID%>").val();
    switch (iType) {
      case "1":
        $("#<%=lstSuppliers.ClientID%> :first-
child").addClass("highlight");
        break;
      case "2":
        $("#<%=lstSuppliers.ClientID%> :last-
child").addClass("highlight");
        break;
      case "3":
        $("#<%=lstSuppliers.ClientID%>
:lt(4)").addClass("highlight");
        break;
      case "4":
        $("#<%=lstSuppliers.ClientID%>
:gt(7)").addClass("highlight");
        break;
      case "5":
```

```
        $("#<%=lstSuppliers.ClientID%> :nth-
child(5)").addClass("highlight");
        break;
      case "6":
        $("#<%=lstSuppliers.ClientID%> :nth-
child(even)").addClass("highlight");
        break;
      case "7":
        $("#<%=lstSuppliers.ClientID%> :nth-
child(odd)").addClass("highlight");
        break;
      default:
        alert("Please select the type of element");
    }
    evt.preventDefault();
  });
});
</script>
```

How it works...

The web page works as follows:

1. Run the application and right-click on the page in the browser to go to **View Source**. At runtime, the `ListBox` control will be rendered as the `select` and `option` HTML elements, as shown here:

```
63    <select size="4" name="lstSuppliers" id="lstSuppliers" style="height:450px;width:300px;">
64    <option value="18">Aux joyeux ecclésiastiques</option>
65    <option value="16">Bigfoot Breweries</option>
66    <option value="5">Cooperativa de Quesos &#39;Las Cabras&#39;</option>
67    <option value="27">Escargots Nouveaux</option>
68    <option value="1">Exotic Liquids</option>
69    <option value="29">Forêts d&#39;érables</option>
70    <option value="14">Formaggi Fortini s.r.l.</option>
71    <option value="28">Gai pâturage</option>
72    <option value="24">G&#39;day, Mate</option>
73    <option value="3">Grandma Kelly&#39;s Homestead</option>
74    <option value="11">Heli Süßwaren GmbH &amp; Co. KG</option>
75    <option value="23">Karkki Oy</option>
76    <option value="20">Leka Trading</option>
```

2. The entire action of the page lies in the event handler for the `click` event of the **Select Items** button:

```
$("#<%=btnSelect.ClientID%>").click(function (evt) {…});
```

When you click on this button, first of all, the CSS style of all child elements of the `ListBox` control (the `option` element) is reset using the `removeClass` function:

```
$("#<%=lstSuppliers.ClientID%> >
*").removeClass("highlight");
```

3. The selected value of the `DropDownList` control is retrieved to find the type of selection required:

```
var iType = $("#<%=ddlType.ClientID%>").val();
```

4. A switch-case statement helps you to choose different selections of the child elements based on the item selected in the dropdown list:

   1. If the item selected in the dropdown list is **First**, the first option element is highlighted using the following code:

      ```
      $("#<%=lstSuppliers.ClientID%> :first-
      child").addClass("highlight");
      ```

   2. If the item selected is **Last**, the last option element is highlighted using this code:

      ```
      $("#<%=lstSuppliers.ClientID%> :last-
      child").addClass("highlight");
      ```

   3. If the item selected is **Less Than**, all option elements that are less than index 4—that is, items with indices 0 to 3, are highlighted using the following code:

      ```
      $("#<%=lstSuppliers.ClientID%>
      :lt(4)").addClass("highlight");
      ```

The index is hard coded here for simplicity.

   4. If the item selected is **Greater Than**, all option elements that are greater than index 7—that is, items excluding those with indices 0 to 7, are highlighted using this code:

      ```
      $("#<%=lstSuppliers.ClientID%>
      :gt(7)").addClass("highlight");
      ```

The index is hardcoded here for simplicity.

5. If the item selected is **Nth Item**, the fifth option element is highlighted using the following code:

```
$("#<%=lstSuppliers.ClientID%> :nth-
child(5)").addClass("highlight");
```

> The index is hardcoded here for simplicity.

6. If the item selected is **Even Items**, all option elements with even indices are highlighted using this code:

```
$("#<%=lstSuppliers.ClientID%> :nth-
child(even)").addClass("highlight");
```

7. If the item selected is **Odd Items**, all option elements with odd indices are highlighted using the following code:

```
$("#<%=lstSuppliers.ClientID%> :nth-
child(odd)").addClass("highlight");
```

5. Lastly, executing `evt.preventDefault()` prevents the submission of the page because of the button `click` event.

See also

▶ The *Selecting a control using an ID and displaying its value* recipe

Enabling/disabling controls on a web form

This recipe demonstrates how to enable/disable controls dynamically on a web form in response to events triggered by other controls on the form. The constructs used in this example are as follows:

Construct	Type	Description
`$("#identifier")`	jQuery selector	This selects an element based on its ID
`$(this)`	jQuery object	This refers to the current jQuery object
`:checked`	jQuery selector	This selects checked input elements
`.click()`	jQuery event binder	This binds a handler to the `click` event of an element
`.find()`	jQuery method	This finds all elements matching the filter
`.is()`	jQuery method	This returns a Boolean value if the matched element satisfies a given condition

Construct	Type	Description
`prop(propertyName)` or `.prop(propertyName, value)`	jQuery method	This returns the value of the specified property for the first matched element or sets the value of the specified property for all matched elements
`.val()`	jQuery method	This returns the value of the first matched element or sets the value of every matched element

Getting ready

Let's create a job application form that shows enabling and disabling of ASP.NET controls:

1. We will build a simple job application form for a company, as shown here:

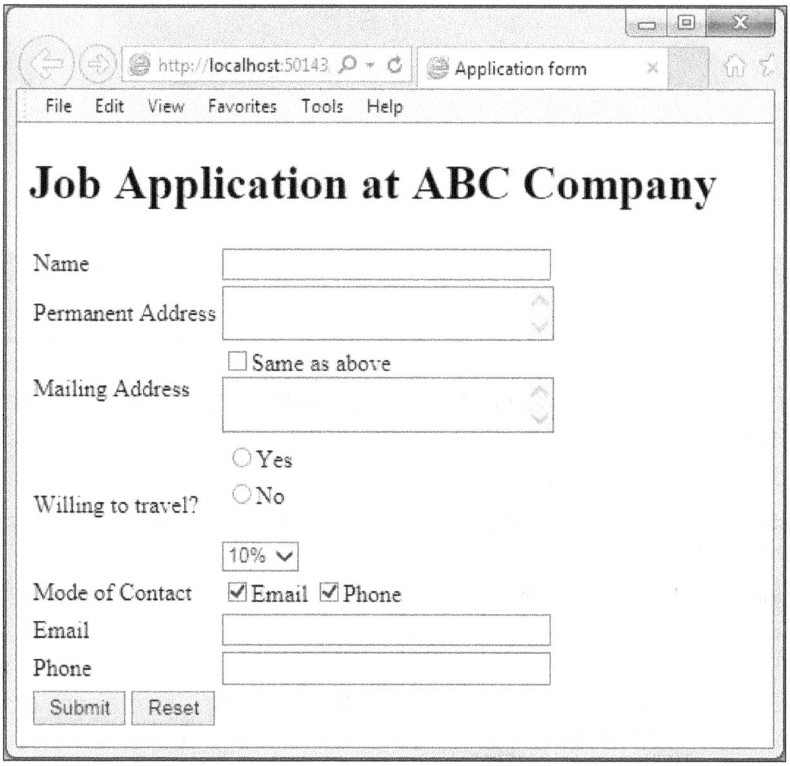

2. Clicking on certain controls disables other controls on the form, as shown in the following screenshot:

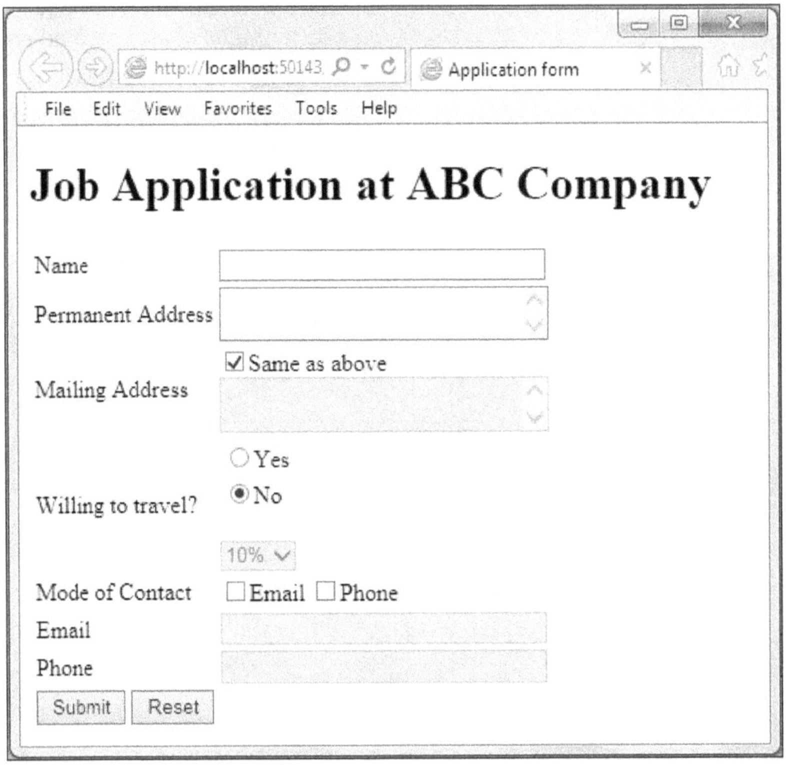

3. To get started, create an **ASP.NET Web Application** project using the **Empty** template, and **name** the project Recipe6 (or any other suitable name).

4. Add a **Web Form** to the project and **name** it Default.aspx.

5. Create a Scripts folder and add jQuery files (debug and release versions of a library) to it.

6. Include the jQuery library in the form using either the <script> block or the ScriptManager control, as described in *Chapter 1, Getting Started with jQuery in ASP.NET*.

7. Open the Default.aspx web form in the **Design** mode, and drag and drop the required controls by navigating to **Toolbox | Standard** to create the web form, as shown in the preceding screenshots. The markup of the web form is as follows:

```
<table>
  <tr>
    <td>
```

```
      <asp:Label ID="lblName" runat="server"
Text="Name"></asp:Label>
    </td>
    <td>
      <asp:TextBox ID="txtName" runat="server"
Width="220px"></asp:TextBox>
    </td>
  </tr>
  <tr>
    <td>
      <asp:Label ID="lblPermAddr" runat="server"
Text="Permanent Address"></asp:Label>
    </td>
    <td>
      <asp:TextBox ID="txtPermAddr" runat="server"
Width="220px" TextMode="MultiLine"></asp:TextBox>
    </td>
  </tr>
  <tr>
    <td>
      <asp:Label ID="lblMailingAddr" runat="server"
Text="Mailing Address" />
    </td>
    <td>
      <asp:CheckBox ID="chkMailingAddr" runat="server"
Text="Same as above" />
      <br />
      <asp:TextBox ID="txtMailingAddr" runat="server"
Width="220px" TextMode="MultiLine"></asp:TextBox>
    </td>
  </tr>
  <tr>
    <td>
      <asp:Label ID="lblTravel" runat="server"
Text="Willing to travel?" />
    </td>
    <td>
      <asp:RadioButtonList ID="rdTravel" runat="server">
        <asp:ListItem Text="Yes"
Value="Yes"></asp:ListItem>
        <asp:ListItem Text="No" Value="No"></asp:ListItem>
      </asp:RadioButtonList>
      <br />
      <asp:DropDownList ID="ddlTravel" runat="server">
        <asp:ListItem Text="10%"></asp:ListItem>
```

```
          <asp:ListItem Text="25%"></asp:ListItem>
          <asp:ListItem Text="50%"></asp:ListItem>
          <asp:ListItem Text="75%"></asp:ListItem>
        </asp:DropDownList>
        <br />
      </td>
    </tr>
    <tr>
      <td>
        <asp:Label ID="lblMode" runat="server" Text="Mode of
Contact" />
      </td>
      <td>
        <asp:CheckBox ID="chkEmail" runat="server"
Text="Email" Value="Email" Checked="true" />
        <asp:CheckBox ID="chkPhone" runat="server"
Text="Phone" Value="Phone" Checked="true" />
      </td>
    </tr>
    <tr>
      <td>
        <asp:Label ID="lblEmail" runat="server" Text="Email"
/>
      </td>
      <td>
        <asp:TextBox ID="txtEmail" runat="server"
Width="220px"></asp:TextBox>
      </td>
    </tr>
    <tr>
      <td>
        <asp:Label ID="lblPhone" runat="server" Text="Phone"
/>
      </td>
      <td>
        <asp:TextBox ID="txtPhone" runat="server"
Width="220px"></asp:TextBox>
      </td>
    </tr>
    <tr>
      <td colspan="2">
        <asp:Button ID="btnSubmit" runat="server"
Text="Submit" />
```

```
        <asp:Button ID="btnReset" runat="server" Text="Reset"
    />
        </td>
      </tr>
    </table>
```

How to do it...

Include the following jQuery code in a `<script>` block after the library is included in the page:

```
<script type="text/javascript">
$(document).ready(function() {
  $("#<%=chkMailingAddr.ClientID%>").click(function() {
    if ($(this).is(":checked"))
      $("#<%=txtMailingAddr.ClientID%>").prop("disabled", true);
    else
      $("#<%=txtMailingAddr.ClientID%>").prop("disabled", false);
  });
  $("#<%=rdTravel.ClientID%>").click(function() {
    var strTravel = $(this).find(":checked").val();
    if (strTravel == "No")
      $("#<%=ddlTravel.ClientID%>").prop("disabled", true);
    else
      $("#<%=ddlTravel.ClientID%>").prop("disabled", false);
  });
  $("#<%=chkEmail.ClientID%>").click(function() {
    if (!$(this).is(":checked"))
      $("#<%=txtEmail.ClientID%>").prop("disabled", true);
    else
      $("#<%=txtEmail.ClientID%>").prop("disabled", false);
  });
  $("#<%=chkPhone.ClientID%>").click(function() {
    if (!$(this).is(":checked"))
      $("#<%=txtPhone.ClientID%>").prop("disabled", true);
    else
      $("#<%=txtPhone.ClientID%>").prop("disabled", false);
  });
});
</script>
```

How it works...

The web page works as follows:

1. Save the application and launch it using *F5*. In the **Mailing Address** section, on checking the **Same as above** field, the **Mailing Address** textbox is disabled as follows:

    > Similarly, on unchecking the field, the **Mailing Address** textbox is enabled.

2. This is made possible by writing an event handler for the `click` event of the `CheckBox` control. The `click` event is triggered when the checkbox is either checked or unchecked:

    ```
    $("#<%=chkMailingAddr.ClientID%>").click(function () {…});
    ```

3. In the preceding event handler, firstly, it is determined whether the field is checked using the following code:

    ```
    if ($(this).is(":checked"))
    ```

    If the preceding condition is `true`, in order to disable the **Mailing Address** textbox, the `prop()` method is used to assign a `true` value to its `disabled` property as follows:

    ```
    $("#<%=txtMailingAddr.ClientID%>").prop("disabled", true);
    ```

    Similarly, if the checkbox is unchecked, the **Mailing Address** textbox is enabled by assigning a `false` value to its `disabled` property as follows:

    ```
    $("#<%=txtMailingAddr.ClientID%>").prop("disabled", false);
    ```

4. For the **Willing to Travel** radio button, when the **No** option is selected, the dropdown list below the field is disabled, as shown in the following figure:

5. This is made possible by attaching an event handler to the `click` event of the `RadioButtonList`:

```
$("#<%=rdTravel.ClientID%>").click(function () {…});
```

6. When the preceding event handler is invoked, the selected value is first determined using this code:

```
var strTravel = $(this).find(":checked").val();
```

   If the selected value is **No,** the dropdown list is disabled by attaching a `true` value to its `disabled` property, as follows:

```
if (strTravel == "No")
  $("#<%=ddlTravel.ClientID%>").prop("disabled", true);
```

   Otherwise, the dropdown list is enabled by attaching a `false` **value** to its `disabled` property, as follows:

```
else
  $("#<%=ddlTravel.ClientID%>").prop("disabled", false);
```

7. When the two checkbox controls in the **Mode of Contact** field are unchecked, the corresponding textbox field is disabled, that is, unchecking the **Email** checkbox disables the **Email** textbox. Similarly, unchecking the **Phone** checkbox disables the **Phone** textbox as follows:

Mode of Contact	☐ Email ☐ Phone
Email	
Phone	

8. This is made possible by attaching respective event handlers to the `Email` and `Phone` checkbox controls as follows:

```
$("#<%=chkEmail.ClientID%>").click(function () {…});
$("#<%=chkPhone.ClientID%>").click(function () {…});
```

9. In the preceding event handlers, it is first required to determine whether the respective `CheckBox` control is unchecked using the following code:

```
if (!$(this).is(":checked"))
```

If the respective checkbox is unchecked, then the `TextBox` control is disabled by attaching the `true` value to the `disabled` property of the `TextBox` control as follows:

- For the `Email` field:

```
$("#<%=txtEmail.ClientID%>").prop("disabled", true);
```

- For the `Phone` field:

```
$("#<%=txtPhone.ClientID%>").prop("disabled", true);
```

Otherwise, the respective `TextBox` control is enabled by attaching the `false` value to the `disabled` property, as follows:

- For the `Email` field:

```
$("#<%=txtEmail.ClientID%>").prop("disabled", false);
```

- For the `Phone` field:

```
$("#<%=txtPhone.ClientID%>").prop("disabled", false);
```

See also

▶ The *Selecting a control by its attribute* recipe

Using selectors in MVC applications

So far, all recipes are based on using selectors with ASP.NET web forms. Next, we introduce an example to demonstrate the use of selectors in an ASP.NET MVC application. The constructs used in this example are as follows:

Construct	Type	Description
`$(#identifier)`	jQuery selector	This selects an element based on its `ID`
`$(this)`	jQuery object	This refers to the current jQuery object
`:checked`	jQuery selector	This selects checked input elements
`.click()`	jQuery event binder	This binds a handler to the `click` event of an element
`.css()`	jQuery method	This gets the CSS property of the first matched element or sets one or more CSS properties for every matched element
`.each()`	jQuery method	This iterates over the matched elements and executes a function for each element
`event.preventDefault()`	jQuery method	This prevents the default action of the event from being triggered

Construct	Type	Description
`.html()`	jQuery method	This returns the HTML content of the first matched element or sets the HTML content of every matched element
`.prop(propertyName)` or `.prop(propertyName, value)`	jQuery method	This returns the value of the specified property for the first matched element or sets the value of the specified property for all matched elements
`:radio`	jQuery selector	This selects input elements of type radio
`.val()`	jQuery method	This returns the value of the first matched element or sets the value of every matched element

Getting ready

To use selectors in a MVC application, follow these steps:

1. Let's create a simple MVC application for a **Feedback Form** to be completed by a user, as shown in the following screenshot:

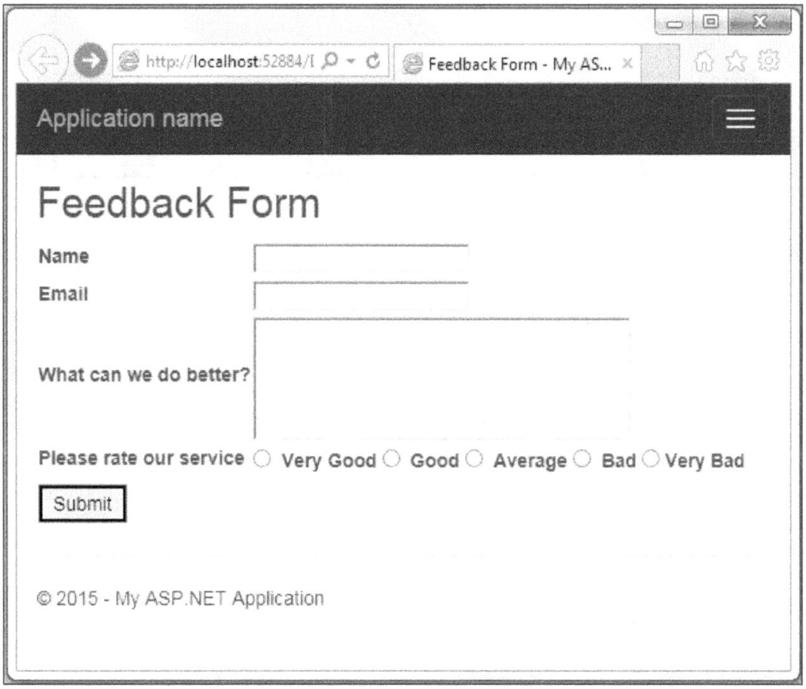

2. When you click on the **Submit** button, the validation of the form fields is done using jQuery, and the page will throw an error message giving the details of the fields that are required to be completed, as shown here:

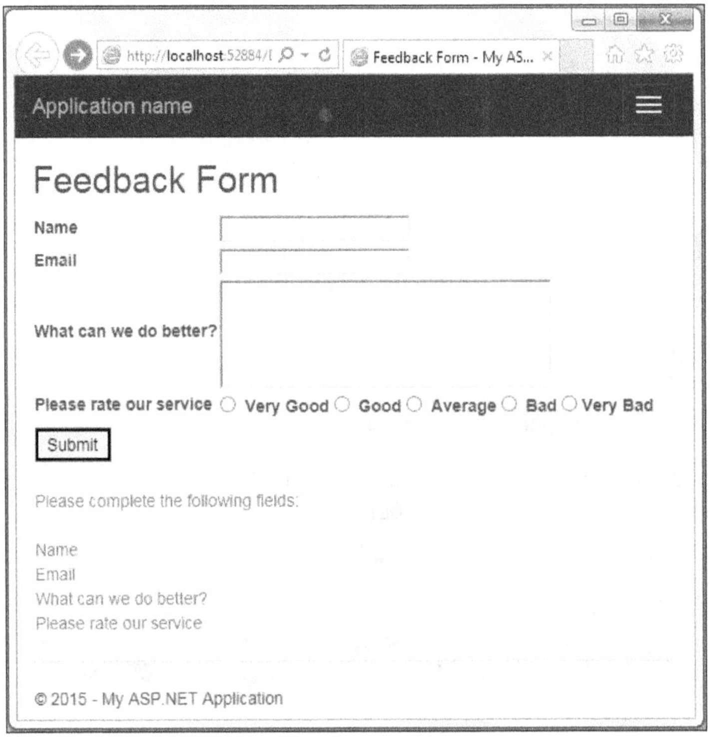

3. If all the fields are completed, the validation will go through, and the user will see a confirmation screen, as shown here:

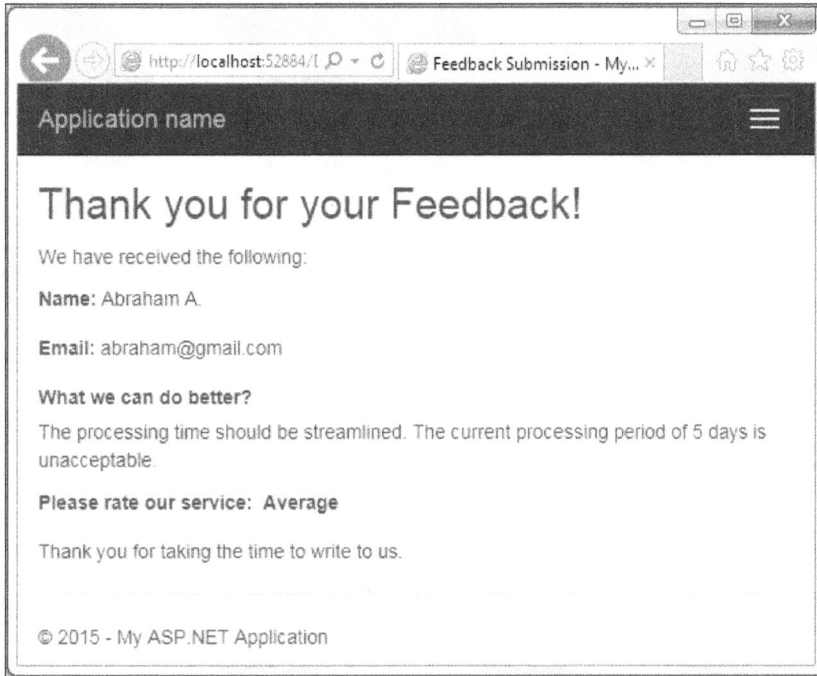

4. To get started, create a new project in Visual Studio by navigating to **File** | **New** | **Project**. From the dialog box, select **ASP.NET Web Application**, and type `Recipe7` (or any other suitable name) for the **name** of the application.

5. From the following dialog box, select the **Empty** template and the **MVC** checkbox, as shown in the following screenshot, and click on the **OK** button:

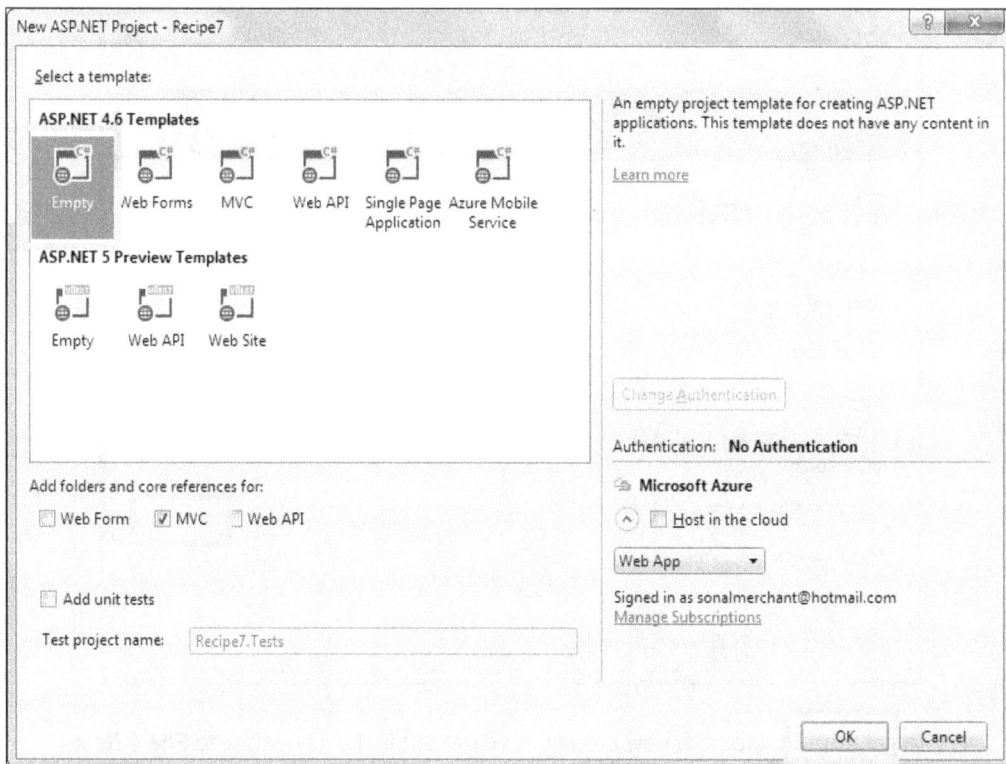

6. We need to add a model to the feedback form, two views (corresponding to the two screens in the application) and a controller. Let's start by adding a model by right-clicking on the **Models** folder in **Solution Explorer** and navigating to **New | Class. name** the class FeedbackForm.vb (VB) or FeedbackForm.cs (C#), and add the following properties that correspond to the fields on the feedback form:

For VB, the code is as follows:

```
Public Class FeedbackForm
    Public Property Name As String
    Public Property Email As String
    Public Property ImprovementArea As String
    Public Property Rating As String
End Class
```

For C#, the code is as follows:

```
public class FeedbackForm
{
```

```
        public string Name { get; set; }
        public string Email { get; set; }
        public string ImprovementArea { get; set; }
        public string Rating { get; set; }
    }
```

7. Now, add a controller by right-clicking on the **Controllers** folder in **Solution Explorer** and navigating to **New | Controller**. From the dialog box, select **MVC 5 Controller – Empty**, and click on the **Add** button:

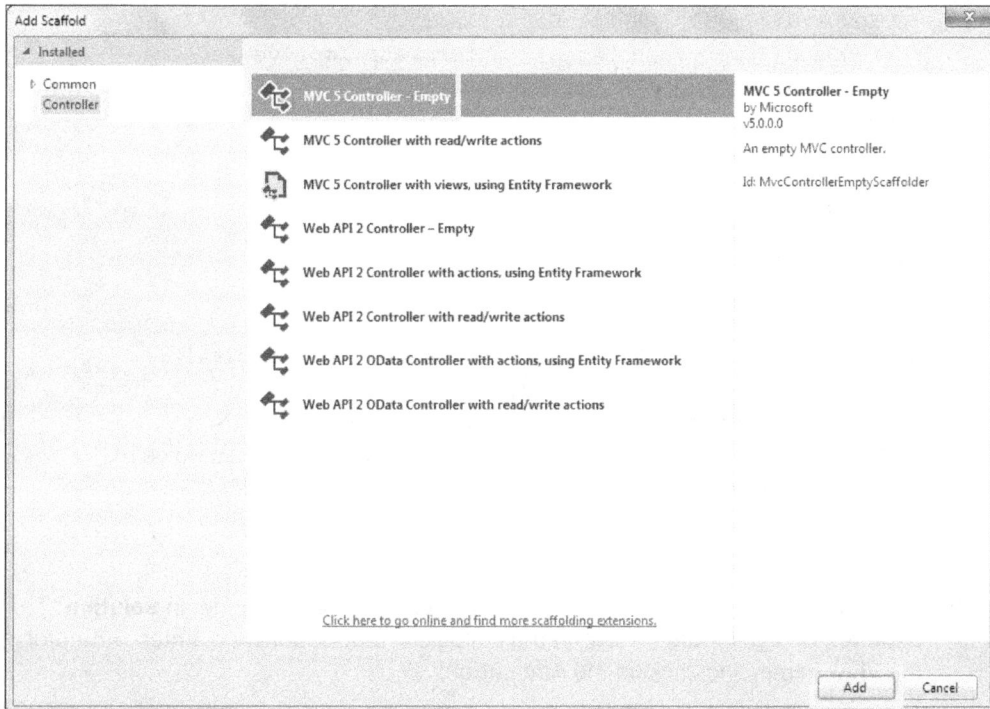

8. In the following dialog box, enter `DefaultController` in the **Controller name** field, and click on the **Add** button:

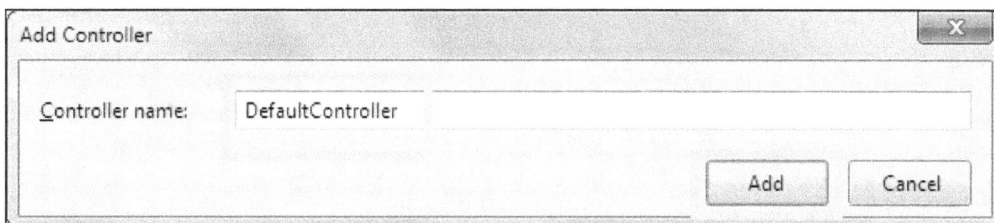

9. Add the following `Action` method in `DefaultController.vb` (VB) or `DefaultController.cs` (C#):

   For VB, the code is as follows:

   ```
   Function Index() As ActionResult
     Return View()
   End Function
   Function HandleForm(ByVal formData As FeedbackForm) As
   ActionResult
     ViewData("Name") = formData.Name
     ViewData("Email") = formData.Email
     ViewData("ImprovementArea") = formData.ImprovementArea
     ViewData("Rating") = formData.Rating
     Return View()
   End Function
   ```

   For C#, the code is as follows:

   ```
   public ActionResult Index() {
     return View();
   }
   public ActionResult HandleForm(FeedbackForm formData) {
     ViewData["Name"] = formData.Name;
     ViewData["Email"] = formData.Email;
     ViewData["ImprovementArea"] = formData.ImprovementArea;
     ViewData["Rating"] = formData.Rating;
     return View();
   }
   ```

10. To add a view, right-click by navigating to the **Views | Default** folder in **Solution Explorer**, and go to **Add | View**. In the dialog box that is launched, enter `Index` for the **View name**, and click on the **Add** button:

Add View ✕

View <u>n</u>ame: Index

<u>T</u>emplate: Empty (without model) ▼

<u>M</u>odel class:

Options:

☐ <u>C</u>reate as a partial view

☐ <u>R</u>eference script libraries

☑ <u>U</u>se a layout page:

⋯

(Leave empty if it is set in a Razor _viewstart file)

Add   Cancel

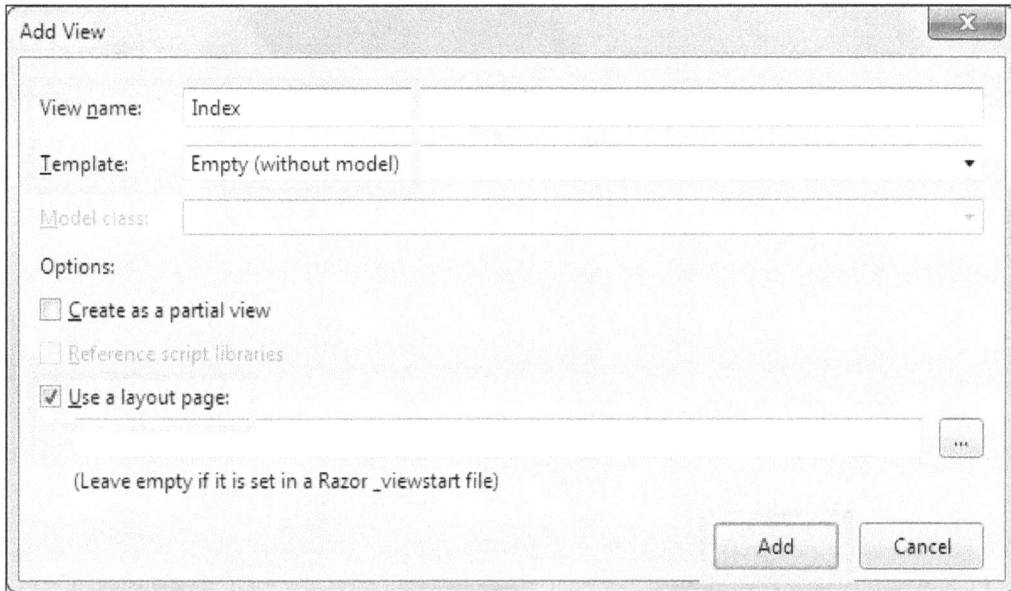

11. Similarly, add one more view by navigating to the **Views | Default** folder, and name the view `HandleForm`. This view is the confirmation page that is launched once the feedback form has been submitted by the user.

12. Create a `Scripts` folder in the project and include the jQuery library files in this folder.

13. Include the jQuery library in the Index view using the bundling method, as described in *Chapter 1, Getting Started with jQuery in ASP.NET,* or by using a `<script>` tag.

14. Add a `<form>` element to the Index view using HTML extensions with the Razor syntax, as follows:

For VB, the code is as follows:

```
@Imports System.Web.Optimization
@Code
ViewData("Title") = "Feedback Form"
End Code
@Scripts.Render("~/Scripts/jquery")
<h2>Feedback Form</h2>
<table>
  @Using Html.BeginForm("HandleForm", "Default")
  @
```

```
<text>
  <tr>
    <td>@Html.Label("Name")</td>
    <td>@Html.TextBox("Name")</td>
  </tr>
  <tr>
    <td>@Html.Label("Email")</td>
    <td>@Html.TextBox("Email")</td>
  </tr>
  <tr>
    <td>@Html.Label("What can we do better?")</td>
    <td>@Html.TextArea("ImprovementArea", New With {.cols
= 50, .rows = 5})</td>
  </tr>
  <tr>
    <td>@Html.Label("Please rate our service")</td>
    <td>
      @Html.RadioButton("Rating", "5")<label> Very
Good</label>
      @Html.RadioButton("Rating",
"4")<label> Good</label>
      @Html.RadioButton("Rating",
"3")<label> Average</label>
      @Html.RadioButton("Rating",
"2")<label> Bad</label>
      @Html.RadioButton("Rating", "1")<label> Very
Bad</label>
    </td>
  </tr>
  <tr>
    <td colspan = "2"> <input id="btnSubmit"
type="submit" value="Submit" /></td>
  </tr>
  <tr>
    <td colspan = "2" >
      <div id="ErrorMessage"></div>
    </td>
  </tr>
</text>
End Using
</table>
```

For C#, the code is as follows:

```
@using System.Web.Optimization;
@{
```

```
ViewBag.Title = "Feedback Form";
}
@Scripts.Render("~/Scripts/jquery")
<h2>Feedback Form</h2>
<table>
  @using (Html.BeginForm("HandleForm","Default"))
  {
  <tr>
    <td>@Html.Label("Name")</td>
    <td>@Html.TextBox("Name")</td>
  </tr>
  <tr>
    <td>@Html.Label("Email")</td>
    <td>@Html.TextBox("Email")</td>
  </tr>
  <tr>
    <td>@Html.Label("What can we do better?")</td>
    <td>@Html.TextArea("ImprovementArea",new { @cols=50,
@rows=5})   </td>
  </tr>
  <tr>
    <td>@Html.Label("Please rate our service")</td>
    <td>@Html.RadioButton("Rating", "5") <label> Very
Good</label>
      @Html.RadioButton("Rating", "4")
<label> Good</label>
      @Html.RadioButton("Rating", "3")
<label> Average</label>
      @Html.RadioButton("Rating", "2")
<label> Bad</label>
      @Html.RadioButton("Rating", "1")<label> Very
Bad</label>
    </td>
  </tr>
  <tr>
    <td colspan="2"><input id="btnSubmit" type="submit"
value="Submit" /></td>
  </tr>
  <tr>
    <td colspan="2">
      <div id="ErrorMessage"></div>
    </td>
  </tr>
  }
</table>
```

15. Add the following markup to the `HandleForm` view:

For VB, the code is as follows:

```
@Code
ViewData("Title") = "Feedback Submission"
End Code
<h2>Thank you for your Feedback!</h2>
<p>We have received the following:</p>
<p><label>Name: </label>@Html.Encode(ViewData("Name"))</p>
<p><label>Email: </label>@Html.Encode(ViewData("Email"))</p>
<p>
   <label>What we can do better?</label><br />
   @Html.Encode(ViewData("ImprovementArea"))
</p>
<p>
   <label>Please rate our service: </label>
   @If ViewData("Rating").Equals("5") Then
   @:<label>Very Good</label>
   ElseIf ViewData("Rating").Equals("4")
   @:<label>Good</label>
   ElseIf ViewData("Rating").Equals("3")
   @:<label>Average</label>
   ElseIf ViewData("Rating").Equals("2")
   @: <label>Bad</label>
   ElseIf ViewData("Rating").Equals("1")
   @: <label>Very Bad</label>
   End If
</p>
<p> Thank you For taking the time To write To us.</p>
```

For C#, the code is as follows:

```
@{
   ViewBag.Title = "Feedback Submission";
}
<h2>Thank you for your Feedback!</h2>
<p>We have received the following:</p>
<p><label>Name: </label>@Html.Encode(ViewData["Name"])</p>
<p><label>Email: </label>@Html.Encode(ViewData["Email"])</p>
<p><label>What we can do better?</label><br/>
   @Html.Encode(ViewData["ImprovementArea"])
</p>
<p><label>Please rate our service: </label>
   @if (ViewData["Rating"].Equals("5"))
   {
```

```
        <label>Very Good</label>
    }
    else if (ViewData["Rating"].Equals("4"))
    {
        <label>Good</label>
    }
      else if (ViewData["Rating"].Equals("3"))
    {
        <label>Average</label>
    }
    else if  (ViewData["Rating"].Equals("2")){
        <label>Bad</label>
    }
    else if  (ViewData["Rating"].Equals("1")){
        <label>Very Bad</label>
    }
</p>
<p> Thank you for taking the time to write to us.</p>
```

How to do it...

Include the following jQuery code in a `<script>` block after the library has been included on the page:

```
<script type="text/javascript">
  $(document).ready(function () {
    $("#btnSubmit").click(function (evt) {
      var strMessage = "";
      if ($("#Name").val() == "")
        strMessage = strMessage + "Name<br/>";
      if ($("#Email").val() == "")
        strMessage = strMessage + "Email<br/>";
      if ($("#ImprovementArea").val() == "")
        strMessage = strMessage + "What can we do better?<br/>";
      var bChecked = false;
      $(":radio").each(function () {
        if ($(this).prop("checked")){
          bChecked = true;
        }
      });
      if (!bChecked)
        strMessage = strMessage + "Please rate our service<br/>";
      if (strMessage != "") {
```

```
          strMessage = "<br/>Please complete the following fields:
<br/><br/>" + strMessage;
          $("#ErrorMessage").html(strMessage);
          $("#ErrorMessage").css("color", "#FF0000");
          evt.preventDefault();
        }
      });
    });
</script>
```

How it works...

The feedback form in MVC works as follows:

1. To run the application, right-click on the **Index** view in the **Solution Explorer**, and select **View in Browser**. As a result, the feedback form loads in the browser window.

2. When the user clicks on the **Submit** button, the event handler for the button `click` is executed:

   ```
   $("#btnSubmit").click(function (evt) {…});
   ```

3. The jQuery code validates each field in the form. A `strMessage` string variable keeps track of all fields that are not filled:

   ```
   var strMessage = "";
   if ($("#Name").val() == "")
     strMessage = strMessage + "Name<br/>";
   if ($("#Email").val() == "")
     strMessage = strMessage + "Email<br/>";
   if ($("#ImprovementArea").val() == "")
     strMessage = strMessage + "What can we do better?<br/>";
   ```

4. To test if the radio button list is checked, we loop through each radio button, and use the `.prop()` method to determine whether the checked property is `true`:

   ```
   var bChecked = false;
   $(":radio").each(function() {
     if ($(this).prop("checked")) {
       bChecked = true;
     }
   });
   if (!bChecked)
     strMessage = strMessage + "Please rate our service<br/>";
   ```

5. Lastly, if validation errors are found on the page—that is, if `strMessage` is nonempty, the error is displayed in the div area at the end of the form. The font color of the error message is changed to red using the `.css()` method:

```
if (strMessage != "") {
   strMessage = "<br/>Please complete the following fields:
<br/><br/>" + strMessage;
    $("#ErrorMessage").html(strMessage);
    $("#ErrorMessage").css("color", "#FF0000");
    evt.preventDefault();
}
```

6. To prevent the form from submission when validation errors are present, the `.preventDefault()` method is used.

See also

▶ The *Selecting a control using an ID and displaying its value* recipe

3

Event Handling
Using jQuery

This chapter introduces the important concepts when handling events in ASP.NET using jQuery. The following recipes are discussed in this chapter:

- ▶ Responding to mouse events
- ▶ Responding to keyboard events
- ▶ Responding to form events
- ▶ Using event delegation to attach events to future controls
- ▶ Running an event only once
- ▶ Triggering an event programmatically
- ▶ Passing data with events and using event namespacing
- ▶ Detaching events

Introduction

An event is an action that occurs when the user interacts with the web page or when certain milestones are completed such as loading a page in the browser. Moving the mouse, pressing a key, clicking on a button or link, keying in text in a field, or submitting a form, all correspond to common events that are raised during the life cycle of a page. These events can either be user- or system-initiated.

An event handler is a function that is executed when a specific event occurs. Writing an event handler for a particular event is called wiring or binding an event. Event handlers help developers harness events and program the desired actions.

When working with events, it is important to familiarize you with a mechanism called **event delegation**. This feature enables you to attach a single event handler to a parent instead of attaching individual event handlers to each child element. For example, consider an unordered list, that is, a `ul` element consisting of 100 list items. Instead of attaching 100 individual event handlers to the page, that is, one for each list item, a single event handler can be attached to the parent, that is, to the unordered list instead. In addition to optimizing the number of event handlers required on the page, event delegation also helps you wire the event to child elements that do not exist now but will be added in future.

Event delegation is made possible because of **event bubbling**. Event bubbling is the process by which an event that occurs in a child element travels to its parent, then to its parent's parent, and so on, until it reaches the root element: the window. Let's say we have a table element on a page. When you click on a table cell, that is, when you click on the `td` element, the `click` event will bubble all the way up the DOM tree, that is `td` -> `tr` -> `table` -> `body` -> `html` -> `window`, as shown in the following figure:

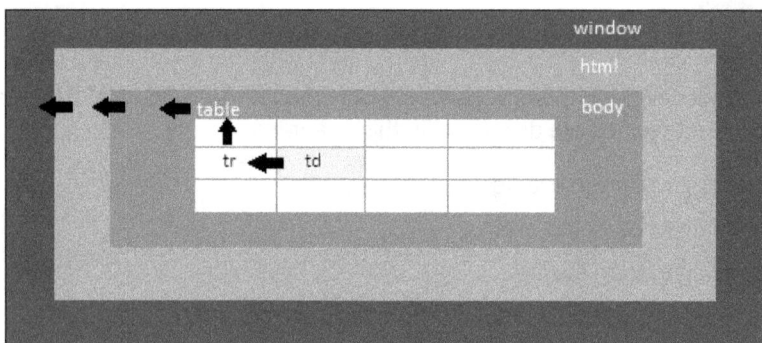

Hence, the `click` event for `td` elements can be intercepted by the parent `table` element, and a single handler attached to the table can act as a representative for all the individual table cells.

Certain applications, however, may require event bubbling to be terminated at a particular level. Hence, jQuery provides a `.stopPropagation()` method to the event that causes the event to stop bubbling up the DOM tree.

> Find out more about jQuery events at
> `https://api.jquery.com/category/events`.

jQuery event binders

jQuery 1.7+ provides the `.on()` method to respond to events. Prior to this method, other event binders such as `.bind()`, `.live()`, and `.delegate()`, were used. However, these methods have been deprecated, and it is recommended that you use `.on()` in jQuery 1.7+ for event binding. There are various ways of using this method, which are as follows:

- Attaching a single event to a handler

  For example, attaching a handler to the `click` event of a button control as follows:

  ```
  $ ("#btnTest").on ("click",function (){...});
  ```

- Attaching multiple events to a handler

  For example, attaching the same handler to the `mouseover` and `mouseout` events of an image control as follows:

  ```
  $ ("#imgTest").on ("mouseover mouseout", function (){...});
  ```

- Attaching different events to different handlers

  For example, attaching different handlers to the `mouseover` and `mouseout` events of an image control as follows:

  ```
  $ ("#imgTest").on ({
    mouseover: function (){...}, mouseout: function (){...}
  });
  ```

- Event delegation

  For example, attaching an event handler to the parent table instead of each individual table row as follows:

  ```
  $("#tblTest").on("click", "tr", function(){...});
  ```

- Passing data to events

  For example, passing data to an event as a JSON string as follows:

  ```
  $("btnTest").on("click",{var1: "val1", var2: "val2"},
  function(event){...});
  ```

Now, let's move on to the recipes to take a closer look at binding.

Responding to mouse events

This recipe demonstrates how to write event handlers for common mouse events that occur on a web page, such as `mouseover` and `mouseout`. The constructs used in this example are summarized as follows:

Construct	Type	Description
`$(".class")`	jQuery selector	This matches all elements with the specified CSS class.
`$(this)`	jQuery object	This refers to the current jQuery object
`.attr("name")` or `.attr("name", "value")`	jQuery method	This returns a string with the value of the required attribute of the first matched element. It can also be used to set the attribute to the required value.
`.appendTo()`	jQuery method	This appends each matched element to the end of the target element.
`input`	jQuery selector	This selects all input elements.
`mouseout`	jQuery event	This is fired when the mouse pointer leaves a control. It corresponds to the JavaScript `mouseout` event.
`mouseover`	jQuery event	This is fired when the mouse pointer enters a control. It corresponds to the JavaScript `mouseover` event.
`.on()`	jQuery event binder	This attaches an event handler for one or more events to the matched elements.
`.parents()`	jQuery method	This selects the ancestors of the matched elements in the DOM tree.
`.remove()`	jQuery method	This removes the matched elements from the DOM.
`.removeAttr()`	jQuery method	This removes the specific attribute from the matched elements.
`.text()`	jQuery method	This returns the combined text content of each of the matched elements or sets the text content of every matched element.
`:text`	jQuery selector	This selects all input elements of type equal to text.

To show the handling of mouse events on a page, follow these steps:

1. Let's start by creating a simple registration page for students, as shown in the following screenshot:

2. By moving the mouse pointer over any TextBox control on the page, the corresponding tooltip is displayed using jQuery, as shown here:

3. When the mouse pointer moves out of the respective TextBox control, the tooltip becomes invisible.

> When the `ToolTip` property of a control is used, ASP.NET displays a simple tooltip by default. This recipe enhances the default tooltip and applies custom styles to it.

4. To build this page, create an **ASP.NET Web Application** project in Visual Studio using the **Empty** template, and name the project `Recipe1` (or any other suitable name).

5. Add the jQuery library to the project in the `Scripts` folder.

6. Create a new web form, and include the jQuery library in the form.

7. Add the following markup to the form to create the registration fields:

```
<table>
  <tr><td>Student Name:</td>
    <td><asp:TextBox ID="txtStudentName" runat="server"
      ToolTip="Name as in your Student
      Card"></asp:TextBox>
    </td>
  </tr>
  <tr><td>Student ID:</td>
    <td><asp:TextBox ID="txtStudentID" runat="server"
      ToolTip="Enter your 10 digit Student
      ID"></asp:TextBox>
    </td>
  </tr>
  <tr><td>Email:</td>
    <td><asp:TextBox ID="txtEmail" runat="server"
      ToolTip="Email address for receiving registration
      notification"></asp:TextBox>
    </td>
  </tr>
  <tr>
    <td colspan="2">
      <asp:Button ID="btnRegister" runat="server"
        Text="Register" />
    </td>
  </tr>
</table>
```

Note that each `TextBox` control has a `ToolTip` text defined. This is the text that will be displayed when the user moves the mouse pointer to the respective `TextBox` control.

8. In the `head` element of the page, add a `style` element to the tooltip, as shown in the following code:

```css
<style type="text/css">
  tooltip{
    border: 1px solid;
    font-family:'Times New Roman', Times, serif;
    font-size:smaller;
    font-weight:700;
    background-color:crimson;
    color:white;
    position:absolute;
    padding:3px;
  }
</style>
```

How to do it...

Add the following jQuery code to a `<script>` block on the page:

```javascript
<script type="text/javascript">
  $(document).ready(function () {
    $("input:text").on("mouseover",function(){
      var strTitle = $(this).attr("title");
      $(this).removeAttr("title");
      $("<div class='tooltip'></div>")
        .text(strTitle).appendTo($(this).parents("tr"));
    });
    $("input:text").on("mouseout", function () {
      var strTitle = $(".tooltip").text();
      $(this).attr("title", strTitle);
      $(".tooltip").remove();
    });
  });
</script>
```

How it works...

The web page works as follows:

1. Save the application using *Ctrl + S*, and run it using *F5*. The page gets loaded in the browser window, and the respective tooltips can be seen next to the `TextBox` control by moving the mouse pointer inside the control. By moving the mouse pointer out of the control, the tooltip disappears.

2. This is made possible by attaching events to both the `mouseover` and `mouseout` properties of the `TextBox` controls as follows:

```
$("input:text").on("mouseover",function(){…});
$("input:text").on("mouseout", function(){…});
```

> Instead of using the `.on()` event binder with the `mouseover` and `mouseout` events, a hover can be used that provides a shortcut mechanism to wire events for the mouse pointer that enters and leaves the element.

3. In the event handler for `mouseover`, we need to retrieve the `ToolTip` text and display it in a `div` area next to the `TextBox` control. At runtime, the `ToolTip` property of an ASP.NET control is rendered as a `title` property. Thus, the `title` attribute of the control is retrieved and saved in a local variable:

```
var strTitle = $(this).attr("title");
```

To prevent ASP.NET from displaying the default tooltip, remove the `title` attribute from the respective control. To remove the attribute is fine since we have already saved its value in the `strTitle` variable:

```
$(this).removeAttr("title");
```

4. Now, create a `div` element with a `tooltip` CSS class. This class contains the necessary cosmetics used to display the tooltip. Set its text to the tooltip text, `strTitle`. Append this `div` element to the parent table row, that is, the `tr` element of the `TextBox` control:

```
$("<div class='tooltip'></div>")
.text(strTitle).appendTo($(this).parents("tr"));
```

5. In the event handler for `mouseout`, we need to delete the `div` element created in step 4 and restore the `title` attribute of the control. Hence, firstly, retrieve the tooltip text using the CSS class selector:

```
var strTitle = $(".tooltip").text();
```

6. Add this tooltip text to the `title` attribute of the `TextBox` control. This is to ensure that the tooltip text for a particular `TextBox` control is not lost:

```
$(this).attr("title", strTitle);
```

Now, the `div` element created in step 4 can be safely deleted so that it disappears by moving out the mouse pointer. Once again, the CSS class selector is used to access the `div` element during deletion:

```
$(".tooltip").remove();
```

See also

The *Responding to keyboard events* recipe

Responding to keyboard events

This recipe demonstrates how to write an event handler for a common keyboard event, `keyup`, which is triggered when a key is released. The constructs used in this example are as follows:

Construct	Type	Description
`$("#identifier")`	jQuery selector	This selects an element using its ID.
`$(this)`	jQuery object	This refers to the current jQuery object.
`.addClass()`	jQuery method	This adds the specified CSS class to each matched element.
`keyup`	jQuery event	This is fired when a key is released. It corresponds to the JavaScript `keyup` event.
`.length`	JavaScript property	This returns the length of the string.
`.on()`	jQuery event binder	This attaches an event handler for one or more events to the matched elements.
`.prop(propertyName)` or `.prop(propertyName, value)`	jQuery method	This returns the value of the specified property for the first matched element or sets the value of the specified property for all matched elements.
`.substring()`	JavaScript function	This extracts a substring of a string.
`.text()`	jQuery method	This returns the combined text content of each of the matched elements or sets the text content of every matched element.
`.toString()`	JavaScript function	This converts an object to a string data type.
`.val()`	jQuery method	This returns the value of the first matched element or sets the value of every matched element.

Getting ready

For creating a page that responds to keyboard events, follow these steps:

1. We will create the following form that keeps a check on the number of characters entered by a user in a multiline textbox field. When characters are entered in the field, the second textbox displays the number of the remaining characters that can be entered, with the limit set to **100**, as shown in the following screenshot:

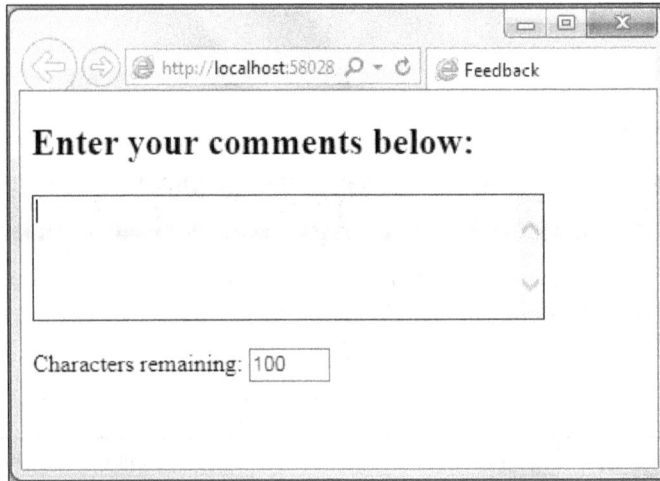

When the maximum number of characters, that is, 100 is reached, the count reduces to 0, and the multiline textbox field prevents any more characters from being entered, as shown in the following screenshot:

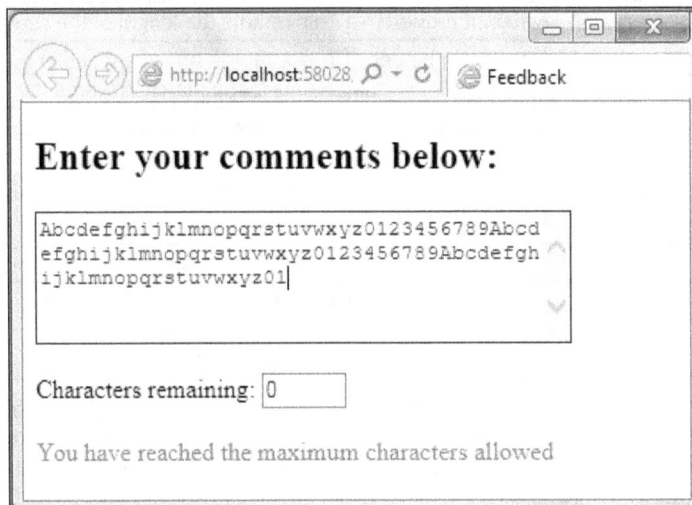

2. To get started with this application, create a new **ASP.NET Web Application** project in Visual Studio using the **Empty** template, and name it `Recipe2` (or any other suitable name).

3. Create a `Scripts` folder in the project and copy the jQuery library files to this folder.

4. Add a new web form to the project and include the jQuery library on the form.

5. Add the following markup to the web form to create the page, as shown in the preceding screenshot:

```
<h2> Enter your comments below:</h2>
<asp:TextBox ID="txtComments" runat="server" Columns="40"
  Rows="5" TextMode="MultiLine"></asp:TextBox>
<br/><br/>
<asp:Label ID="lblCount" runat="server" Text="Characters
  remaining: "></asp:Label><asp:TextBox ID="txtCount"
  runat="server" MaxLength="3" Width="50px"></asp:TextBox>
<br/><br/>
<asp:Label ID="lblError" runat="server"></asp:Label>
```

Note that the `TextMode` property of the `txtComments` field is set to `MultiLine`. The `txtCount` textbox that is used to display the count of the remaining characters has `MaxLength` set to 3 since it will be used to display numbers from 0 to 100 only. There is a `lblError` label control at the end of the form that is used to display an error message once the character count exceeds the maximum allowable limit.

6. Add the following CSS style to the page:

```
<style type="text/css">
  .red{
    color:red;
  }
</style>
```

This style will be applied to the error message.

How to do it...

Include the following jQuery code in a `<script>` block on the page:

```
<script type="text/javascript">
  $(document).ready(function () {
    $("#<%=txtCount.ClientID%>").val("100");
    $("#<%=txtCount.ClientID%>").prop("readonly",true);
    $("#<%=lblError.ClientID%>").addClass("red");
    $("#<%=txtComments.ClientID%>").on("keyup", function ()
```

```
        {
          var maxChars = 100;
          var count = $(this).val().length;
          var remChars = maxChars - count;
          if (remChars >= 0) {
            $("#<%=txtCount.ClientID%>").val(remChars.toString());
          }else{
            $(this).val($(this).val().substring(0,maxChars));
            $("#<%=txtCount.ClientID%>").val("0");
            $("#<%=lblError.ClientID%>").text("You have reached
              the maximum characters allowed");
          }
        });
      });
    </script>
```

How it works...

The page works as follows:

1. Save the page using *Ctrl + S*, and run it using *F5*. When the document is ready, the number of remaining characters in the textbox below the comments field is set to 100 characters in the following statement:

   ```
   $("#<%=txtCount.ClientID%>").val("100");
   ```

   This textbox is also set to readonly so that the user cannot make changes to its contents:

   ```
   $("#<%=txtCount.ClientID%>").prop("readonly",true);
   ```

2. A CSS class is added to the error label so that it displays the error message in red:

   ```
   $("#<%=lblError.ClientID%>").addClass("red");
   ```

3. An event handler is wired to the keyup event of the multiline textbox using the .on() method as follows:

   ```
   $("#<%=txtComments.ClientID%>").on("keyup", function ()
   {...});
   ```

> The keyup event is used instead of the keydown and keypress events so that the character count calculation can be done after the character has been added to the textbox. When using keydown or keypress, the jQuery code is executed before the character has been added to the textbox, thus giving an incorrect character count. Try changing keyup to keydown or keypress by yourself.

4. In the preceding event handler, firstly, a variable is declared to store the maximum allowable characters in the multiline textbox and its value is set to **100** characters:

```
var maxChars = 100;
```

5. The number of characters in the multiline textbox at any point of time is saved in another variable:

```
var count = $(this).val().length;
```

6. The difference between the maximum and actual number of characters is calculated and saved in a third variable:

```
var remChars = maxChars - count;
```

7. If the difference is positive or zero, the number of available characters, that is, the difference calculated earlier, is displayed in the second textbox below the comments field:

```
if (remChars >= 0) {
    $("#<%=txtCount.ClientID%>").val(remChars.toString());
}
```

Otherwise, only the first 100 characters are extracted from the comments field using the `substring` function and displayed in the field. The count of characters is set to 0 in the second textbox, and an error message is displayed using the label control at the end of the page:

```
else{
    $(this).val($(this).val().substring(0,maxChars));
    $("#<%=txtCount.ClientID%>").val("0");
    $("#<%=lblError.ClientID%>").text("You have reached the
       maximum characters allowed");
}
```

See also

The *Responding to form events* recipe

Responding to form events

This recipe demonstrates how to respond to events such as `focus` and `blur` that are triggered on controls on the web form. The constructs used in this example are as follows:

Construct	Type	Description
`$(this)`	jQuery object	This refers to the current jQuery object.
`.addClass()`	jQuery method	This adds the specified CSS class to each matched element.
`[attribute!= "value"]`	jQuery selector	This selects elements with the specified attribute that is not equal to the `value` string.
`blur`	jQuery event	This is fired when an element loses focus. It corresponds to the JavaScript `blur` event.
`.each()`	jQuery method	This iterates over the matched elements and executes a function for each element.
`focus`	jQuery event	This is fired when an element gets focus. It corresponds to the JavaScript `focus` event.
`:input`	jQuery selector	This matches the `input`, `button`, `select`, and `textarea` elements.
`.on()`	jQuery event binder	This attaches an event handler for one or more events to the matched elements.
`.prop(propertyName)` or `.prop(propertyName, value)`	jQuery method	This returns the value of the specified property for the first matched element or sets the value of the specified property for all matched elements.
`.removeClass()`	jQuery method	This removes the specified CSS class from each matched element.
`.val()`	jQuery method	This returns the value of the first matched element or sets the value of every matched element.

Getting ready

Follow these steps to create a form for event handling:

1. We will build a very basic account registration form, as shown in the following screenshot:

The textbox fields on the form display default text. When the cursor is focused on a particular `TextBox` control, the default text disappears and the control is highlighted in blue, as shown in the preceding screenshot. Similarly, highlighting is also applied to the `DropDownList` control when it is active.

When the cursor moves out of the control, and if the control is empty, that is, if no data is entered into the control, it is highlighted in red to indicate a validation error, as shown in the following screenshot:

2. To get started, first create an **ASP.NET Web Application** project in Visual Studio using the **Empty** template and name it `Recipe3` (or any other suitable name).

3. Create a `Scripts` folder in the project and copy the jQuery library files to this folder.

4. Add a new web form to the project and include the jQuery library in the page.

5. Add the following markup to the web form:

```
<table>
  <tr>
    <td colspan="2"><asp:Label ID="lblName"
      runat="server" Text="Name"></asp:Label>
    </td>
  </tr>
  <tr>
    <td><asp:TextBox ID="txtFirst" runat="server"
      ToolTip="First"></asp:TextBox>
    </td>
    <td><asp:TextBox ID="txtLast" runat="server"
      ToolTip="Last"></asp:TextBox>
    </td>
```

```
    </tr>
    <tr>
      <td colspan="2"><asp:Label ID="lblEmail"
        runat="server" Text="Email"></asp:Label>
      </td>
    </tr>
    <tr>
      <td colspan="2"><asp:TextBox ID="txtEmail"
        runat="server" ToolTip="@email.com"></asp:TextBox>
      </td>
    </tr>
    <tr>
      <td colspan="2"><asp:Label ID="lblPassword"
        runat="server" Text="Password"></asp:Label>
      </td>
    </tr>
    <tr>
      <td colspan="2"><asp:TextBox ID="txtPassword"
        runat="server" TextMode="Password"></asp:TextBox>
      </td>
    </tr>
    <tr>
      <td colspan="2"><asp:Label ID="lblConfirmPassword"
        runat="server" Text="Confirm Password"></asp:Label>
      </td>
    </tr>
    <tr>
      <td colspan="2"><asp:TextBox ID="txtConfirmPassword"
        runat="server" TextMode="Password"></asp:TextBox>
      </td>
    </tr>
    <tr>
      <td colspan="2"><asp:Label ID="lblGender"
        runat="server" Text="Gender"></asp:Label>
      </td>
    </tr>
    <tr>
      <td colspan="2">
        <asp:DropDownList ID="ddlGender"
        runat="server">
          <asp:ListItem Text="--Please select--"
          Value=""></asp:ListItem>
          <asp:ListItem Text="Male"
          Value="Male"></asp:ListItem>
```

```
      <asp:ListItem Text="Female"
      Value="Female"></asp:ListItem>
    </asp:DropDownList>
  </td>
</tr>
<tr>
  <td colspan="2">
    <asp:Button ID="btnSubmit" runat="server"
      Text="Submit" />
    <asp:Button ID="btnReset" runat="server" Text="Reset" />
  </td>
</tr>
</table>
```

6. Include the following styles in the `head` element of the page:

```css
<style type="text/css">
  .active{
    border-color:blue;
  }
  .invalid{
    border-color:red;
  }
  .backgroundtext{
    color:grey;
  }
</style>
```

The `active` style is applied to the current control on the page, that is, the control that has the cursor. The `invalid` style is applied to invalid controls: controls in which no data has been entered. The `backgroundtext` style is applied to the default text displayed in the `TextBox` controls.

How to do it...

Include the following jQuery code in a `<script>` block on the page:

```javascript
<script type="text/javascript">
  $(document).ready(function () {
    $(":input[type!=submit]").each(function () {
      if ($(this).val() == "") {
        $(this).addClass("backgroundtext");
        $(this).val($(this).prop("title"));
      }
    });
```

```
$(":input[type!=submit]").on({
  focus: function () {
    if ($(this).val() == $(this).prop("title")) {
      $(this).removeClass("backgroundtext");
      $(this).removeClass("invalid");
      $(this).val("");
    }
    $(this).addClass("active");
  },
  blur: function () {
    $(this).removeClass("active");
    if ($(this).val() == "") {
      $(this).addClass("backgroundtext");
      $(this).addClass("invalid");
      $(this).val($(this).prop("title"));
    }else {
      $(this).removeClass("invalid");
    }
  }
});
});
</script>
```

How it works...

The page works as follows:

1. When the form loads at runtime, all controls except the button controls are initialized by executing the `.each()` method:

    ```
    $(":input[type!=submit]").each(function () {...});
    ```

    The attribute filter ensures that the `input` elements of the `type = submit` i.e. the button controls are excluded from the initialization.

2. For each control on the form filtered using the preceding selector, if the control is empty, then the default text is displayed by setting the `ToolTip` text to its text value. The CSS class of the control is also set to `backgroundtext`:

    ```
    if ($(this).val() == "") {
      $(this).addClass("backgroundtext");
      $(this).val($(this).prop("title"));
    }
    ```

[📝 At runtime, the ToolTip is rendered as the `title` attribute.
Hence, `$(this).prop("title")` gives the ToolTip text.]

3. For all the controls on the form, excluding the button controls, the `.on()` method is used to bind event handlers to the `focus` and `blur` events, as follows:

```
$(":input[type!=submit]").on({focus: function () {...},
   blur: function () {...}});
```

Here, the binder is used to attach different event handlers to the `focus` and `blur` events, respectively.

4. Now, let's discuss the individual event handlers, starting with the one for the focus event. When any control receives focus, we want the border color to change to blue, indicating that this is the current or active control. Also, if the control is empty, that is, if its text is set to the default value, then the default text should be cleared and any other styles should be removed. This can be achieved as follows:

```
focus: function () {
   $(this).addClass("active");
   if ($(this).val() == $(this).prop("title")) {
     $(this).val("");
     $(this).removeClass("backgroundtext");
     $(this).removeClass("invalid");
   }
}
```

In the event handler for `blur`, firstly, since the control is no longer the active control, the corresponding style should be removed. Secondly, we need to check whether data has been entered into the control or not. If the field is empty, its border color is changed to red. Also, the default text is displayed with the corresponding styling:

```
blur: function () {
   $(this).removeClass("active");
   if ($(this).val() == "") {
     $(this).addClass("backgroundtext");
     $(this).addClass("invalid");
     $(this).val($(this).prop("title"));
   }else {
     $(this).removeClass("invalid");
   }
}
```

See also

The *Detaching events* recipe

Using event delegation to attach events to future controls

This recipe demonstrates event delegation and event bubbling. By adding elements at runtime, we will also demonstrate how delegation helps you attach events to future controls. The constructs used in this example are as follows:

Construct	Type	Description
`$("html_tag")`	jQuery selector	This selects all elements with the specified HTML tag.
`.addClass()`	jQuery method	This adds the specified CSS class to each matched element.
`.append()`	jQuery method	This attaches elements at the end of each matched element.
`[attribute= "value"]`	jQuery selector	This selects an element with the specified attribute equal to the `value` string.
`click`	jQuery event	This is fired when you click on an element. It corresponds to the JavaScript `click` event.
`dblclick`	jQuery event	This is fired when you double-click on an element is. It corresponds to the JavaScript `dblclick` event.
`.on()`	jQuery event binder	This attaches an event handler for one or more events to the matched elements.
`.removeClass()`	jQuery method	This removes the specified CSS class from each matched element.

Getting ready

Follow the steps listed below to create a form to demonstrate event bubbling and delegation:

1. We will create a simple web page that displays data rows from an XML file. A new data row is added at runtime so that we can see the impact with and without delegation:

ID	Student Name	Module	Score
HT2015098	Amaan M.	Java	72
HT2015034	Zain M.	Physics	71
HT2015001	Ayaan M.	ISR	77
HT2015051	Abraham A.	ISR	70

When you double-click on a row, it is highlighted, as shown in the following screenshot. With a single mouse click on the same row, the highlight can be removed:

ID	Student Name	Module	Score
HT2015098	Amaan M.	Java	72
HT2015034	Zain M.	Physics	71
HT2015001	Ayaan M.	ISR	77
HT2015051	Abraham A.	ISR	70

2. To create the preceding page, launch a new **ASP.NET Web Application** project in Visual Studio using the **Empty** template and name it `Recipe4` (or any other suitable name).

3. Create a `Scripts` folder in the project and add the jQuery library files to this folder.

4. Add the `App_Data` folder to the project by right-clicking on the project in **Solution Explorer** tab and navigating to **Add | Add ASP.NET Folder | App_Data**.

5. Right-click on the `App_Data` folder, and go to **Add | XML File**. In the dialog box that is displayed, name the file `StudentData.xml`, and click on the **OK** button.

6. Now, double-click on the previous XML file in **Solution Explorer** tab to open the file. Enter some sample student records with the following structure:

```
<StudentData>
  <Student>
    <ID>...</ID>
    <Name>...</Name>
    <Score>...</Score>
    <Module>...</Module>
  </Student>
  ...
</StudentData>
```

7. Add a new web form to the project and include the jQuery library in the page.

8. Navigate to **Toolbox | Data**, and add the `XMLDataSource` and `Repeater` controls to the form.

9. In the **Design** view of the web form, click on the small arrow icon in the top-right corner of the **XMLDataSource** option to open its configuration menu, as shown here:

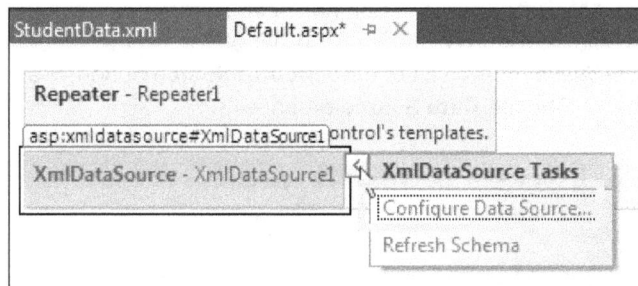

10. From the preceding menu, select **Configure Data Source**, go to the path of the `StudentData.xml` file, and set its XPath to `/StudentData/Student`, as shown in the following screenshot. Click on the **OK** button:

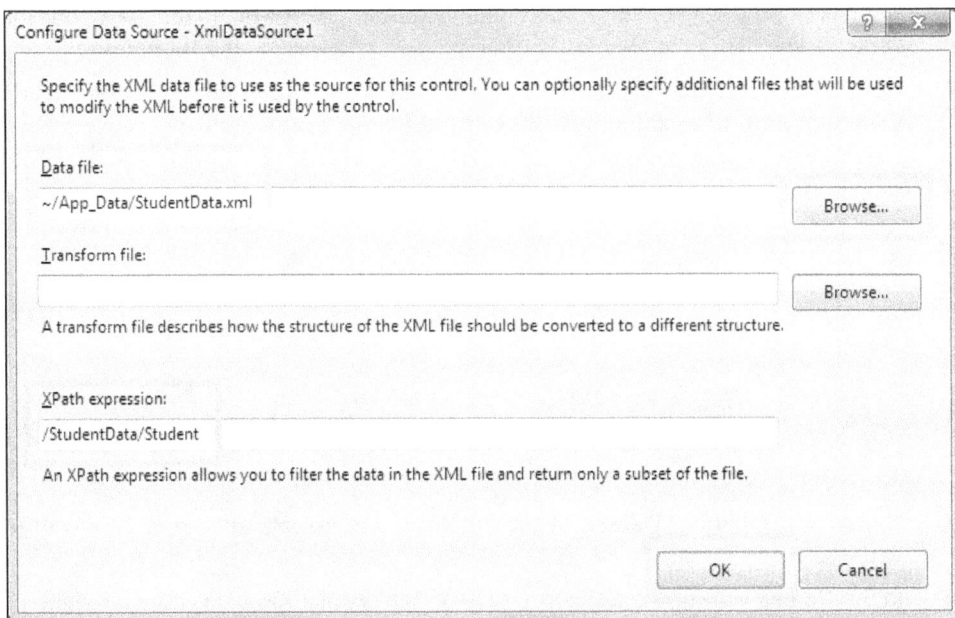

11. Now that the **XMLDataSource** option has been configured in the **Design** view, click on the small arrow in the top-right corner of the `Repeater` control to open the **Repeater Tasks** menu. Select the **XMLDataSource** option, that was configured earlier, from the **Choose Data Source** dropdown:

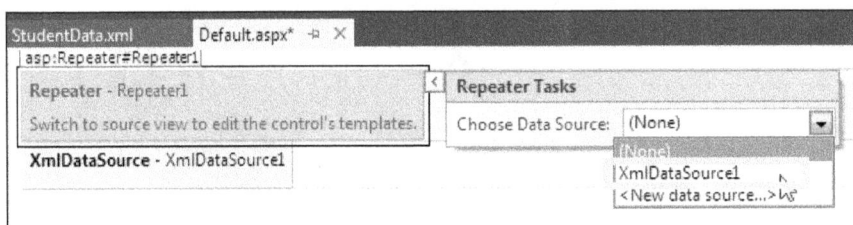

12. Add the following markup to the `Repeater` control so that it displays the fields of the student record:

```
<asp:Repeater ID="Repeater1" runat="server"
  DataSourceID="XmlDataSource1">
  <HeaderTemplate>
    <table id="StudentData">
    <thead>
```

```
      <tr>
        <th>ID</th>
        <th>Student Name</th>
        <th>Module</th>
        <th>Score</th>
      </tr>
    </thead>
  </HeaderTemplate>
  <ItemTemplate>
    <tr>
      <td><%# XPath("ID") %></td>
      <td><%# XPath("Name") %></td>
      <td><%# XPath("Module") %></td>
      <td><%# XPath("Score") %></td>
    </tr>
  </ItemTemplate>
  <FooterTemplate>
  </table>
  </FooterTemplate>
</asp:Repeater>
```

13. Include the following style in the `head` element on the page. This style will be applied to rows that require to be highlighted:

```
<style type="text/css">
  .highlight{
    background-color:greenyellow;
  }
</style>
```

How to do it...

Include the following jQuery code in a `<script>` block on the web page:

```
<script type="text/javascript">
  $(document).ready(function () {
    $("table[id=StudentData] ").on("dblclick","tr", function () {
      $(this).addClass("highlight");
    });
    $("table[id=StudentData] ").on("click", "tr", function () {
      $(this).removeClass("highlight");
    });
    $("table[id=StudentData]").append("<tr><td>HT2015051</td><td>Abrah
      am A.</td><td>ISR</td><td>70</td></tr>");
  });
</script>
```

How it works...

The page works as follows:

1. Save the page using *Ctrl + S* and run it using *F5*. The page loads up, and the `Repeater` control displays the student data from the XML file.

2. Instead of attaching the double-click event to the table row, the `.on()` event binder is used to attach the event handler to the parent table instead. The `tr` element is specified as the selector to filter the descendant elements that are allowed to trigger the event. So, when you double-click on a table row, the event bubbles up to the parent table and the respective `dblclick` event handler is executed:

```
$("table[id=StudentData] ").on("dblclick","tr", function () {
    $(this).addClass("highlight");
});
```

3. Similarly, the `click` event handler is attached to the parent table instead of the `tr` element. By clicking on any row, the highlighting can be removed as follows:

```
$("table[id=StudentData] ").on("click", "tr", function () {
    $(this).removeClass("highlight");
});
```

4. At runtime, a new table row can be appended using the `.append()` function as follows:

```
$("table[id=StudentData]").append("<tr><td>HT2015051</td>
    <td>Abraham A.</td><td>ISR</td><td>70</td></tr>");
```

   This row exhibits the same behavior as any other row; that is, you can double-click on it to add a background color and click on it once to remove the background color.

5. Now, to see the behavior of a dynamically added row in the absence of event delegation, modify the event bindings to attach the events to the table row instead of the parent table, as follows:

```
$("table[id=StudentData]   tr").on("dblclick", function () {
    $(this).addClass("highlight");
});
$("table[id=StudentData] tr").on("click", function () {
    $(this).removeClass("highlight");
});
```

   Now, when a new row is added at runtime, it does not display the required behavior on `click` and `dbclick` events.

See also

The *Responding to mouse events* recipe

Running an event only once

Certain applications require triggering of event handlers just once. If an event handler is wired using the .on() method, it is triggered every time the event occurs, which may be undesirable in such situations. This recipe demonstrates how to attach an event handler for one-time invocation. The constructs used in this example are summarized as follows:

Construct	Type	Description
$(".class")	jQuery selector	This matches all elements with the specified CSS class.
$("html_tag")	jQuery selector	This selects all elements with the specified HTML tag.
[attribute= "value"]	jQuery selector	This selects an element with the specified attribute equal to the value string.
click	jQuery event	This is fired when you click on an element. It corresponds to the JavaScript click event.
.hide()	jQuery method	This hides the matched elements.
.one()	jQuery event binder	This attaches an event handler for one or more events to the matched elements. The handler is executed at most once.
.show()	jQuery method	This displays the matched elements.

Getting ready

To create a form that executes an event handler just once, follow these steps:

1. We will build the web form, as shown in the following screenshot, to display the `Employee` records from the Northwind database. The page has a **See More...** link to display additional details about the employee:

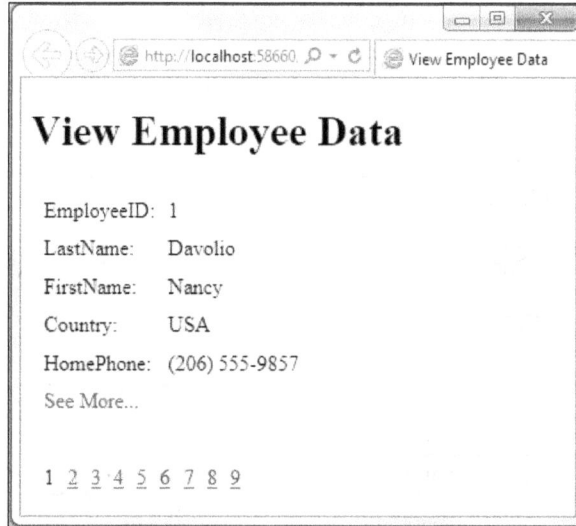

When you click on the link, the additional details will be displayed on the page, as shown in the following screenshot:

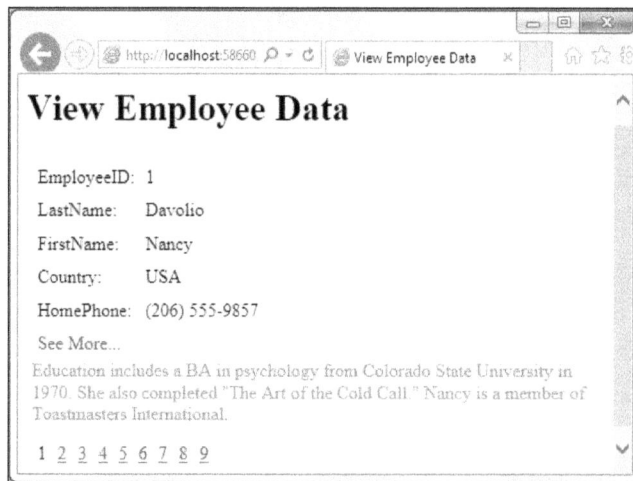

The **See More...** link is designed to work only once. Subsequent clicking of the link will not trigger any event handlers.

Northwind is an open source database that can be downloaded from `https://northwinddatabase.codeplex.com`.
Read more about *How to install sample databases* from the MSDN page at `https://msdn.microsoft.com/en-us/library/8b6y4c7s.aspx`.

2. To build the preceding page, we need to create an **ASP.NET Web Application** project in Visual Studio and name it `Recipe5` (or any other suitable name).

3. Add a `Scripts` folder to the project and add the jQuery library to the folder.

4. Add a new web form to the project. Include the jQuery library on the form.

5. Open the form in the **Design** mode. Go to **Toolbox | Data**, and add a `SqlDataSource` control to the form.

6. In the **Design** mode, click on the small arrow icon that appears in the top-right corner of the `SqlDataSource` control on `mouseover`. Click on **Configure Data Source**, as shown here:

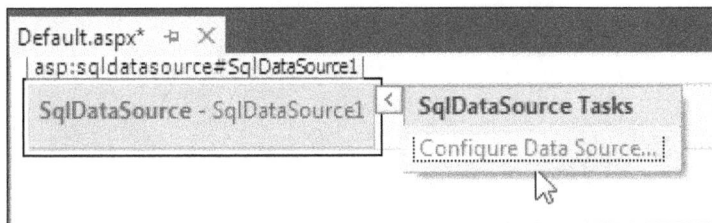

7. Follow the wizard, and add a new database connection. In the dialog box, enter your server name, select the **Northwind** catalog, and click on **OK**:

Add Connection

Enter information to connect to the selected data source or click "Change" to choose a different data source and/or provider.

Data source:

Microsoft SQL Server (SqlClient)   Change...

Server name:

LOCALHOST   ▼   Refresh

Log on to the server

◉ Use Windows Authentication

○ Use SQL Server Authentication

User name:

Password:

☐ Save my password

Connect to a database

◉ Select or enter a database name:

Northwind   ▼

○ Attach a database file:

Browse...

Logical name:

Advanced...

Test Connection   OK   Cancel

> Note that we are using Windows Authentication for all database driven examples in this book. Hence in the MS SQL Server, it is important to give permission to the windows account to access the Northwind database.

8. In the **Configure the Select Statement** dialog box, as shown in the following screenshot, choose **Specify columns from a table or view** from the radio button list, and select the `Employees` table from the drop-down menu. Check the columns required to be displayed on the page, such as `EmployeeID`, `LastName`, `FirstName`, `Country`, `HomePhone`, and `Notes`. Click on the **Next** button:

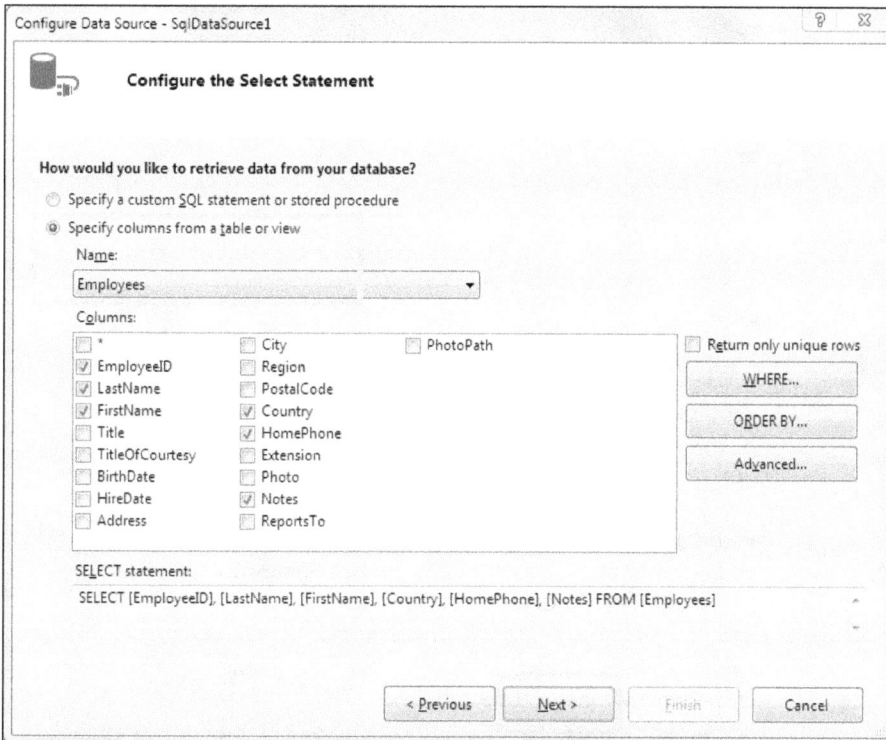

Test the query, and complete the wizard by clicking on the **Finish** button.

9. Now, in the **Design** mode, drag and drop a `FormView` control by navigating to **Toolbox | Data**. Click on the small arrow icon that appears in the top-right corner of the `FormView` control on `mouseover`, and click on **Choose Data Source**. Select `SqlDataSource1` from the drop-down menu, as shown here:

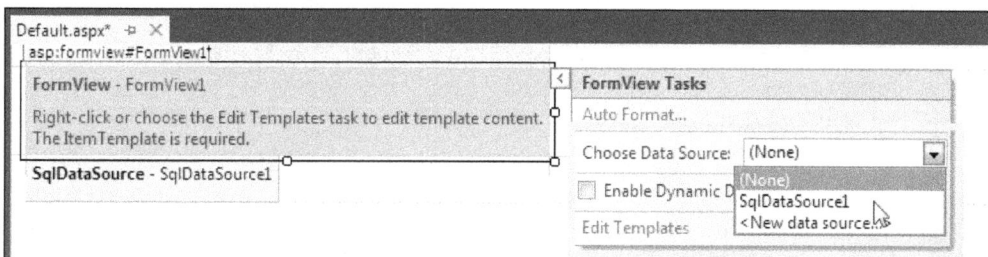

10. Add the following markup to the `FormView` control in **Source** mode:

```
<asp:FormView ID="FormView1" runat="server"
AllowPaging="True" DataKeyNames="EmployeeID"
DataSourceID="SqlDataSource1">
  <ItemTemplate>
    <table id="EmployeeData">
      <tr>
        <td>EmployeeID:</td>
        <td><asp:Label ID="EmployeeIDLabel" runat="server"
          Text='<%# Eval("EmployeeID") %>' /></td>
      </tr>
      <tr>
        <td>Last Name:</td>
        <td><asp:Label ID="LastNameLabel" runat="server"
          Text='<%# Bind("LastName") %>' /></td>
      </tr>
      <tr>
        <td>First Name:</td>
        <td><asp:Label ID="FirstNameLabel" runat="server"
          Text='<%# Bind("FirstName") %>' /></td>
      </tr>
      <tr>
        <td>Country:</td>
        <td><asp:Label ID="CountryLabel" runat="server"
          Text='<%# Bind("Country") %>' /></td>
      </tr>
      <tr>
        <td>Home Phone:</td>
        <td><asp:Label ID="HomePhoneLabel" runat="server"
          Text='<%# Bind("HomePhone") %>' /></td></tr>
      <tr>
        <td colspan="2">
          <asp:HyperLink ID="lnkMore" runat="server"
            CssClass="morelink">See More...</asp:HyperLink>
        </td>
      </tr>
    </table>
    <asp:Label ID="lblMoreData" CssClass="moredata"
      runat="server" Text='<%#Bind("Notes") %>'></asp:Label>
    <br/>
  </ItemTemplate>
</asp:FormView>
```

11. Add the following styles to the head element of the page:

```
<style type="text/css">
  .moredata{
    color:grey;
  }
  .morelink{
    cursor:pointer;
    color:maroon;
    text-decoration:underline;
  }
</style>
```

The moredata CSS class is applied to the additional details of the employee displayed on the page. The morelink CSS class is used to style the **See More...** link.

How to do it...

Add the following jQuery code to a `<script>` block on the page:

```
<script type="text/javascript">
  $(document).ready(function () {
    $(".moredata").hide();
    $("table[id=EmployeeData]").one("click", "a.morelink",
      function () {
      $(".moredata").show();
    });
  });
</script>
```

How it works...

The page works as follows:

1. Save the application and run it using *F5*. The page loads the first record from the Employees table and displays it in the FormView control. Navigation through the records is possible using the page numbers at the bottom of the page.

2. Each page displays the basic employee details, such as the name, country, and home phone number. The notes related to the employee are hidden using the following code:

    ```
    $(".moredata").hide();
    ```

    The preceding selector uses the CSS class assigned to the lblMoreData label control in the FormView item template.

3. A **See More...** hyperlink provided in the **FormView** option enables you to view the notes related to the employee record. This is done using the `.one()` event binder attached to the parent table:

```
$("table[id=EmployeeData]").one("click", "a.morelink",
    function () {
    $(".moredata").show();
});
```

Using `.one()` instead of `.on()` enables you to call the event handler at most once. Once the event handler is executed, it is detached from the element so that it cannot be reinvoked.

Note that the event handler is attached to the parent element instead of attaching it to the hyperlink directly. The `anchor` element with the `morelink` CSS class is passed as the child selector that can raise the event.

Once the `click` event is raised, the `label` control containing the notes is displayed using the `.show()` method.

See also

The *Passing data with events and using event namespacing* recipe

Triggering an event programmatically

This recipe demonstrates the use of the `.trigger()` method to invoke events programmatically. The constructs used in this example are as follows:

Construct	Type	Description
`$(".class")`	jQuery selector	This matches all elements with the specified CSS class.
`$("html_tag")`	jQuery selector	This selects all elements with the specified HTML tag.
`$(this)`	jQuery object	This refers to the current jQuery object.
`.attr("name")` or `.attr("name", "value")`	jQuery method	This returns a string with the required attribute value of the first matched element. It can also be used to set the attribute to the required value.
`[attribute= "value"]`	jQuery selector	This selects an element with the specified attribute equal to the `value` string.
`click`	jQuery event	This is fired when you click on an element. It corresponds to the JavaScript `click` event.

Construct	Type	Description
dblclick	jQuery event	This is fired when you double-click on an element. It corresponds to the JavaScript double-click event.
eval()	JavaScript function	This executes the JavaScript expression.
.find()	jQuery method	This finds all elements matching the filter.
.on()	jQuery event binder	This attaches an event handler for one or more events to the matched elements.
.trigger()	jQuery method	This executes handlers and behaviors attached to the matched elements.

Getting ready

To create a web page that triggers events programmatically, follow these steps:

1. We will build a web page, as shown in the following screenshot. The page displays the list of products from the Northwind database in a GridView control. The GridView control has an **Edit** column containing a LinkButton control to edit any particular row of data:

Generally, when you click on the **Edit** link in any particular row, the record goes into the edit mode, and the **Update** and **Cancel** links are shown. In our case, we will use jQuery to trigger the clicking of the **Edit** link when the user double-clicks on a particular row. So, programmatically, the edit mode of the specific row will be activated, as shown in the following screenshot:

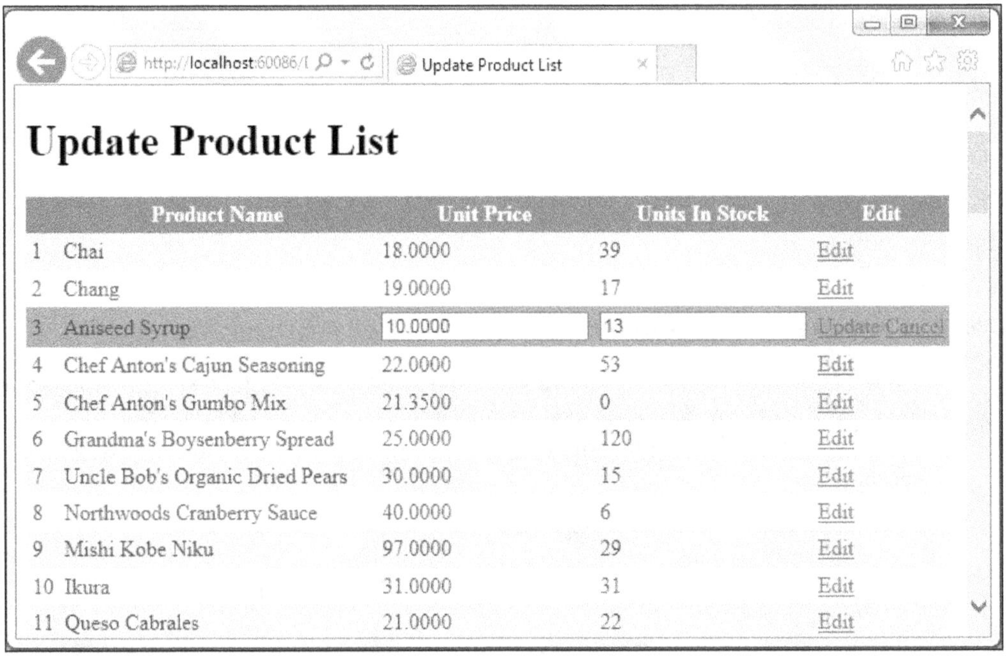

2. To build the preceding page, create an **ASP.NET Web Application** project in Visual Studio and name it `Recipe6` (or any other suitable name).

3. Add a `Scripts` folder to the project, and add the jQuery library to the folder.

4. Add a new web form to the project. Include the jQuery library on the web form.

5. Now, right-click on the project in **Solution Explorer**, and go to **Add | New Item**. From the dialog box, select **Data** in the left-hand side panel and **ADO.NET Entity Data Model** in the middle panel. Enter the name `ProductModel` in the text field shown in the following screenshot, and click on the **Add** button:

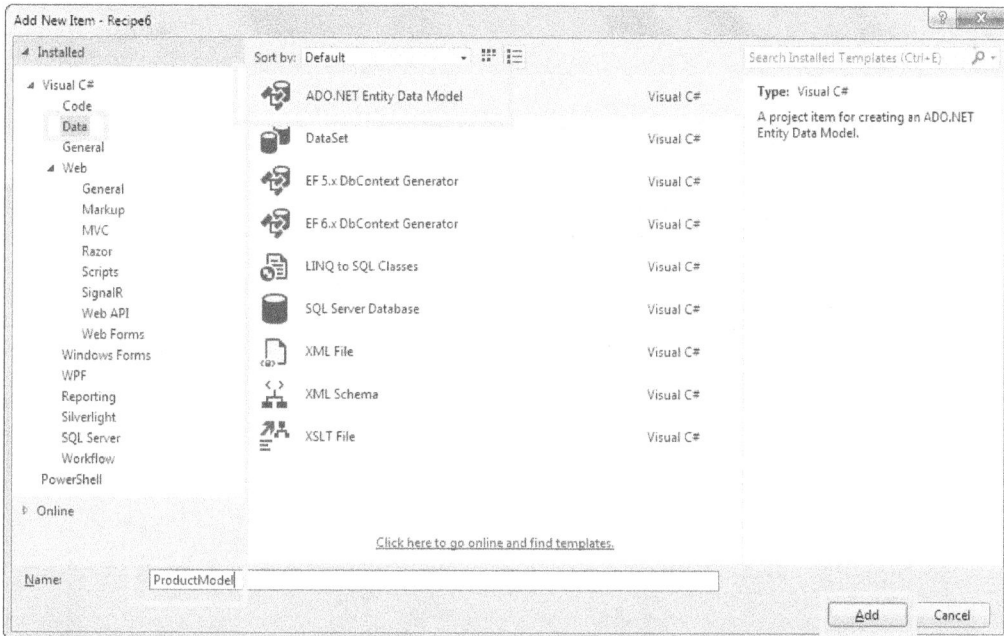

6. In the **Entity Data Model Wizard**, select **EF Designer from database**, and click on the **Next** button:

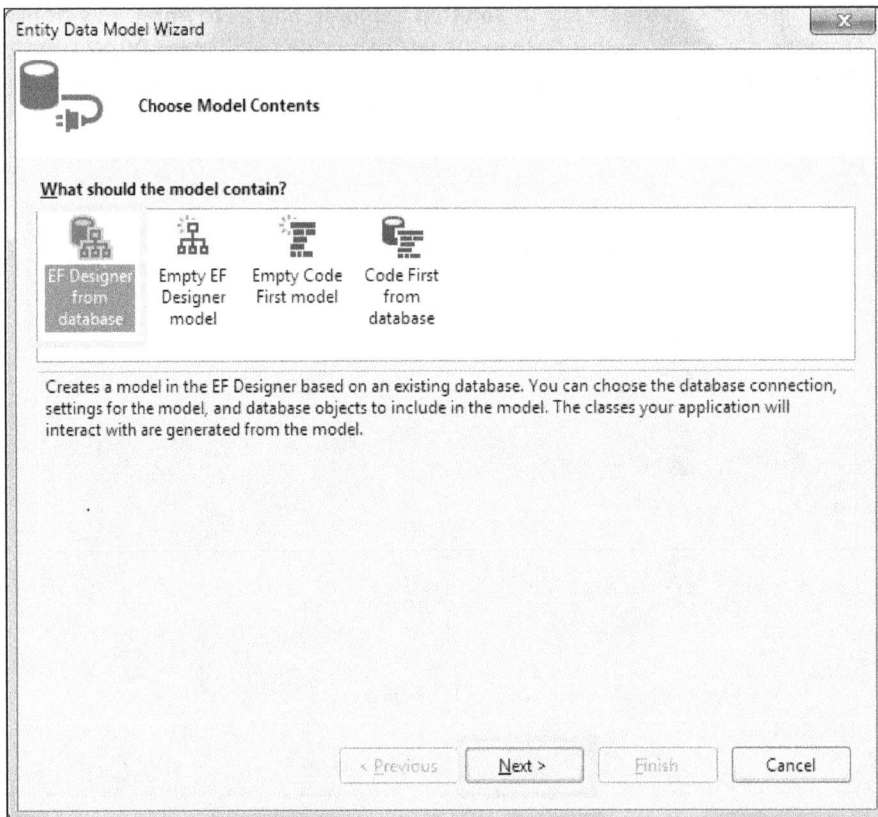

7. Create a connection to the Northwind database running on MS SQL Server, and save the connection string in `web.config` as `NorthwindEntities`. Click on the **Next** button:

Entity Data Model Wizard

Choose Your Data Connection

Which data connection should your application use to connect to the database?

| pc.Northwind.dbo ▼ | New Connection... |

This connection string appears to contain sensitive data (for example, a password) that is required to connect to the database. Storing sensitive data in the connection string can be a security risk. Do you want to include this sensitive data in the connection string?

  ○ No, exclude sensitive data from the connection string. I will set it in my application code.

  ○ Yes, include the sensitive data in the connection string.

Connection string:

```
metadata=res://*/ProductModel.csdl|res://*/ProductModel.ssdl|
res://*/ProductModel.msl;provider=System.Data.SqlClient;provider connection string="data
source=PC;initial catalog=Northwind;integrated
security=True;MultipleActiveResultSets=True;App=EntityFramework"
```

☑ Save connection settings in Web.Config as:

NorthwindEntities

| < Previous | Next > | Finish | Cancel |

8. On the next screen, which displays the database objects, check the **Products** table by navigating to **Tables | dbo | Products**, and click on the **Finish** button:

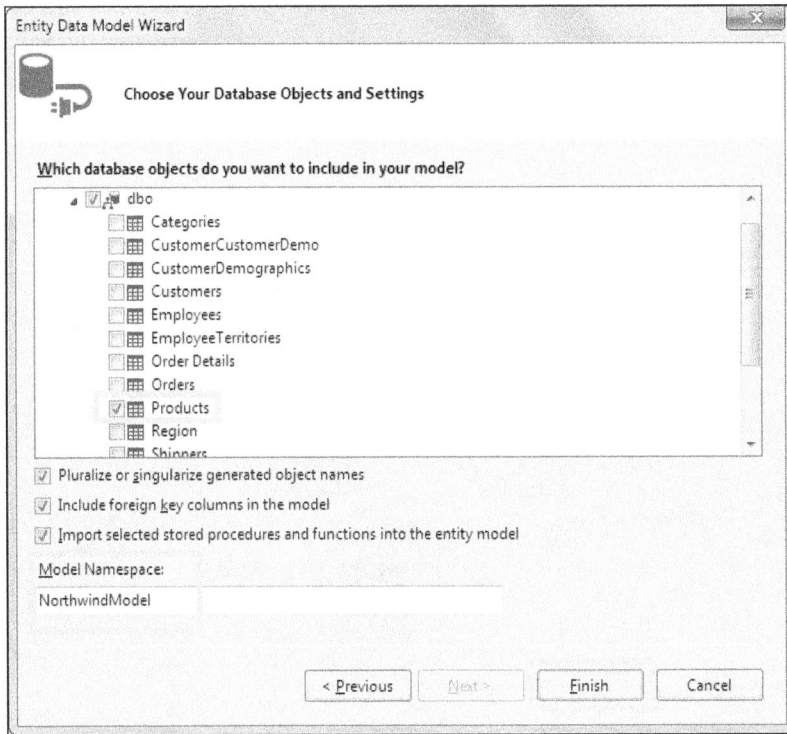

9. Now, add a `GridView` control to the web form by navigating to **Toolbox | Data**.

10. In the code-behind file (`Default.aspx.vb` or `Default.aspx.cs`), add the following method to retrieve records from the Products table.

For VB, the code is as follows:

```
Public Function GridView1_GetData() As IQueryable
  Dim db As NorthwindEntities = New NorthwindEntities()
  Dim queryResults = From prod In db.Products
    Order By prod.ProductID
    Select prod.ProductID, prod.ProductName,
      prod.UnitPrice, prod.UnitsInStock
  Return queryResults
End Function
```

For C#, the code is as follows:

```
public IQueryable GridView1_GetData()
{
```

```
NorthwindEntities db = new NorthwindEntities();
var query = from prod in db.Products
  orderby prod.ProductID
  select new
  ProductID = prod.ProductID,
  ProductName = prod.ProductName,
  UnitPrice = prod.UnitPrice,
  UnitsInStock = prod.UnitsInStock
  };
  return query;
}
```

11. Set `SelectMethod` of `GridView` to the preceding method in the `GridView` markup as follows:

```
SelectMethod="GridView1_GetData"
```

12. Define a CSS style for the **Edit** link in the `GridView` in the `head` element of the page:

```
<style type="text/css">
  .edit{
    color:blue;
    cursor:pointer;
  }
</style>
```

13. The complete markup of the page (excluding the styles applied to `GridView`) is as follows:

```
<asp:GridView ID="GridView1" runat="server"
  AutoGenerateColumns="False"
  SelectMethod="GridView1_GetData">
  <Columns>
  <asp:BoundField DataField="ProductID" ReadOnly="true"/>
  <asp:BoundField DataField="ProductName" ReadOnly="true"
    HeaderText="Product Name"/>
    <asp:TemplateField HeaderText="Unit Price">
      <ItemTemplate>
        <asp:Label ID="lblUnitPrice" runat="server" Text='<%#
          Bind("UnitPrice")%>'></asp:Label>
      </ItemTemplate>
      <EditItemTemplate>
        <asp:TextBox ID="txtUnitPrice" runat="server"    Text='<%#
          Bind("UnitPrice")%>'></asp:TextBox>
      </EditItemTemplate>
    </asp:TemplateField>
    <asp:TemplateField HeaderText="Units In Stock">
      <ItemTemplate>
```

```
        <asp:Label ID="lblUnitsInStock" runat="server"
          Text='<%# Bind("UnitsInStock")%>'></asp:Label>
      </ItemTemplate>
      <EditItemTemplate>
        <asp:TextBox ID="txtUnitsInStock" runat="server"
          Text='<%# Bind("UnitsInStock")%>'></asp:TextBox>
      </EditItemTemplate>
    </asp:TemplateField>
    <asp:TemplateField HeaderText="Edit">
      <ItemTemplate>
        <asp:LinkButton ID="btnEdit" CssClass="edit"
          CommandName="Edit"    runat="server">Edit</
asp:LinkButton>
      </ItemTemplate>
      <EditItemTemplate>
        <asp:LinkButton ID="btnUpdate" CommandName="Update"
runat="server">Update</asp:LinkButton>
        <asp:LinkButton ID="btnCancel" CommandName="Cancel"
          runat="server">Cancel</asp:LinkButton>
      </EditItemTemplate>
    </asp:TemplateField>
  </Columns>
</asp:GridView>
```

How to do it...

Add the following jQuery code to a `<script>` block on the page:

```
<script type="text/javascript">
  $(document).ready(function () {
    $("table[id=GridView1]").on("dblclick", "tr", function () {
      $(this).find(".edit").trigger("click");
    });
    $(".edit").click(function () {
      eval($(this).attr('href'));
    });
  });
</script>
```

How it works...

The page works as follows:

1. When you run the page, the product list is displayed in the GridView control.

2. Now, double-click on any row. You will notice that this will simulate clicking on the **Edit** link in that specific row. This is possible by attaching an event handler to the dblclick event of the row element as follows:

   ```
   $("table[id=GridView1]").on("dblclick", "tr", function ()
   {...});
   ```

3. The event handler uses the edit CSS class to select the **Edit** link in that row, and the .trigger() method is used to call the click event on this link, as follows:

   ```
   $(this).find(".edit").trigger("click");
   ```

4. Finally, an event handler is attached to the click event of the Edit link:

   ```
   $(".edit").click(function () {...});
   ```

   This event handler uses the JavaScript eval() function to call the href attribute attached to the **Edit** link:

   ```
   eval($(this).attr('href'));
   ```

See also

The *Using event delegation to attach events to future controls* recipe

Passing data with events and using event namespacing

In this recipe, we will demonstrate how to pass event data with the .trigger() method. The event data will be defined in the **JavaScript Object Notation** (**JSON**) format, which is simply a collection of name/value pairs. We will also see how to use namespacing on the same event type to execute different handlers. The constructs used in this example are as follows:

Construct	Type	Description
$(this)	jQuery object	This refers to the current jQuery object.
:checked	jQuery selector	This selects all checked checkboxes and radio buttons.
click	jQuery event	This is fired when you click on an element. It corresponds to the JavaScript click event.

Construct	Type	Description
`.find()`	jQuery method	This finds all elements matching the filter.
`.on()`	jQuery event binder	This attaches an event handler for one or more events to the matched elements.
`.trigger()`	jQuery method	This executes handlers and behaviors attached to the matched elements.
`.val()`	jQuery method	This returns the value of the first matched element or sets the value of every matched element.

Getting ready

To pass data with events and to use event namespacing, follow these steps:

1. We will create a simple web page with two `RadioButtonList` controls and one `Button` control as follows:

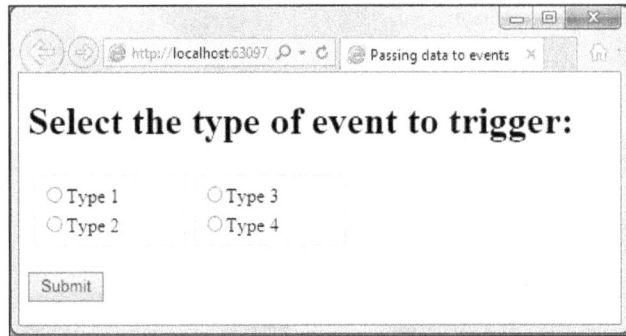

When you click on any radio button in the first `RadioButtonList` control, the `click` event of the `Button` control is called programmatically and information on the selected radio button is passed to the event handler. The event data is displayed in a JavaScript alert message, as shown in the following screenshot:

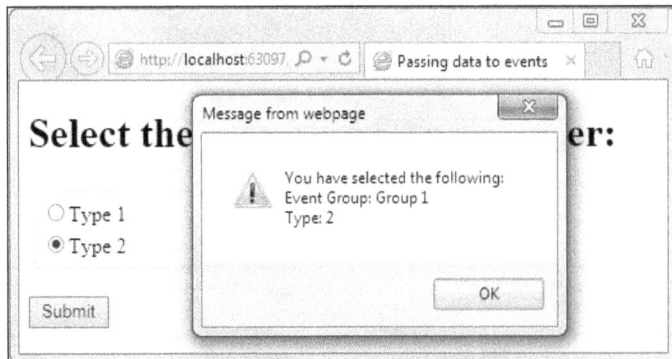

When you click on any radio button from the second `RadioButtonList` control, once again the `click` event handler of the `Button` control is called programmatically and event data is passed. However, this time a different handler is executed and the event data is displayed in a JavaScript confirm box, as follows:

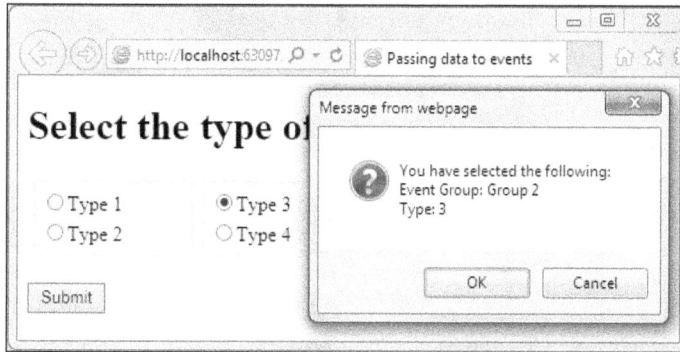

2. To get started, create an **ASP.NET Web Application** project in Visual Studio and name it `Recipe7` (or any other suitable name).

3. Add a `Scripts` folder to the project, and add the jQuery library to the folder.

4. Add a new web form to the project. Include the jQuery library on the form.

5. Add the following markup to the page:

```
<table>
  <tr>
    <td><fieldset>
      <asp:RadioButtonList ID="RadioButtonList1"
        runat="server" Width="120px">
        <asp:ListItem Text="Type 1"
          Value="1"></asp:ListItem>
        <asp:ListItem Text="Type 2"
          Value="2"></asp:ListItem>
      </asp:RadioButtonList>
    </fieldset></td>
    <td><fieldset>
      <asp:RadioButtonList ID="RadioButtonList2"
        runat="server" Width="120px">
        <asp:ListItem Text="Type 3"
          Value="3"></asp:ListItem>
        <asp:ListItem Text="Type 4"
          Value="4"></asp:ListItem>
      </asp:RadioButtonList>
    </fieldset></td>
  </tr>
</table><br />
<asp:Button ID="btnSubmit" runat="server" Text="Submit" />
```

How to do it...

Include the following jQuery code in a `<script>` block on the page:

```
<script type="text/javascript">
  $(document).ready(function () {
    $("#<%=RadioButtonList1.ClientID%>").on("click", function () {
      var strValContent = $(this).find(":checked").val();
      var data = { txtContent: "Group 1", valContent:
        strValContent };
      $("#<%=btnSubmit.ClientID%>").trigger("click.radioclick1",
        data);
    });
    $("#<%=RadioButtonList2.ClientID%>").on("click", function () {
      var strValContent = $(this).find(":checked").val();
      var data = { txtContent: "Group 2",  valContent:
        strValContent };
      $("#<%=btnSubmit.ClientID%>").trigger("click.radioclick2",
        data);
    });
    $("#<%=btnSubmit.ClientID%>").on("click.radioclick1", function
      (evt,data) {
      if (data != null){
        var strMessage = "You have selected the following: \r\n"+
          "Event Group: " + data.txtContent + "\r\n"    +
          "Type: " + data.valContent ;
        alert(strMessage);
      }
    });
    $("#<%=btnSubmit.ClientID%>").on("click.radioclick2", function
      (evt, data) {
      if (data != null){
        var strMessage = "You have selected the following: \r\n" +
          "Event Group: " + data.txtContent + "\r\n" +
          "Type: " + data.valContent;
        window.confirm(strMessage);
      }
    });
  });
</script>
```

How it works...

1. When the page loads and when you click on any radio button in the first `RadioButtonList` control, the event handler corresponding to its `click` event is executed:

   ```
   $("#<%=RadioButtonList1.ClientID%>").on("click", function
      () {...});
   ```

2. The preceding event handler first reads the selected value of the radio button:

   ```
   var strValContent = $(this).find(":checked").val();
   ```

   It then forms a JSON string to pass the preceding value as the event data:

   ```
   var data = { txtContent: "Group 1", valContent:
     strValContent };
   ```

   Finally, it triggers the `click` event of the `Button` control with the required `click.radioclick1` namespace and passes the required event data:

   ```
   $("#<%=btnSubmit.ClientID%>").trigger("click.radioclick1",
     data);
   ```

3. When the `click` event is invoked programmatically, its corresponding event handler with the `click.radioclick1` namespace is executed:

   ```
   $("#<%=btnSubmit.ClientID%>").on("click.radioclick1",
   function (evt,data) {...});
   ```

   This handler reads the event data. If the data is not null, it is displayed in an alert message as follows:

   ```
   if (data != null){
     var strMessage = "You have selected the following: \r\n"+
       "Event Group: " + data.txtContent + "\r\n" +
       "Type: " + data.valContent ;
     alert(strMessage);
   }
   ```

4. Similarly, when you click on a radio button in the second `RadioButtonList` control, the event handler corresponding to its `click` event is executed:

   ```
   $("#<%=RadioButtonList2.ClientID%>").on("click", function
   (  ) {...});
   ```

5. The preceding event handler first reads the selected value of the radio button:

   ```
   var strValContent = $(this).find(":checked").val();
   ```

It then forms a JSON string to be passed as the event data:

```
var data = { txtContent: "Group 2",  valContent:
  strValContent };
```

Finally, it triggers the `click` event of the `Button` control with the required `click.radioclick2` namespace and passes the required event data:

```
$("#<%=btnSubmit.ClientID%>").trigger("click.radioclick2",
  data);
```

6. When the `click` button is invoked programmatically, this time, the event handler with the `click.radioclick2` namespace is executed:

```
$("#<%=btnSubmit.ClientID%>").on("click.radioclick2",
  function (evt,data) {...});
```

This handler reads the event data. If the data is not `null`, it displays the information in a `confirm` message this time as follows:

```
if (data != null){
  var strMessage = "You have selected the following: \r\n"
+
    "Event Group: " + data.txtContent + "\r\n" +
    "Type: " + data.valContent;
  window.confirm(strMessage);
}
```

See also

The *Triggering an event programmatically* recipe

Detaching events

This recipe demonstrates the use of the `.off()` method to detach event handlers from page elements. The constructs used in this example are as follows:

Construct	Type	Description
`$("html_tag")`	jQuery selector	This selects all elements with the specified HTML tag.
`$(this)`	jQuery object	This refers to the current jQuery object.
`.addClass()`	jQuery method	This adds the specified CSS class to each matched element.
`blur`	jQuery event	This is fired when an element loses focus. It corresponds to the JavaScript `blur` event.

Construct	Type	Description
`:checked`	jQuery selector	This selects all checked checkboxes and radio buttons.
`click`	jQuery event	This is fired when you click on an element. It corresponds to the JavaScript `click` event.
`focus`	jQuery event	This is fired when an element receives focus. It corresponds to the JavaScript `focus` event.
`:input`	jQuery selector	This matches the `input`, `button`, `select`, and `textarea` elements.
`.is()`	jQuery method	This returns a Boolean value if the matched element satisfies a given condition.
`.off()`	jQuery method	This removes event handlers from the matched elements.
`.on()`	jQuery event binder	This attaches an event handler for one or more events to the matched elements.
`.removeClass()`	jQuery method	This removes the specified CSS class from each matched element.

Getting ready

To create a form for demonstrating detaching of events, follow these steps:

1. Create the following sample page consisting of a few `TextBox` controls. There is a `CheckBox` control on the top of the page. When the `CheckBox` control is checked, the current control with `focus` is highlighted with a blue border, as shown in the following screenshot:

When the `CheckBox` control is unchecked, the active control is not highlighted any more with the blue border as it was in the previous case:

2. To build the preceding page, create an **ASP.NET Web Application** project in Visual Studio and name it `Recipe8` (or any other suitable name).

3. Add a `Scripts` folder to the project, and add the jQuery library to the folder.

4. Add a new web form to the project. Include the jQuery library on the form.

5. Add the following markup to the page:

```
<table>
  <tr>
    <td colspan="2"><asp:CheckBox ID="chkHighlight"
      runat="server" Text="Highlight TextBoxes" />
    </td>
  </tr>
  <tr>
    <td colspan="2"><asp:Label ID="lblName"
      runat="server" Text="Name"></asp:Label>
    </td>
  </tr>
  <tr>
    <td><asp:TextBox ID="txtFirst"
      runat="server"></asp:TextBox>
    </td>
```

```
      <td><asp:TextBox ID="txtLast"
        runat="server"></asp:TextBox>
      </td>
    </tr>
    <tr>
      <td colspan="2"><asp:Label ID="lblEmail" runat="server"
        Text="Email"></asp:Label>
      </td>
    </tr>
    <tr>
      <td colspan="2"><asp:TextBox ID="txtEmail"
        runat="server"></asp:TextBox>
      </td>
    </tr>
    <tr>
      <td colspan="2"><asp:Label ID="lblHomeAddr"
        runat="server" Text="Home Address"></asp:Label>
      </td>
    </tr>
    <tr>
      <td colspan="2"><asp:TextBox ID="txtHomeAddr"
        runat="server"></asp:TextBox>
      </td>
    </tr>
    <tr>
      <td colspan="2"><asp:Label ID="lblMailingAddr"
        runat="server" Text="Mailing Address"></asp:Label>
      </td>
    </tr>
    <tr>
      <td colspan="2"><asp:TextBox ID="txtMailingAddr"
        runat="server"></asp:TextBox>
      </td>
    </tr>
    <tr>
      <td colspan="2"></td>
    </tr>
    <tr>
      <td colspan="2">
        <asp:Button ID="btnSubmit" runat="server"
            Text="Submit" />
        <asp:Button ID="btnReset" runat="server" Text="Reset" />
      </td>
    </tr>
</table>
```

6. Add the following style to the head element to give a blue border to the active element:

```css
<style type="text/css">
  .active{
    border-color:blue;
  }
</style>
```

How to do it...

Include the following jQuery code in a `<script>` block on the page:

```javascript
<script type="text/javascript">
  $(document).ready(function () {
    $("#<%=chkHighlight.ClientID%>").on("click", function () {
      if ($(this).is(":checked")) {
        $("input:text").on("focus", function () {
          $(this).addClass("active");
        });
        $("input:text").on("blur", function () {
          $(this).removeClass("active");
        });
      } else {
        $("input:text").off();
      }
    });
  });
</script>
```

How it works...

The page works as follows:

1. Run the application by pressing the *F5* key. When the page loads up, the checkbox control is unchecked. By checking the checkbox control, its `click` event handler is executed:

```javascript
$("#<%=chkHighlight.ClientID%>").on("click", function ()
{...}
```

2. The `click` event handler first checks whether the control is checked. If it is checked, it adds event handlers to all `TextBox` controls for the `focus` and `blur` events on the form. In the `focus` event handler, the `TextBox` control is highlighted, and in `blur`, the highlighting is removed as follows:

```
if ($(this).is(":checked")) {
  $("input:text").on("focus", function () {
    $(this).addClass("active");
  });
  $("input:text").on("blur", function () {
    $(this).removeClass("active");
  });
}
```

3. If the `CheckBox` control is unchecked, all events handlers tied to the `TextBox` controls are removed using the `.off()` method as follows:

```
else {
  $("input:text").off();
}
```

See also

The *Running an event only once* recipe

4

DOM Traversal and Manipulation in ASP.NET

This chapter looks at methods used for traversing the DOM tree and the techniques that can be used for manipulating them. We will discuss the following recipes in this chapter:

- ▶ Adding/removing DOM elements
- ▶ Accessing parent and child controls
- ▶ Accessing sibling controls
- ▶ Refining selection using a filter
- ▶ Adding items to controls at runtime

Introduction

The **Document Object Model** (**DOM**) provides a representation for web pages as structured documents with a tree-like format. Each node in the tree is tied to properties, methods, and event handlers. The web page is itself referred to as the `document` object and can be accessed from the `window` object using `window.document`. The HTML elements on the page become element nodes such as a `head` element or `body` element. These nodes, in turn, can have children nodes such as `table`, `div`, `input`, and so on. Some nodes may be text nodes while some may also be comment nodes.

It is important to note that the DOM is not a programming language but rather an object-oriented model that can be used across various languages, such as JavaScript, HTML, and XML. Thus, it is language-independent and provides a common **Application Programming Interface (API)** that can be implemented by various languages. By connecting web pages to programming languages, you can manipulate their style, structure, and content.

jQuery provides many methods for traversing the DOM tree such as accessing the parent, children, sibling, or next/previous elements. Using jQuery, DOM elements can be added, removed, or cloned at runtime using the client code. In this chapter, we will see how this can be accomplished.

Adding/removing DOM elements

This recipe demonstrates how to clone elements on the DOM. We will also see how to remove elements completely from the DOM tree. The programming constructs used in this example are summarized in the following table:

Construct	Type	Description
`$("#identifier")`	jQuery selector	This selects an element based on its ID
`$("html_tag")`	jQuery selector	This selects all elements with the specified HTML tag.
`.addClass()`	jQuery method	This adds the specified CSS class to each matched element.
`.attr("name")` or `.attr("name", "value")`	jQuery method	This returns a string with the required attribute value of the first matched element. It can also be used to set the attribute to the required value.
`[attribute="value"]`	jQuery selector	This selects an element with the specified attribute equal to the `"value"` string.
`.appendTo()`	jQuery method	This inserts elements at the end of the target.
`click`	jQuery event	This is fired when you click on an element. It corresponds to the JavaScript `click` event.
`.clone()`	jQuery method	This makes a deep copy of the matched elements, that is, the matched elements are copied along with their descendants and text nodes.
`event.preventDefault()`	jQuery method	This prevents the default action of the event from being triggered.
`.find()`	jQuery method	This finds all elements that match the filter.
`.length`	jQuery property	This returns the number of elements in the jQuery object.

Construct	Type	Description
`.on()`	jQuery event binder	This attaches an event handler for one or more events to the matched elements.
`.remove()`	jQuery method	This removes the matched elements as well as their descendants from the document. All the related data and events are also removed.
`.removeClass()`	jQuery method	This removes the specified CSS class from each matched element.
`.val()`	jQuery method	This returns the value of the first matched element or sets the value of every matched element.

Getting ready

Follow these steps to create a page for showing the adding and removing of DOM elements:

1. In this recipe, let's create a subsection of a job application form where the applicant needs to key in the current and past working experience. Since this is a variable section and different applicants can have different number of job experiences, we will let the user add new subsections if required. Once the page is loaded, the following form will be displayed:

2. When you click on the **Add Work Experience** link, a new subsection is added as follows:

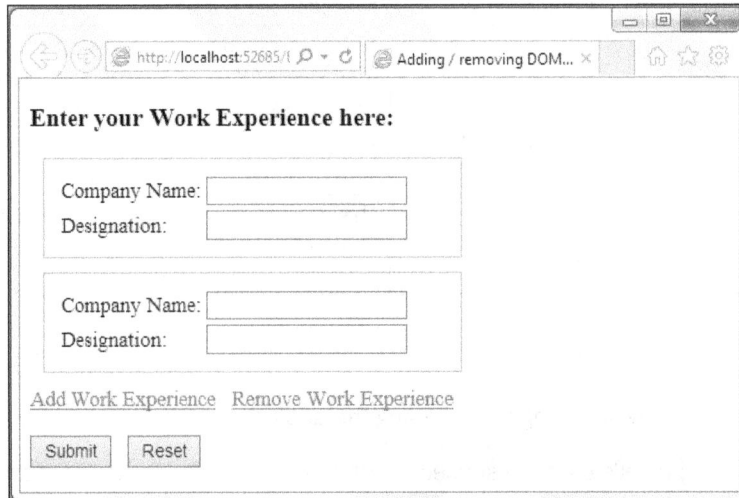

3. When you click on the **Remove Work Experience** link, a prompt message is displayed to the user, as shown in the following screenshot:

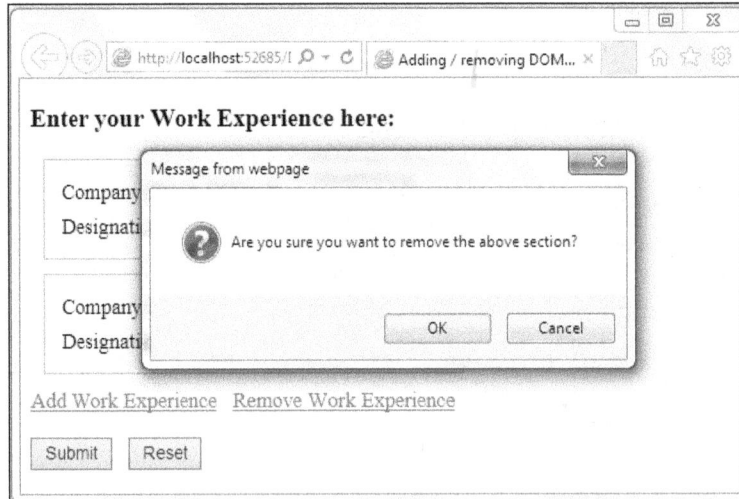

By clicking on **Cancel**, the action is dismissed. By clicking on **OK**, the previous subsection is permanently removed from the form.

4. To get started, create a new **ASP.NET Web Application** project in Visual Studio using the **Empty** template and name it `Recipe1` (or any other suitable name).

5. Add a `Scripts` folder to the project and include the jQuery library files in this folder.

6. Add a new web form and include the jQuery library in this form.

7. Add two form fields: `Company Name` and `Designation` to the form. Drag and drop two **LinkButton** controls below these fields: one to add a new section and the other to remove the previous section. Also, add two Button controls to the form for the `Submit` and `Reset` functions, respectively. Thus, the markup of the form will be as follows:

```
<div id="container">
  <asp:Panel ID="pnlWorkExp" runat="server"
CssClass="addPanel">
    <table>
      <tr>
        <td>
          <asp:Label ID="lblCompany" runat="server"
Text="Company Name:"></asp:Label>
        </td>
        <td>
          <asp:TextBox ID="txtCompany"
runat="server"></asp:TextBox>
        </td>
      </tr>
      <tr>
        <td>
          <asp:Label ID="lblDesignation" runat="server"
Text="Designation:"></asp:Label>
        </td>
        <td>
          <asp:TextBox ID="txtDesignation"
runat="server"></asp:TextBox>
        </td>
      </tr>
    </table>
  </asp:Panel>
</div>
<asp:LinkButton ID="lnkAddWorkExp" runat="server">Add Work
Experience</asp:LinkButton>
  
<asp:LinkButton ID="lnkRemWorkExp" runat="server">Remove
Work Experience</asp:LinkButton>
<br /><br />
<asp:Button ID="btnSubmit" runat="server" Text="Submit" />
  
<asp:Button ID="btnReset" runat="server" Text="Reset" />
```

8. Note that the form has a container div area consisting of a `Panel` control. We will be cloning this `Panel` on every click of the **Add Work Experience** link. Add the following styles to this `Panel`:

```css
.addPanel {
  border: solid;
  border-width: 1 px;
  border-color: darkgray;
  width: 300 px;
  padding: 10 px;
  margin: 10 px;
}
```

9. We will also add a style to `disabled` controls on the page:

```css
.disabled{
  color:gray;
  text-decoration:none;
}
```

How to do it...

Add the following jQuery code to a `<script>` block in the form:

```javascript
<script type="text/javascript">
$(document).ready(function() {
  $("#<%=lnkRemWorkExp.ClientID%>").attr("disabled",
true).addClass("disabled");
  $("#<%=lnkAddWorkExp.ClientID%>").on("click", function(evt) {
    evt.preventDefault();
    var cnt = $(".addPanel").length + 1;
    var clone = $("#<%=pnlWorkExp.ClientID%>").clone();
    clone.attr("ID", "<%=pnlWorkExp.ClientID%>_" + cnt);
    clone.find("#<%=lblCompany.ClientID%>").attr("ID",
"<%=lblCompany.ClientID%>_" + cnt);
    clone.find("#<%=txtCompany.ClientID%>").attr("ID",
"<%=txtCompany.ClientID%>_" + cnt).attr("name",
"<%=txtCompany.ClientID%>_" + cnt).val("");
    clone.find("#<%=lblDesignation.ClientID%>").attr("ID",
"<%=lblDesignation.ClientID%>_" + cnt);
    clone.find("#<%=txtDesignation.ClientID%>").attr("ID",
"<%=txtDesignation.ClientID%>_" + cnt).attr("name",
"<%=txtDesignation.ClientID%>_" + cnt).val("");
    clone.appendTo("#container");
    $("#<%=lnkRemWorkExp.ClientID%>").attr("disabled",
false).removeClass("disabled");
  });
```

```
$("#<%=lnkRemWorkExp.ClientID%>").on("click", function(evt) {
    evt.preventDefault();
    var cnt = $(".addPanel").length;
    if (cnt > 1) {
        if (confirm("Are you sure you want to remove the above
section?")) {
            $("#<%=pnlWorkExp.ClientID%>_" + cnt).remove();
            cnt--;
            if (cnt == 1)
                $("#<%=lnkRemWorkExp.ClientID%>").attr("disabled",
false).addClass("disabled");
        }
    }
});
$("#<%=btnSubmit.ClientID%>").on("click", function(evt) {
    evt.preventDefault();
    //handle form submission using AJAX here
});
$("#<%=btnReset.ClientID%>").on("click", function(evt) {
    evt.preventDefault();
    $("input[type=text]").val("");
});
});
</script>
```

How it works...

Let's see how to add and remove the DOM elements:

1. In the jQuery code, the **Remove Work Experience** link is initially disabled by setting its `disabled` attribute to `true` as follows:

    ```
    $("#<%=lnkRemWorkExp.ClientID%>").attr("disabled",
    true).addClass("disabled");
    ```

    Thus, initially on page load, the link will not be clickable.

2. Event handlers are attached to the `LinkButton` controls to add and remove the subsections as well as the `Button` controls to submit and reset the form:

    ```
    $("#<%=lnkAddWorkExp.ClientID%>").on("click", function
    (evt) {…});
    $("#<%=lnkRemWorkExp.ClientID%>").on("click", function
    (evt) {…});
    $("#<%=btnSubmit.ClientID%>").on("click", function (evt)
    {…});
    $("#<%=btnReset.ClientID%>").on("click", function (evt)
    {…});
    ```

3. In the event handler of the **Add Work Experience** link, we are going to make a deep copy of the `Panel` control using the `.clone()` function. We will need to update the `ID`, `name`, and `value` of each child control to avoid duplicates on the page. To get started with this, first prevent posting of the form due to the button `click` action:

```
evt.preventDefault();
```

Since we need a unique `ID` for each element, let's set the `ID` of each cloned element to `OriginalID_N` where, `OriginalID` is equal to the `ID` of the element that is cloned. `N` is equal to the Nth instance of the original element.

To determine the value of `N`, first determine the total number of `Panel` controls on the form that have the `addPanel` CSS class. Increment this count by `1` to get the number of the next instance, as follows:

```
var cnt = $(".addPanel").length + 1;
```

Make a copy of the original `Panel` control:

```
var clone = $("#<%=pnlWorkExp.ClientID%>").clone();
```

Update the `ID` of the cloned `Panel` to `OriginalID_N`:

```
clone.attr("ID", "<%=pnlWorkExp.ClientID%>_" + cnt);
```

Now, start updating the `ID` and `name` of its child elements to `OriginalID_N`. If any data has been entered into the controls, the data will be replicated as well. Hence, reset the data of the cloned text controls, as follows:

```
clone.find("#<%=lblCompany.ClientID%>").attr("ID",
"<%=lblCompany.ClientID%>_" + cnt);
clone.find("#<%=txtCompany.ClientID%>").attr("ID",
"<%=txtCompany.ClientID%>_" + cnt).attr("name",
"<%=txtCompany.ClientID%>_" + cnt).val("");
clone.find("#<%=lblDesignation.ClientID%>").attr("ID",
"<%=lblDesignation.ClientID%>_" + cnt);
clone.find("#<%=txtDesignation.ClientID%>").attr("ID",
"<%=txtDesignation.ClientID%>_" + cnt).attr("name",
"<%=txtDesignation.ClientID%>_" + cnt).val("");
```

Now, the cloned Panel is ready to be appended to the container div area:

```
clone.appendTo("#container");
```

Enable the **Remove Work Experience** link by updating its `disabled` attribute to `false`:

```
$("#<%=lnkRemWorkExp.ClientID%>").attr("disabled",
false).removeClass("disabled");
```

4. When you click on the **Remove Work Experience** link, we will remove the most recently added `Panel` from the form. To do this, first prevent posting of the form on the `click` event:

```
evt.preventDefault();
```

Get the number of the last added `Panel` on the form, as follows:

```
var cnt = $(".addPanel").length;
```

If the panel is the original element, that is, the first panel on the form, it will not be removed. If there are more than one Panel controls on the form, we need to show the confirmation dialog box to the user. The user can dismiss the dialog box by clicking on **Cancel**. If the user clicks on **OK**, we use the `.remove()` function to delete the Panel as well its child elements.

Since the number of Panels is reduced by 1, we can decrease the count by 1. If only one panel is left behind, disable the `remove` link to avoid removing the original panel:

```
if (cnt > 1) {
   if (confirm("Are you sure you want to remove the above
section?")){
      $("#<%=pnlWorkExp.ClientID%>_" + cnt).remove();
      cnt--;
      if (cnt == 1)
         $("#<%=lnkRemWorkExp.ClientID%>").attr("disabled",
false).addClass("disabled");
   }
}
```

> Since DOM elements are added using the client code, they are not accessible by the server side. Hence, in the event handler of the **Submit** button, retrieve the contents of all DOM elements and post them to the server using **AJAX**. This technique of posting form contents is demonstrated in the *Serializing form data* recipe in *Chapter 9, Useful jQuery Recipes for ASP.NET Sites*, which is available at: `https://www.packtpub.com/sites/default/files/downloads/4836OT_Chapter_09`.

5. In the event handler of the **Reset** button, prevent posting of the form and reset the value of all text controls as follows:

```
evt.preventDefault();
$("input[type=text]").val("");
```

See also

The *Accessing sibling controls* recipe

Accessing parent and child controls

This recipe demonstrates how to access parent and child elements in the DOM when performing client-side validation of a sample form. The constructs used in this example are summarized as follows:

Construct	Type	Description
`$("#identifier")`	jQuery selector	This selects an element based on its `ID`
`$("html_tag")`	jQuery selector	This selects all elements with the specified HTML tag
`$(this)`	jQuery object	This refers to the current jQuery object
`.addClass()`	jQuery method	This adds the specified `CSS` class to each matched element
`:checked`	jQuery selector	This selects checked input elements
`.children()`	jQuery method	This returns the immediate descendant element of the matched elements
`.each()`	jQuery method	This iterates over the matched elements and executes a function for each element
`event.preventDefault()`	jQuery method	This prevents the default action of the event from being triggered
`.find()`	jQuery method	This finds all elements that match the filter
`.length`	jQuery property	This returns the number of elements in the jQuery object
`.parent()`	jQuery method	This returns the immediate parent element of the matched elements
`.prop(propertyName)` or `.prop(propertyName, value)`	jQuery method	This returns the value of the specified property for the first matched element or sets the value of the specified property for all matched elements
`.removeClass()`	jQuery method	This removes the specified CSS class from each matched element
`:selected`	jQuery selector	This retrieves the selected input elements
`.val()`	jQuery method	This returns the value of the first matched element or sets the value of every matched element

Getting ready

Following are the steps to build a page to demonstrate accessing of parent and child controls:

1. We will be validating a form that registers interested volunteers with the school museum. The form consists of the following fields:

When you click on the **Submit** button, the fields are validated according to the following rules:

- All fields are compulsory, that is, they should be nonempty
- The **Availability** field should have at least three entries selected

Fields that fail the validation are highlighted in red, as shown here:

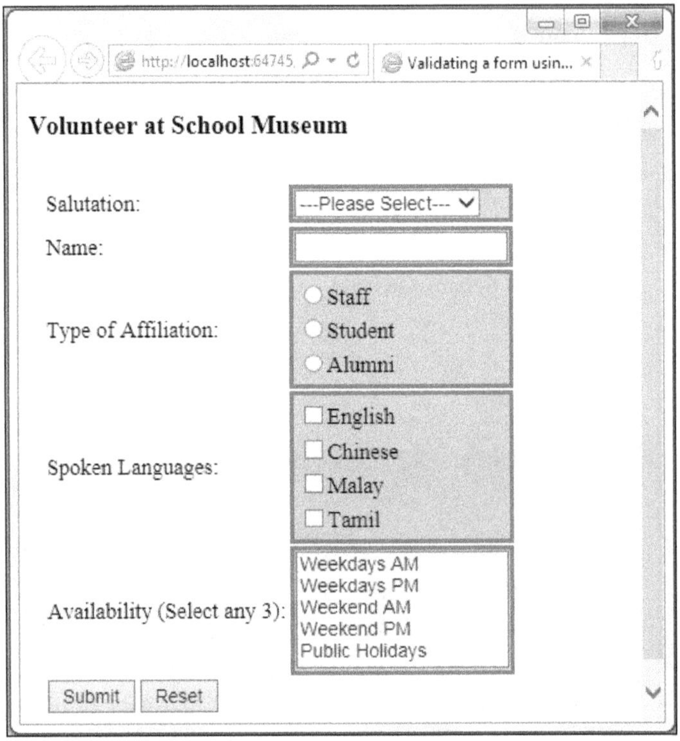

2. To create this form, launch a new **ASP.NET Web Application** in Visual Studio using the **Empty** template and name it Recipe2 (or any other suitable name).

3. Add a Scripts folder and include the jQuery library in this folder.

4. Create a web form and include the jQuery library in the form.

5. Add the following markup to the page:

```
<table id="container">
<tr><td>
<asp:Label ID="lblSalutation" runat="server"
Text="Salutation:"></asp:Label></td>
<td><asp:DropDownList ID="ddlSalutation" runat="server">
<asp:ListItem Text="---Please Select---"
  Value=""></asp:ListItem>
<asp:ListItem Text="Mr" Value="Mr"></asp:ListItem>
<asp:ListItem Text="Ms" Value="Ms"></asp:ListItem>
<asp:ListItem Text="Mrs"
  Value="Mrs"></asp:ListItem>
<asp:ListItem Text="Dr" Value="Dr"></asp:ListItem>
```

```
<asp:ListItem Text="Prof"
  Value="Prof"></asp:ListItem>
</asp:DropDownList>
</td>
</tr>
<tr>
  <td>
    <asp:Label ID="lblName" runat="server"
      Text="Name:"></asp:Label>
  </td>
  <td>
    <asp:TextBox ID="txtName"
      runat="server"></asp:TextBox>
  </td>
</tr>
<tr>
  <td>
    <asp:Label ID="lblAffiliation" runat="server"
      Text="Type of Affiliation:"></asp:Label>
  </td>
  <td>
    <asp:RadioButtonList ID="rdlAffiliation"
      runat="server">
      <asp:ListItem Text="Staff"
        Value="Staff"></asp:ListItem>
      <asp:ListItem Text="Student"
        Value="Student"></asp:ListItem>
      <asp:ListItem Text="Alumni"
        Value="Alumni"></asp:ListItem>
    </asp:RadioButtonList>
  </td>
</tr>
<tr>
  <td>
    <asp:Label ID="lblLanguages" runat="server"
      Text="Spoken Languages:"></asp:Label>
  </td>
  <td>
    <asp:CheckBoxList ID="chkLanguages" runat="server">
      <asp:ListItem Text="English"
        Value="English"></asp:ListItem>
      <asp:ListItem Text="Chinese"
        Value="Chinese"></asp:ListItem>
      <asp:ListItem Text="Malay"
```

```
          Value="Malay"></asp:ListItem>
        <asp:ListItem Text="Tamil"
          Value="Tamil"></asp:ListItem>
      </asp:CheckBoxList>
    </td>
  </tr>
  <tr>
    <td>
      <asp:Label ID="lblAvailability" runat="server"
        Text="Availability (Select any 3):"></asp:Label>
    </td>
    <td>
      <asp:ListBox ID="lstAvailability" runat="server"
        SelectionMode="Multiple" Width="100%" Height="82px" >
        <asp:ListItem Text="Weekdays AM"
          Value="WeekdaysAM"></asp:ListItem>
        <asp:ListItem Text="Weekdays PM"
          Value="WeekdaysPM"></asp:ListItem>
        <asp:ListItem Text="Weekend AM"
          Value="WeekendAM"></asp:ListItem>
        <asp:ListItem Text="Weekend PM"
          Value="WeekendPM"></asp:ListItem>
        <asp:ListItem Text="Public Holidays"
          Value="PublicHolidays"></asp:ListItem>
      </asp:ListBox>
    </td>
  </tr>
  <tr>
    <td colspan="2">
      <asp:Button ID="btnSubmit" runat="server"
        Text="Submit" />
      <asp:Button ID="btnReset" runat="server" Text="Reset"
        />
    </td>
  </tr>
</table>
```

6. To show a border and background color for controls that are invalid, include the following style:

```
.error{
  border-style:solid;
  border-color:red;
  background-color:lightpink;
}
```

7. Add the following style to the `container` table to give sufficient `padding` between the controls:

```
#container{
  padding:10px;
}
```

How to do it...

Add the following jQuery code to a `<script>` block on the form:

```
<script type="text/javascript">
$(document).ready(function() {
  $("#<%=btnSubmit.ClientID%>").click(function(evt) {
    evt.preventDefault();
    //Salutation field
    if ($("#<%=ddlSalutation.ClientID%>").val() == "")
$("#<%=ddlSalutation.ClientID%>").parent().addClass("error");
    else
$("#<%=ddlSalutation.ClientID%>").parent().removeClass("error");
    //Name field
    if ($("#<%=txtName.ClientID%>").val() == "")
      $("#<%=txtName.ClientID%>").parent().addClass("error");
    else
      $("#<%=txtName.ClientID%>").parent().removeClass("error");
    //Affiliation field
    var rdlAffCount =
$("#<%=rdlAffiliation.ClientID%>").find("input:checked").length;
    if (rdlAffCount == 0)
$("#<%=rdlAffiliation.ClientID%>").parent().addClass("error");
    else
$("#<%=rdlAffiliation.ClientID%>").parent().removeClass("error");
    //Languages field
    var chkLanguagesCount =
$("#<%=chkLanguages.ClientID%>").find("input:checked").length;
    if (chkLanguagesCount == 0)
$("#<%=chkLanguages.ClientID%>").parent().addClass("error");
    else
$("#<%=chkLanguages.ClientID%>").parent().removeClass("error");
    //Availability field
    var lstAvailCount =
$("#<%=lstAvailability.ClientID%>").children("option:selected").
length;
    if (lstAvailCount != 3)
$("#<%=lstAvailability.ClientID%>").parent().addClass("error");
```

```
      else $("#<%=lstAvailability.ClientID%>").parent().
removeClass("error");
    });
    $("#<%=btnReset.ClientID%>").click(function(evt) {
      evt.preventDefault();
      //Salutation field
      $("#<%=ddlSalutation.ClientID%>").val("");
      $("#<%=ddlSalutation.ClientID%>").parent().removeClass("error");
      //Name field
      $("#<%=txtName.ClientID%>").val("");
      $("#<%=txtName.ClientID%>").parent().removeClass("error");
      //Affiliation field
      $("#<%=rdlAffiliation.ClientID%> input").each(function() {
        $(this).prop("checked", false);
      });
      $("#<%=rdlAffiliation.ClientID%>").parent().removeClass("error");
      //Languages field
      $("#<%=chkLanguages.ClientID%> input").each(function() {
        $(this).prop("checked", false);
      });
      $("#<%=chkLanguages.ClientID%>").parent().removeClass("error");
      //Availability field
      $("#<%=lstAvailability.ClientID%> option").each(function() {
        $(this).prop("selected", false);
      });
      $("#<%=lstAvailability.ClientID%>").parent().removeClass("error");
    });
  });
</script>
```

How it works...

Let's see how to access the parent and child controls:

1. When you click on the **Submit** button, the page is prevented from posting back to the server:

   ```
   evt.preventDefault();
   ```

2. Next, the fields are validated step by step, starting with the first control, which is a `DropDownList` control. If no option is selected from this control, we will need to mark it as invalid. To do this, get its `parent` element—that is, the table cell container and highlight it by adding the `error` CSS style. If, however, the field is not empty, then any highlighting should be removed from the `parent` table cell:

```
if ($("#<%=ddlSalutation.ClientID%>").val() == "")
$("#<%=ddlSalutation.ClientID%>").parent().addClass("error"
);
else
$("#<%=ddlSalutation.ClientID%>").parent().removeClass("err
or");
```

3. Next, validate the textbox field. If the field is empty, get its `parent` element—that is, the container table cell, and add the `error` CSS style to it. If the field is not empty, remove any highlighting attached to it:

```
if ($("#<%=txtName.ClientID%>").val() == "")
$("#<%=txtName.ClientID%>").parent().addClass("error");
else
$("#<%=txtName.ClientID%>").parent().removeClass("error");
```

4. The third field on the form is the `Affiliation` field, which is defined as a `RadioButtonList` control. To determine whether any radio button is selected, we use the `:checked` selector:

```
var rdlAffCount =
$("#<%=rdlAffiliation.ClientID%>").find("input:checked").le
ngth;
```

Note that, at runtime, the `RadioButtonList` control is rendered as a table element, and each `ListItem` control is rendered as an input element with `type = radio` in a table row element, as shown in the following HTML source:

```
126                    <table id="rdlAffiliation">
127        <tr>
128            <td><input id="rdlAffiliation_0" type="radio" name="rdlAffiliation"
     value="Staff" /><label for="rdlAffiliation_0">Staff</label></td>
129        </tr><tr>
130            <td><input id="rdlAffiliation_1" type="radio" name="rdlAffiliation"
     value="Student" /><label for="rdlAffiliation_1">Student</label></td>
131        </tr><tr>
132            <td><input id="rdlAffiliation_2" type="radio" name="rdlAffiliation"
     value="Alumni" /><label for="rdlAffiliation_2">Alumni</label></td>
133        </tr>
134 </table></td>
```

Hence, we use the `.find()` function to search through the descendants of the table to find the required input elements.

If no option is selected, the `parent` table cell is highlighted to indicate that it is an invalid field. Otherwise, any highlighting attached to the cell can be removed:

```
if (rdlAffCount == 0)
$("#<%=rdlAffiliation.ClientID%>").parent().addClass("error
");
else
$("#<%=rdlAffiliation.ClientID%>").parent().removeClass("er
ror");
```

5. Next, we will validate the **Spoken Languages** field, which is defined as a `CheckBoxList` control. At runtime, the `CheckBoxList` control is rendered as a table element, and each `ListItem` control is rendered as an input element with `type = checkbox` in a table row element, as shown in the following HTML source:

```
140                    <table id="chkLanguages">
141        <tr>
142            <td><input id="chkLanguages_0" type="checkbox" name="chkLanguages$0"
    value="English" /><label for="chkLanguages_0">English</label></td>
143        </tr><tr>
144            <td><input id="chkLanguages_1" type="checkbox" name="chkLanguages$1"
    value="Chinese" /><label for="chkLanguages_1">Chinese</label></td>
145        </tr><tr>
146            <td><input id="chkLanguages_2" type="checkbox" name="chkLanguages$2"
    value="Malay" /><label for="chkLanguages_2">Malay</label></td>
147        </tr><tr>
148            <td><input id="chkLanguages_3" type="checkbox" name="chkLanguages$3"
    value="Tamil" /><label for="chkLanguages_3">Tamil</label></td>
149        </tr>
150 </table></td>
```

So, once again, we use the `.find()` function to search through the descendants of the table to determine the input elements, as follows:

```
var chkLanguagesCount =
$("#<%=chkLanguages.ClientID%>").find("input:checked").leng
th;
```

If no checkbox has been checked, then mark the field as invalid; otherwise, mark it as valid, as follows:

```
if (chkLanguagesCount == 0)
$("#<%=chkLanguages.ClientID%>").parent().addClass("error");
else
$("#<%=chkLanguages.ClientID%>").parent().removeClass("erro
r");
```

6. Lastly, we check the **Availability** field, which is defined as a `ListBox` control. Here, the condition for a successful validation is that at least three entries should be selected. So, first find out the total number of selected choices by filtering the options using the `:selected` selector:

```
var lstAvailCount =
$("#<%=lstAvailability.ClientID%>").children("option:select
ed").length;
```

Note that, at runtime, the `ListBox` control is rendered as a `select` element, and each `ListItem` control is rendered as an `option` element, as follows:

```
156                    <select size="4" name="lstAvailability" multiple="multiple"
       id="lstAvailability" style="height:82px;width:100%;">
157        <option value="WeekdaysAM">Weekdays AM</option>
158        <option value="WeekdaysPM">Weekdays PM</option>
159        <option value="WeekendAM">Weekend AM</option>
160        <option value="WeekendPM">Weekend PM</option>
161        <option value="PublicHolidays">Public Holidays</option>
162
163 </select>
```

The `.children()` function is used since the `option` element is an immediate descendant of the `select` element, and we do not need to search through all the descendants.

If the number of selected options is not equal to 3, then mark the field as invalid; otherwise, mark it as valid as follows:

```
if (lstAvailCount != 3)
$("#<%=lstAvailability.ClientID%>").parent().addClass("erro
r");
else
$("#<%=lstAvailability.ClientID%>").parent().removeClass("e
rror");
```

7. When you click on the **Reset** button, we need to clear the data entered into the form fields (if any). At the same time, the `error` CSS class attached to any table cell should also be removed.

8. When you click on the **Reset** button, first prevent posting of the form to the server:

```
evt.preventDefault();
```

9. Next, reset the value of the first `DropDownList` field, and remove any error styles attached to it:

```
$("#<%=ddlSalutation.ClientID%>").val("");
$("#<%=ddlSalutation.ClientID%>").parent().removeClass("error");
```

10. Next, repeat the same process for the `TextBox` field:

```
$("#<%=txtName.ClientID%>").val(""); $("#<%=txtName.ClientID%>").
parent().removeClass("error");
```

11. For the `RadioButtonList`, `CheckBoxList`, and `ListBox` controls, loop through each option and reset the selection (if any). Also, remove the error styles (if any):

```
$("#<%=rdlAffiliation.ClientID%> input").each(function() {
    $(this).prop("checked", false);
});
$("#<%=rdlAffiliation.ClientID%>").parent().removeClass("er
ror");
$("#<%=chkLanguages.ClientID%> input").each(function() {
    $(this).prop("checked", false);
});
$("#<%=chkLanguages.ClientID%>").parent().removeClass("erro
r");
$("#<%=lstAvailability.ClientID%> option").each(function()
{
    $(this).prop("selected", false);
});
$("#<%=lstAvailability.ClientID%>").parent().removeClass("e
rror");
```

See also

The *Adding / removing DOM elements* recipe

Accessing sibling controls

In the previous recipe, we traversed upwards and downwards from an element in the DOM tree. In this recipe, let's traverse to other controls on the same level. The constructs used in this example are summarized as follows:

Construct	Type	Description
`$(".class")`	jQuery selector	This matches all elements with the specified CSS class
`$("html_tag")`	jQuery selector	This selects all elements with the specified HTML tag
`$(this)`	jQuery object	This refers to the current jQuery object
`.click()`	jQuery event binder	This binds a handler to the click event of an element
`event.preventDefault()`	jQuery method	This prevents the default action of the event from being triggered

Construct	Type	Description
`.focus()`	jQuery event binder	This triggers the focus event of an element or binds an event handler to the focus event
`.prop(propertyName)` or `.prop(propertyName, value)`	jQuery method	This returns the value of the specified property for the first matched element or sets the value of the specified property for all matched elements
`.siblings()`	jQuery method	This retrieves the siblings of the matched elements
`.text()`	jQuery method	This returns the combined text content of each of the matched elements or sets the text content of every matched element

Getting ready

Follow these steps to build a page for accessing sibling controls:

1. To demonstrate how to access sibling controls, create the following content management interface to edit reports. All text sections are read-only and are provided with **EDIT** links for any updates required, as shown in the following screenshot:

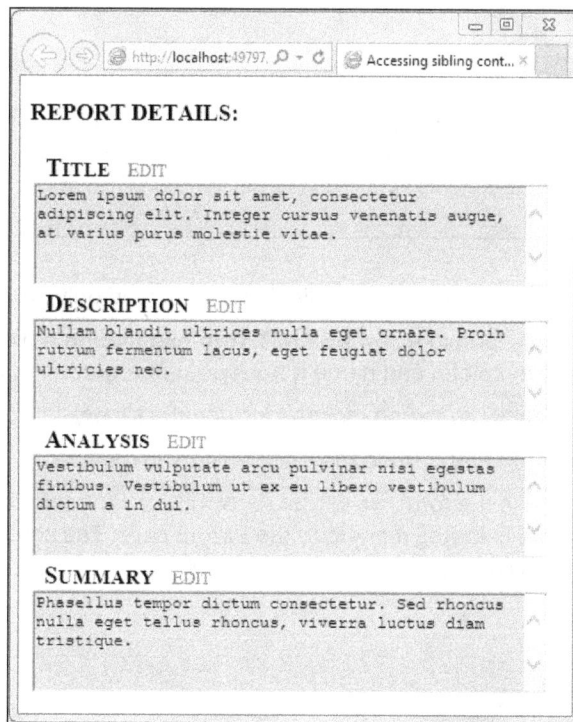

2. When you click on any **EDIT** link, the corresponding sibling text field is made editable as follows:

3. By clicking on the **SAVE** link, the text field becomes read-only once again.

4. To create this form, launch a new **ASP.NET Web Application** project in Visual Studio using the **Empty** template, and name it `Recipe3` (or any other suitable name).

5. Add a `Scripts` folder to the project and include the jQuery library in this folder.

6. Add a new web form and include the jQuery library in the form.

7. For each text field in the form, we will use a `TextBox` control in the `MultiLine` mode. So, add the following markup to the `.aspx` page. The content of the `TextBox` controls can be any random text, as follows:

```
<table>
  <tr>
    <td>
```

```
        <asp:Label ID="lblTitle" runat="server" Text="Title"
CssClass="sectionHeader"></asp:Label>
        <asp:LinkButton ID="lnkEdit1" CssClass="edit"
runat="server">Edit</asp:LinkButton><br />
        <asp:TextBox ID="txtTitle" runat="server"
TextMode="MultiLine" Rows="5" Columns="50">Lorem ipsum
dolor sit amet...</asp:TextBox>
    </td>
  </tr>
  <tr>
    <td>
        <asp:Label ID="lblDescription" runat="server"
Text="Description" CssClass="sectionHeader"></asp:Label>
        <asp:LinkButton ID="lnkEdit2" CssClass="edit"
runat="server">Edit</asp:LinkButton><br />
        <asp:TextBox ID="txtDescription" runat="server"
TextMode="MultiLine" Rows="5" Columns="50">Nullam
blandit...</asp:TextBox>
    </td>
  </tr>
  <tr>
    <td>
        <asp:Label ID="lblAnalysis" runat="server"
Text="Analysis" CssClass="sectionHeader"></asp:Label>
        <asp:LinkButton ID="lnkEdit3" CssClass="edit"
runat="server">Edit</asp:LinkButton><br />
        <asp:TextBox ID="txtAnalysis" runat="server"
TextMode="MultiLine" Rows="5" Columns="50">Vestibulum
vulputate... </asp:TextBox>
    </td>
  </tr>
  <tr>
    <td>
        <asp:Label ID="lblSummary" runat="server"
Text="Summary" CssClass="sectionHeader"></asp:Label>
        <asp:LinkButton ID="lnkEdit4" CssClass="edit"
runat="server">Edit</asp:LinkButton><br />
        <asp:TextBox ID="txtSummary" runat="server"
TextMode="MultiLine" Rows="5" Columns="50">Phasellus
tempor...</asp:TextBox>
    </td>
  </tr>
</table>
```

8. To differentiate between the read-only and update modes, in read-only mode, we can give a background color to the `TextBox` controls by adding the following style:

```
.readtext{
  background-color:powderblue;
}
```

9. Also, add the following styles to the **EDIT/SAVE** links and section headers:

```
.edit {
  font-variant: small - caps;
  text-decoration: none;
}
.sectionHeader {
  font-size: 20 px;
  font-variant: small-caps;
  font-weight: 700;
  padding: 10 px;
}
```

How to do it...

Add the following jQuery code to a `<script>` block on the form:

```
<script type="text/javascript">
$(document).ready(function() {
  $("textarea").prop("readonly", true).addClass("readtext");
  $(".edit").click(function(evt) {
    evt.preventDefault();
    var lnkText = $(this).text();
    if (lnkText == "Edit") {
      $(this).siblings("textarea").prop("readonly",
false).removeClass("readtext").focus();
      $(this).text("Save");
    } else if (lnkText == "Save") {
      $(this).siblings("textarea").prop("readonly",
true).addClass("readtext");
      $(this).text("Edit");
    }
  });
});
</script>
```

How it works...

Let's see how to access the sibling controls:

1. Initially, when the page loads in the browser, all `TextBox` controls are made uneditable by setting their `readonly` property to `true`. At runtime, the `TextBox` controls in the `MultiLine` mode are rendered as `textarea` elements. Hence, we can use the `.prop()` method as follows:

    ```
    $("textarea").prop("readonly", true).addClass("readtext");
    ```

    > The CSS class added earlier ensures that a background color is applied to the `TextBox` controls.

2. All **EDIT** `LinkButton` controls are tied to an `edit` CSS class. Hence, we can use the CSS selector to attach a handler to the `click` event of each link as follows:

    ```
    $(".edit").click(function (evt) {..});
    ```

3. When you click on any of the preceding links, firstly, prevent page submission:

    ```
    evt.preventDefault();
    ```

    Secondly, get the `text` of the link. This `text` can be either **EDIT** or **SAVE**, depending on the user's action:

    ```
    var lnkText = $(this).text();
    ```

4. If the link text is **EDIT**, we use the `.siblings()` method to traverse through other elements on the same level until we come across a `textarea` element. Once the element is located, the following needs to be done:

    ❑   Set the `readonly` property of the `textarea` element to `false`, that is, make the field editable

    ❑   Remove the background color by removing the corresponding style

    ❑   Focus the cursor on the field

    This can be done by chaining the methods in a single statement:

    ```
    $(this).siblings("textarea").prop("readonly",
    false).removeClass("readtext").focus();
    ```

    Lastly, update the `text` of the link to `SAVE`:

    ```
    $(this).text("Save");
    ```

5. If you click on the **SAVE** link, the following needs to be done:

   ❑ Set the `readonly` property of the sibling `textarea` element to `true`, that is, make the field uneditable

   ❑ Add a background color to the `textarea` element

This can be done by chaining the methods in the following statement:

```
$(this).siblings("textarea").prop("readonly",
true).addClass("readtext");
```

Next, update the link `text` to display `EDIT` instead:

```
$(this).text("Edit");
```

> Note that, by clicking on the **SAVE** link, you might also need to perform some server-side action such as saving the content to a database or file using AJAX.

There's more...

Let's use the developer tools in the browser window to view the changes in the properties of the active `textarea` field. The developer tools can be launched as follows:

▸ In Internet Explorer, from the main menu, go to **Tools | F12 Developer Tools**

▸ In Firefox, from the main menu, go to **Developer | Toggle Tools | Debugger** (*Ctrl + Shift + I*)

▸ In Google Chrome, from the main menu, go to **More tools | Developer tools** (*Ctrl + Shift + I*)

Add the required breakpoints to the jQuery script, as shown in the following screenshot:

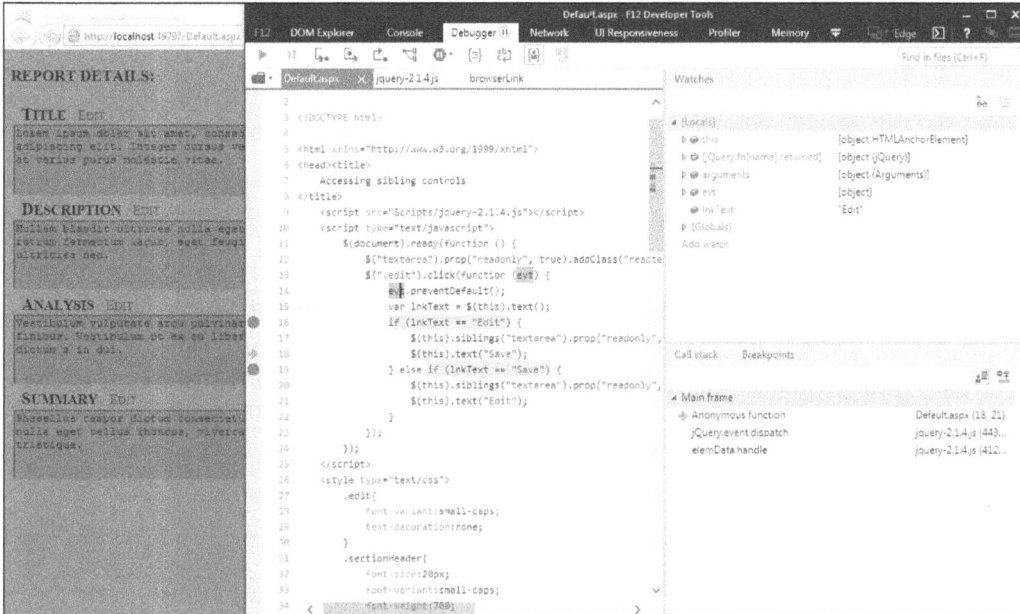

Step through the code to see the change in the `readonly` property and background color of the active `textarea` element.

See also

The *Accessing parent and child controls* recipe

Refining selection using a filter

jQuery provides a useful `.filter()` method to filter elements using a `selector` or `custom` function. In this recipe, we will filter the rows of a `GridView` control on the client side using this method. The constructs used in this example are summarized in the following table:

Construct	Type	Description
`$(#identifier)`	jQuery selector	This selects an element based on its `ID`
`$(".class")`	jQuery selector	This matches all elements with the specified CSS class
`$("html_tag")`	jQuery selector	This selects all elements with the specified HTML tag
`$(this)`	jQuery object	This refers to the current jQuery object

Construct	Type	Description
`.click()`	jQuery event binder	This binds a handler to the `click` event of an element
`:eq(i)`	jQuery selector	This selects all elements with the index equal to `i`.
`event.preventDefault()`	jQuery method	This prevents the default action of the event from being triggered
`.filter()`	jQuery method	This returns elements that match a selector or custom function
`.find()`	jQuery method	This finds all elements that match the filter
`:first-child`	jQuery selector	This selects elements that are the first child of the parent elements
`.hide()`	jQuery method	This hides the matched elements
`:not(selector)`	jQuery selector	This selects elements that do not match the specified selector
`.show()`	jQuery method	This displays the matched elements
`.substring(startIndex, [endIndex])`	JavaScript function	This returns a substring of a given string from `startIndex` to `endIndex` or to the end of the string
`.text()`	jQuery method	This returns the combined text content of each of the matched elements or sets the text content of every matched element
`:visible`	jQuery selector	This selects elements that are visible, that is, elements with a width or height > 0

Getting ready

Let's build a page to refine selection using a filter:

1. Let's create a web page with a `GridView` control that reads data from the Products table in the Northwind database. When you run the page, all records are retrieved and displayed, as shown here:

A B C D E F G H I J K L M N O P Q R S T U V W X Y Z

Product ID	Product Name	Unit Price	Units In Stock
1	Chai	18.0000	39
2	Chang	19.0000	17
3	Aniseed Syrup	10.0000	13
4	Chef Anton's Cajun Seasoning	22.0000	53
5	Chef Anton's Gumbo Mix	21.3500	0
6	Grandma's Boysenberry Spread	25.0000	120
7	Uncle Bob's Organic Dried Pears	30.0000	15
8	Northwoods Cranberry Sauce	40.0000	6
9	Mishi Kobe Niku	97.0000	29
10	Ikura	31.0000	31
11	Queso Cabrales	21.0000	22

2. When you click on any letter from **A** to **Z** above the GridView control, the rows are filtered to show the product names that begin with the selected letter. For example, when you click on the letter R, the page will display all product names beginning with the letter R, as shown in the following screenshot:

A B C D E F G H I J K L M N O P Q R S T U V W X Y Z

Product ID	Product Name	Unit Price	Units In Stock
28	Rössle Sauerkraut	45.6000	26
45	Rogede sild	9.5000	5
57	Ravioli Angelo	19.5000	36
59	Raclette Courdavault	55.0000	79
73	Röd Kaviar	15.0000	101
75	Rhönbräu Klosterbier	7.7500	125

If there are no product names that start with the selected letter, a message is displayed to the user, as shown in the following screenshot:

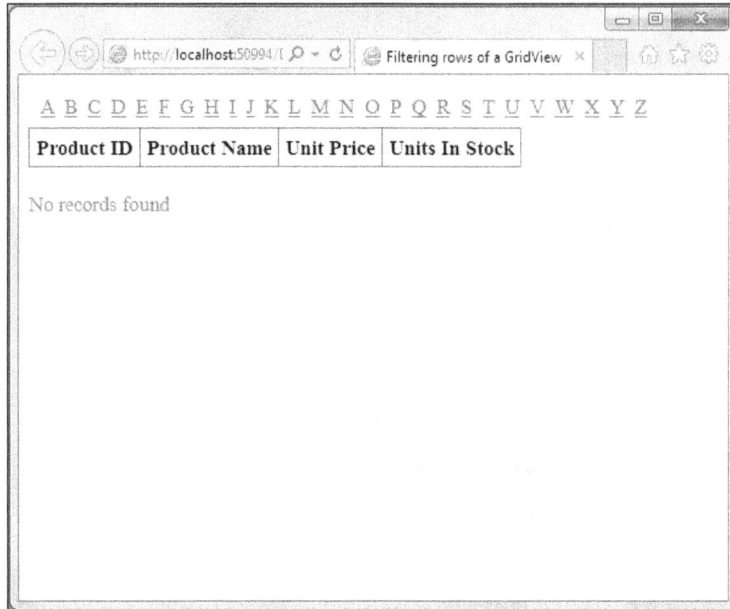

3. To get started, create a new **ASP.NET Web Application** project in Visual Studio using the **Empty** template and name it `Recipe4` (or any other suitable name).

4. Add a `Scripts` folder to the project and include the jQuery library files in this folder.

5. Create a new web form and add the jQuery library to the form.

6. Go to **Toolbox | Data**, and drag and drop a **GridView** control onto the form.

7. In the **Design** mode, mouse over the **GridView** control until a small arrow icon appears in the top-right corner of the screen. Click on the arrow to show the **GridView Tasks** menu, as shown here:

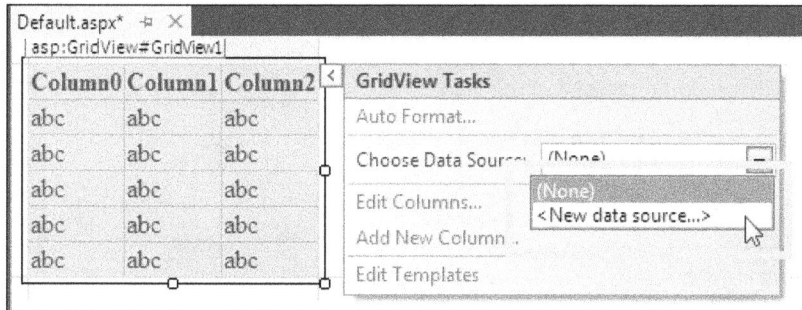

8. Select the **<New data source...>** option from the **Choose Data Source** field from the preceding menu. This will launch the **Data Source Configuration Wizard**, Select **SQL Database** from the available options, and click on **OK** to proceed:

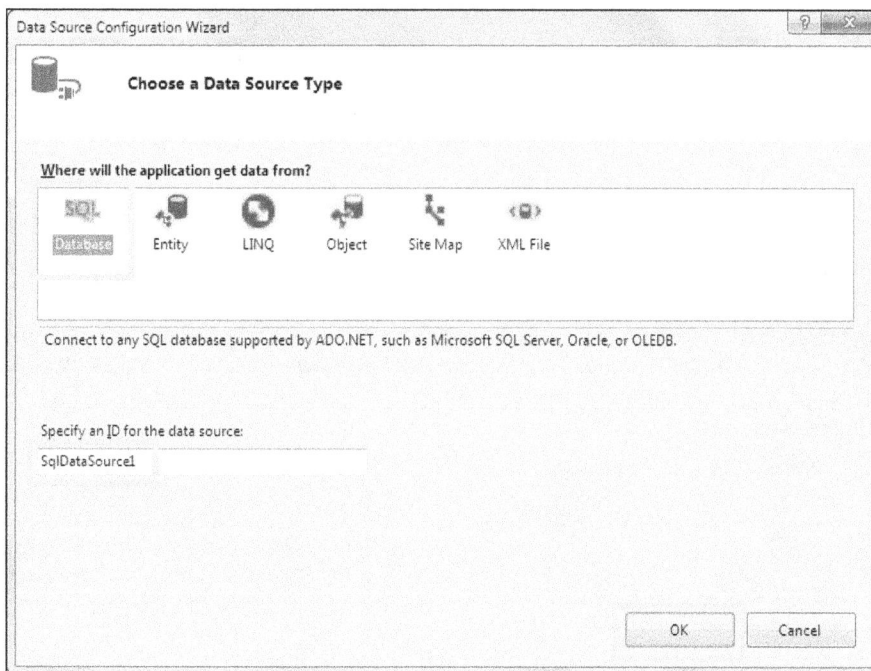

9. On the next screen, add a connection to the Northwind database. This will launch the **Configure the Select Statement** screen, as shown in the following screenshot. Select the **Products** table, and choose few columns for display such as **ProductID**, **ProductName**, **UnitPrice**, and **UnitsInStock**. Click on **Next** to proceed. Test the query to complete the wizard.

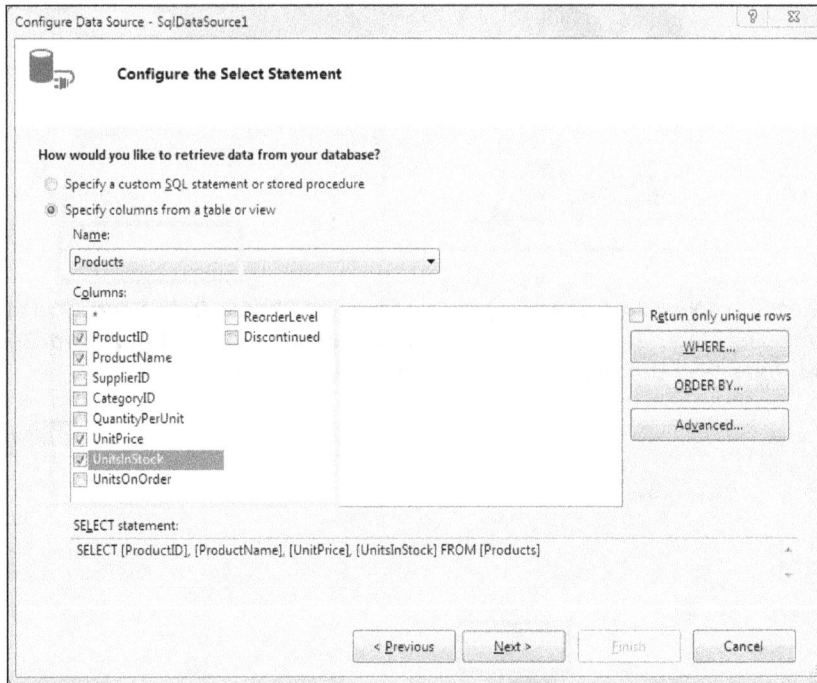

10. To display a list of letters from **A** to **Z** for filtering the GridView control, we will use a Repeater control. Hence, drag and drop a **Repeater** control by navigating to **Toolbox | Data**. In the code-behind file, populate the Repeater control using DataTable as follows:

    For VB, the code is as follows:

```
Private Sub Repeater1_BindData()
  Dim dt As DataTable = New DataTable()
  dt.Columns.Add("Alphabet")
  Dim cnt As Integer

  For cnt = 65 To 90 Step 1
    dt.Rows.Add(Chr(cnt))
  Next
```

```
    dt.AcceptChanges()
    Repeater1.DataSource = dt
    Repeater1.DataBind()
End Sub
```

For C#, the code is as follows:

```
private void Repeater1_BindData()
{
  DataTable dt = new DataTable();
  dt.Columns.Add("Alphabet");

  for (int cnt= 65; cnt <= 90; ++cnt)
    dt.Rows.Add((char)cnt);

  dt.AcceptChanges();
  Repeater1.DataSource = dt;
  Repeater1.DataBind();
}
```

In the preceding procedure, we use the ASCII code to generate the alphabet list. Since the ASCII code of A is 65 and that of Z is 90, the loop runs from 65 to 90, generating the required character from the ASCII code. The generated characters are stored in an Alphabet column in the DataTable. This column will be used in the Repeater markup for displaying.

11. To populate the Repeater control, call the preceding procedure on loading the page:

    For VB, the code is as follows:

    ```
    Protected Sub Page_Load(ByVal sender As Object, ByVal e As
    System.EventArgs) Handles Me.Load
      Repeater1_BindData
    End Sub
    ```

    For C#, the code is as follows:

    ```
    protected void Page_Load(object sender, EventArgs e)
    {
      Repeater1_BindData();
    }
    ```

12. In the **Design** mode, in the <ItemTemplate> element of the Repeater control, add a LinkButton control to display each letter as a link button.

13. Also, add a Label control to the form. This Label will be displayed when no records are retrieved for a particular filter.

14. The final markup of the `.aspx` page will be as follows:

```
<table>
  <tr>
    <td>
      <asp:Repeater ID="Repeater1" runat="server" >
        <ItemTemplate>
          <asp:LinkButton CssClass="filterLink"
runat="server"><%#Eval("Alphabet") %></asp:LinkButton>
        </ItemTemplate>
      </asp:Repeater>
    </td>
  </tr>
</table>
<asp:GridView ID="GridView1" runat="server"
AutoGenerateColumns="False" DataKeyNames="ProductID"
DataSourceID="SqlDataSource1">
  <Columns>
    <asp:BoundField DataField="ProductID"
HeaderText="Product ID" InsertVisible="False"
ReadOnly="True" SortExpression="ProductID" />
    <asp:BoundField DataField="ProductName"
HeaderText="Product Name" SortExpression="ProductName" />
    <asp:BoundField DataField="UnitPrice" HeaderText="Unit
Price" SortExpression="UnitPrice" />
    <asp:BoundField DataField="UnitsInStock"
HeaderText="Units In Stock" SortExpression="UnitsInStock"
/>
  </Columns>
</asp:GridView>
<br />
<asp:Label ID="lblMessage" runat="server" Text="No records
found" CssClass="message"></asp:Label>
```

15. Add the following style to display information messages to the user:

```
.message{
  color:red;
}
```
The following style will give the padding to the respective elements:
```
.filterLink{
  padding:2px;
}
th,td{
  padding:5px;
}
```

How to do it...

Add the following jQuery code to a `<script>` block on the form:

```
<script type="text/javascript">
$(document).ready(function () {
  $("#<%=lblMessage.ClientID%>").hide();
  $(".filterLink").click(function (evt) {
    evt.preventDefault();
    var filterLetter = $(this).text();
    $("#<%=GridView1.ClientID%> tr:not(:first-
child)").hide().filter(function () {
      if ($(this).find("td:eq(1)").text().substring(0, 1) ==
filterLetter)
        return this;
      }).show();
    if (($("#<%=GridView1.ClientID%> tr:visible").length - 1) ==
0)
    $("#<%=lblMessage.ClientID%>").show();
    else
    $("#<%=lblMessage.ClientID%>").hide();
  });
});
</script>
```

How it works...

Following steps shows the refining of selection using filter:

1. When the page is launched in the browser, initially, the `Label` control that is used to display information messages to the user is hidden:

   ```
   $("#<%=lblMessage.ClientID%>").hide();
   ```

2. Each letter from **A** to **Z** above the `GridView` control is assigned a `filterLink` CSS class. An event handler is attached to the `click` event of these links using the CSS selector as follows:

   ```
   $(".filterLink").click(function (evt) {..});
   ```

3. If you click on any of the preceding links, the page will be prevented from posting back, as follows:

   ```
   evt.preventDefault();
   ```

Next, retrieve the letter that was clicked. This can be done by retrieving the `text` link:

```
var filterLetter = $(this).text();
```

To return only the rows that have product names beginning with the clicked letter, select all rows except the header row using the `tr:not(:first-child)` selector. These rows are hidden initially:

```
$("#<%=GridView1.ClientID%> tr:not(:first-child)").hide()
```

Next, apply the `filter()` method. The `td:eq(1)` product name cell is read, and we compare if its character begins with the clicked letter:

```
.filter(function () {
   if ($(this).find("td:eq(1)").text().substring(0, 1) ==
filterLetter)
      return this;
})
```

Only rows that satisfy the `.filter()` method are returned and displayed:

```
.show();
```

4. Next, to display the information message if no rows are retrieved from the filtering, we use the `:visible` filter to check the number of rows that are visible. If only the header row is visible, we can display the message to inform the user that no rows have been returned:

```
if (($("#<%=GridView1.ClientID%> tr:visible").length - 1)
== 0)
   $("#<%=lblMessage.ClientID%>").show();
Otherwise, the message is hidden:
else
   $("#<%=lblMessage.ClientID%>").hide();
```

There's more...

The `.children()` method is an alternative to using the `.find()` method. The difference between the two methods is that the `.children()` method travels only one level down the DOM tree. Since the `td` elements are the immediate descendants of the `tr` elements, let's take a look at the following statement in the `<script>` block:

```
if ($(this).find("td:eq(1)").text().substring(0, 1) ==
filterLetter)
```

This can be modified using the `children()` method, as follows:

```
if ($(this).children("td:eq(1)").text().substring(0, 1) ==
filterLetter)
```

See also

The *Adding/removing DOM elements* recipe

Adding items to controls at runtime

In this recipe, we will use jQuery to add items to different ASP.NET controls, such as `DropDownList`, `ListBox`, and `BulletedList` at runtime. The constructs used in this example are summarized as follows:

Construct	Type	Description
`$("#identifier")`	jQuery selector	This selects an element using its `ID`
`$.map()`	jQuery function	This transforms an array or object into another array
`.append()`	jQuery method	This inserts content at the end of each matched element
`.click()`	jQuery event binder	This binds a handler to the `click` event of an element
`event.preventDefault()`	JavaScript function	This prevents the default action of the event from being triggered
`.focus()`	jQuery event binder	This triggers the focus event of an element or binds an event handler to the focus event
`.prepend()`	jQuery method	This inserts content at the beginning of each matched element
`.split()`	JavaScript function	This splits a string into substrings using the specified character as a delimiter
`.trim()`	JavaScript function	This removes a whitespace from the beginning and end of a string
`.val()`	jQuery method	This returns the value of the first matched element or sets the value of every matched element

Getting ready

Let's build a page to add items to controls at runtime:

1. In this recipe, let's create a web page with different types of controls to which items will be added at runtime. We will also provide a textbox field where the user can enter the items that need to be added.

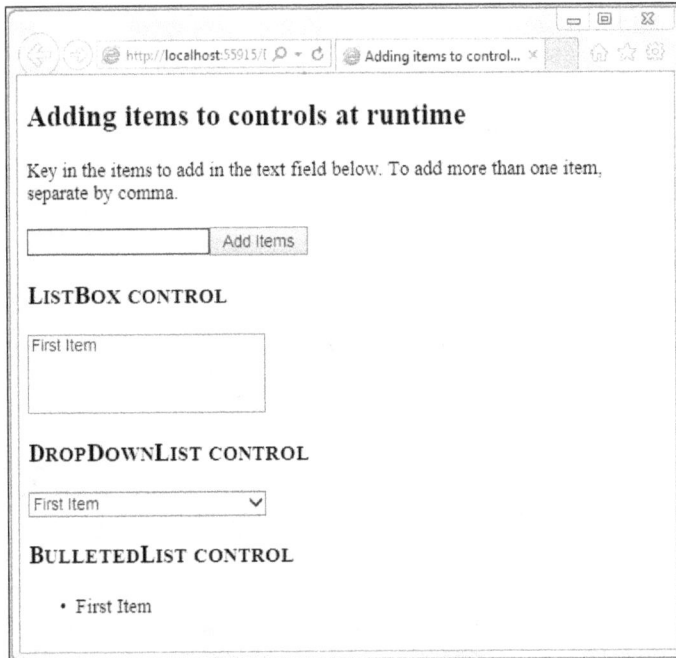

Let's say the user needs to add more than one item to the controls. This can be done by keying in the items separated by comma, as shown in the following screenshot:

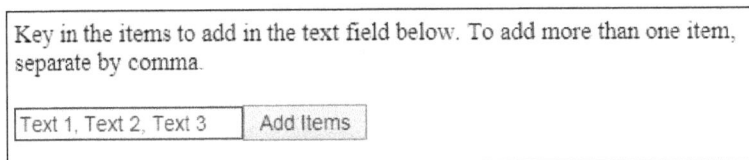

2. When you click on the **Add Items** button, the new items are reflected in the controls, as shown in the following screenshot:

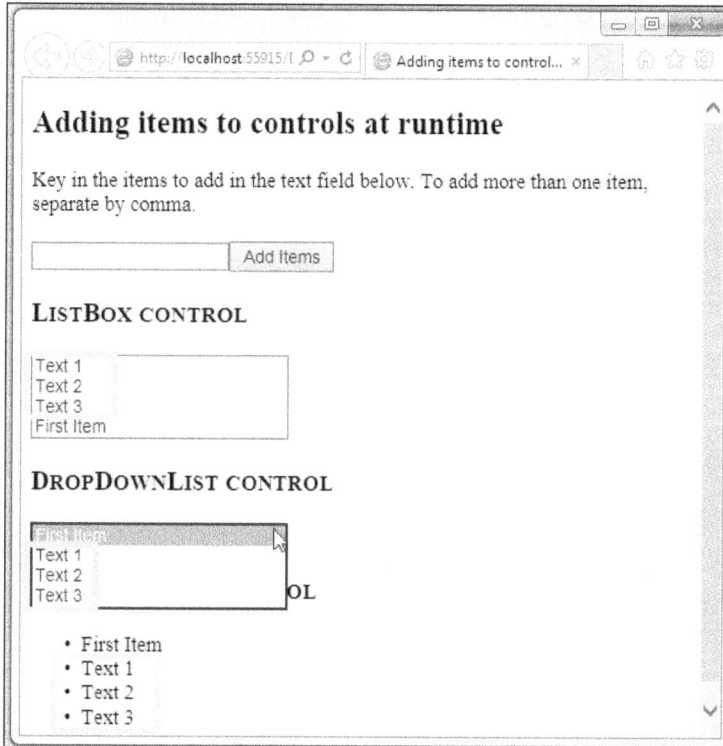

3. Let's get started by creating a new **ASP.NET Web Application** project in Visual Studio using the **Empty** template and name it Recipe5 (or any other suitable name).

4. Create a Scripts folder in the project and add the jQuery library to this folder.

5. Create a new web form and include the jQuery library in the form.

6. Drag and drop the required controls on the form to create the following markup on the page:

```
<div>
   <asp:Label ID="lblDescription" runat="server" Text="Key
in the items to add in the text field below. To add more
than one item, separate by comma."></asp:Label>
   <br /><br />
   <asp:TextBox ID="txtAddItem"
runat="server"></asp:TextBox>
```

```
<asp:Button ID="btnAdd" runat="server" Text="Add Items"
  />
<br />
<p class="sectionHeader">ListBox control</p>
<asp:ListBox ID="lstBox" runat="server" Width="200px">
  <asp:ListItem Text="First Item" Value="First
Item"></asp:ListItem>
</asp:ListBox>
<br />
<p class="sectionHeader">DropDownList control</p>
<asp:DropDownList ID="ddlList" runat="server"
Width="200px">
  <asp:ListItem Text="First Item" Value="First
Item"></asp:ListItem>
</asp:DropDownList>
<br />
<p class="sectionHeader">BulletedList control</p>
<asp:BulletedList ID="lstList" runat="server">
  <asp:ListItem Text="First Item" Value="First
Item"></asp:ListItem>
</asp:BulletedList>
</div>
```

7. Add some styling to the section headers:

```
.sectionHeader{
  font-size:20px;
  font-variant:small-caps;
  font-weight:700;
}
```

How to do it...

Add the following jQuery code to a `<script>` block on the form:

```
<script type="text/javascript">
$(document).ready(function() {
  $("#<%=txtAddItem.ClientID%>").focus();
  $("#<%=btnAdd.ClientID%>").click(function(evt) {
    evt.preventDefault();
    var addItemText = $("#<%=txtAddItem.ClientID%>").val().trim();
    if (addItemText != "") {
      var arrString = addItemText.split(",");
      $("#<%=lstBox.ClientID%>").prepend(
        $.map(arrString, function(v) {
```

```
        return $("<option value=" + v.trim() + ">" + v.trim() +
"</option>");
        }));
    $("#<%=ddlList.ClientID%>").append(
        $.map(arrString, function(v) {
            return $("<option>").val(v.trim()).text(v.trim());
        }));
    $("#<%=lstList.ClientID%>").append(
        $.map(arrString, function(v) {
            return $("<li>" + v.trim() + "</li>");
        }));
    }
    $("#<%=txtAddItem.ClientID%>").val("").focus();
  });
});
</script>
```

How it works...

Following are the steps to add items to controls at runtime:

1. On loading the page in the browser, the cursor is focused in the text field by using the `.focus()` function:

   ```
   $("#<%=txtAddItem.ClientID%>").focus();
   ```

2. An event handler is attached to the `click` event of the **Add Items** button:

   ```
   $("#<%=btnAdd.ClientID%>").click(function (evt) {…});
   ```

3. If you click on the preceding button, the first task is to prevent posting of the page to the server:

   ```
   evt.preventDefault();
   ```

4. Next, retrieve the content of the text field and `trim` it to remove whitespaces:

   ```
   var addItemText =
   $("#<%=txtAddItem.ClientID%>").val().trim();
   ```

5. Check whether the content of the preceding field is empty:

   ```
   if (addItemText != "")
   ```

   If it is not empty, build an array from the entered text by splitting the string using commas as delimiters:

   ```
   var arrString = addItemText.split(",");
   ```

> If there are no commas in the string, the array will consist of a single element.

6. Now, use the `.map()` function to transform this array into a list of `<option>` elements such that both the text and value of the `<option>` element are equal to the array element at that index.

7. Prepend this list of `option` elements to the `ListBox` control, that is, the new elements will appear as the starting elements inside the `ListBox` control:

```
$("#<%=lstBox.ClientID%>").prepend($.map(arrString,
function (v) {
   return $("<option value=" + v.trim() + ">" + v.trim() +
"</option>");
}));
```

8. The same list of `option` elements can also be appended to the `DropDownList` control. When the `.append()` function is used, the new items will appear at the end of the list:

```
$("#<%=ddlList.ClientID%>").append($.map(arrString,
function (v) {
   return $("<option>").val(v.trim()).text(v.trim());
}));
```

9. To append items to the `BulletedList` control, we use the `.map()` function to build a list of `<li>` elements since, at runtime, a `BulletedList` control renders each `ListItem` control as an `<li>` element. So, the items are added as follows:

```
$("#<%=lstList.ClientID%>").append($.map(arrString,
function(v){
   return $("<li>" + v.trim() + "</li>");
}));
```

10. Lastly, after adding the elements to the preceding controls, clear the text field and focus the cursor on the field so that it is ready to take in the next set of inputs:

```
$("#<%=txtAddItem.ClientID%>").val("").focus();
```

See also

The *Adding / removing DOM elements* recipe

5
Visual Effects in ASP.NET Sites

This chapter explores the various visual effects and animations that can be applied to ASP.NET controls using jQuery. The following recipes will be covered in this chapter:

- Animating the Menu control
- Animating a Label control to create a digital clock
- Animating the alt text of the AdRotator control
- Animating images in the TreeView control
- Creating scrolling text in a Panel control
- Creating a vertical accordion menu using Panel controls
- Showing/hiding the GridView control with the explode effect

Introduction

jQuery has simplified the adding of attractive visual effects on web pages. The library provides many supporting methods used to show, hide, fade, slide, toggle, and other custom animations. Let's briefly run through these methods:

- Showing and hiding elements:

jQuery method	Description
.show()	This displays the matched elements
.hide()	This hides the matched elements
.toggle()	This displays or hides the matched elements

▶ Fading elements:

jQuery method	Description
.fadeIn()	This animates the opacity of the matched elements by increasing them gradually until they reaches a value of 1, that is, they become opaque.
.fadeOut()	This animates the opacity of the matched elements by decreasing them gradually until they reaches a value of 0, that is, they become transparent.
.fadeTo()	This animates the opacity of the matched elements to the specified value.
.fadeToggle()	This animates the opacity of the matched elements to hide or display them.

▶ Sliding elements:

jQuery method	Description
.slideUp()	This hides elements with an upward slide motion.
.slideDown()	This displays elements with a download slide motion.
.slideToggle()	This hides or displays the matched elements with a sliding motion.

▶ Custom effects:

jQuery method	Description
.animate()	This performs a custom animation on the specified CSS properties. The properties that can be animated are mostly numeric CSS properties, such as the font size, width, height, opacity, top, left, right, and so on.

All the preceding supporting methods allow you to specify the duration of the animation in milliseconds. The default duration for all animations is 400 ms. jQuery also provides keywords, such as slow (600 ms) and fast (200 ms) to specify the duration. A larger value for the duration indicates a slower animation as compared to a smaller value.

▸ Stopping animations:

jQuery method	Description
.stop()	This stops all running animations
.finish()	This stops the running animations, removes queued animations, and completes the animations on the matched elements

Animating the Menu control

The ASP.NET Menu control enables quick building of menus on websites. This recipe demonstrates how to add text animations, such as a blink effect and change of font color of a menu item on mouseover. The constructs used in this example are summarized in the following table:

Construct	Type	Description
$(".class")	jQuery selector	This matches all elements with the specified CSS class.
$("html_tag")	jQuery selector	This selects all elements with the specified HTML tag.
$(this)	jQuery object	This refers to the current jQuery object.
.css()	jQuery method	This gets the style property for the first matched element or sets the style property for every matched element.
.fadeIn()	jQuery method	This animates the opacity of the matched element by increasing it gradually until it reaches a value of 1, that is, it becomes opaque.
.fadeOut()	jQuery method	This animates the opacity of the matched element by decreasing it gradually until it reaches a value of 0, that is, it becomes transparent.
mouseout	jQuery event	This is fired when the mouse pointer leaves a control. It corresponds to the JavaScript mouseout event.
mouseover	jQuery event	This is fired when the mouse pointer enters a control. It corresponds to the JavaScript mouseover event.
.on()	jQuery event binder	This attaches an event handler for one or more events to the matched elements.

Getting ready

Follow these steps to create a Menu to which animation effects will be applied:

1. Let's create a web page with a horizontal menu, as shown in the following screenshot. By moving the mouse pointer on any main menu item, the font color changes and the text blinks once.

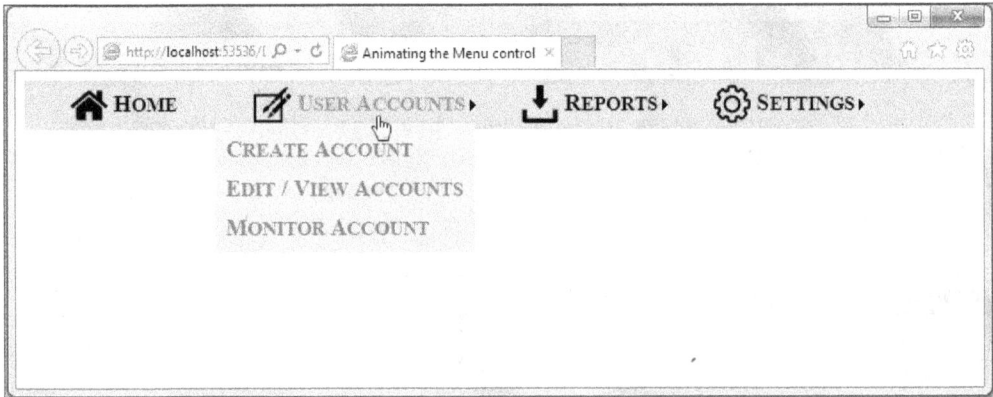

    Similarly, by moving the mouse pointer on any submenu item, the font color changes and the text blinks:

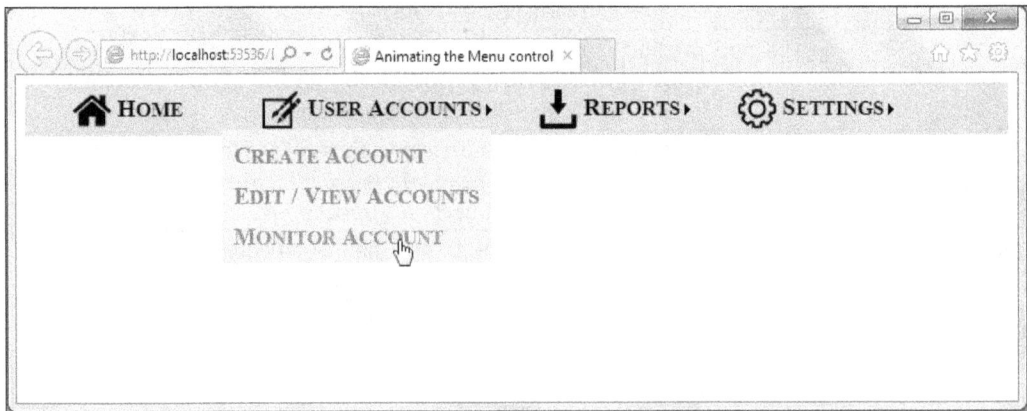

    The original font color is restored by moving the mouse pointer out of the main menu or submenu item.

2. To build this web page, create a new **ASP.NET Web Application** project in Visual Studio using the **Empty** template and name it `Recipe1` (or any other suitable name).

3. Add the jQuery library to the `Scripts` folder.

4. Create a new web form and include the jQuery library in the form.

5. Go to **Toolbox** | **Navigation**, and drag and drop a `Menu` control on the form.

6. In the **Properties** window of the `Menu` control, set the **Layout** | **Orientation** property to **Horizontal**, as shown here:

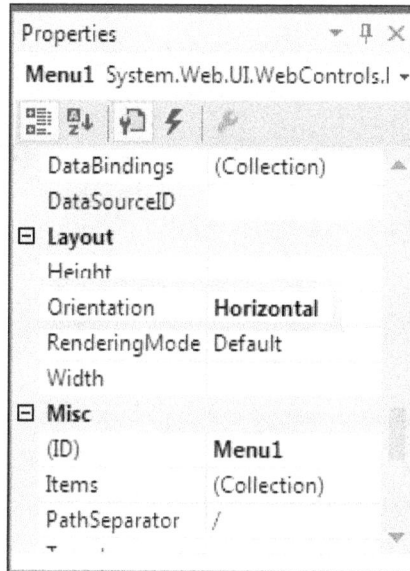

Properties	▾ ⇲ ×
Menu1 System.Web.UI.WebControls.l ▾	

▤▤ ᵶ↓ ⟆ ⚡ ⚲

DataBindings	(Collection) ▲
DataSourceID	
⊟ **Layout**	
Heiaht	
Orientation	**Horizontal**
RenderingMode	Default
Width	
⊟ **Misc**	
(ID)	**Menu1**
Items	(Collection)
PathSeparator	/

7. In the **Design** mode, move the mouse pointer on the `Menu` control until a small arrow icon appears on the top-right corner of the control. Click on the arrow to open the **Menu Tasks** window, as shown here:

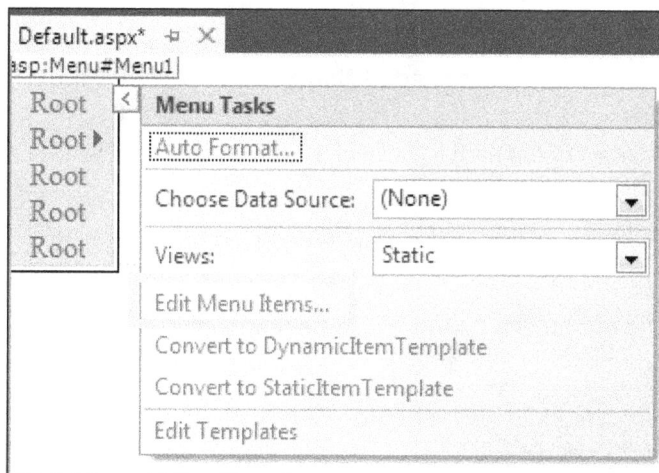

Default.aspx* ⇲ ✕
asp:Menu#Menu1|

Root   <

Root ▸

Root

Root

Root

Menu Tasks

Auto Format...

Choose Data Source: (None) ▾

Views: Static ▾

Edit Menu Items...

Convert to DynamicItemTemplate

Convert to StaticItemTemplate

Edit Templates

8. Click on the **Edit Menu Items** link in the preceding **Menu Tasks** window to open the **Menu Item Editor** window. Create the root and child menu items, as shown in the following screenshot. You will need to update the **ImageUrl**, **Text**, and **Value** properties of the main menu (root) items, for example, **Home**, **User Accounts**, **Reports**, and **Settings**. For the submenu items, you will need to update just the **Text** and **Value** properties:

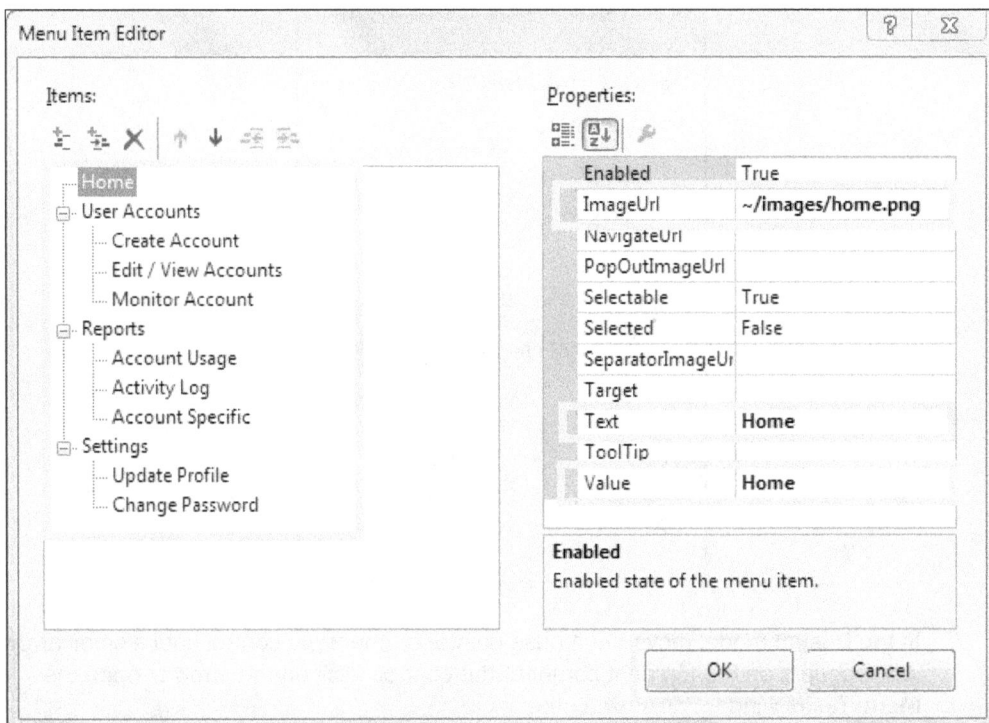

9. Add an `images` folder to the project by right-clicking on the project in the **Solution Explorer** tab and navigating to **Add | New Folder**. Include the icons for the main menu items.

10. The final markup of the form is as follows:

```
<div id="container">
  <asp:Menu ID="Menu1" runat="server"
    Orientation="Horizontal">
    <Items>
      <asp:MenuItem Text="Home" Value="Home"
        ImageUrl="~/images/home.png"></asp:MenuItem>
      <asp:MenuItem Text="User Accounts" Value="User
        Accounts" ImageUrl="~/images/accounts.png">
        <asp:MenuItem Text="Create Account" Value="Create
          Account"></asp:MenuItem>
```

```
            <asp:MenuItem Text="Edit / View Accounts" Value="Edit
                / View Accounts"></asp:MenuItem>
            <asp:MenuItem Text="Monitor Account" Value="Monitor
                Account"></asp:MenuItem>
        </asp:MenuItem>
        <asp:MenuItem Text="Reports" Value="Reports"
            ImageUrl="~/images/reports.png">
            <asp:MenuItem Text="Account Usage" Value="Account
                Usage"></asp:MenuItem>
            <asp:MenuItem Text="Activity Log" Value="Activity
                Log"></asp:MenuItem>
            <asp:MenuItem Text="Account Specific"
                Value="Account Specific"></asp:MenuItem>
        </asp:MenuItem>
        <asp:MenuItem Text="Settings" Value="Settings"
            ImageUrl="~/images/settings.png">
            <asp:MenuItem Text="Update Profile" Value="Update
                Profile"></asp:MenuItem>
            <asp:MenuItem Text="Change Password" Value="Change
                Password"></asp:MenuItem>
        </asp:MenuItem>
    </Items>
    <StaticMenuItemStyle HorizontalPadding="35px" />
  </asp:Menu>
</div>
```

11. Note that in the preceding markup, the `Menu` control is included in a `div` container. Apply the following style to this `div` container:

```
#container {
  background-color:lightgray;
  width:100%;
}
```

This will give a background color to the entire `Menu` control and keep its width at 100% of the page width.

12. At runtime, the `Menu` control renders the `level1` CSS class for the main menu items and `level2` for the submenu items. Hence, apply the following styles to these items:

```
#Menu1 .level1{
  padding:5px;
  font-variant:small-caps;
  color:black;
  font-size:20px;
  font-weight:700;
  font-family:'Times New Roman', Times, serif;
}
```

```
#Menu1 .level2{
  background-color:aquamarine;
  color:green;
  padding:5px;
}
```

13. To create spacing between the image and the text in the main menu items, add the following style to the page:

```
#Menu1 img{
  padding-right:5px;
}
```

How to do it...

Add the following jQuery code to a `script` block on the page:

```
<script type="text/javascript">
  $(document).ready(function() {
    $(".level1 a, .level2 a").on("mouseover", function() {
      $(this).css("color", "red");
      $(this).fadeOut("fast").fadeIn("fast");
    });
    $(".level1 a").on("mouseout", function() {
      $(this).css("color", "black");
    });
    $(".level2 a").on("mouseout", function() {
      $(this).css("color", "green");
    });
  });
</script>
```

How it works...

The Menu animation works in the following manner:

1. Save the page using *Ctrl + S* and run it using *F5*. This will launch the menu on the web page.

2. When you move the mouse over any main menu or submenu item, the following corresponding event handler will be executed:

```
$(".level1 a, .level2 a").on("mouseover", function () {…});
```

The preceding selector attaches the event handler of the `mouseover` event on both the `level1` and `level2` hyperlinks.

3. In the preceding event handler, firstly, the font color is changed to red by updating the css property as follows:

```
$(this).css("color", "red");
```

Secondly, a blink effect is added to the text by fading it out completely so that it is hidden, and then, the control is gradually made visible by fading in as follows:

```
$(this).fadeOut("fast").fadeIn("fast");
```

Thus, the fading out and fading in effects are chained to give a blink effect to the text. Both the fadeOut() and fadeIn() methods are called with a fast duration, 200 ms.

4. When the mouse pointer is moved out of a main menu or submenu item, the corresponding mouseout event handler is executed. This event handler will restore the font color to the original value as follows:

```
$(".level1 a").on("mouseout", function () {
    $(this).css("color", "black");
});
$(".level2 a").on("mouseout", function () {
    $(this).css("color", "green");
});
```

See also

The *Creating a vertical accordion menu using Panel controls* recipe

Animating a Label control to create a digital clock

This recipe uses custom animation effects to create a blinking digital clock to display the current time in the hh:mm:ss format. The constructs used in this example are summarized in the following table:

Construct	Type	Description
$("#identifier")	jQuery selector	This selects an element using its ID.
.animate()	jQuery method	This performs a custom animation on the specified CSS properties.
Date	JavaScript object	This is an object that stores date/time information: year, month, day, hours, minutes, and seconds.

Construct	Type	Description
`Date.getHours()`	JavaScript function	This returns the number of hours from 0 to 23.
`Date.getMinutes()`	JavaScript function	This returns the number of minutes from 0 to 59.
`Date.getSeconds()`	JavaScript function	This returns the number of seconds from 0 to 59.
`opacity`	CSS property	This is the degree of transparency of the element.
`setInterval(function, delay)`	JavaScript function	This executes a function repeatedly after the specified delay in milliseconds.
`.slice()`	JavaScript function	This extracts part of a string. A negative number passed as a parameter to the function extracts the required number of characters from the end of the string.
`.text()`	jQuery method	This returns the combined text content of each of the matched elements or sets the text content of every matched element.

Getting ready

Follow these steps to create a digital clock with jQuery animation:

1. Let's build the digital clock by animating a `Label` control. The control will display the current time in the hh:mm:ss format at any point of time. Once every second, the `Label` control will be cleared and the new time will be displayed, giving the clock a blink effect.

2. To get started, add a new **ASP.NET Web Application** project in Visual Studio using the **Empty** template and name it `Recipe2` (or any other suitable name).

3. Add a `Scripts` folder to the project and add the jQuery library files to the folder.

4. Add a new web form to the project. Include the jQuery library in the Web form.

5. Add a `Label` control inside a `Panel` control, as shown in the following markup:

```
<asp:Panel ID="pnlContainer" runat="server"
  CssClass="container">
  <asp:Label ID="lblTime" runat="server" ></asp:Label>
</asp:Panel>
```

6. Add the following CSS style to the containing `Panel` control:

```
.container{
  background-color:lightgray;
  font-size:24px;
  font-family:'Times New Roman', Times, serif;
  color:black;
  border:solid;
  border-color:darkblue;
  border-width:1px;
  width:150px;
  text-align:center;
}
```

How to do it...

Include the following jQuery code in a `script` block on the page:

```
<script type="text/javascript">
  $(document).ready(function() {
    setInterval(animateLabel, 1000);
    function animateLabel() {
      var time = getCurrentTime();
      $("#<%=lblTime.ClientID%>").text(time);
      $("#<%=lblTime.ClientID%>").animate({
        opacity: 0
      }, 950).animate({
        opacity: 1
      }, 50);
    }
    function getCurrentTime() {
      var dt = new Date();
      var dtHour = dt.getHours(); // returns a number from 0 to 23
      var dtMinutes = ("0" + dt.getMinutes()).slice(-2);
      var dtSeconds = ("0" + dt.getSeconds()).slice(-2);
      var strAmPm = "";
```

```
        if (dtHour >= 12)
          strAmPm = "PM";
        else
          strAmPm = "AM";
        if (dtHour > 12)
          dtHour -= 12;
        var time = dtHour + ":" + dtMinutes + ":" + dtSeconds + " "
          + strAmPm;
        return time;
      }
    });
  </script>
```

How it works...

The digital clock works as follows:

1. Save and run the page. When the document is ready, the setInterval JavaScript function calls the animateLabel method every 1000 ms, that is, once every second:

   ```
   setInterval(animateLabel, 1000);
   ```

2. The animateLabel method gets the current time using the getCurrentTime method, which we shall see shortly:

   ```
   var time = getCurrentTime();
   ```

3. Next, the text of the Label control is set to the time retrieved in the preceding step:

   ```
   $("#<%=lblTime.ClientID%>").text(time);
   ```

4. The opacity of the Label control is animated to reach 0 in 950 ms so that Label is completely invisible at the end of the animation. The next animation is chained at the end of this animation, and the opacity of the Label control is increased to 1 in 50 ms so that the Label control is completely opaque after a blink effect:

   ```
   $("#<%=lblTime.ClientID%>").animate({ opacity: 0 },
   950).animate({ opacity: 1 }, 50);
   ```

   Thus, the 1000 ms interval is broken into two parts, 950 ms and 50 ms.

> The opacity of an element is the degree of transparency of that element. Opacity can take any value from 0 to 1.
>
> When the opacity is 1, the element is opaque.
>
> When the opacity is 0, the element is transparent, that is, invisible.
>
> When the opacity is > 0 and < 1, it is translucent, that is, its background is visible.

5. Next, let's take a look at the `getCurrentTime` method that returns the current time in the hh:mm:ss format. This method first creates a `Date` object:

```
var dt = new Date();
```

Next, get the hours from the date object as an integer value from 0 to 23:

```
var dtHour = dt.getHours();
```

Get the minutes from the date object. The minutes can be a single digit so pad it with a zero in front and extract the last two characters using `slice` as follows:

```
var dtMinutes = ("0" + dt.getMinutes()).slice(-2);
```

Get the seconds from the date object. The seconds can also be a single digit so pad it with a zero in front and extract the last two characters using `slice` as follows:

```
var dtSeconds = ("0" + dt.getSeconds()).slice(-2);
```

6. Let a `strAmPm` variable store AM or PM as required. Initialize this variable to an empty string:

```
var strAmPm = "";
```

If the number of hours is more than or equal to `12`, set `strAMPM` to `PM`, else set it to `AM`:

```
if (dtHour >= 12)
    strAmPm = "PM";
else
    strAmPm = "AM";
```

7. Also, display the hours from 0 to 12 instead of 0 to 23 as follows:

```
if (dtHour > 12)
    dtHour -= 12;
```

Now, build a string formatted as hours:minutes:seconds with the values computed earlier. Return the `time` string

```
var time = dtHour + ":" + dtMinutes + ":" + dtSeconds + " "
    + strAmPm;
return time;
```

See also

The *Creating scrolling text in a Panel control* recipe

Animating the alt text of the AdRotator control

The `AdRotator` control is used to display advertisement banners on web pages. The control loads a new banner each time the page is refreshed. In this demonstration, let's enhance the `AdRotator` control to display the alt text of an ad banner with the sliding animation. The constructs used in this example are as follows:

Construct	Type	Description
`$("#identifier")`	jQuery selector	This selects an element using its ID
`$("html_tag")`	jQuery selector	This selects all elements with the specified HTML tag
`.addClass()`	jQuery method	This adds the specified CSS class to each matched element
`.animate()`	jQuery method	This performs a custom animation on the specified CSS properties
`.css()`	jQuery method	This gets the CSS property of the first matched element or sets one or more CSS properties for every matched element
`event.pageX`	jQuery event property	This returns the mouse position relative to the left edge of the document
`event.pageY`	jQuery event property	This returns the mouse position relative to the top edge of the document
`.hide()`	jQuery method	This hides the matched elements
`.hover()`	jQuery event binder	This binds event handlers for the `mouseover` and `mouseout` events
`left`	CSS property	This is the position of the left edge of the element
`opacity`	CSS property	This is the degree of transparency of the element
`.prop(propertyName)` or `.prop(propertyName, value)`	jQuery method	This returns the value of the specified property for the first matched element or sets the value of the specified property for all matched elements
`.slideDown()`	jQuery method	This displays elements with a download slide motion
`.text()`	jQuery method	This returns the combined text content of each of the matched elements or sets the text content of every matched element
`top`	CSS property	This is the position of the top edge of the element

Getting ready

Follow these steps for building a web page with an AdRotator:

1. We will create a web page with an `AdRotator` control that displays ad banners from an advertisement XML file. The alt text for each banner is also saved in the XML file. At runtime, when the mouse pointer is moved on the banner, its opacity reduces, and the alt text is displayed in a sliding panel, as shown in the following screenshot:

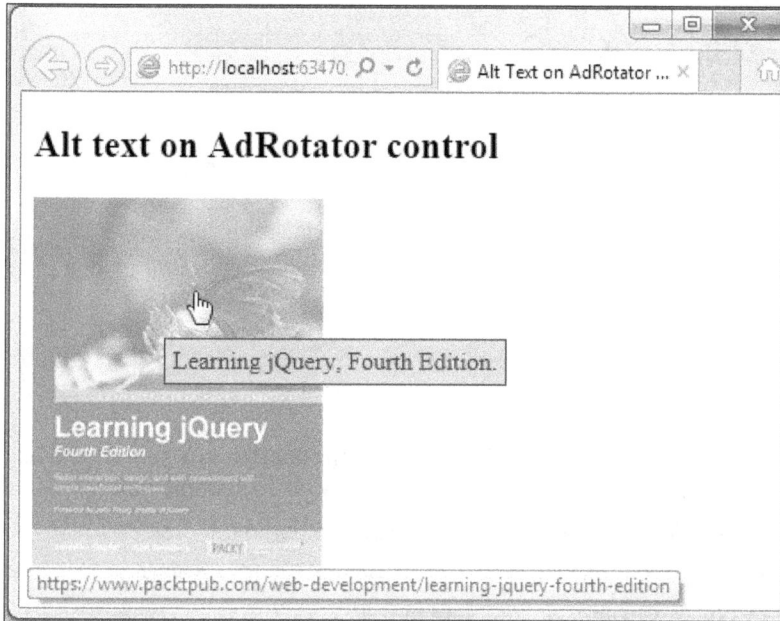

When the page is refreshed, the control loads another ad banner from the XML file. The same effect can be seen on the updated banner, as shown here:

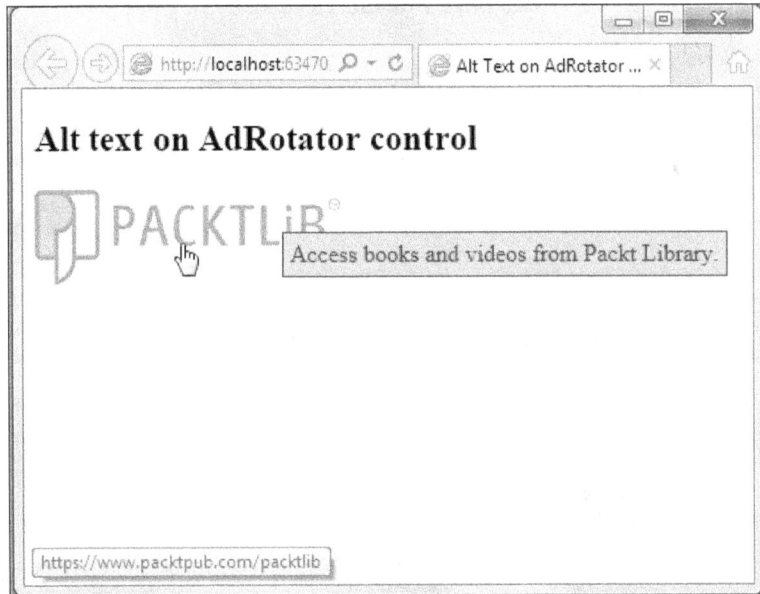

2. To get started, create a new **ASP.NET Web Application** in Visual Studio using the **Empty** template and name it `Recipe3` (or any other suitable name).

3. Include the jQuery library files in a `Scripts` folder in the project.

4. Add a new web form to the project, and include the jQuery library in the form.

5. Go to **Toolbox | Standard**, and drag and drop an `AdRotator` control on the form. Also, add a `Panel` control to the form below the `AdRotator` control. This panel will be used to display the alt text on the ad banner.

6. In the **Solution Explorer** tab, right-click on the project, and go to **Add | Add ASP.NET Folder** and select `App_Data` folder. This will add the `App_Data` folder to the project if it does not already exist.

7. Right-click on the `App_Data` folder, and go to **Add | XML File**. In the dialog box, key in `AdsFile.xml`. This XML file will be used to store the advertisement data that is to be displayed in the `AdRotator` control.

8. Add the following content to the XML file. Note that the root node is `Advertisements` and the details of each ad are saved in the `Ad` node:

```
<Advertisements>
  <Ad>
    <ImageUrl>~/images/packtlib-logo-dark.png</ImageUrl>
    <height>56</height>
```

```
      <width>115</width>
      <NavigateUrl>https://www.packtpub.com/packtlib</NavigateUrl>
      <AlternateText>Access books and videos from Packt
        Library.</AlternateText>
      <Impressions>80</Impressions>
      <Keyword>Packt</Keyword>
    </Ad>
    <Ad>
      <ImageUrl>~/images/learning_jquery.jpg</ImageUrl>
      <height>92</height>
      <width>115</width>
      <NavigateUrl>https://www.packtpub.com/web-
        development/learning-jquery-fourth-
        edition</NavigateUrl>
      <AlternateText>Learning jQuery, Fourth
Edition.</AlternateText>
      <Impressions>80</Impressions>
      <Keyword>Packt</Keyword>
    </Ad>
</Advertisements>
```

Each child node within an `Ad` node offers a unique functionality, which is summarized as follows:

Node	Description
ImageUrl	This is the URL of the image to be displayed.
Height	This is the height of the image in pixels.
Width	This is the width of the image in pixels.
NavigateUrl	This is the URL of the page to be loaded when you click on the ad banner.
AlternateText	This is the text that is displayed when the image is not available.
Impressions	This is the likelihood of the image being displayed that is expressed as a number.
Keyword	This is the category of the image. This field can be used to filter specific ads.

9. Set the `AdvertisementFile` property of the `AdRotator` control to the preceding file. So, the markup of the form is as follows:

```
<asp:AdRotator ID="AdRotator1"
  AdvertisementFile="~/App_Data/AdsFile.xml" runat="server"
/>
<asp:Panel ID="pnlDescription" runat="server"></asp:Panel>
```

10. Add the following CSS class to the page in the `head` element. This style will be applied to the `Panel` control when we display the alt text of the banner:

```css
<style type="text/css">
  .altTextStyle {
    background-color:lightblue;
    border-color:blue;
    border-style:solid;
    border-width:1px;
    position:absolute;
    color:indigo;
    padding:5px;
  }
</style>
```

11. Add a new `images` folder to the project, and add the required ad banners to this folder.

How to do it...

Include the following jQuery code in a `script` block on the page:

```javascript
<script type="text/javascript">
  $(document).ready(onReady);
  function onReady() {
    $("#<%=pnlDescription.ClientID%>").addClass("altTextStyle").hide()
;
    $("#<%=AdRotator1.ClientID%>").hover(
      function(evt) {
        var altText = $("#<%=AdRotator1.ClientID%>
          img").prop("alt");
        $("#<%=pnlDescription.ClientID%>").text(altText).css("left",
          evt.pageX).css("top", evt.pageY);
        $("#<%=pnlDescription.ClientID%>").slideDown("slow");
        $("#<%=AdRotator1.ClientID%> img").animate({
          opacity: 0.5
        }, "slow");
      },
      function() {
        $("#<%=pnlDescription.ClientID%>").hide();
        $("#<%=AdRotator1.ClientID%> img").animate({
          opacity: 1
        }, "slow");
      });
  }
</script>
```

How it works...

The AdRotator works as follows:

1. When the page is launched in the browser, the `onReady` function is called when the document is ready:

    ```
    $(document).ready(onReady);
    ```

2. In the `onReady` function, the `altTextStyle` CSS class is added to the `Panel` control and the control is then hidden:

    ```
    $("#<%=pnlDescription.ClientID%>").addClass("altTextStyle")
    .hide();
    ```

3. The `hover` event binder is used to attach event handlers for the `mouseover` and `mouseout` events as follows:

    ```
    $("#<%=AdRotator1.ClientID%>").hover(function(){...},
    function(){...});
    ```

    Here, the first function is the handler for the `mouseover` event while the second is the handler for the `mouseout` event.

4. At runtime, the `AdRotator` control is rendered as an `<img>` element enclosed within an `<a>` element, as shown in the following figure. To view the HTML source of the page, right-click on the browser window, and select **View Source**:

    ```
    <a id="AdRotator1" href="https://www.packtpub.com/web-
    development/aspnet-jquery-cookbook" target="_top"><img
    src="/images/aspnet_jquery.jpg" alt="ASP.NET jQuery Cookbook, First Edition" />
    </a>
    ```

    Hence, the event handler for `mouseover` can retrieve the alt text property of the banner from the rendered image as follows:

    ```
    var altText = $("#<%=AdRotator1.ClientID%>
      img").prop("alt");
    ```

5. The text of the `Panel` control is set to the preceding text. The location of the mouse is retrieved using the `event.pageX` and `event.pageY` properties. The left and top locations of the `Panel` control can now be set to these coordinates so that the `Panel` hovers over the mouse pointer:

    ```
    $("#<%=pnlDescription.ClientID%>").text(altText).css("left"
      , evt.pageX).css("top", evt.pageY);
    ```

Now that the text and position of the `Panel` control are initialized, it is animated using the `slideDown` function with the `slow` duration:

```
$("#<%=pnlDescription.ClientID%>").slideDown("slow");
```

The ad banner is also animated to reduce its opacity to 50% at a `slow` speed:

```
$("#<%=AdRotator1.ClientID%> img").animate({ opacity: 0.5
    }, "slow");
```

6. The `mouseout` event handler accomplishes two tasks. Firstly, the alt text `Panel` is hidden from the view as follows:

```
$("#<%=pnlDescription.ClientID%>").hide();
```

Secondly, the banner is restored to its complete visibility by increasing the opacity to 1 at a slow speed:

```
$("#<%=AdRotator1.ClientID%> img").animate({ opacity: 1 },
    "slow");
```

There's more...

The `AdRotator` control displays a new ad banner only on refreshing the page. To refresh the `AdRotator` control automatically after regular intervals, we can place the control in an `UpdatePanel` control and use AJAX to refresh it. This can be done as follows:

1. Drag and drop a `ScriptManager` control and an `UpdatePanel` control by navigating to **Toolbox | AJAX Extensions**.

2. To refresh the ad banner at regular intervals, we also need a `Timer` control. Hence, drag and drop a `Timer` control by navigating to **Toolbox | AJAX Extensions**.

3. In the **Properties** window, as shown in the following screenshot, set the **Interval** property of the timer to `5000` ms. This will cause the `Timer` control to tick every 5 seconds:

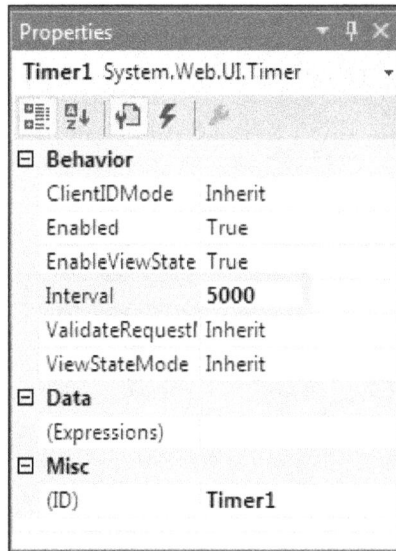

4. Now, open the **Properties** window of the UpdatePanel control, and expand the **Triggers** property, as shown here:

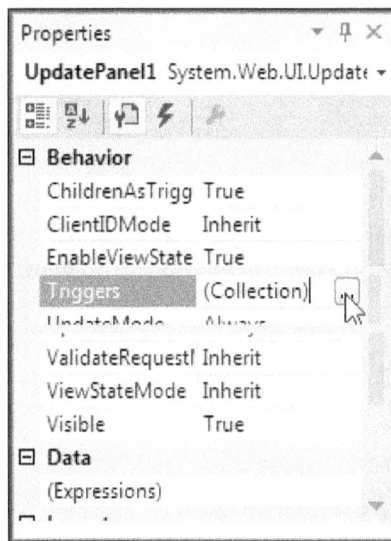

In the **UpdatePanelTrigger Collection Editor** window that is launched, click on the **Add** button to add an `AsyncPostBack` trigger, and set the **ControlID** property to `Timer1` and **EventName** to `Tick`, as shown in the following screenshot. Click on **OK** to close the window:

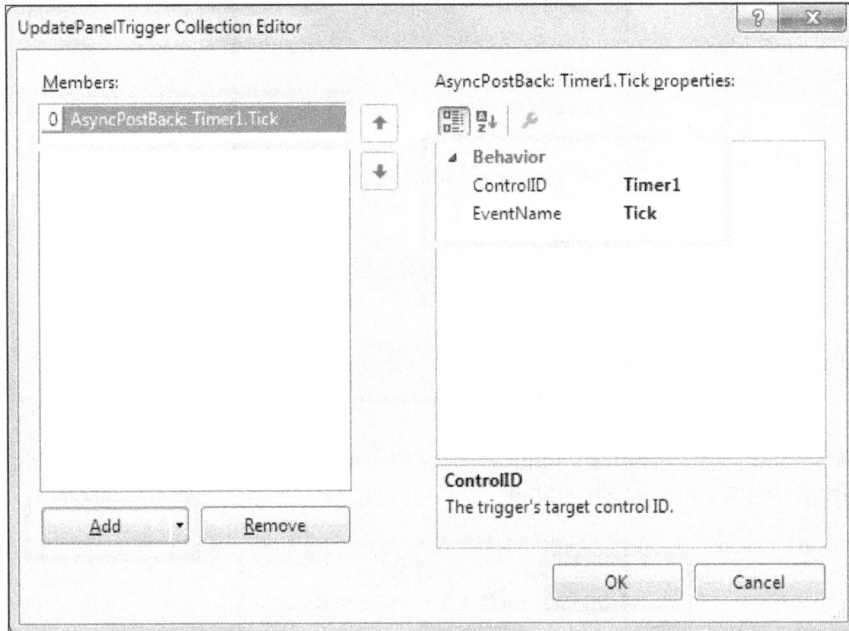

5. Place the `AdRotator` and `Panel` controls in the `ContentTemplate` control of the `UpdatePanel` control.

6. After every AJAX refresh of the `UpdatePanel` control, the client script code is rewritten, and the jQuery code that we wrote to animate the alt text is lost. Hence, we need to rewrite our jQuery code on the page using the `System.Application. add_load` method as follows:

```
<script type="text/javascript">
  Sys.Application.add_load(onReady);
</script>
```

The preceding script is also included in the `ContentTemplate` control of the `UpdatePanel` control.

7. Thus, the form markup will change to the following code:

```
<asp:ScriptManager ID="ScriptManager1"
  runat="server"></asp:ScriptManager>
<asp:Timer ID="Timer1" runat="server"
  Interval="5000"></asp:Timer>
```

```
<asp:UpdatePanel ID="UpdatePanel1" runat="server">
  <Triggers>
    <asp:AsyncPostBackTrigger ControlID="Timer1"
      EventName="Tick" />
  </Triggers>
  <ContentTemplate>
    <script type="text/javascript">
      Sys.Application.add_load(onReady);
    </script>
    <asp:AdRotator ID="AdRotator1" AdvertisementFile="~/App_Data/
AdsFile.xml" runat="server"
/>
    <asp:Panel ID="pnlDescription"
      runat="server"></asp:Panel>
  </ContentTemplate>
</asp:UpdatePanel>
```

See also

The *Animating images in the TreeView control* recipe

Animating images in the TreeView control

A `TreeView` control enables you to display data in a hierarchical format. Let's apply animation to enlarge and shrink images in the nodes of a `TreeView` control. We will also take a look at the mechanism of easing using the jQuery UI library. The constructs used in this example are as follows:

Construct	Type	Description
`$("#identifier")`	jQuery selector	This selects an element using its ID.
`$("html_tag")`	jQuery selector	This selects all elements with the specified HTML tag.
`$(this)`	jQuery object	This refers to the current jQuery object.
`.animate()`	jQuery method	This performs a custom animation on the specified CSS properties.
`[attr$="value"]`	jQuery selector	This selects an element with the specified attribute ending with the `value` string.
`.find()`	jQuery method	This finds all elements that match the filter.
`height`	CSS property	This is the height of the element.
`mouseout`	jQuery event	This is fired when the mouse pointer leaves a control. It corresponds to the JavaScript `mouseout` event.

Construct	Type	Description
`mouseover`	jQuery event	This is fired when the mouse pointer enters a control. It corresponds to the JavaScript `mouseover` event.
`.on()`	jQuery event binder	This attaches an event handler for one or more events to the matched elements.
`.stop()`	jQuery method	This stops all running animations.
`width`	CSS property	This is the width of the element.

Getting ready

Follow these steps to setup a TreeView control on a web page:

1. Let's create a web page to display the list of employees (with their profile photos) in various departments of a company in a tree structure, as shown in the following screenshot:

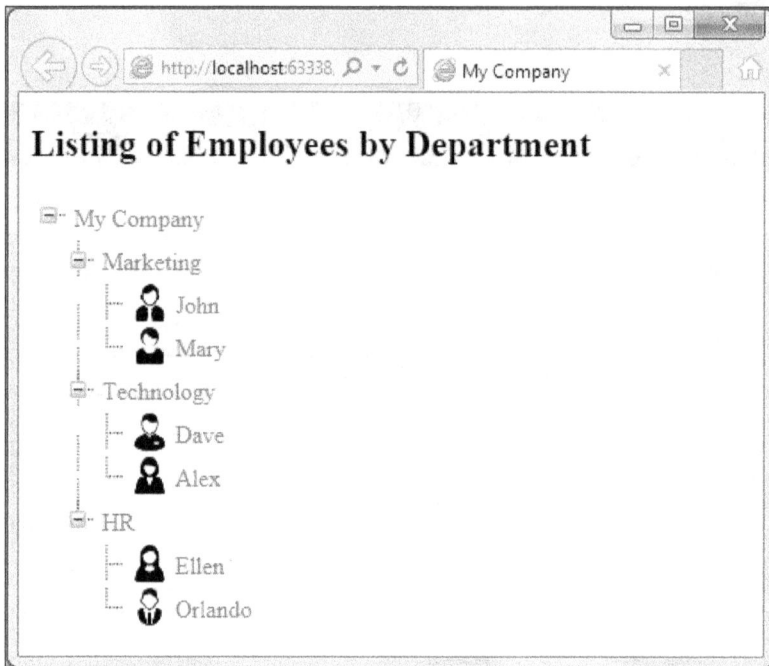

To zoom the profile photo of any particular employee, we just need to move the mouse pointer over the photo, as shown in the following screenshot:

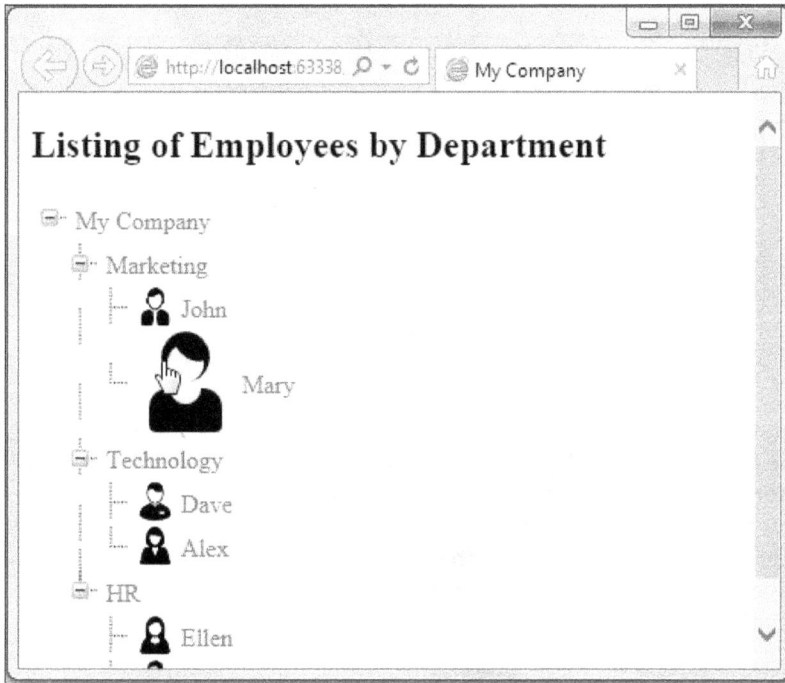

By moving the mouse pointer out of the photo, it shrinks back to the original thumbnail size.

2. Let's get started by creating an **ASP.NET Web Application** project in Visual Studio using the **Empty** template and name it `Recipe4` (or any other suitable name).

3. Add a `Scripts` folder to the project, and add the jQuery library files to this folder.

4. Add a new web form to the project, and include the jQuery library in the form.

5. Drag and drop a `TreeView` control on the form by navigating to **Toolbox | Navigation**.

6. In the **Design** mode, move the mouse pointer over the `TreeView` control until a small arrow icon appears in the top-right corner. Click on this arrow to open the **TreeView Tasks** menu, as shown in the following figure:

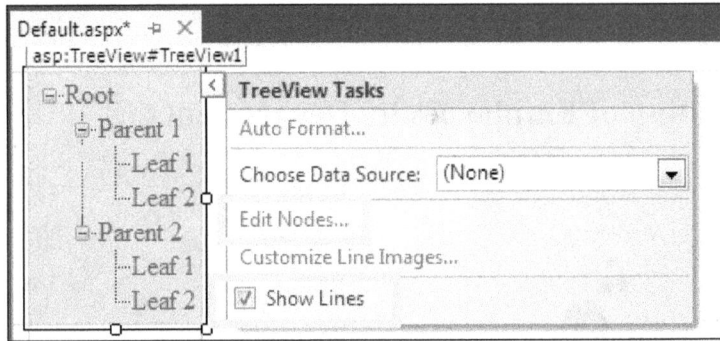

From the **TreeView Tasks** menu, select the **Show Lines** checkbox to display the node connections. Next, click on the **Edit Nodes** link to open the **TreeView Node Editor** dialog box. Add the parent and child nodes to the control, as shown in the following screenshot. For the nodes that display department, update the **Text** and **Value** properties. For the nodes that display employee, update the **Text**, **Value**, and **ImageUrl** properties. The profile photo of the employee will be displayed from the **ImageUrl** property. Click on the **OK** button after adding the nodes:

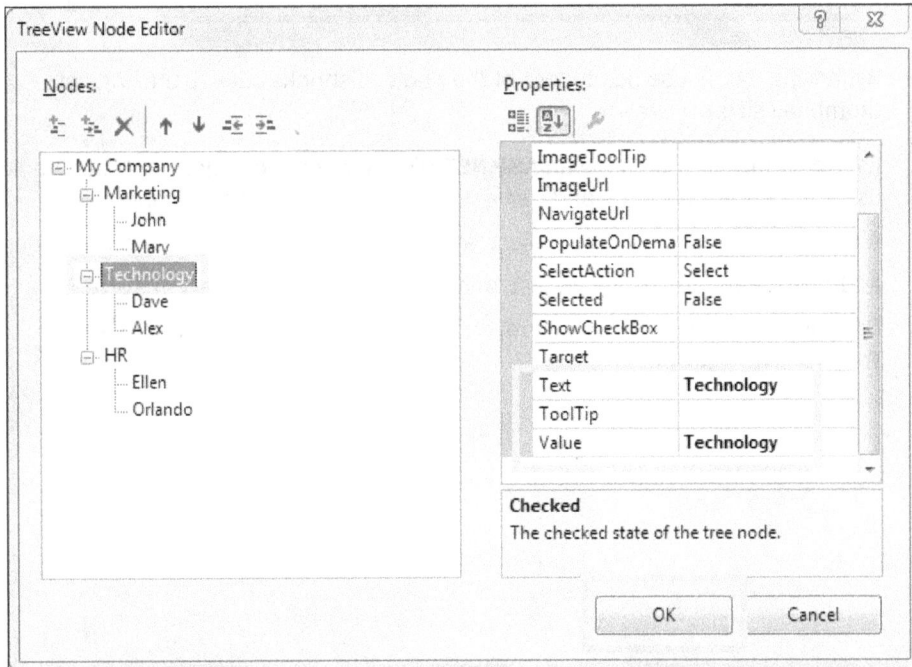

7. This will generate the following markup for the `TreeView` control:

```
<asp:TreeView ID="TreeView1" runat="server"
  ShowLines="True">
  <Nodes>
    <asp:TreeNode Text="My Company" Value="MyCompany">
      <asp:TreeNode Text="Marketing" Value="Marketing">
        <asp:TreeNode Text="John" Value="EMP001"
          ImageUrl="~/images/user1.png"></asp:TreeNode>
        <asp:TreeNode Text="Mary" Value="EMP004"
          ImageUrl="~/images/user4.png"></asp:TreeNode>
      </asp:TreeNode>
      <asp:TreeNode Text="Technology" Value="Technology">
        <asp:TreeNode Text="Dave" Value="EMP003"
          ImageUrl="~/images/user3.png"></asp:TreeNode>
        <asp:TreeNode Text="Alex" Value="EMP006"
          ImageUrl="~/images/user6.png"></asp:TreeNode>
      </asp:TreeNode>
      <asp:TreeNode Text="HR" Value="HR">
        <asp:TreeNode Text="Ellen" Value="EMP002"
          ImageUrl="~/images/user2.png"></asp:TreeNode>
        <asp:TreeNode Text="Orlando" Value="EMP005"
          ImageUrl="~/images/user5.png"></asp:TreeNode>
      </asp:TreeNode>
    </asp:TreeNode>
  </Nodes>
</asp:TreeView>
```

8. Add an `images` folder to the project, and add the required profile photos to the folder.

How to do it...

Include the following jQuery code in a `script` block on the page:

```
<script type="text/javascript">
$(document).ready(function () {
  $("#<%=TreeView1.ClientID%> a").on({
    mouseover: function () {
      $(this).find("img[src$='png']").animate({ width: "64px", height:
"64px" }, "slow", "linear");
    },
    mouseout: function () {
      $(this).find("img[src$='png']").stop().animate({ width:
        "24px", height: "24px" }, "slow", "linear");
    }
  });
});
</script>
```

How it works...

The animation on the TreeView control works as follows:

1. At runtime, the `TreeView` control generates the `<a>` elements for each node of the tree. To zoom the picture of an employee, we attach event handlers for the `mouseover` and `mouseout` events on the `<a>` elements inside the `TreeView` control as follows:

    ```
    $("#<%=TreeView1.ClientID%> a").on({mouseover: function
        (){...}, mouseout: function () {...} });
    ```

2. In the event handler for `mouseover`, firstly, find the image element that ends with the `.png` extension. This is to ensure that expand (**+**) and collapse (**-**) images are not animated. Secondly, a custom animation is applied to increase the `width` and `height` of the image to 64 px each. The duration of the animation is `slow` and the easing is `linear`:

    ```
    $(this).find("img[src$='png']").animate({ width: "64px",
        height: "64px" }, "slow", "linear");
    ```

3. In the event handler for `mouseout`, find the image element that ends with the `.png` extension. Then, stop any existing animations using the `stop` method, and apply a custom animation to reduce the `width` and `height` to the original dimensions, that is, 24 px each. The duration of the animation is `slow` and the easing is `linear`:

    ```
    $(this).find("img[src$='png']").stop().animate({ width:
        "24px", height: "24px" }, "slow", "linear");
    ```

> Instead of `linear`, swing can also be used. Just update `linear` to swing in the `mouseover` and `mouseout` event handlers.

There's more...

Easing is a mechanism of controlling the speed of animation at different points during the progress of an animation. jQuery provides two built-in easing methods: `linear` and `swing`. To add advanced effects, the jQuery UI library can be used. jQuery UI is a JavaScript library that provides many utilities to plug and play on websites. It provides widgets, such as Tabs, Accordion, Progressbar, Slider, and so on, and visual effects such as Bounce, Explode, Color Animation, and so on, among many other features.

In our previous example, let's use jQuery UI's `easeOutBounce` effect by following these steps:

1. Download jQuery UI either from `http://jqueryui.com/download` or the NuGet package manager. To use the NuGet package manager, go to **Tools | NuGet Package Manager | Manage NuGet Packages for Solution**.

2. This will open up the **NuGet Package Manager** screen. Search for
   `jQuery.UI.Effects.Core`, and click on the **Install** button:

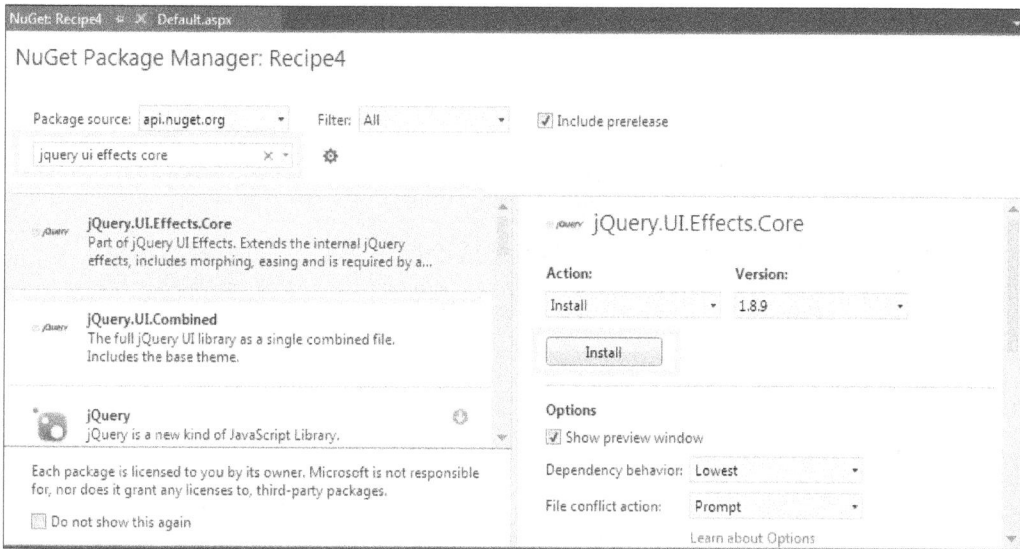

This will download `jquery.effects.core.js` and `jquery.effects.core.min.js` to the `Scripts` folder.

3. Next, search for `jQuery.UI.Effects.Bounce`, and click on the **Install** button:

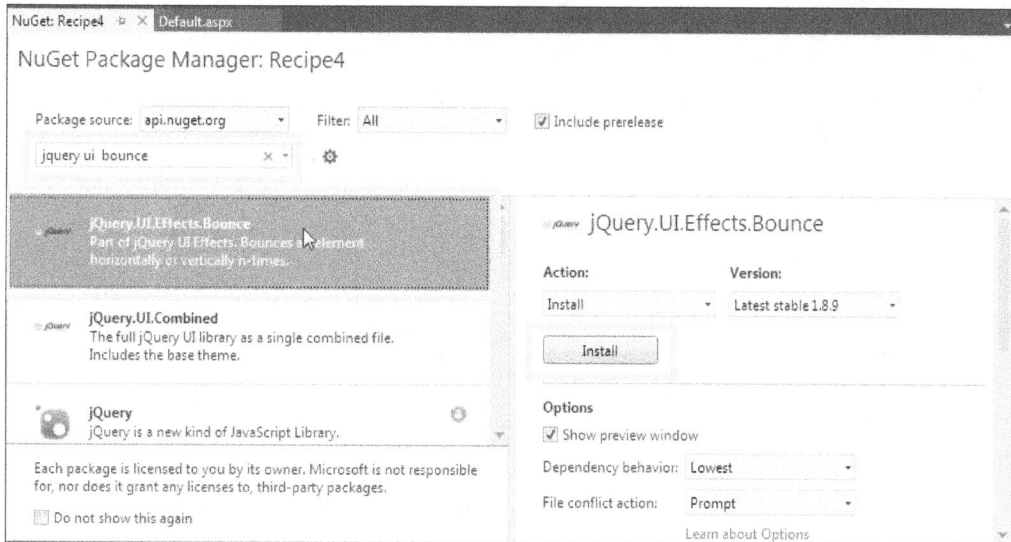

This will download `jquery.effects.bounce.js` and `jquery.effects.bounce.min.js` to the `Scripts` folder.

4. Now, include the debug versions of both the preceding libraries in the web form as follows:

```
<script src="Scripts/jquery.effects.core.js"></script>
<script src="Scripts/jquery.effects.bounce.js"></script>
```

5. In the jQuery code written earlier, update the easing from `linear`/`swing` to `easeOutBounce`, as shown here.

For the `mouseover` event, run the following code:

```
$(this).find("img[src$='png']").animate({ width: "64px",
  height: "64px" }, "slow", "easeOutBounce");
```

For the `mouseout` event, run the following code:

```
$(this).find("img[src$='png']").stop().animate({ width:
  "24px", height: "24px" }, "slow", "easeOutBounce");
```

6. Save and run the page to see the bounce effect on the profile photo when the mouse pointer is moved over it and when the pointer is moved out of it.

See also

The *Animating the alt text of the AdRotator control* recipe

Creating scrolling text in a Panel control

One of the interesting text animations that can be implemented using jQuery is to create a scrolling text. This animation has many applications, such as news scrollers, tickers for stock quotes, and so on. In this demonstration, let's apply this type of animation to the text content in a `Panel` control. We will also demonstrate how to loop animation effects continuously using the callback function parameter of the `.animate()` method. The constructs used in this example are as follows:

Construct	Type	Description
`$("#identifier")`	jQuery selector	This selects an element using its ID
`.animate()`	jQuery method	This performs a custom animation on the specified CSS properties
`.css()`	jQuery method	This gets the CSS property of the first matched element or sets one or more CSS properties for every matched element

Construct	Type	Description
left	CSS property	This is the position of the left boundary of an element from the left boundary of its containing element

Getting ready

Follow these steps to create scrolling text in a Panel control:

1. We will create a web page with a `Panel` control and some text content. The text content will be initially positioned toward the right of the containing panel and will be animated to move toward the left, as shown in the following two screenshots:

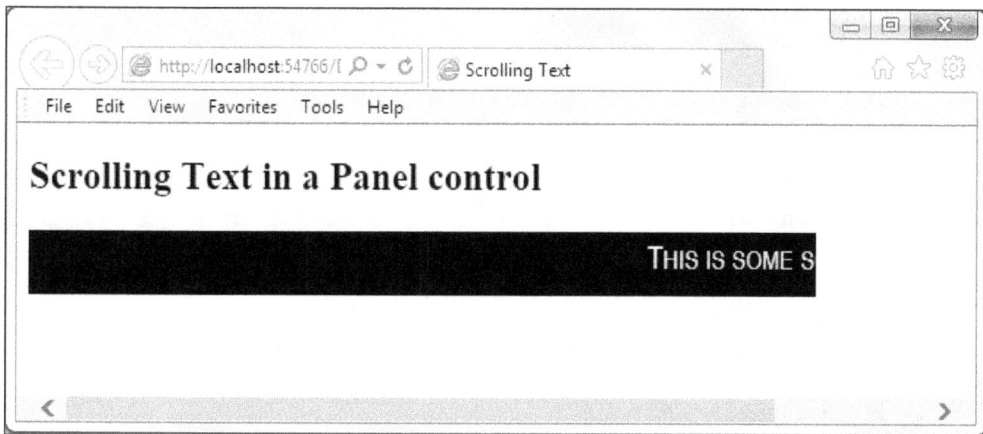

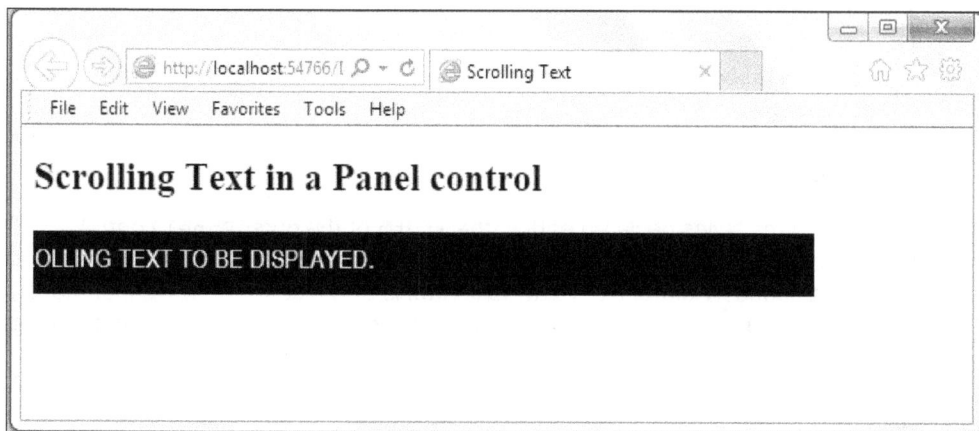

After the text is out of the view, it will restart from the right once again. This process will be executed in a loop.

2. Let's get started by creating a new **ASP.NET Web Application** project in Visual Studio using the **Empty** template and name it `Recipe5` (or any other suitable name).

3. Add a `Scripts` folder to the project, and add the jQuery library files to the folder.

4. Add a new web form and include the jQuery library in the form.

5. Go to **Toolbox | Standard**, and add two nested `Panel` controls to the form as follows. Note that the scrolling text is placed inside the inner `Panel` control:

```
<asp:Panel ID="pnlContainer" runat="server">
  <asp:Panel ID="pnlScollingText" runat="server">
    This is some scrolling text to be displayed.
  </asp:Panel>
</asp:Panel>
```

6. Add the following styles to the respective `Panel` controls:

```
<style type="text/css">
#pnlContainer {
  color:white;
  background-color:black;
  font-family:'Arial Narrow', Arial, sans-serif;
  font-size: 20px;
  font-variant:small-caps;
  padding:5px;
  width:500px;
  height:30px;
  white-space:nowrap;
}
#pnlScollingText{
  position:absolute;
  left:500px;
}
</style>
```

Note that in the styles declared earlier, the `width` of the outer `Panel` control is 500 px. Hence, the `left` position of the inner `Panel` control is initialized to 500 px, that is, the left boundary of the inner `Panel` control is 500 px toward the right of the left boundary of the outer `Panel` control. In other words, the text is positioned at the right edge of the outer `Panel` control.

How to do it...

Add the following jQuery code to a `script` block on the page:

```
<script type="text/javascript">
$(document).ready(function () {
  loopAnimation();
  function loopAnimation() {
    $("#<%=pnlScollingText.ClientID%>").css("left", "500px");
    $("#<%=pnlScollingText.ClientID%>").animate({ left: "-=850px"
      }, 7000, "linear", loopAnimation);
  }
});
</script>
```

How it works...

The scrolling text works as follows:

1. On running the page in the browser, the `loopAnimation` function is called:

    ```
    loopAnimation();
    ```

2. In the `loopAnimation` function, the left position of the inner `Panel` control is reset to 500 px. This ensures that the text always starts scrolling from the right boundary of the outer `Panel` control:

    ```
    $("#<%=pnlScollingText.ClientID%>").css("left", "500px");
    ```

3. The inner `Panel` control is then animated to reduce its left position gradually to a value equal to (width of the outer `Panel` control + width of the scrolling text), that is, (500 px + approx. 350 px): approximately 850 px. This value can be found by trial and error:

    ```
    $("#<%=pnlScollingText.ClientID%>").animate({ left: "-
      =850px" }, 7000, "linear", loopAnimation);
    ```

    The duration of the animation is set to `7000` ms: it takes 7 seconds for the text to scroll from right to left. The easing is set to `linear`. It is important to note that the `loopAnimation` function is passed as a parameter to the callback function value. This ensures that the animation loops continuously and the function calls itself at the end of each animation.

See also

The *Animating a Label control to create a digital clock* recipe

Creating a vertical accordion menu using Panel controls

This example demonstrates sliding animation with `Panel` controls. We will create a vertical accordion menu that allows only one main menu item to be expanded at a time. The constructs used in this example are as follows:

Construct	Type	Description
`$("#identifier")`	jQuery selector	This selects an element using its ID.
`$(".class")`	jQuery selector	This matches all elements with the specified CSS class.
`$(this)`	jQuery object	This refers to the current jQuery object.
`click`	jQuery event	This is fired when you click on an element. It corresponds to the JavaScript click event.
`event.stopPropagation()`	jQuery method	This stops an event from bubbling up the DOM tree.
`.find()`	jQuery method	This finds all elements that match the filter.
`.hide()`	jQuery method	This hides the matched elements.
`.is()`	jQuery method	This returns a Boolean value if the matched element satisfies a given condition.
`.on()`	jQuery event binder	This attaches an event handler for one or more events to the matched elements.
`.slideDown()`	jQuery method	This displays elements with a download slide motion.
`.slideUp()`	jQuery method	This hides elements with an upward slide motion.
`:visible`	jQuery selector	This selects elements that are visible, that is, elements with a width or height > 0.

Getting ready

Follow these steps to create a vertical accordion menu:

1. We will create a web page with the main menu items, as shown in the following screenshot:

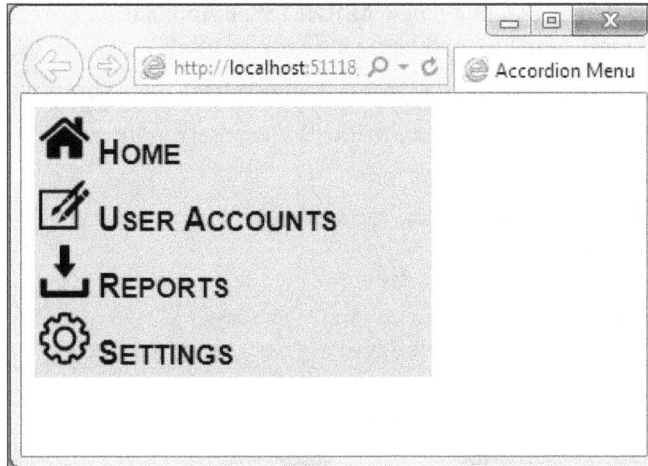

When you click on any main menu item, it expands with a sliding animation to show its corresponding submenu items, as shown here:

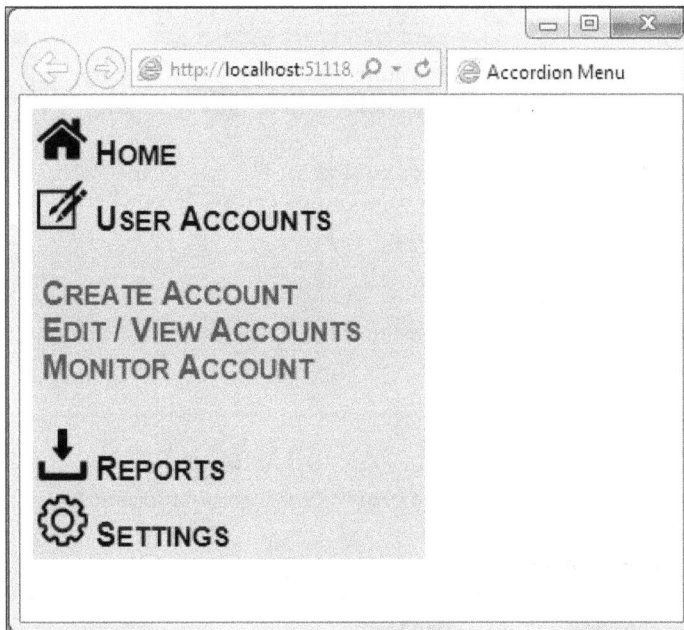

When you click on any other main menu item, the previously expanded submenu slides up, that is, it collapses and the new submenu slides down, that is, it expands.

2. Let's get started by creating a new **ASP.NET Web Application** project in Visual Studio using the **Empty** template and name it `Recipe6` (or any other suitable name).

3. Create a `Scripts` folder in the project and add the jQuery library files to the project.

4. Create a new web form and include the jQuery library in the web form.

5. Add the following markup to the form:

```
<table id="tblMenu" class="mainmenu">
  <tr>
    <td>
      <img src="images/home.png" />Home
      <asp:Panel runat="server" CssClass="submenu">
        <ul>
          <li>Configure Dashboard</li>
          <li>Logout</li>
        </ul>
      </asp:Panel>
    </td>
  </tr>
  <tr>
    <td>
      <img src="images/accounts.png" />User Accounts
      <asp:Panel runat="server" CssClass="submenu">
        <ul>
          <li>Create Account</li>
          <li>Edit / View Accounts</li>
          <li>Monitor Account</li>
        </ul>
      </asp:Panel>
    </td>
  </tr>
  <tr>
    <td>
      <img src="images/reports.png" />Reports
      <asp:Panel runat="server" CssClass="submenu">
        <ul>
          <li>Account Usage</li>
          <li>Activity Log</li>
          <li>Account Specific</li>
        </ul>
      </asp:Panel>
    </td>
  </tr>
  <tr>
    <td>
```

```
      <img src="images/settings.png" />Settings
      <asp:Panel runat="server" CssClass="submenu">
        <ul>
          <li>Update Profile</li>
          <li>Change Password</li>
        </ul>
      </asp:Panel>
    </td>
  </tr>
</table>
```

6. Create an `images` folder, and add the required image files for the main menu items to this folder.

7. To add spacing between the image and the text in the main menu items, include the following style in the page:

```
img{
    padding-right:5px;
}
```

8. Add the following style for the main menu items:

```
.mainmenu{
    cursor:pointer;
    width:250px;
    background-color:lightgray;
    font-variant:small-caps;
    font-size:20px;
    font-family:Arial, sans-serif;
    font-weight:700;
    padding:0px;
}
```

9. Add the following style for the submenu items:

```
.submenu{
    color:blue;
    background-color:lightblue;
    padding-top:3px;
    padding-bottom:2px;
}
.submenu ul{
    width:100%;
    padding-left:3px;
    list-style-type:none;
}
```

How to do it...

Include the following jQuery code in a `script` block on the page:

```
<script type="text/javascript">
$(document).ready(function () {
  $(".submenu").hide();
  $("#tblMenu").on("click", "tr", function () {
    $(".submenu").slideUp("slow");
    var submenuPanel = $(this).find(".submenu");
    if (!$(submenuPanel).is(":visible"))
      $(submenuPanel).slideDown("slow");
  });
  $(".submenu").on("click", "li", function (evt) {
    evt.stopPropagation();
  });
});
</script>
```

How it works...

The vertical accordion menu works as follows:

1. When the page loads in the browser, all submenu panels are hidden using the CSS selector for the submenu items, as follows:

    ```
    $(".submenu").hide();
    ```

2. An event handler for a `click` event is attached to the container table that holds the main menu items. The target element for the `click` event is the table row:

    ```
    $("#tblMenu").on("click", "tr", function () {…});
    ```

3. Since only one submenu should be visible at a time, the preceding event handler will collapse any visible submenu panels with sliding animation:

    ```
    $(".submenu").slideUp("slow");
    ```

4. The `click` event then expands the submenu panel whose main menu item is clicked. To determine the submenu panel that needs to be shown, use the CSS selector on the current object:

    ```
    var submenuPanel = $(this).find(".submenu");
    ```

5. If the required submenu panel is already visible, nothing needs to be done. If however, it is not visible, we need to display it using sliding animation:

    ```
    if (!$(submenuPanel).is(":visible"))
      $(submenuPanel).slideDown("slow");
    ```

6. The submenu items are actually list items. To prevent the submenu items from triggering the expand/collapse menu, we use the `.stopPropagation()` method on the list items. This will prevent the event from bubbling up the DOM tree:

```
$(".submenu").on("click", "li", function (evt) {
  evt.stopPropagation();
});
```

See also

The *Animating the Menu control* recipe

Showing/hiding the GridView control with the explode effect

The jQuery UI library provides many interesting effects that can be easily applied on ASP.NET sites. We have already seen the `bounce` effect when applied to images in an earlier recipe. In this particular example, we will make use of another effect called `explode` and apply it to a `GridView` control. The constructs used in this example are as follows:

Construct	Type	Description
`$("#identifier")`	jQuery selector	This selects an element using its ID.
`event.preventDefault()`	jQuery method	This prevents the default action of the event from being triggered.
`explode`	jQuery UI effect	This splits an element in the specified number of pieces while hiding or showing it.
`.hide()`	jQuery method	This hides the matched elements.
`.is()`	jQuery method	This returns a Boolean value if the matched element satisfies a given condition.
`pieces`	Property of the jQuery UI explode effect	These are the number of pieces to be exploded. Its default value is set to 9.
`.show()`	jQuery method	This displays the matched elements.
`.val()`	jQuery method	This returns the value of the first matched element or sets the value of every matched element.
`:visible`	jQuery selector	This selects elements that are visible, that is, elements with a width or height > 0.

Follow these steps to setup a data driven GridView control on the form:

1. Let's create a page that consists of a `GridView` control that displays the `Employee` data from the Northwind database, as shown in the following screenshot:

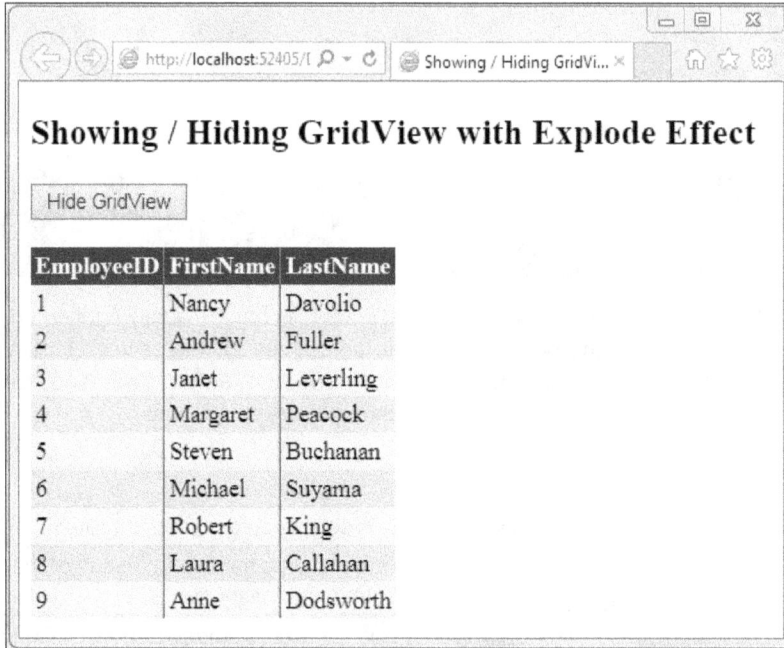

When you click on the **Hide GridView** button at the top of the page, the `GridView` control is hidden gradually with the `explode` effect, as follows:

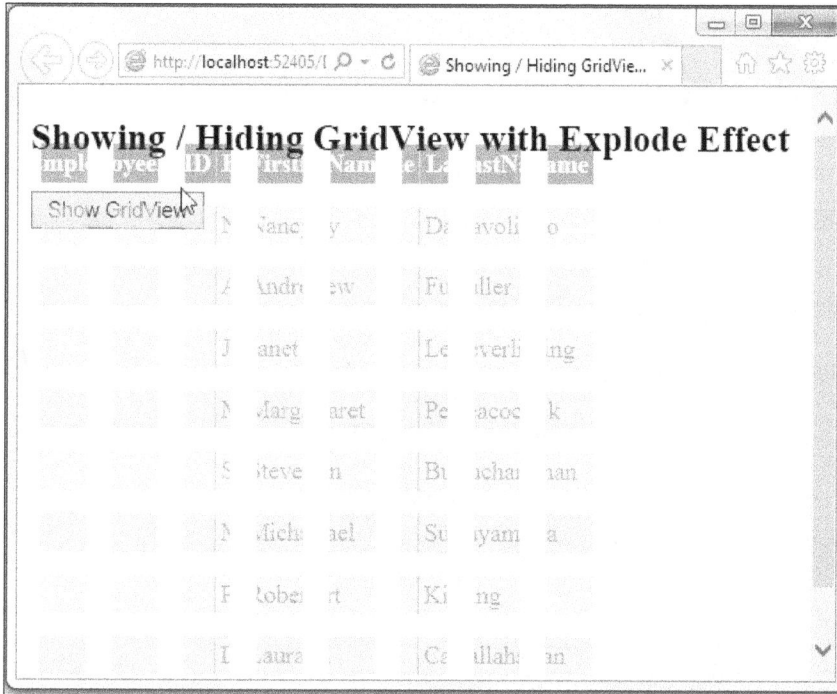

The animation is applied until the `GridView` control is completely hidden, as shown in the following screenshot:

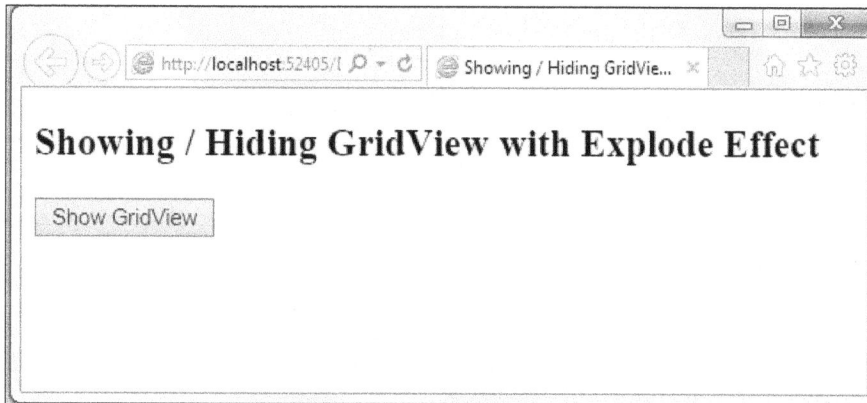

The button now changes to **Show GridView**. When you click on the button, the `GridView` control is gradually made visible using the same effect.

2. To get started, create a new **ASP.NET Web Application** project in Visual Studio using the **Empty** template and name it `Recipe7` (or any other suitable name).

3. Create a `Scripts` folder in the project and add the jQuery library files to the folder.

4. Add a new web form to the project and include the jQuery library in the form.

5. Drag and drop a `GridView` control on the form by navigating to **Toolbox | Data**.

6. In the **Design** mode, move the mouse pointer over the `GridView` control until a small arrow icon appears in the top-right corner. Click on this arrow to open the **GridView Tasks** menu, as shown in the following figure:

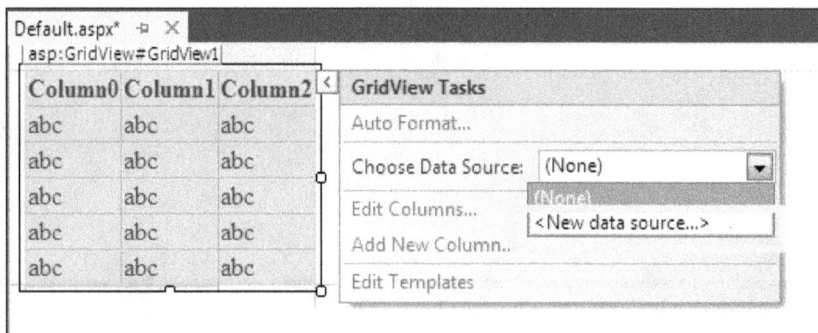

7. From the preceding menu, select **<New data source...>** from the **Choose Data Source** drop-down menu. This will open the **Data Source Configuration Wizard**, as shown in the following screenshot. Select **SQL**, and complete the wizard to connect to the Northwind database running on MS SQL Server:

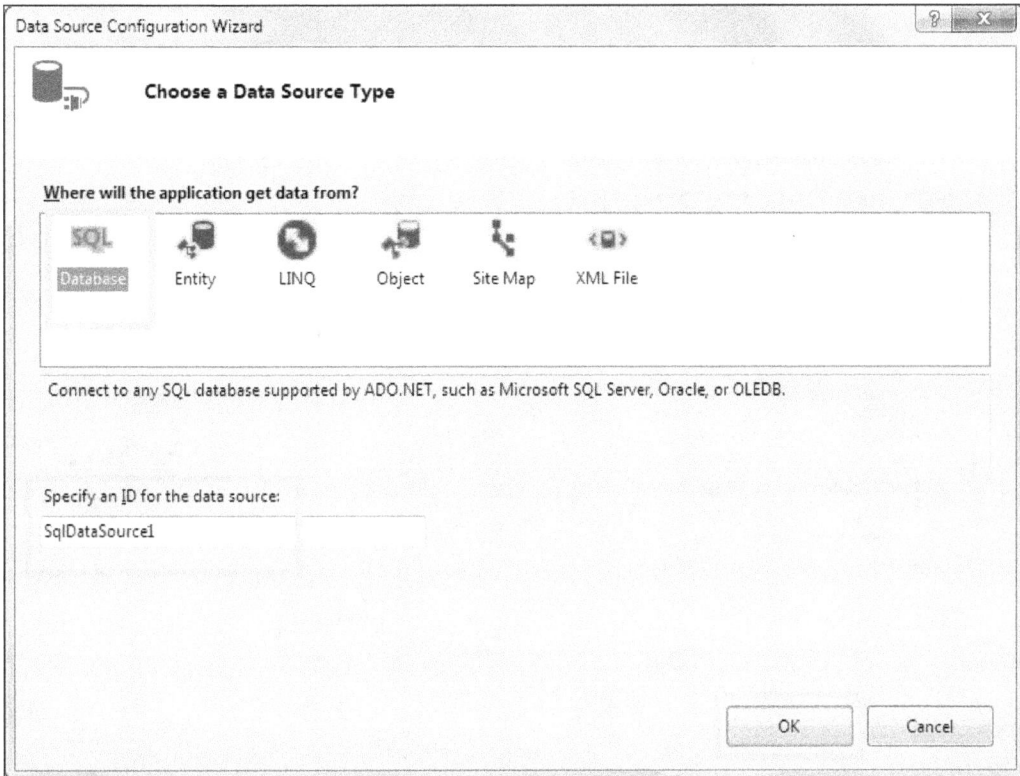

When you configure the **Select Statement** option in the **Data Source Configuration Wizard**, choose the Employees table, and select the EmployeeID, LastName, and FirstName columns:

Note that we are using Windows Authentication for all database driven examples in this book. Hence in the MS SQL Server, it is important to give permission to the windows account to access the Northwind database.

8. To style the GridView control, you can open the **GridView Tasks** menu once again, and click on **Auto Format**. Choose the required formatting scheme, and click on **Apply** to format the GridView control:

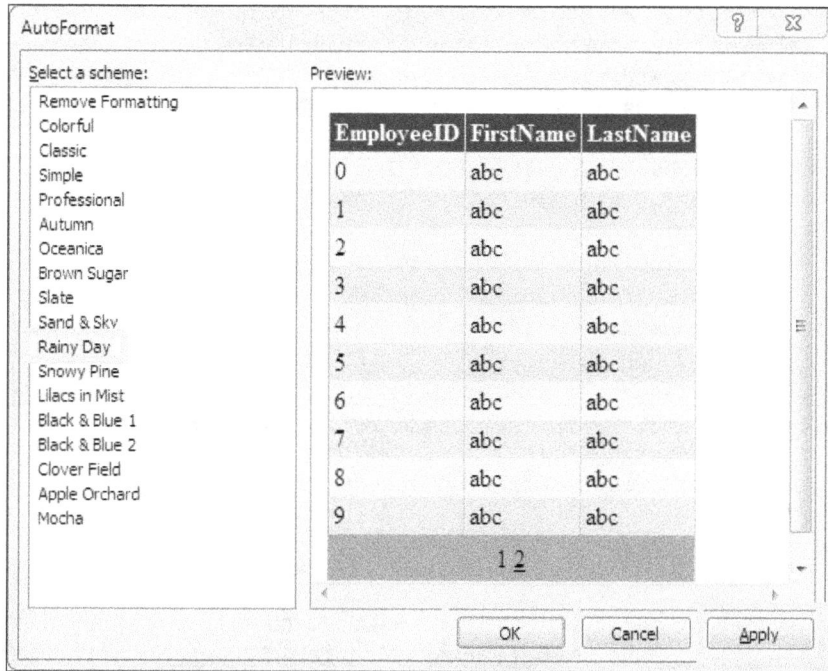

9. Also, add a `Button` control to the form by navigating to **Toolbox | Standard**. This button will be used to hide/show the `GridView` control as required.

10. Thus, the markup of the form is as follows:

```
<asp:Button ID="btnShowHide" runat="server" Text="Hide
  GridView" />
<br /><br />
<asp:GridView ID="GridView1" runat="server"
  AutoGenerateColumns="False" DataKeyNames="EmployeeID"
  DataSourceID="SqlDataSource1" AllowPaging="True"
  CellPadding="3" GridLines="Vertical" BackColor="White"
  BorderColor="#999999" BorderStyle="None" BorderWidth="1px">
  <AlternatingRowStyle BackColor="#DCDCDC" />
  <Columns>
    <asp:BoundField DataField="EmployeeID"
      HeaderText="EmployeeID" InsertVisible="False"
      ReadOnly="True" SortExpression="EmployeeID" />
    <asp:BoundField DataField="FirstName"
      HeaderText="FirstName" SortExpression="FirstName" />
    <asp:BoundField DataField="LastName"
      HeaderText="LastName" SortExpression="LastName" />
  </Columns>
```

```
<FooterStyle BackColor="#CCCCCC" ForeColor="Black" />
<HeaderStyle BackColor="#000084" Font-Bold="True"
  ForeColor="White" />
<PagerStyle BackColor="#999999" ForeColor="Black"
  HorizontalAlign="Center" />
<RowStyle BackColor="#EEEEEE" ForeColor="Black" />
<SelectedRowStyle BackColor="#008A8C" Font-Bold="True"
  ForeColor="White" />
<SortedAscendingCellStyle BackColor="#F1F1F1" />
<SortedAscendingHeaderStyle BackColor="#0000A9" />
<SortedDescendingCellStyle BackColor="#CAC9C9" />
<SortedDescendingHeaderStyle BackColor="#000065" />
</asp:GridView>
<asp:SqlDataSource ID="SqlDataSource1" runat="server"
  ConnectionString="<%$
  ConnectionStrings:NorthwindConnectionString %>"
  SelectCommand="SELECT [FirstName], [LastName],
  [EmployeeID]
  FROM [Employees]"></asp:SqlDataSource>
```

11. To use the `explode` effect, we need to download the necessary jQuery UI files by navigating to **Tools | NuGet Package Manager | Manage NuGet Packages for Solution**. In the **Nuget Package Manager** screen, as shown in the following screenshot, search for `jQuery.UI.Effects.Core`, and click on **Install**. This will add both the debug and release versions: `jquery.effects.core.js` and `jquery.effects.core.min.js` to the `Scripts` folder:

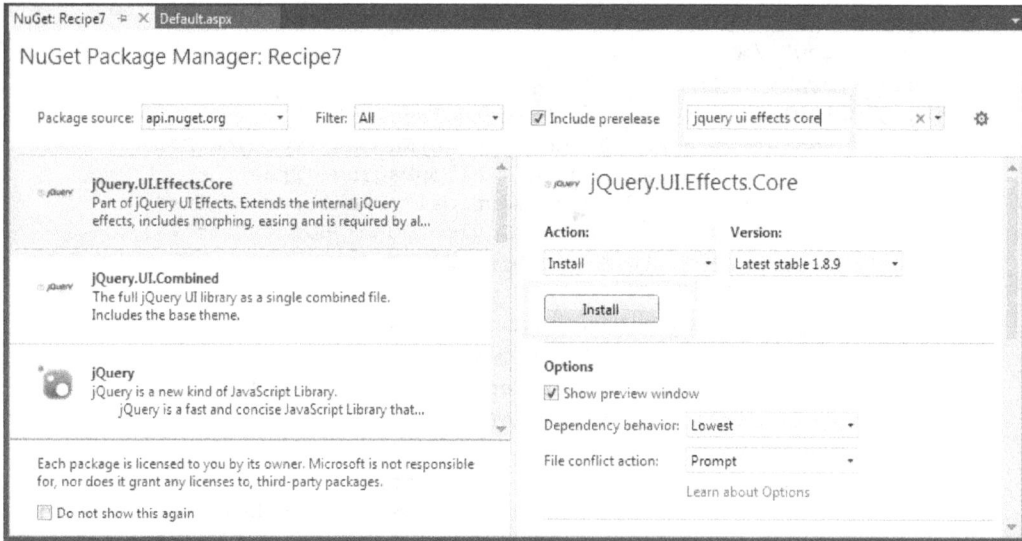

12. Next, search for `jQuery.UI.Effects.Explode`, and click on **Install**. This will add `jquery.effects.explode.js` and `jquery.effects.explode.min.js` to the `Scripts` folder:

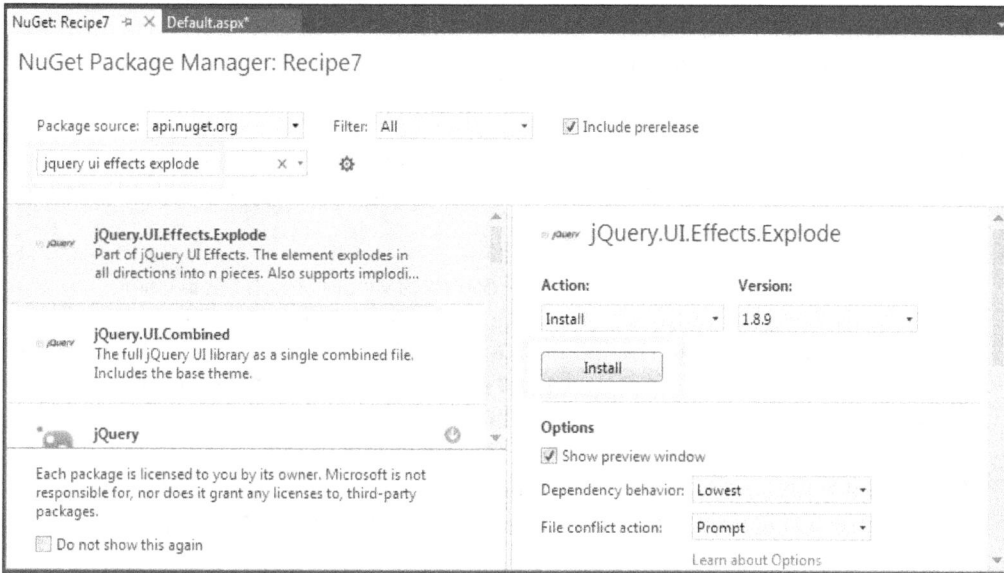

13. Include the debug versions for both `jQuery.UI.Effects.Core` and `jQuery.UI.Effects.Explode` in the Web form as follows:

```html
<script src="Scripts/jquery.effects.core.js"></script>
<script src="Scripts/jquery.effects.explode.js"></script>
```

How to do it...

Include the following jQuery code in a `script` block on the page:

```html
<script type="text/javascript">
  $(document).ready(function () {
    $("#<%=btnShowHide.ClientID%>").click(function (evt) {
      evt.preventDefault();
      if ($("#GridView1").is(":visible")) {
        $("#GridView1").hide("explode", { pieces: 100 }, 5000);
        $("#<%=btnShowHide.ClientID%>").val("Show GridView");
      }else {
        $("#GridView1").show("explode", { pieces: 100 }, 5000);
        $("#<%=btnShowHide.ClientID%>").val("Hide GridView");
      }
    });
  });
</script>
```

How it works...

The explode effect on the GridView control works as follows:

1. When the page is launched in the browser, an event handler is attached to the click event of the `Button` control as follows:

    ```
    $("#<%=btnShowHide.ClientID%>").click(function (evt) {…});
    ```

2. In this event handler, first of all the default behavior of the `Button` control is prevented, that is, the page is prevented from being submitted on the `Button` click:

    ```
    evt.preventDefault();
    ```

3. Next, we check whether the `GridView` control is visible or not. If it is visible, then it is hidden gradually using the `explode` effect of jQuery UI. The number of `pieces` is set to `100` and the duration of animation is set to `5000` ms; the `GridView` control will explode into 100 pieces and gradually disappear in 5 seconds. The `Text` property of the `Button` control is also updated accordingly:

    ```
    if ($("#GridView1").is(":visible")) {
      $("#GridView1").hide("explode", { pieces: 100 }, 5000);
      $("#<%=btnShowHide.ClientID%>").val("Show GridView");
    }
    ```

4. If the `GridView` control is not visible, it is gradually shown using the explode effect of jQuery UI. The number of `pieces` is once again set to `100` and the duration of animation is set to `5000` ms; the `GridView` control is assembled from 100 pieces and made visible in 5 seconds. The `Text` property of the `Button` control is also updated accordingly:

    ```
    else {
      $("#GridView1").show("explode", { pieces: 100 }, 5000);
      $("#<%=btnShowHide.ClientID%>").val("Hide GridView");
    }
    ```

See also

The *Animating images in the TreeView control* recipe

6
Working with Graphics in ASP.NET Sites

This chapter explores the use of jQuery for embedding graphics in ASP.NET websites and MVC. We will cover the following recipes in this chapter:

- ▶ Creating a spotlight effect on images
- ▶ Zooming images on mouseover
- ▶ Creating an image scroller
- ▶ Building a photo gallery using z-index property
- ▶ Building a photo gallery using ImageMap control
- ▶ Using images to create effects in the Menu control
- ▶ Creating a 5 star rating control
- ▶ Previewing image uploads in MVC

Introduction

The Web is all about content and presentation of the content to an audience. The visual representation and interactivity of content along with its user friendliness are important factors to be considered when building websites. The use of graphics in the web content adds to its visual appeal and enhances the experience of the end user. Examples of graphics include images, animated gif, flash, charts, image buttons, and so on.

jQuery eases the process of integrating graphics into web content. It provides utilities for creating effects and animations on web elements. Event handlers can be easily attached and client-side handling improves the performance by preventing a round trip to the server.

Using jQuery, ASP.NET server controls such as `Image`, `ImageButton`, and `ImageMap` can be enhanced with effects, animations, and event handlers. Plain HTML elements, such as the image element can also be manipulated using jQuery. This approach is useful in MVC applications since MVC uses HTML elements instead of server controls.

In this chapter, we will take look at some common uses of jQuery to work with graphic elements.

Creating a spotlight effect on images

Creating a spotlight on a focused item, such as text or any graphic element on a web page, is often required to draw attention to that item. In this recipe, let's see how such an effect can be created on a collection of images. The constructs used in this example are summarized in the following table:

Construct	Type	Description
`$("#identifier")`	jQuery selector	This selects an element based on its ID
`$("html_tag")`	jQuery selector	This selects all elements with the specified HTML tag
`$(this)`	jQuery object	This refers to the current jQuery object
`.addClass()`	jQuery method	This adds the specified CSS class to each matched element
`.css()`	jQuery method	This gets the style property for the first matched element or sets the style property for every matched element
`.hover()`	jQuery event binder	This binds event handlers for `mouseover` and `mouseout` events
`.removeClass()`	jQuery method	This removes the specified CSS class from each matched element

Getting ready

Let's build a web page with images for the spotlight effect:

1. Let's create a web page with a collection of image controls arranged in a grid format, as shown in the following screenshot:

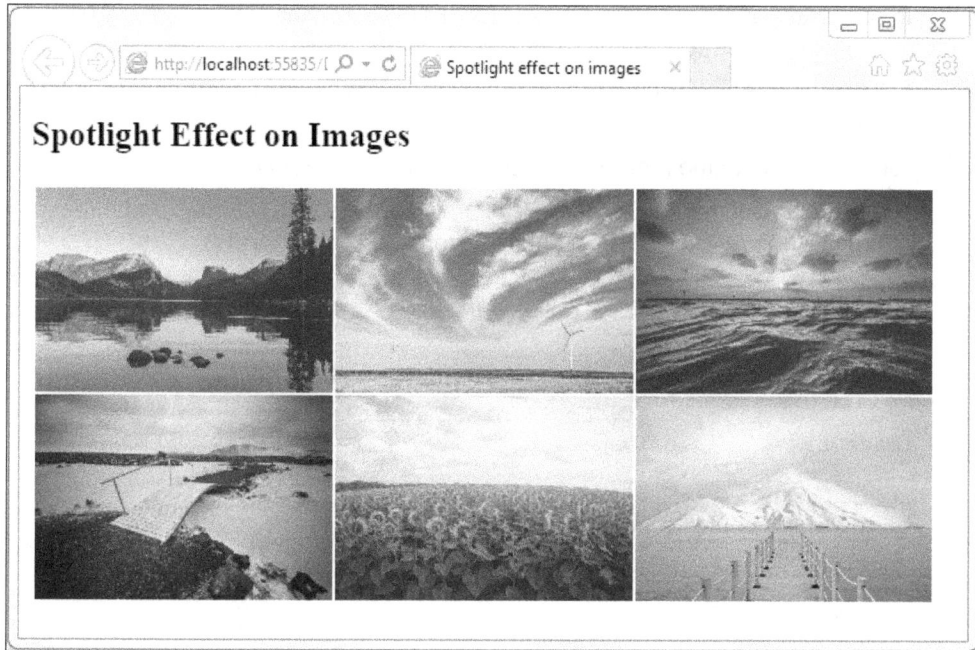

2. On moving the mouse pointer over any image in the grid, the focused item receives a spotlight with the remaining items fading out, as shown in this screenshot:

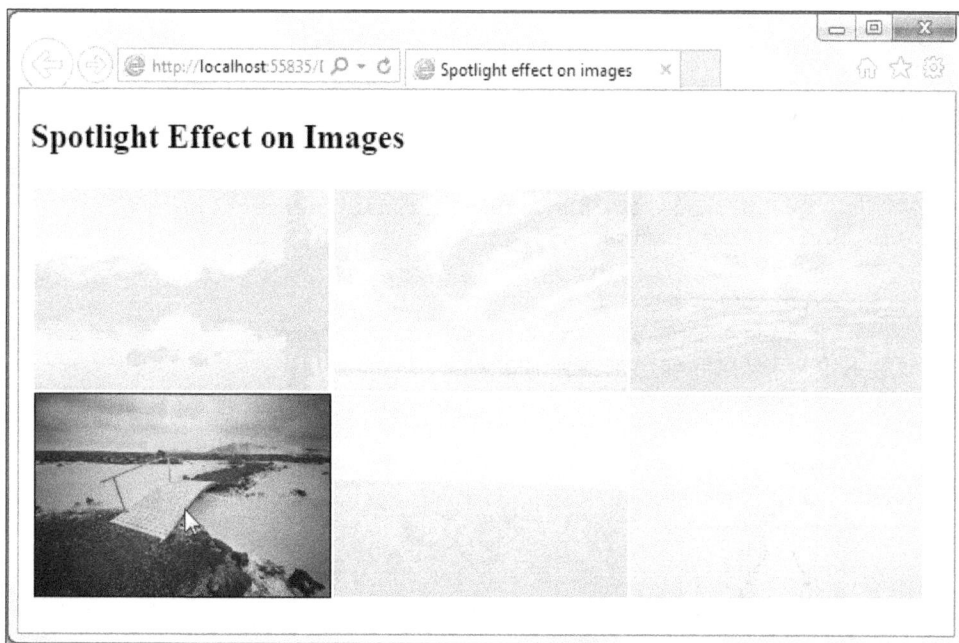

3. To create this application, launch an **ASP.NET Web Application** project in Visual Studio using the **Empty** template and name it `Recipe1` (or any other suitable name).

4. Add the jQuery library to the project in a `Scripts` folder. Add some sample images to an `images` folder.

5. Add a web form to the project and include the jQuery library in the form.

6. Add the following markup to the page to create a table with two rows and three columns. An `Image` control is added to each table cell:

```
<div id="container">
  <table>
    <tr>
      <td>
        <asp:Image ID="imgSample1" runat="server"
ImageUrl="~/images/image1.jpg" />
      </td>
      <td>
        <asp:Image ID="imgSample2" runat="server"
ImageUrl="~/images/image2.jpg"/>
      </td>
      <td>
        <asp:Image ID="imgSample3" runat="server"
ImageUrl="~/images/image3.jpg" />
      </td>
    </tr>
    <tr>
      <td>
        <asp:Image ID="imgSample4" runat="server"
ImageUrl="~/images/image4.jpg"/>
      </td>
      <td>
        <asp:Image ID="imgSample5" runat="server"
ImageUrl="~/images/image5.jpg"/>
      </td>
      <td>
        <asp:Image ID="imgSample6" runat="server"
ImageUrl="~/images/image6.jpg"/>
      </td>
    </tr>
  </table>
</div>
```

7. Include the following styles on the page to set the display dimensions of the images and padding/margins for the table element:

```css
<style type="text/css">
#container img {
  width: 213px;
  height: 142px;
  display: block;
}

#container table {
  padding: 1px;
}

#container td {
  padding: 0px;
  margin: 0px;
}

.highlight {
  border-color: #000000;
  border-width: 1px;
  border-style: solid;
}
</style>
```

The highlight CSS class defined earlier will be used to attach a border to the focused image.

How to do it...

Add the following jQuery code to a `<script>` block on the page:

```javascript
<script type="text/javascript">
$(document).ready(function() {
  $("#container img").hover(
    function() {
      $("#container img").css("opacity", "0.2");
      $(this).css("opacity", "1");
      $(this).addClass("highlight");
    },
    function() {
      $("#container img").css("opacity", "1");
      $(this).removeClass("highlight");
    });
});
</script>
```

How it works...

The spotlight effect on images is achieved as follows:

1. Save the page using *Ctrl + S* and run it using *F5*. This will launch the page in the browser window and the images will be displayed in the grid.

2. The `mouseover` and `mouseout` event handlers are tied to the images using the `.hover()` method, as follows:

   ```
   $("#container img").hover(function(){…},function(){…});
   ```

3. On moving the mouse pointer over any image, the `mouseover` event handler is triggered. This handler, first of all, fades all images in the grid by setting their `opacity` to `0.2`:

   ```
   $("#container img").css("opacity", "0.2");
   ```

   Only the focused image, that is, the one with the spotlight is made completely opaque by setting its `opacity` to `1`:

   ```
   $(this).css("opacity", "1");
   ```

   A solid border is also applied to the focused image by adding the `highlight` CSS class to it:

   ```
   $(this).addClass("highlight");
   ```

4. On moving the mouse pointer outwards from the spotlight, the `mouseout` event handler is triggered. This event handler restores the `opacity` of all images in the grid to `1`:

   ```
   $("#container img").css("opacity", "1");
   ```

   It also removes the solid border from the focused image:

   ```
   $(this).removeClass("highlight");
   ```

See also

The *Using images to create effects in the Menu control* recipe

Zooming images on mouseover

Some applications require zooming or magnification of images at certain locations. In this recipe, we will zoom an image at the location where the mouse enters the image. The constructs used in this example are as follows:

Construct	Type	Description
`$("#identifier")`	jQuery selector	This selects an element based on its ID.
`$(this)`	jQuery object	This refers to the current jQuery object.
`.css()`	jQuery method	This gets the style property for the first matched element or sets the style property for every matched element.
`height`	CSS property	This is the height of the element.
`left`	CSS property	This is the position of the left edge of the element. For absolutely positioned elements, it indicates the position of the left edge with respect to the parent element.
`mousemove`	jQuery event	This is fired when the mouse pointer moves inside an element. It corresponds to the JavaScript `mousemove` event.
`mouseout`	jQuery event	This is fired when the mouse pointer leaves an element. It corresponds to the JavaScript `mouseout` event.
`mouseover`	jQuery event	This is fired when the mouse pointer enters an element. It corresponds to the JavaScript `mouseover` event.
`.on()`	jQuery event binder	This attaches an event handler for one or more events to the matched elements.
`pageX`	jQuery event property	This returns the position of the mouse pointer with respect to the left edge of the document.
`pageY`	jQuery event property	This returns the position of the mouse pointer with respect to the top edge of the document.
`.prop(propertyName)` or `.prop(propertyName, value)`	jQuery method	This returns the value of the specified property for the first matched element or sets the value of the specified property for all matched elements.
`top`	CSS property	This is the position of the top edge of the element. For absolutely positioned elements, it indicates the position of the top edge with respect to the parent element.
`width`	CSS property	This is the width of the element.

Getting ready

Let's build a page for zooming an image on mouseover:

1. In this example, we will create a page with a single image control, as shown in the following screenshot:

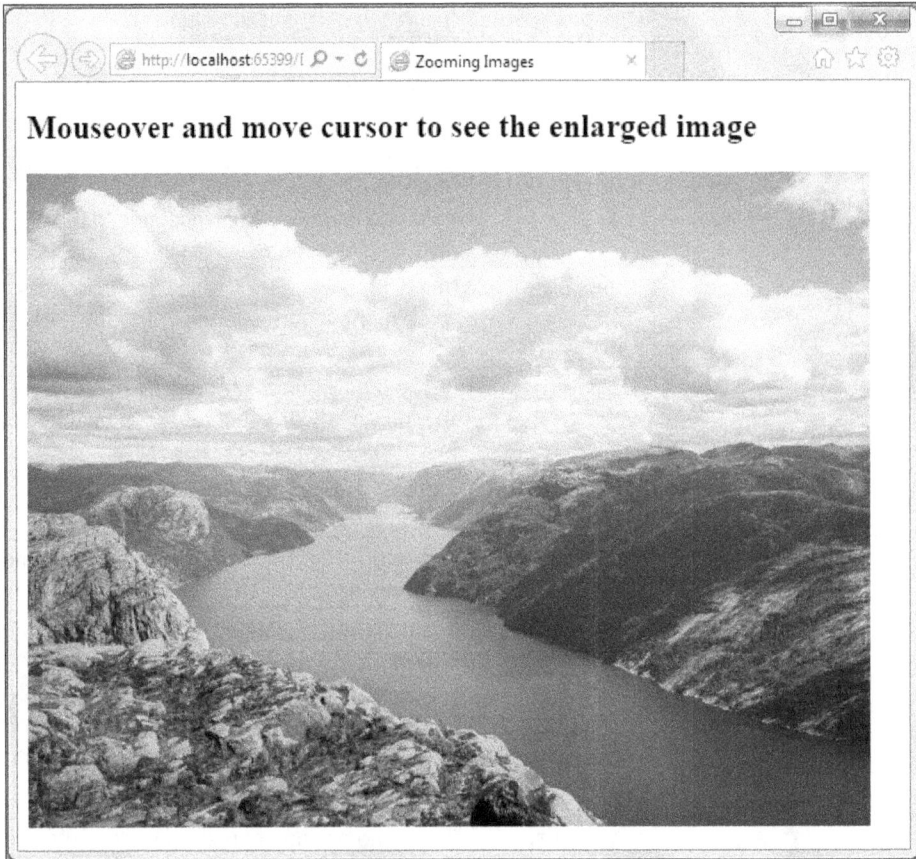

On moving the mouse over the image, it zooms at the location where the mouse pointer first entered the image, as shown here:

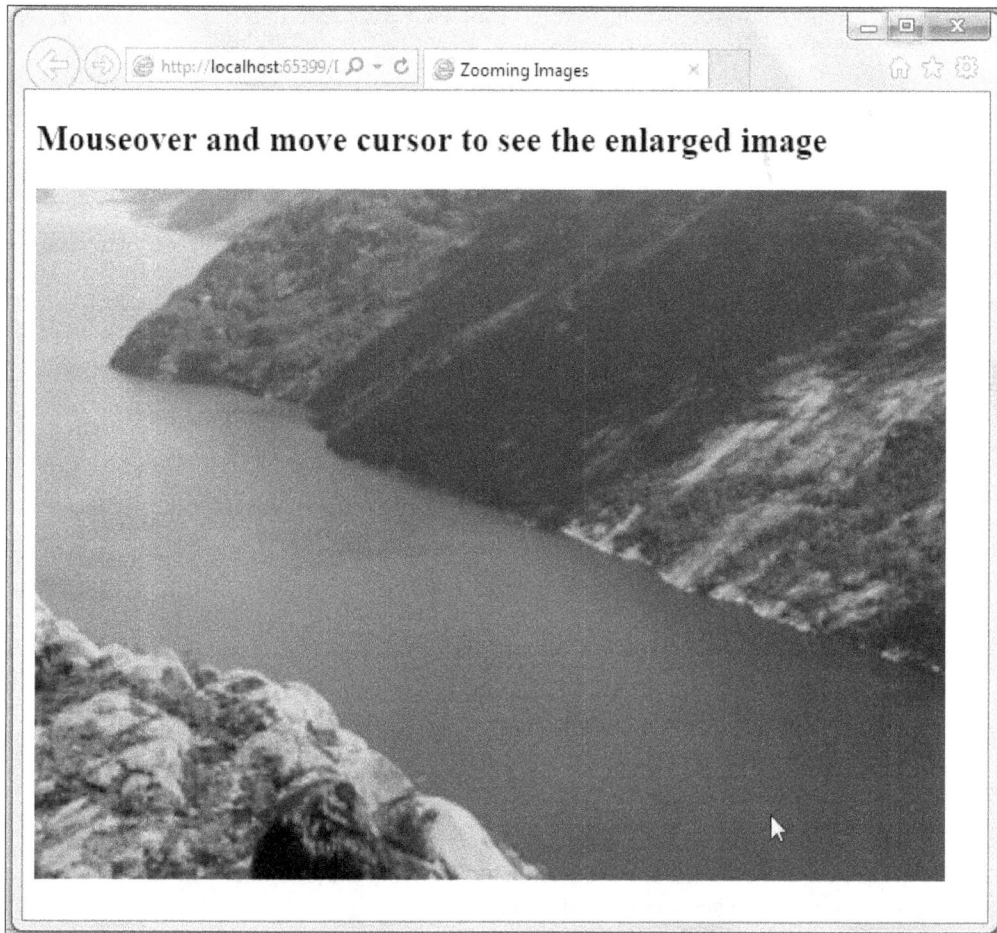

Moving the mouse pointer over the image enables you to scroll the enlarged image in the direction of the mouse.

2. To get started, use the **Empty** template of the **ASP.NET Web Application** project in Visual Studio and name the project Recipe2 (or any other suitable name).

3. Add the jQuery library to a Scripts folder in the project. Include a test image in the images folder.

4. Create a web form and include the jQuery library in the form.

5. Add an **Image** control by navigating to **Toolbox | Standard** to a `container div` element to create the following markup:

```
<div id="container">
  <asp:Image ID="imgSample" ImageUrl="~/images/image1.jpg"
Width="640" Height="480" runat="server" />
</div>
```

6. To set the dimensions of the `container div`, include the following CSS on the page:

```
<style type="" text/css "">
#container {
  width: 640px;
  height: 480px;
  overflow: hidden;
  position: relative;
}

#imgSample {
  position: absolute;
}
</style>
```

7. Note that the `position` of the `container div` is set to `relative` while the `position` of the `Image` control is set to `absolute`. To be able to move an absolutely positioned child element within a parent element, the parent element should be relatively positioned.

   The `overflow` of the `container div` is set to `hidden` so that the enlarged image is retained within it and any overflow is hidden from the end user. The image can be scrolled around to see the hidden areas.

How to do it...

Add the following jQuery code to a `<script>` block on the page:

```
<script type="text/javascript">
$(document).ready(function() {
  $("#<%=imgSample.ClientID%>").on("mouseover", function(evt) {
    var zoomIndex = 2;
    var iWidth = $(this).prop("width");
    var iHeight = $(this).prop("height");
    var newWidth = iWidth * zoomIndex;
    var newHeight = iHeight * zoomIndex;
    var posX = evt.pageX;
    var posY = evt.pageY;
    $(this).css({
```

```
      width: newWidth,
      height: newHeight,
      left: -posX,
      top: -posY
    });
  });
  $("#<%=imgSample.ClientID%>").on("mousemove", function(evt) {
    var posX = evt.pageX;
    var posY = evt.pageY;
    $(this).css({
      left: -posX,
      top: -posY
    });
  });
  $("#<%=imgSample.ClientID%>").on("mouseout", function() {
    $(this).css({
      width: "640px",
      height: "480px",
      left: 0,
      top: 0
    });
  });
});
</script>
```

How it works...

The zooming of the image on mouseover is achieved as follows:

1. The jQuery code attaches event handlers to the image control for `mouseover`, `mousemove`, and `mouseout` events using the following code:

   ```
   $("#<%=imgSample.ClientID%>").on("mouseover", function
   (evt) {…});
   $("#<%=imgSample.ClientID%>").on("mousemove", function
   (evt) {…});
   $("#<%=imgSample.ClientID%>").on("mouseout", function ()
   {…});
   ```

2. In the `mouseover` event handler, the image is enlarged and the position of the image is shifted so that the image appears to zoom at the location where the mouse pointer enters the image. The amount of zoom is determined by the `zoomIndex` variable, as follows:

   ```
   var zoomIndex = 2;
   ```

   Here, the image is zoomed to twice its original dimensions.

The original dimensions of the image are retrieved using the `.prop()` method and the new dimensions are calculated using the `zoomIndex` variable:

```
var iWidth = $(this).prop("width");
var iHeight = $(this).prop("height");
var newWidth = iWidth * zoomIndex;
var newHeight = iHeight * zoomIndex;
```

The *x* and *y* coordinates of the mouse pointer are determined using the `pageX` and `pageY` properties of the `mouseover` event given by the `evt` event variable:

```
var posX = evt.pageX;
var posY = evt.pageY;
```

The new dimensions and position of the image are then set using the `css()` method. The left and top positions of the image are altered so that it shifts and appears to zoom at the location of the mouse pointer. We can use any constant values for this shift or make use of the `posX` and `posY` values, as shown in the following code:

```
$(this).css({
   width: newWidth,
   height: newHeight,
   left: -posX,
   top: -posY
});
```

3. In the `mousemove` event handler, the enlarged image is scrolled in the direction of the mouse pointer. This is done by first retrieving the *x* and *y* coordinates of the mouse pointer:

```
var posX = evt.pageX;
var posY = evt.pageY;
```

The left and top position of the image is then updated using the preceding values in the `css()` method:

```
$(this).css({
  left: -posX,
  top: -posY
});
```

4. In the `mouseout` event handler, the image is reset to its original dimension and position using the `.css()` method:

```
$(this).css({
   width: "640px",
   height: "480px",
   left: 0,
   top:0
});
```

Thus, the image is shrunk to its original size and absolutely positioned, that is, at `left` equal to 0 and `top` equal to 0 of the `container` div.

> The `zoomIndex` variable controls the amount of zoom in the presented code sample. We have used `zoomIndex = 2`. You can experiment with different values of `zoomIndex` in the script. Alternatively, allow the user to enter the amount of magnification by providing a `DropDownList` control or any other suitable control.

See also

The *Building a photo gallery using the z-index property* recipe

Creating an image scroller

This recipe demonstrates horizontal scrolling of a sequence of images toward the left or right by animating the left position of the parent container element. The constructs used in this example are summarized as follows:

Construct	Type	Description
`$("#identifier")`	jQuery selector	This selects an element based on its ID.
`.animate()`	jQuery method	This performs a custom animation on the specified CSS properties.
`click`	jQuery event	This is fired when you click on an element. It corresponds to the JavaScript `click` event.
`event.preventDefault()`	jQuery method	This prevents the default action of the event from being triggered.
`left`	CSS property	This is the position of the left edge of the element.
`.on()`	jQuery event binder	This attaches an event handler to the matched elements for one or more events.
`z-index`	CSS property	This is the z-order of an element. When elements overlap, the one with the higher z-order appears above the one with the lower z-order.

Getting ready

Let's create a page for the image scroller through the following steps:

1. Let's get started by creating a new **ASP.NET Web Application** project in Visual Studio using the **Empty** template and name it `Recipe3` (or any other suitable name).

2. Add a `Scripts` folder to the project and include the jQuery library in this folder.

3. Add few sample images to an `images` folder in the project.

4. Add a new web form and include the jQuery library on the form.

5. Include the following markup on the form:

```
<div id="container">
  <asp:ImageButton ID="btnLeftScroll" runat="server"
ImageUrl="~/images/arrow-left-icon.png" />
  <asp:ImageButton ID="btnRightScroll" runat="server"
ImageUrl="~/images/arrow-right-icon.png" />
   <table id="tblImages">
     <tr>
       <td>
         <asp:Image ID="imgSample1" runat="server"
ImageUrl="~/images/image1.jpg" Width="640" Height="425" />
       </td>
       <td>
         <asp:Image ID="imgSample2" runat="server"
ImageUrl="~/images/image2.jpg" Width="640" Height="427" />
       </td>
       <td>
         <asp:Image ID="imgSample3" runat="server"
ImageUrl="~/images/image3.JPG" Width="640" Height="360" />
       </td>
       <td>
         <asp:Image ID="imgSample4" runat="server"
ImageUrl="~/images/image4.JPG" Width="640" Height="427" />
       </td>
       <td>
         <asp:Image ID="imgSample5" runat="server"
ImageUrl="~/images/image5.JPG" Width="640" Height="427" />
       </td>
       <td>
         <asp:Image ID="imgSample6" runat="server"
ImageUrl="~/images/image6.JPG" Width="640" Height="427" />
       </td>
       <td>
```

```
        <asp:Image ID="imgSample7" runat="server"
ImageUrl="~/images/image7.JPG" Width="640" Height="427" />
      </td>
    </tr>
  </table>
</div>
```

This will create a `container` div element consisting of a `table` with seven columns and one row. Each table cell contains one `Image` control. The images may/may not be of different dimensions.

Two `ImageButton` controls are provided for scrolling toward the left and right, respectively. These `ImageButton` controls are superimposed on top of the displayed image using CSS.

6. Apply the following styles to the preceding markup:

```
<style type="text/css">
#container{
  position:relative;
  overflow:hidden;
  width:640px;
  height:427px;
  vertical-align:central;
  margin:0;
}
#tblImages{
  position:absolute;
  padding:0px;
  margin:0px;
  border-collapse:collapse;
}
#tblImages td{
  padding:0px;
}
#btnLeftScroll{
  position:absolute;
  left:10px;
  top:200px;
  z-index:2;
  width:48px;
  height:48px;
}
#btnRightScroll{
  position:absolute;
```

```
        left:580px;
        top:200px;
        z-index:2;
        width:48px;
        height:48px;
    }
    </style>
```

> Note that the position of the container div is set to relative while the position of the table containing the images is set to absolute so that the table can be moved within the container div. The position of the left and right buttons is also set to absolute with a z-index of 2 so that the buttons appear on top of the displayed image.

7. Thus, the page will appear, as shown in the following screenshot:

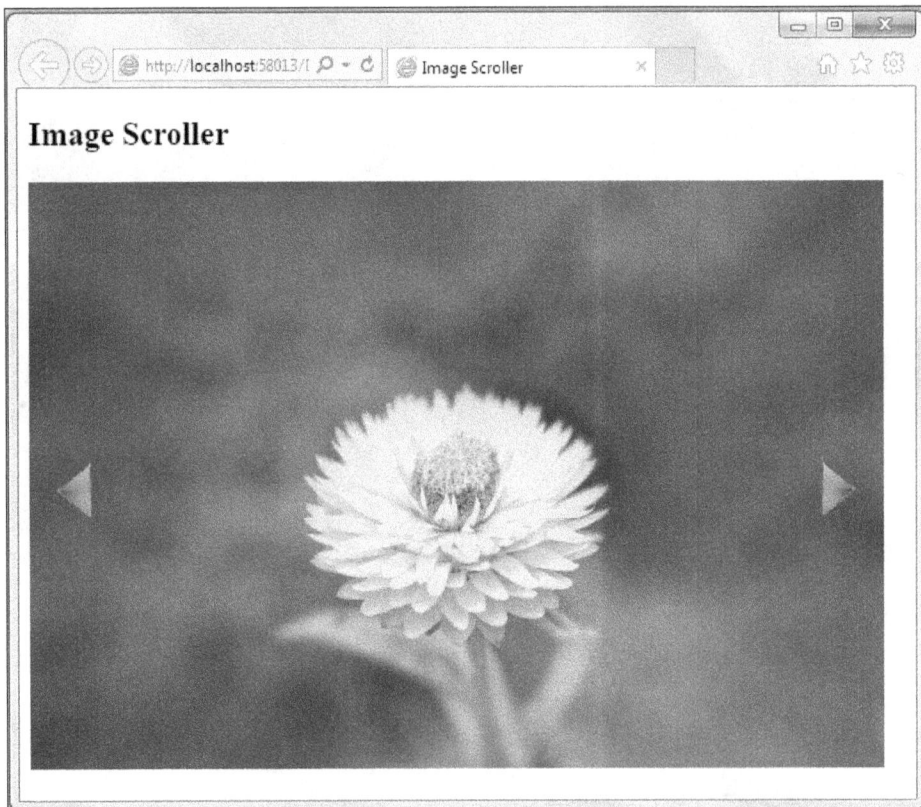

After clicking on the left button, the sequence moves toward the left, as shown in the following screenshot:

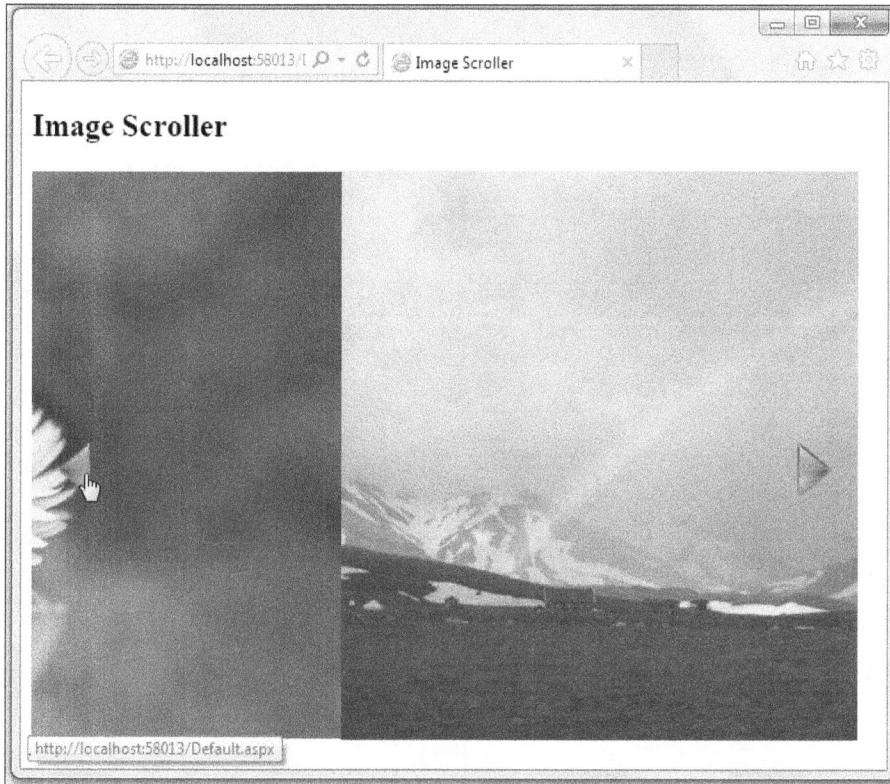

Similarly, after clicking on the right button, the sequence scrolls to the right, as shown here:

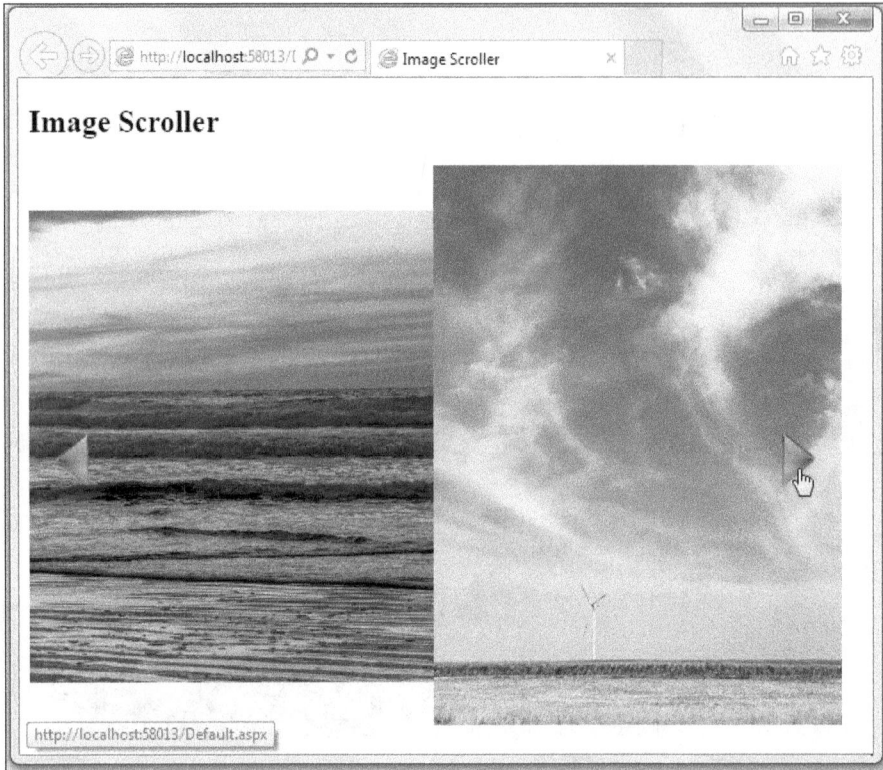

How to do it...

Add the following jQuery code to a `<script>` block on the page:

```
<script type="text/javascript">
$(document).ready(function() {
  var containerWidth = 640;
  var totalImgWidth = 640 * 7;
  var leftEdgePos = 0;
  var rightEdgePos = totalImgWidth - 50;
  $("#<%=btnLeftScroll.ClientID%>").on("click", function(evt) {
    evt.preventDefault();
    scrollLeft();
  });
```

```
$("#<%=btnRightScroll.ClientID%>").on("click", function(evt) {
    evt.preventDefault();
    scrollRight();
});

function scrollLeft() {
    if (rightEdgePos > containerWidth) {
        rightEdgePos -= 200;
        leftEdgePos -= 200;
        $("#tblImages").animate({
            left: '-=200px'
        }, 1500, "linear");
    }
}

function scrollRight() {
    if (leftEdgePos < 0) {
        leftEdgePos += 200;
        rightEdgePos += 200;
        $("#tblImages").animate({
            left: '+=200px'
        }, 1500,
        "linear");
    }
}
});
</script>
```

How it works...

The image scroller works as follows:

1. Save the page using *Ctrl + S* and run it using *F5*. This will launch the application in a browser window. On loading, the page displays the first image in a sequence along with the left and right arrow buttons. To scroll, click on the respective button. Note that scrolling stops once the left edge of the first image coincides with the left edge of the container div when scrolling toward the right. Similarly, when scrolling toward the left, the scrolling stops when the right edge of the last image coincides with the right edge of the container div.

2. The .aspx markup consists of a container div with a fixed width of 640 px and fixed height of 427 px. Its position is defined as relative so that the child elements can be absolutely positioned within it. The overflow is defined as hidden so that at a time, we can view only 640 px * 427 px window of the child elements.

3. The `container div` has a child `table` element with an ID equal to `tblImages`. This table contains the images arranged column-wise. These are the images that we need to scroll. The table is absolutely positioned so that it's left edge can be animated. At any time, the user will see only the **CONTAINER DIV**, that is, the blue shaded area in the following diagram, and the table will scroll in the background:

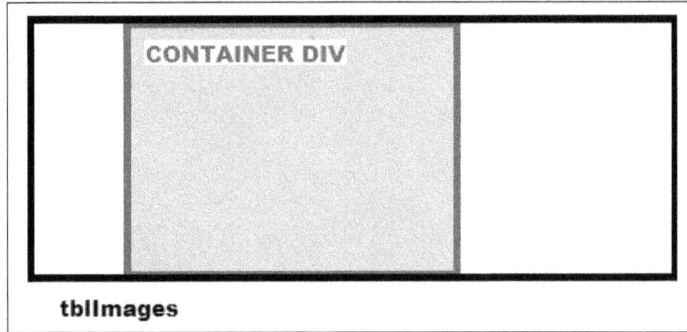

tblImages

4. In the jQuery script, the `container div` width is kept constant at `640` px:

   ```
   var containerWidth = 640;
   ```

   Since there are seven images, each of `640` px in width, the total table width can be determined, as follows:

   ```
   var totalImgWidth = 640 * 7;
   ```

   The position of the left edge of **tblImages** is initialized to coincide with the left edge of the container div:

   ```
   var leftEdgePos = 0;
   ```

   The position of the right edge of **tblImages** is initialized to coincide with the total table width minus `50` px to prevent the right edge from scrolling past the right edge of the container div:

   ```
   var rightEdgePos = totalImgWidth - 50;
   ```

5. An event handler for the `click` event is attached to each `ImageButton` control, that is, the left and right buttons. The left button calls the `scrollLeft` function while the right button calls the `scrollRight` function. Both event handlers call `event.preventDefault()` method to prevent the page from posting back:

   ```
   $("#<%=btnLeftScroll.ClientID%>").on("click", function
   (evt) {
     evt.preventDefault();
     scrollLeft();
   });
   ```

```
$("#<%=btnRightScroll.ClientID%>").on("click", function
(evt) {
    evt.preventDefault();
    scrollRight();
});
```

6. Let's take a look at what happens in the `scrollLeft()` function. First of all, we need to check the position of the right edge of the scrolling table. If the right edge lies to the right of the right edge of the `container div`, we can animate the table and slide it toward the left. For each click of the left button, we will shift the table toward the left by `200 px` in `1500 ms`. The left and right edges positions are adjusted by `200` px, as shown in the following code:

```
function scrollLeft() {
    if (rightEdgePos > containerWidth) {
        rightEdgePos -= 200;
        leftEdgePos -= 200;
        $("#tblImages").animate({ left: '-=200px' }, 1500,
"linear");
    }
}
```

7. Similarly, in the `scrollRight` function, we check the position of the left edge of the scrolling table. If the left edge lies to the left of the left edge of the `container div`, we can animate the table and slide it toward the right. For each click of the right button, we shift the table toward the right by `200 px` in `1500 ms`. The left and right edge positions of the table are also adjusted by `200` px accordingly:

```
function scrollRight() {
    if (leftEdgePos < 0) {
        leftEdgePos += 200;
        rightEdgePos += 200;
        $("#tblImages").animate({ left: '+=200px' }, 1500,
"linear");
    }
}
```

See also

The *Creating a spotlight effect on images* recipe

Building a photo gallery using z-index property

A photo gallery is a common feature on most social media sites. There are many ways of building these galleries using jQuery. In this recipe, let's use the z-index CSS property to build one such application. The following table shows a summary of the constructs used in this example:

Construct	Type	Description
`$("#identifier")`	jQuery selector	This selects an element based on its ID.
`$("html_tag")`	jQuery selector	This selects all elements with the specified HTML tag.
`$(this)`	jQuery object	This refers to the current jQuery object.
`click`	jQuery event	This is fired when you click on an element. It corresponds to the JavaScript `click` event.
`.css()`	jQuery method	This gets the style property for the first matched element or sets the style property for every matched element.
`.each()`	jQuery method	This iterates over the matched elements and executes a function for each element.
`event.preventDefault ()`	jQuery method	This prevents the default action of the event from being triggered.
`.length`	jQuery property	This returns the number of elements in the jQuery object.
`.on()`	jQuery event binder	This attaches an event handler to the matched elements for one or more events.
`parseInt(string)`	JavaScript function	This converts a string into an integer.
`z-index`	CSS property	This is the z-order of an element. When elements overlap, the one with the higher z-order appears above the one with the lower z-order.

Getting ready

Follow these steps to build a page with a photo gallery using z-index property:

1. We aim to create a page that displays one image at a time from a sequence of images. Navigation in the sequence is possible by clicking on the previous and next buttons. The images are displayed in a loop, so clicking on the next button on the last image displays the first image and clicking on the previous button on the first image displays the last image:

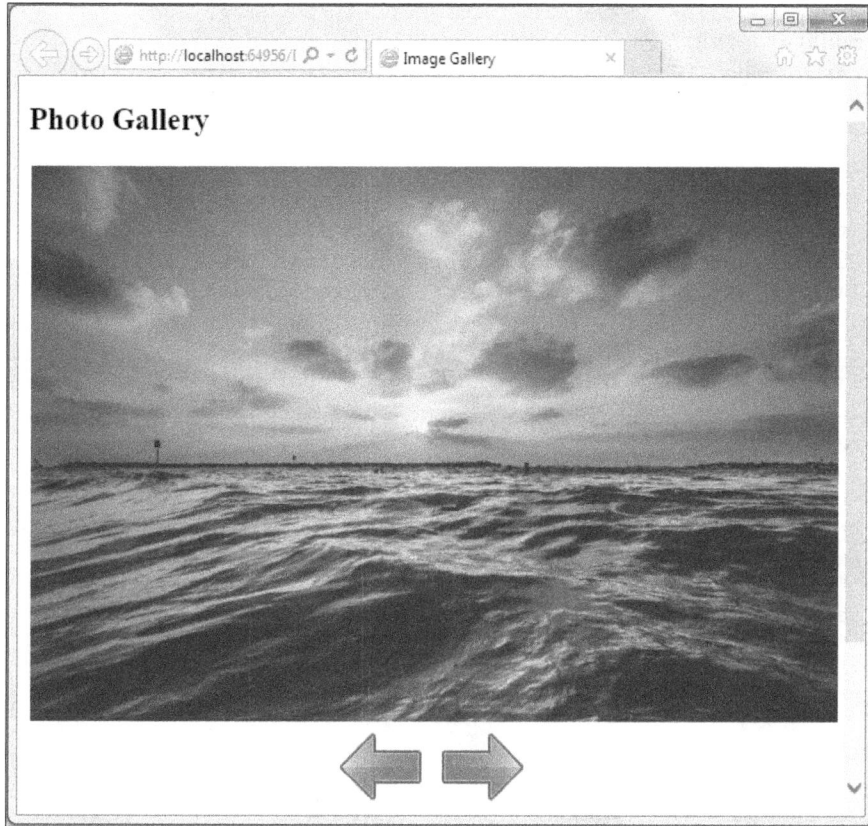

2. To create this gallery, launch a new **ASP.NET Web Application** project in Visual Studio using the **Empty** template and name it `Recipe4` (or any other suitable name).

3. Create a `Scripts` folder in the project and add the jQuery library to the folder. Include some sample images in an `images` folder.

4. Create a new web form and include the jQuery library on the form.

5. We will create an HTML `<table>` element consisting of two rows and one column. The first row will have six `Image` controls that are added to the table cell with `id = container`. The second row will have two `ImageButton` controls for the previous and next image navigation. Hence, add the following markup to the form:

```
<table><tr><td id="container">
<asp:Image ID="imgSample1" ImageUrl="~/images/image1.jpg"
runat="server" />
<asp:Image ID="imgSample2" ImageUrl="~/images/image2.jpg"
runat="server" />
<asp:Image ID="imgSample3" ImageUrl="~/images/image3.jpg"
runat="server" />
```

```
<asp:Image ID="imgSample4" ImageUrl="~/images/image4.jpg"
runat="server" />
<asp:Image ID="imgSample5" ImageUrl="~/images/image5.jpg"
runat="server" />
<asp:Image ID="imgSample6" ImageUrl="~/images/image6.jpg"
runat="server" />
</td></tr>
<tr><td>
<asp:ImageButton ID="btnPrevious" CssClass="buttonStyle"
ImageUrl="~/images/backward.ico" runat="server"
ToolTip="View previous photo" />  
<asp:ImageButton ID="btnNext" CssClass="buttonStyle"
ImageUrl="~/images/forward.ico" runat="server"
ToolTip="View next photo"/>
</td></tr>
</table>
```

6. Include the following styles on the page in order to set the dimensions of the elements and their respective positions:

```
<style type="text/css">
  buttonStyle{
    width:68px;
    height:68px;
  }
  #container{
    position:relative;
    width:640px;
    height:425px;
  }
  #container img{
    position:absolute;
    top:0px;
    left:0px;
  }
  td{
    text-align:center;
  }
</style>
```

> Note that the container table cell has its position property defined as relative. This enables its child elements to be absolutely positioned. Its dimensions are kept constant and all images are displayed in the gallery with these dimensions.

How to do it...

Add the following jQuery code to a `<script>` block on the page:

```
<script type="text/javascript">
$(document).ready(function() {
  var maxZIndex = $("#container img").length;
  var tempZIndex = maxZIndex;
  $("#container img").each(function() {
    $(this).css("z-index", tempZIndex);
    tempZIndex--;
  });
  $("#<%=btnPrevious.ClientID%>").on("click",
    function(evt) {
      evt.preventDefault();
      $("#container img").each(function() {
        var currZIndex = parseInt($(this).css("z-index"));
        if (currZIndex == 1)
          $(this).css("z-index", maxZIndex);
        else
          $(this).css("z-index", currZIndex - 1);
      });
    });
  $("#<%=btnNext.ClientID%>").on("click",
    function(evt) {
      evt.preventDefault();
      $("#container img").each(function() {
        var currZIndex = parseInt($(this).css("z-index"));
        if (currZIndex == maxZIndex)
          $(this).css("z-index", 1);
        else
          $(this).css("z-index", currZIndex + 1);
      });
    });
});
</script>
```

How it works...

The photo gallery works as follows:

1. On launching the page in the browser, the gallery displays the first image in the markup. After clicking on the previous or next button, it navigates to the required images, as shown in the following screenshot:

2. In the jQuery code, we assign a z-index construct to each image, ranging from 1 to the maximum number of images. The image with the highest z-index at any point in time will be displayed in the gallery. To do this, first determine the total number of images:

```
var maxZIndex = $("#container img").length;
```

Now assign a z-index to each image element by assigning the highest index to the first image and then decrementing by 1 for each element in the loop:

```
var tempZIndex = maxZIndex;
$("#container img").each(function () {
  $(this).css("z-index", tempZIndex);
  tempZIndex--;
});
```

3. An event handler is attached to the previous button for the click event, as follows:

```
$("#<%=btnPrevious.ClientID%>").on("click", function (evt) {…});
```

In this event handler, first of all, we prevent the page from posting back on the button click:

```
evt.preventDefault();
```

Then, the z-index of each image element is decreased by 1. If the z-index of any element has the lowest value, that is, 1, it is reset to the maximum value. This ensures that the images are displayed in a loop; when you click on the previous button, the first image will display the last image:

```
$("#container img").each(function () {
  var currZIndex = parseInt($(this).css("z-index"));
  if (currZIndex == 1)
    $(this).css("z-index", maxZIndex);
  else
    $(this).css("z-index", currZIndex-1);
});
```

4. An event handler is attached to the next button for the click event, as follows:

```
$("#<%=btnNext.ClientID%>").on("click", function (evt)
{…});
```

In this event handler, the page is first prevented from posting back:

```
evt.preventDefault();
```

The z-index of each image element is incremented by 1. If the z-index of an element has the maximum value, it is reset to 1. This ensures that when you click on the next button, the last image will display the first image:

```
$("#container img").each(function () {
  var currZIndex = parseInt($(this).css("z-index"));
  if (currZIndex == maxZIndex)
    $(this).css("z-index", 1);
  else
    $(this).css("z-index", currZIndex + 1);
});
```

See also

The *Building a photo gallery using the ImageMap control* recipe

Building a photo gallery using ImageMap control

Since photo galleries can be built using many different methods, let's make use of the ASP. NET ImageMap control in this recipe to build a gallery. The following table lists the summary of constructs used in this example:

Construct	Type	Description
$("#identifier")	jQuery selector	This selects an element based on its ID.
$("html_tag")	jQuery selector	This selects all elements with the specified HTML tag.
[attribute= "value"]	jQuery selector	This selects an element with the specified attribute equal to the "value" string.
click	jQuery event	This is fired when you click on an element. It corresponds to the JavaScript click event.
event. preventDefault()	jQuery method	This prevents the default action of the event from being triggered.
.hide()	jQuery method	This hides the matched elements.
.hover()	jQuery event binder	This binds event handlers for mouseover and mouseout events.
.on()	jQuery event binder	This attaches an event handler to the matched elements for one or more events.

Construct	Type	Description
`.prop(propertyName)` or `.prop(propertyName, value)`	jQuery method	This returns the value of the specified property for the first matched element or sets the value of the specified property for all matched elements.
`.show()`	jQuery method	This displays the matched elements.

Getting ready

Follow these steps to build a page with an ImageMap control:

1. Create a new **ASP.NET Web Application** project in Visual Studio using the **Empty** template and name it `Recipe5` (or any other suitable name).

2. Add a `Scripts` folder and include the jQuery library in the folder.

3. Add an `images` folder to the project. Add some sample images to the folder.

4. Create a web form and include the jQuery library on the form.

5. Go to **Toolbox | Standard**, add an `ImageMap` and two `Image` controls to the form. The `ImageMap` will be used for the display image in the photo gallery while the `Image` controls will be used to display the left and right direction arrows.

6. Define two rectangular hotspots on the `ImageMap` control with the dimension `50 * 58`, assuming that the image is of the dimension `680 * 425`. The position of the two hotspots is shown in the following image:

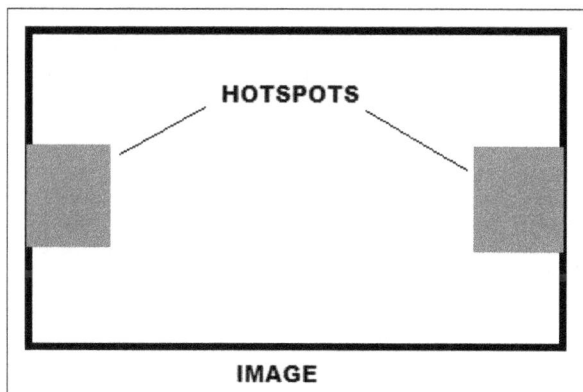

This can be done by adding the following markup to the `.aspx` page:

```
<div id="container">
   <asp:Image ID="imgPrevious" ImageUrl="~/images/Arrows-
Back-icon.png" runat="server" />
   <asp:Image ID="imgNext" ImageUrl="~/images/Arrows-
Forward-icon.png" runat="server" />
   <asp:ImageMap ID="imgMap" ImageUrl="~/images/image1.jpg"
runat="server">
      <asp:RectangleHotSpot HotSpotMode="NotSet" Left="0"
Right="50" Top="212" Bottom="270" AlternateText="Previous"
/>
      <asp:RectangleHotSpot HotSpotMode="NotSet" Left="630"
Right="680" Top="212" Bottom="270" AlternateText="Next" />
   </asp:ImageMap>
</div>
```

7. To set the dimensions and positions of the elements, include the following styles on the page:

```
<style type="text/css">
#container{
   position:relative;
}
#imgMap{
   width:680px;
   height:425px;
   position:absolute;
   top:0px;
   left:50px;
}
#imgPrevious{
   top:212px;
   left:0px;
   position:absolute;
   width:48px;
   height:48px;
}
#imgNext{
   top:212px;
   left:750px;
   position:absolute;
   width:48px;
   height:48px;
}
</style>
```

The `container div` is relatively positioned while all the other controls within this `div` are absolutely positioned.

8. On launching the browser, the page will display the first image in the gallery, as shown in the following screenshot. On mouseover on the hotspot on the left, the left direction arrow will appear:

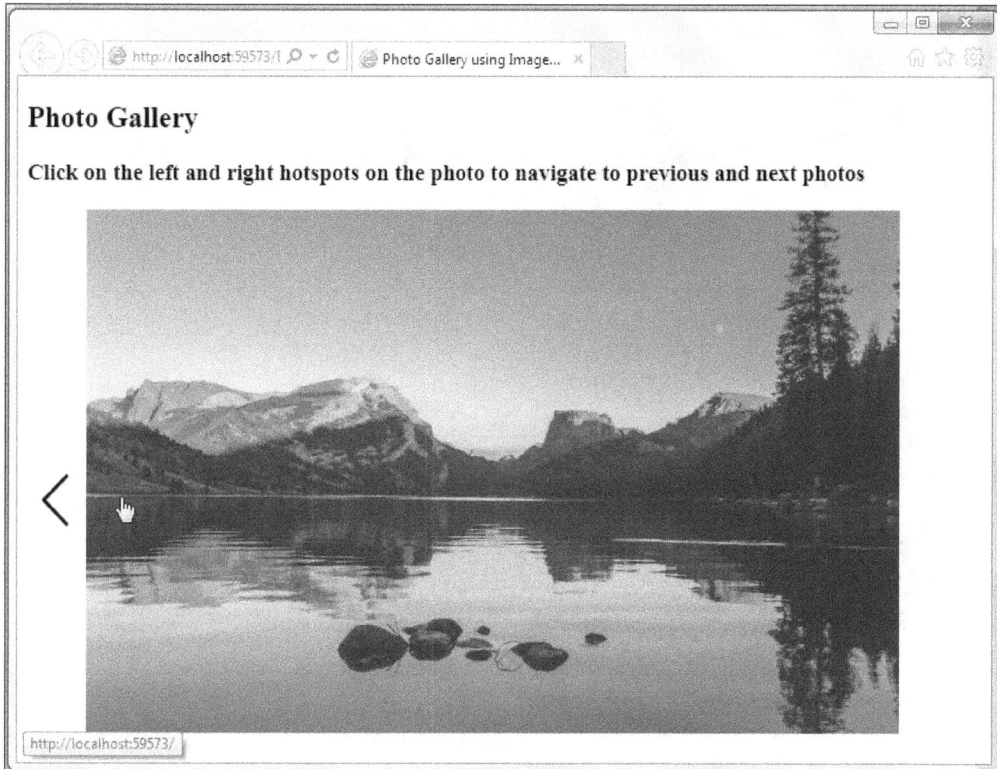

Similarly, on mouseover on the right hotspot, the right direction arrow will appear, as shown in the following screenshot:

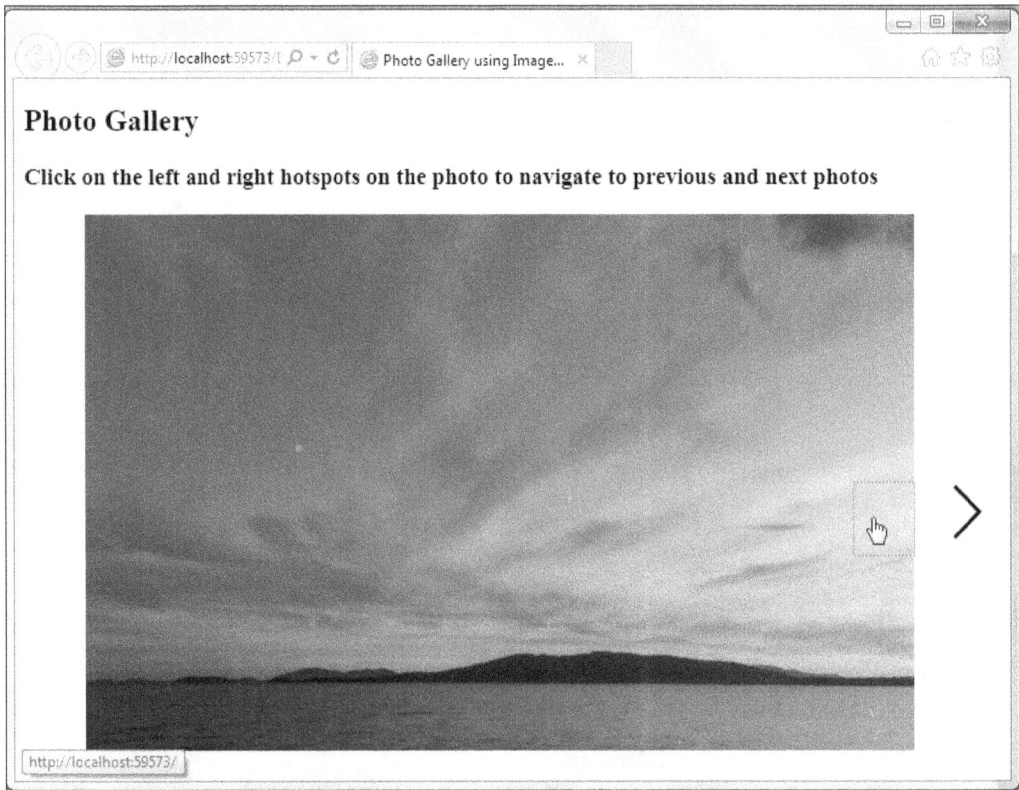

In the next section, we will add the jQuery code that will display the previous or next image after clicking on the respective hotspot.

How to do it...

Add the following jQuery code to a `<script>` block on the page:

```
<script type="text/javascript">
$(document).ready(function() {
  var imgArr = ["image1.jpg", "image2.jpg", "image3.jpg",
    "image4.jpg", "image5.jpg", "image6.jpg"
  ];
  var minIndex = 0;
  var maxIndex = imgArr.length - 1;
  var currIndex = 0;
  var basePath = "/images/";
```

```
$("#<%=imgPrevious.ClientID%>").hide();
$("#<%=imgNext.ClientID%>").hide();
$("map area[title='Previous'").hover(
  function() {
    $("#<%=imgPrevious.ClientID%>").show();
  },
  function() {
    $("#<%=imgPrevious.ClientID%>").hide();
  });
$("map area[title='Next'").hover(
  function() {
    $("#<%=imgNext.ClientID%>").show();
  },
  function() {
    $("#<%=imgNext.ClientID%>").hide();
  });
$("map area[title='Previous'").on("click", function(evt) {
  evt.preventDefault();
  if (currIndex == minIndex)
    currIndex = maxIndex;
  else
    currIndex--;
  var imgPath = basePath + imgArr[currIndex];
  $("#<%=imgMap.ClientID%>").prop("src", imgPath);
});
$("map area[title='Next'").on("click", function(evt) {
  evt.preventDefault();
  if (currIndex == maxIndex)
    currIndex = minIndex;
  else
    currIndex++;
  var imgPath = basePath + imgArr[currIndex];
  $("#<%=imgMap.ClientID%>").prop("src", imgPath);
});
});
</script>
```

How it works...

The image gallery works as follows:

1. In the jQuery code, define an array to store the names of all image files that are required to be displayed in the gallery:

   ```
   var imgArr = ["image1.jpg", "image2.jpg", "image3.jpg",
   "image4.jpg", "image5.jpg", "image6.jpg"];
   ```

The minimum and maximum index of this array is then initialized:

```
var minIndex = 0;
var maxIndex = imgArr.length - 1;
```

The current index, that is, the index of the image that is currently displayed in the gallery at any point of time, is initialized to 0:

```
var currIndex = 0;
```

2. Next, initialize the base path of the folder containing the display images:

```
var basePath = "/images/";
```

3. Hide the left and right arrows initially. These will only be displayed on mouseover on the respective hotspots:

```
$("#<%=imgPrevious.ClientID%>").hide();
$("#<%=imgNext.ClientID%>").hide();
```

4. Use the .hover() method to attach the mouseover and mouseout event handlers on the hotspots. At runtime, the ImageMap control is rendered as an img element and a map element, as shown in the following code:

```
<img id="imgMap" src="images/image1.jpg"
usemap="#ImageMapimgMap" />
<map name="ImageMapimgMap" id="ImageMapimgMap">
<area shape="rect" coords="0,212,50,270" href=""
title="Previous" alt="Previous" />
<area shape="rect" coords="630,212,680,270" href=""
title="Next" alt="Next" />
</map>
```

The hotspots can be distinguished using the title attribute. Thus, the left hotspot can be selected using $("map area[title='Previous']") and the right hotspot using $("map area[title='Next']").

Hence, the .hover() method can be used with the left hotspot to show/hide the left direction arrow, as follows:

```
$("map area[title='Previous']").hover(
  function () {
    $("#<%=imgPrevious.ClientID%>").show();
  },
  function () {
    $("#<%=imgPrevious.ClientID%>").hide();
  });
```

Similarly, it can be used with the right hotspot to show/hide the right direction arrow, as follows:

```
$("map area[title='Next']").hover(
  function () {
    $("#<%=imgNext.ClientID%>").show();
  },
  function () {
    $("#<%=imgNext.ClientID%>").hide();
});
```

In the preceding code, on mouseover, the required arrow image is displayed and on mouseout, it is hidden.

5. We also attach event handlers for the `click` event of the hotspots, as follows:

```
$("map area[title='Previous'").on("click", function (evt)
{…});
$("map area[title='Next'").on("click", function (evt) {…});
```

6. After clicking on the left hotspot, the previous image is displayed. In the `click` event handler for the left hotspot, first of all, the page is prevented from posting back using the following code:

```
evt.preventDefault();
```

To ensure that the images are displayed in a loop, if the display image is the first image, its previous image should be the last image in the array. Hence, the current index is updated, as follows:

```
if (currIndex == minIndex)
  currIndex = maxIndex;
```

For all the other display images, the current index is simply decremented by 1:

```
else
  currIndex--;
```

The image path is then built using the base path:

```
var imgPath = basePath + imgArr[currIndex];
```

The source property of the image control is then set to the preceding path:

```
$("#<%=imgMap.ClientID%>").prop("src",imgPath);
```

7. After clicking on the right hotspot, the next image is displayed. In the `click` event handler for the right hotspot, first of all, the page is prevented from posting back using this code:

```
evt.preventDefault();
```

If the display image is the last image, its next image should be the first image in the array in order to ensure that the images are displayed in a loop. Hence, the current index is updated, as follows:

```
if (currIndex == maxIndex)
    currIndex = minIndex;
```

For all the other display images, the current index is simply incremented by 1:

```
else
    currIndex++;
```

The image path is then built using the base path:

```
var imgPath = basePath + imgArr[currIndex];
```

The source property of the image control is then set to the preceding path:

```
$("#<%=imgMap.ClientID%>").prop("src",imgPath);
```

This enables navigation of the images in a loop in the forward or reverse direction as required.

See also

The *Building a photo gallery using the z-index property* recipe

Using images to create effects in the Menu control

In *Chapter 5, Visual Effects in ASP.NET Sites*, we have seen how the ASP.NET Menu control can be animated using the fade and other CSS effects were explored. In this example, let's use images instead of text for the main menu and submenu items in the Menu control. These images will be updated on `mouseover` and `mouseout` events. The constructs used in this example are summarized as follows:

Construct	Type	Description
`$(".class")`	jQuery selector	This matches all elements with the specified CSS class.
`$("html_tag")`	jQuery selector	This selects all elements with the specified HTML tag.
`$(this)`	jQuery object	This refers to the current jQuery object.
`.indexOf (searchString, [startIndex])`	JavaScript function	This returns the index of the first occurrence of the `searchString` within the given string starting at the `startIndex` position (optional).
`mouseout`	jQuery event	This is fired when the mouse pointer leaves a control. It corresponds to the JavaScript `mouseout` event.
`mouseover`	jQuery event	This is fired when the mouse pointer enters a control. It corresponds to the JavaScript `mouseover` event.
`.on()`	jQuery event binder	This attaches an event handler to the matched elements for one or more events.
`.prop(propertyName)` or `.prop(propertyName, value)`	jQuery method	This returns the value of the specified property for the first matched element or sets the value of the specified property for all matched elements.
`.replace(subString, newString)`	JavaScript function	This replaces all occurrences of `subString` with `newString`.
`.substring(startIndex, [endIndex])`	JavaScript function	This returns a substring of a given string from `startIndex` to `endIndex` or to the end of the string.

Getting ready

Let's build a page to use images to create the effects in the Menu control:

1. In this example, let's recreate the menu, as described in *Chapter 5*, *Visual Effects in ASP.NET Sites* in the *Animating the Menu control* recipe, but this time, using images instead of text. Let's start by creating an **ASP.NET Web Application** project in Visual Studio using the **Empty** template and name it `Recipe6` (or any other suitable name).

2. Add the jQuery library to a `Scripts` folder in the project.

3. Add an `images` folder and include images for the main menu and submenu items in this folder. Also, add the mouseover images for the respective menu items to this folder. The convention that we will use to name the mouseover images is `*_mouseover.png`. For example, if an image is named `Home.png`, its mouseover image will be named `Home_mouseover.png`.

4. Add a new web form and include the jQuery library on the form.

5. Drag and drop a **Menu** control by navigating to the **Toolbox | Navigation** section.

6. Add the following markup to the form:

```
<div id="container">
  <asp:Menu ID="Menu1" runat="server"
Orientation="Horizontal">
    <Items>
      <asp:MenuItem ImageUrl="~/images/Home.png"></asp:MenuItem>
      <asp:MenuItem ImageUrl="~/images/UserAccounts.png">
        <asp:MenuItem ImageUrl="~/images/UserAccounts_1.png"></
asp:MenuItem>
        <asp:MenuItem ImageUrl="~/images/UserAccounts_2.png"></
asp:MenuItem>
        <asp:MenuItem ImageUrl="~/images/UserAccounts_3.png"></
asp:MenuItem>
      </asp:MenuItem>
      <asp:MenuItem ImageUrl="~/images/Reports.png">
        <asp:MenuItem ImageUrl="~/images/Reports_1.png"></
asp:MenuItem>
        <asp:MenuItem ImageUrl="~/images/Reports_2.png"></
asp:MenuItem>
        <asp:MenuItem ImageUrl="~/images/Reports_3.png"></
asp:MenuItem>
      </asp:MenuItem>
      <asp:MenuItem ImageUrl="~/images/Settings.png">
        <asp:MenuItem ImageUrl="~/images/Settings_1.png"></
asp:MenuItem>
        <asp:MenuItem ImageUrl="~/images/Settings_2.png"></
asp:MenuItem>
      </asp:MenuItem>
    </Items>
  </asp:Menu>
</div>
```

7. The `container` div area is given a background color using the following style:

```
#container{
  background-color:lightgray;
}
```

8. The ASP.NET engine renders the main menu items with a CSS class called `level1` at runtime. Add the following styles to this class:

```
#Menu1 .level1{
   padding:0px;
   margin:0px;
}
```

> Note that the submenu items are rendered with a CSS class called `level2`.

9. Now, we will use jQuery to update the main menu image on `mouseover`, as shown in the following screenshot. On `mouseout`, the image is restored to the original one.

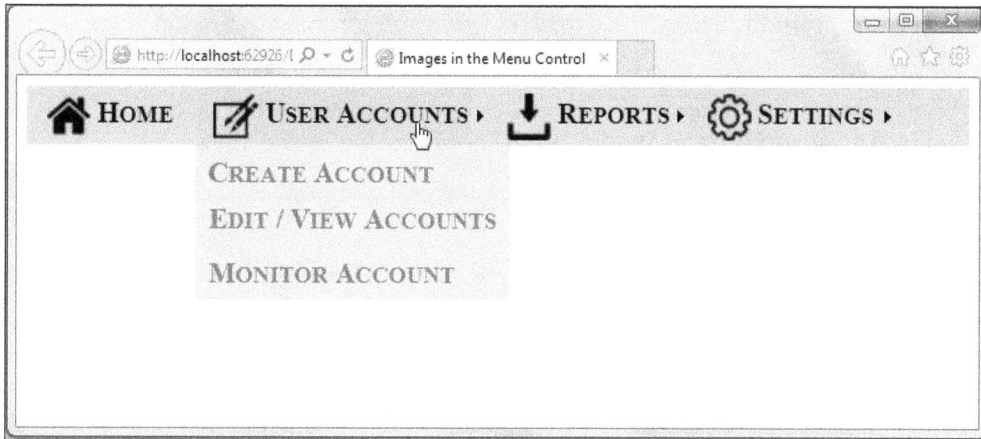

Similarly, on `mouseover` on any submenu item, the respective image is updated, as shown in the following screenshot:

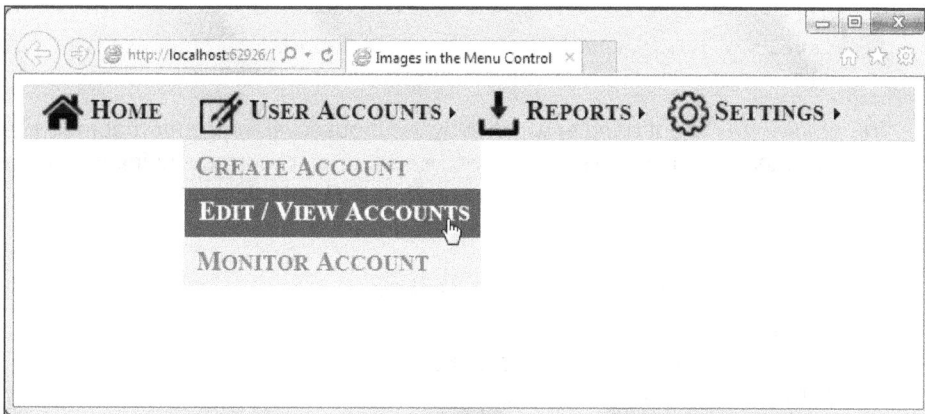

On `mouseout`, the image is restored to the original one thus creating the required visual effect on the menu items.

How to do it...

Add the following jQuery code to a `<script>` block on the page:

```
<script type="text/javascript">
$(document).ready(function() {
  $(".level1 a img, .level2 a img").on("mouseover", function() var
imageSource = $(this).prop("src");
    var pos = imageSource.indexOf(".");
    var strFileExt = imageSource.substring(pos, imageSource.length);
imageSource = imageSource.replace(strFileExt,
"_mouseover" + strFileExt); $(this).prop("src", imageSource);
  }); $(".level1 a img, .level2 a img").on("mouseout", function()
{
  var imageSource = $(this).prop("src");
  imageSource = imageSource.replace("_mouseover", "");
  $(this).prop("src", imageSource);
});
});
</script>
```

How it works...

The effect on the Menu control works as follows:

1. At runtime, the Menu control renders the main menu items with the `level1` CSS class and submenu items with the `level2` CSS class. Thus, we bind event handlers for the `mouseover` and `mouseout` events for the `level1` and `level2` hyperlinked images, as follows:

   ```
   $(".level1 a img, .level2 a img").on("mouseover", function
   () {...});
   $(".level1 a img, .level2 a img").on("mouseout", function
   () {...});
   ```

2. The `mouseover` event handler will display the mouseover image for that menu item. Assuming that when an image is named `image.png`, its corresponding mouseover image will be `image_mouseover.png`, and we first get the image source:

   ```
   var imageSource = $(this).prop("src");
   ```

   Then, determine the file extension of the image:

   ```
   var pos = imageSource.indexOf(".");
   var strFileExt = imageSource.substring(pos,
   imageSource.length);
   ```

Replace the original file extension with the `_mouseover` string followed by the respective file extension. For example, if the file extension is `.png`, then it is replaced by `_mouseover.png` in the image source string:

```
imageSource = imageSource.replace(strFileExt, "_mouseover"
+ strFileExt);
```

Now, replace the image source with this updated image source:

```
$(this).prop("src", imageSource);
```

3. When the mouse pointer moves out from the image, get the source of the image using the `.prop()` method as follows:

```
var imageSource = $(this).prop("src");
```

Replace the `_mouseover` string with an empty string:

```
imageSource = imageSource.replace("_mouseover", "");
```

Update the image source once again using the `prop()` method:

```
$(this).prop("src", imageSource);
```

See also

The *Previewing image uploads in MVC* recipe

Creating a 5 star rating control

A 5 star rating control is a useful feature when you need to review an item, such as a book, movie, product, and so on. In this example, let's use jQuery to create this application as an ASP.NET User Control. The constructs used in this example are as follows:

Construct	Type	Description
`$("#identifier")`	jQuery selector	This selects an element based on its ID.
`$("html_tag")`	jQuery selector	This selects all elements with the specified HTML tag.
`$(this)`	jQuery object	This refers to the current jQuery object.
`[attribute$="value"]`	jQuery selector	This selects an element with the specified attribute ending with the `"value"` string.
`click`	jQuery event	This is fired when you click on an element. It corresponds to the JavaScript `click` event.

Construct	Type	Description
`.indexOf (searchString, [startIndex])`	JavaScript function	This returns the index of the first occurrence of the `searchString` within the given string starting at the `startIndex` position (optional).
`.length`	jQuery property	This returns the number of elements in the jQuery object.
`.nextAll()`	jQuery method	This gets all the succeeding siblings of the matched elements. A selector can be provided optionally.
`.on()`	jQuery event binder	This attaches an event handler to the matched elements for one or more events.
`.prevAll()`	jQuery method	This gets all the previous siblings of the matched elements. A selector can be provided optionally.
`.prop(propertyName)` or `.prop(propertyName, value)`	jQuery method	This returns the value of the specified property for the first matched element or sets the value of the specified property for all matched elements.
`.text()`	jQuery method	This returns the combined text content of each of the matched elements or sets the text content of every matched element.

Getting ready

Follow these steps to create a page with a 5 star rating control:

1. Let's create a page consisting of five star images arranged in a row. When the stars are unselected, they appear in a grey background, as shown in the following screenshot:

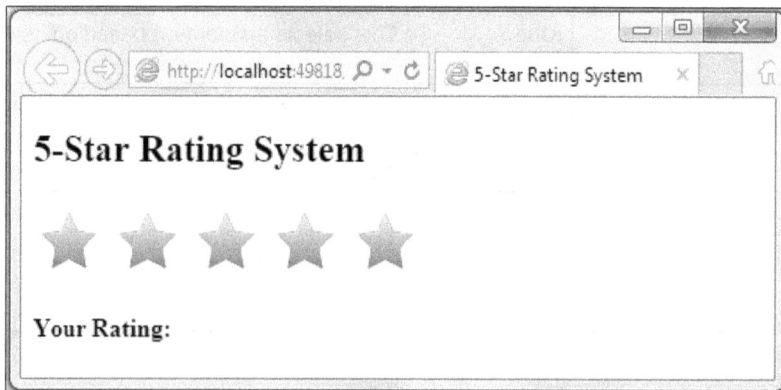

After clicking on a particular star, all the star images until the clicked image are selected and appear in a golden background. For example, if we click on the fourth star, the first four stars will light up and show a rating of 4, as shown in the following screenshot:

Now, if you click on the first star, starting in the reverse direction, all the stars until the first star will switch off and show a rating of 1, as shown in the following screenshot:

2. To create this application, launch an **ASP.NET Web Application** project in Visual Studio using the **Empty** template and name it `Recipe7` (or any other suitable name).

3. Add the jQuery library to the `Scripts` folder in the project.

4. Add an `images` folder to the project. Include the two types of images in this folder, that is, a star image with a grey background and a star image with a golden background.

5. Add a web form to the project and include the jQuery library on the form.

6. Since we want to create the 5-star rating system as a standalone control, add a `Controls` folder to the project. Now, right-click on this folder in the **Solution Explorer** tab and go to **Add | New Item**. From the dialog box that is launched, select **Web Forms User Control** and name the control `RatingControl.acsx`, as shown in the following screenshot. Click on the **Add** button.

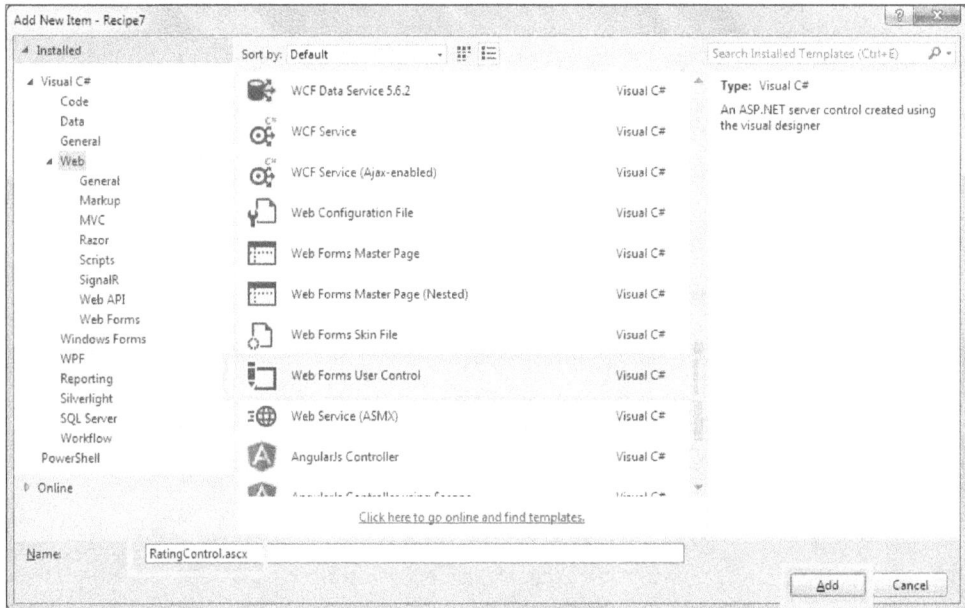

7. Open the `RatingControl` control in the **Source** mode. Go to **Toolbox | Standard**, drag and drop a `Panel` control on the user control. Drag and drop five `Image` controls inside the `Panel` control. Also, add two `Label` controls below the `Panel` control to display the current rating. This will create the following markup in the user control:

```
<asp:Panel ID="pnlImgContainer" runat="server">
  <asp:Image ID="imgStar1" runat="server"
ImageUrl="~/images/star_grey.png" />
  <asp:Image ID="imgStar2" runat="server"
ImageUrl="~/images/star_grey.png" />
  <asp:Image ID="imgStar3" runat="server"
ImageUrl="~/images/star_grey.png" />
  <asp:Image ID="imgStar4" runat="server"
ImageUrl="~/images/star_grey.png" />
  <asp:Image ID="imgStar5" runat="server"
ImageUrl="~/images/star_grey.png" />
</asp:Panel><br />
<asp:Label ID="lblLabel" runat="server" Text="Your Rating:
" AssociatedControlID="lblStarRating" Font-Bold="True"></
asp:Label>
<asp:Label ID="lblStarRating" runat="server"></asp:Label>
```

8. Register the user control by adding the following code to the `web.config` file in the `system.web` node:

```
<pages>
<controls>
<add tagPrefix="uc1" tagName="RatingControl"
src="~/Controls/RatingControl.ascx"/>
</controls>
</pages>
```

9. Now, open the web form in the Design or Source mode, and drag and drop the **RatingControl** control on the form area. This will add the following markup to the web form:

```
<uc1:RatingControl runat="server" id="RatingControl" />
```

Also, note that the following `@Register` directive is added to the page:

```
<%@ Register Src="~/Controls/RatingControl.ascx"
TagPrefix="uc1" TagName="RatingControl" %>
```

How to do it...

Add the following jQuery code to a `<script>` block on the user control after the `@Control` directive:

```
<script type="text/javascript">
$(document).ready(function() {
  var BasePath = "images/";
  var greyImg = "star_grey.png";
  var goldImg = "star_golden.png";
  $("#<%=pnlImgContainer.ClientID%> img").on("click",
    function() {
       if ($(this).prop("src").indexOf(greyImg) > -1) {
         $(this).prop("src", BasePath + goldImg);
         $(this).prevAll("img").prop("src", BasePath + goldImg);
       } else {
         $(this).prop("src", BasePath + greyImg);
         $(this).nextAll("img").prop("src", BasePath + greyImg);
       }
       var rating = $("# <%=pnlImgContainer.ClientID%> img[src$='"
+ goldImg + "']").length;
       $("#<%=lblStarRating.ClientID%>").text(rating);
    });
});
</script>
```

How it works...

The 5 star rating control is designed as follows:

1. In the jQuery code, set the base path of the images as well as the respective image names for the on (a golden background) and off (a grey background) images:

```
var BasePath = "images/";
var greyImg = "star_grey.png";
var goldImg = "star_golden.png";
```

2. Attach a click event handler to each image in the container panel, as follows:

```
$("#<%=pnlImgContainer.ClientID%> img").on("click",
function () {…});
```

3. In the preceding handler, determine whether the clicked image is the grey background image, as follows:

```
if ($(this).prop("src").indexOf(greyImg) > -1)
```

4. If the preceding condition is `true`, then update the clicked image to display the golden background image, as follows:

```
$(this).prop("src", BasePath + goldImg);
```

    At the same time, change all the preceding images to the golden background image as well:

```
$(this).prevAll("img").prop("src", BasePath + goldImg);
```

5. If the condition in step 3 is `false`, update the clicked image to display the grey background image, as follows:

```
$(this).prop("src", BasePath + greyImg);
```

    At the same time, change all the succeeding images to a grey background image as well:

```
$(this).nextAll("img").prop("src", BasePath + greyImg);
```

6. Determine the rating by counting the number of golden stars using the source property of each Image control:

```
var rating = $("# <%=pnlImgContainer.ClientID%> img[src$='"
+ goldImg + "']").length;
```

    Display this rating in the Label control on the page:

```
$("#<%=lblStarRating.ClientID%>").text(rating);
```

Since the rating control is implemented as an independent user control, multiple instances of it can be added to the web form. So, drag and drop another instance on the form so that there are two such controls on the page:

```
<uc1:RatingControl runat="server" id="RatingControl" />
<uc1:RatingControl runat="server" id="RatingControl2" />
```

The page will now display the two standalone controls, as shown in the following screenshot. Each control can be used independently of the other.

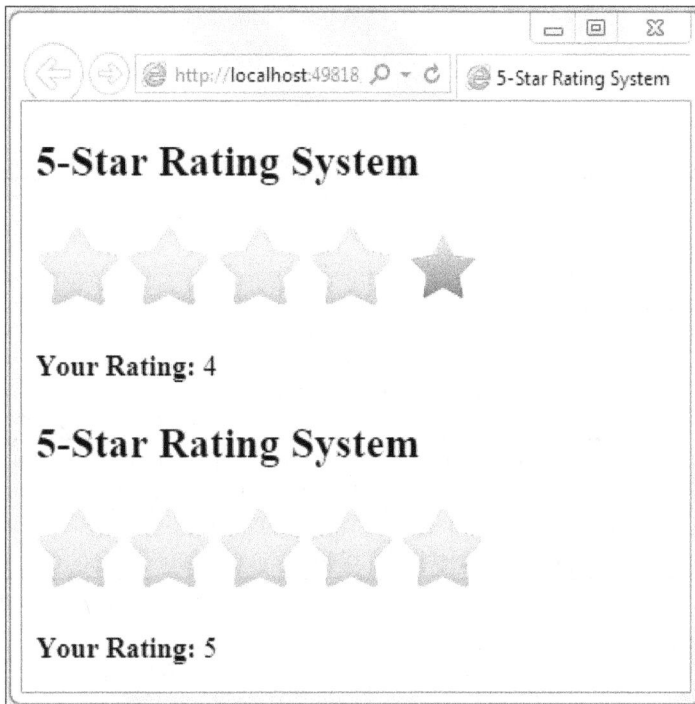

See also

The *Previewing image uploads in MVC* recipe

Previewing image uploads in MVC

In this example, let's create an MVC application that can preview images using a client script prior to uploading it on the server. Note that this recipe only covers the client script, and the server code for the upload is not dealt with. The following table shows a quick summary of the constructs used in this example:

Construct	Type	Description
`$("#identifier")`	jQuery selector	This selects an element based on its ID.
`.attr("name")` OR `.attr("name", "value")`	jQuery method	This returns a string with the required attribute value of a matched element. It can also be used to set the attribute to the required value.
`change`	jQuery event	This is fired when the value of an element changes. It corresponds to the JavaScript `change` event.
`FileReader.onloadend`	Event handler provided by the FileReader interface	This defines the event handler for the `loadend` event. It is executed each time the event is completed.
`FileReader.readAsDataUrl()`	Method provided by the FileReader interface	This reads the contents of a file or blob (a file-like object of immutable, raw data). After the reading is completed, the result attribute returns a URL of the read file data.
`FileUpload.files`	FileList object	The selected files from the file upload element that is returned as a `FileList` object.
`FileUpload.files.length`	Property of the FileList object	This is the number of files in the `FileList` object.
`FileUpload.file.type`	Property of the FileList object	This returns the file type for the given file object.
`.match(regexp)`	JavaScript function	This matches a string against a regular expression.
`.on()`	jQuery event binder	This attaches an event handler for one or more events to the matched elements.
`window.File`	Interface provided by the File API	This provides informational attributes of a file such as a name, last modified date, and so on.
`window.FileReader`	Interface provided by the File API	This enables reading the contents of a file or blob (a file-like object of immutable, raw data).

Follow these steps to build an MVC application for an image preview:

1. Let's create an MVC application with an image preview area and file upload control, as shown in the following screenshot:

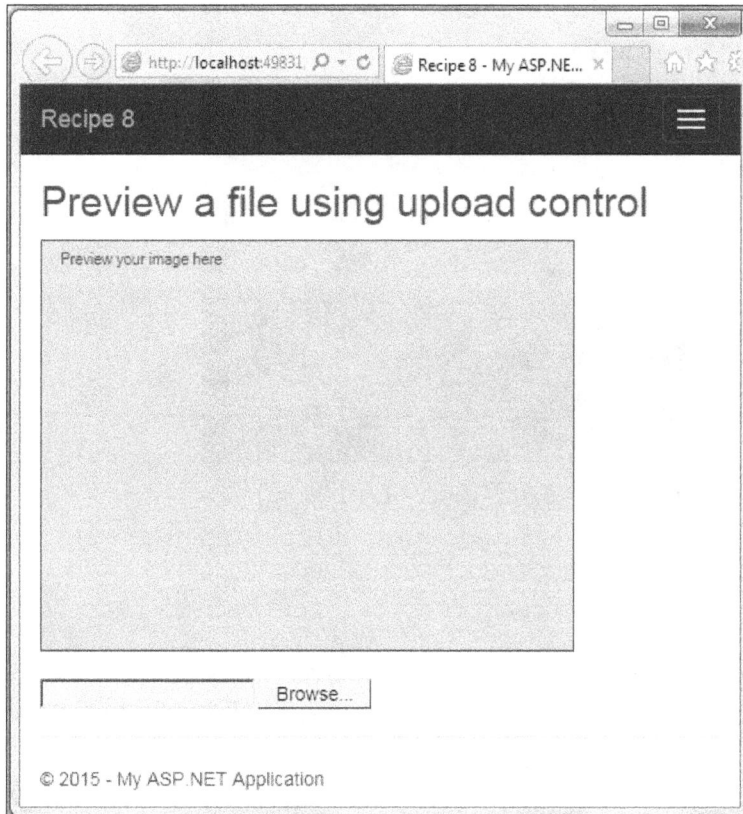

2. On browsing and selecting an image file, a preview of the image can be seen in the shaded area on the page, as shown in the following screenshot:

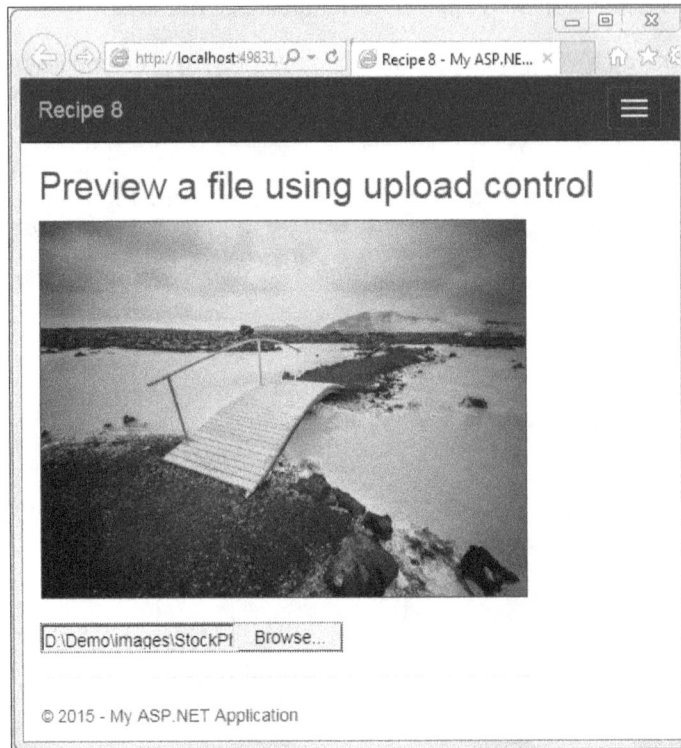

3. To create the preceding page, launch a new **ASP.NET Web Application** project in Visual Studio. Select the **Empty** template and ensure that the **MVC** checkbox is selected, as shown in the following screenshot. Name the application Recipe8 (or any other suitable name).

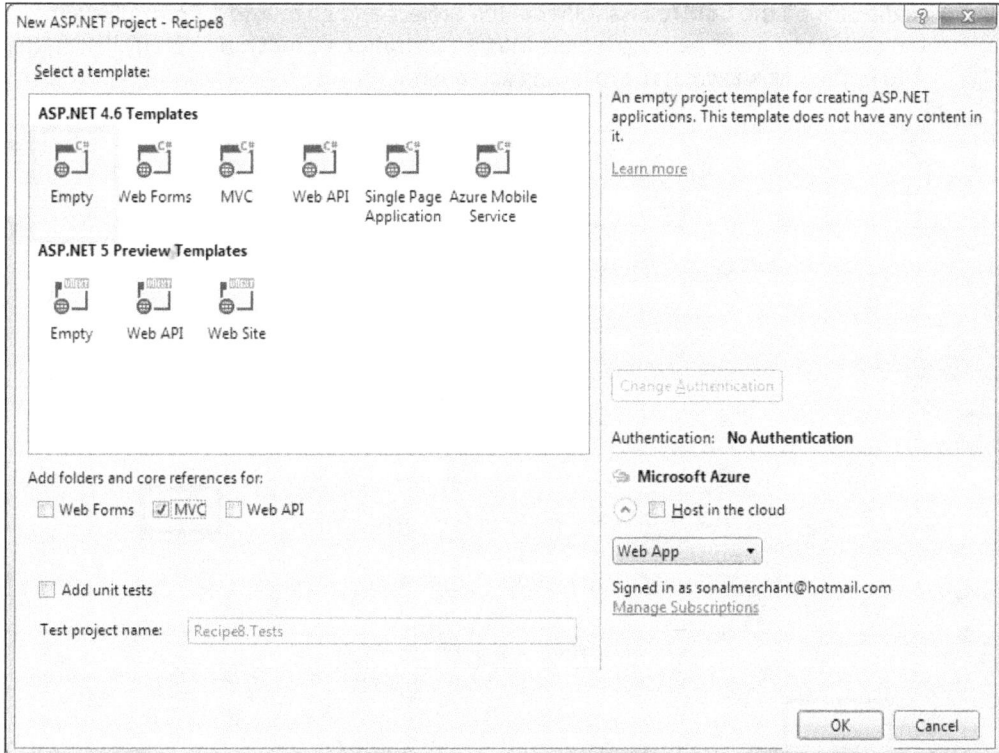

4. ASP.NET automatically adds a `Scripts` folder to the MVC project with the jQuery library files. You can retain these files or replace them with the latest version.

5. Right-click on the **Controllers** folder in the project and go to **Add | Controller**. From the dialog box that opens up, select **MVC5 Controller – Empty,** and then click on the **Add** button, as shown in the following screenshot:

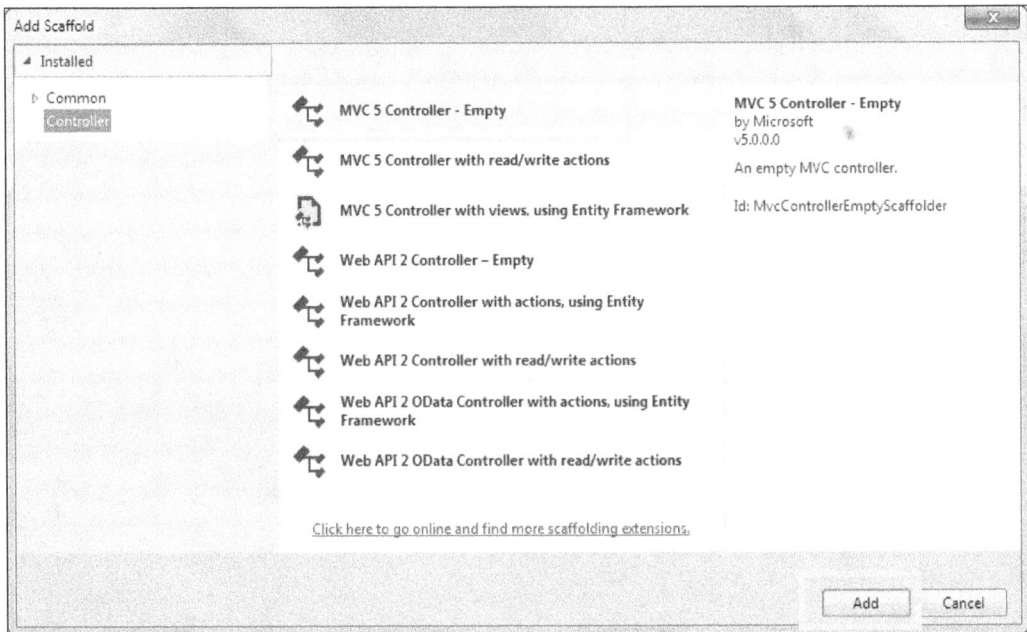

6. Name the controller `DefaultController`. By default, Visual Studio adds the `Index ActionResult` to the controller.

7. In the **Solution Explorer** tab, right-click by navigating to **Views | Default** and go to **Add | View**. Enter `Index` for the **View name**, and click on the **Add** button on the **Add View** dialog box, as shown in the following screenshot. Note that the **Template** selected is **Empty (without model)**:

Add View

View **n**ame:	Index
Template:	Empty (without model) ▾
Model class:	▾

Options:

☐ **C**reate as a partial view

☐ **R**eference script libraries

☑ **U**se a layout page:

|_____| [...]

(Leave empty if it is set in a Razor _viewstart file)

            [Add] [Cancel]

8. Add an image element and a file upload element to the View. Also, include the jQuery library. Thus, the markup of the View will be as follows:

```html
<h2>Preview a file using upload control</h2>
<script src="~/Scripts/jquery-2.1.4.js"></script>
<div>
<img id="imgPreview" alt="Preview your image here"
width="400" height="300" /><br/><br/>
<input type="file" id="FileUpload1" />
</div>
```

9. Include a background color for the preceding image element by adding the following style:

```css
<style type="text/css">
#imgPreview{
   background-color:lightgray;
   border-width:1px;
   border-style:solid;
}
</style>
```

How to do it...

Add the following jQuery code to a `<script>` block on the View:

```
<script type="text/javascript">
$(document).ready(function() {
  $("#FileUpload1").on("change", function() {
    if (this.files.length == 0) {
      alert("No image is selected");
      return;
    }
    if (!window.File || !window.FileReader) {
      alert("File API is not supported in this browser");
      return;
    }
    if (this.files[0].type.match("image.*")) {
      var reader = new FileReader();
      reader.readAsDataURL(this.files[0]);
      reader.onloadend = function() {
        $("#imgPreview").attr("src", this.result);
      }
    }
  });
});
</script>
```

How it works...

The image preview works as follows:

1. To run the application, in the **Solution Explorer** tab, right-click by navigating to **Views | Default | Index.cshtml**, and click on **View in Browser (Internet Explorer)**. After successfully loading the page in the browser, browse the image file required to be uploaded. The page will display the image in the preview area.

2. This is accomplished by attaching an event hander for the `change` event of the file upload control, as follows:

    ```
    $("#FileUpload1").on("change", function () {…});
    ```

    This event is triggered each time a file is browsed and selected in the file upload control.

3. In the preceding handler, firstly, we check whether the file upload control returns an empty object, as follows:

```
if (this.files.length == 0) {
  alert("No image is selected");
  return;
}
```

4. Secondly, we also need to verify that the browser supports the `File API` or not. This can be done using the following checks:

```
if (!window.File || !window.FileReader) {
  alert("File API is not supported in this browser");
  return;
}
```

5. Next, check whether the selected file is an image or not using a regular expression on the file type:

```
if (this.files[0].type.match("image.*"))
```

> Since the file upload element returns a `FileList` object, we can select the first file using `index 0`, that is, `files[0]`. We then match the regular expression `image.*` on the file type to filter only image files.

If the selected file is an image file, create a `FileReader` object to read the file:

```
var reader = new FileReader();
```

Now, using the `FileReader` object, read the contents of the file:

```
reader.readAsDataURL(this.files[0]);
```

Write the event handler for the `loadend` event. This will be executed when the file has been read completely:

```
reader.onloadend = function () {…}
```

In the preceding `loadend` event handler, since the result attribute contains the URL of the file data, we can set the source attribute of the image element to this URL, as follows:

```
$("#imgPreview").attr("src", this.result);
```

See also

The *Using images to create effects in the Menu control* recipe

7

Ajax Using jQuery

This chapter demonstrates the use of jQuery to post asynchronous requests using Ajax. The list of recipes covered is as follows:

- ▶ Setting up Ajax with ASP.NET using jQuery
- ▶ Consuming page methods
- ▶ Consuming Web services
- ▶ Consuming WCF services
- ▶ Retrieving data from a Web API
- ▶ Making Ajax calls to a controller action
- ▶ Making Ajax calls to a HTTP handler

Introduction

AJAX (Asynchronous JavaScript and XML) is a term coined by Jesse James Garrett of Adaptive Path. It stands for a combination of different technologies that help you communicate seamlessly with the server without the need for a page refresh. Ajax applications involve the following technologies:

- ▶ JavaScript for running the core Ajax engine
- ▶ The `XmlHttpRequest` object to communicate with the server
- ▶ A web presentation using HTML and CSS or XSLT
- ▶ DOM to work with the HTML structure
- ▶ XML and JSON for data interchange

The `XmlHttpRequest` object is used to post HTTP/HTTPS requests to the server. Most modern browsers have a built-in `XmlHttpRequest` object.

> **JSON** (**JavaScript Object Notation**) is a lightweight data interchange format and is increasingly used in Ajax applications. It is basically a collection of name/value pairs and can be used with different data types, such as a string, number, Boolean, arrays, and objects.

In a typical web application, the client submits data to the server for processing and the server sends back the refreshed content to the client. This causes a visible page refresh, and the user needs to wait for a page reload before there is any further interaction with the page. This flow of request/response is demonstrated in the following figure:

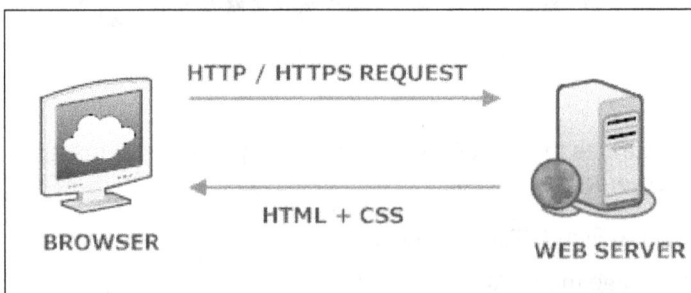

Ajax provides a new paradigm for communication between the browser and the server. Using Ajax, parts of a web page can be updated without sending the entire page to the server. By communicating behind the scenes, the need for an explicit page refresh is eliminated. The user can continue to work with the web page without having to wait for a response from the server, as demonstrated in the following figure:

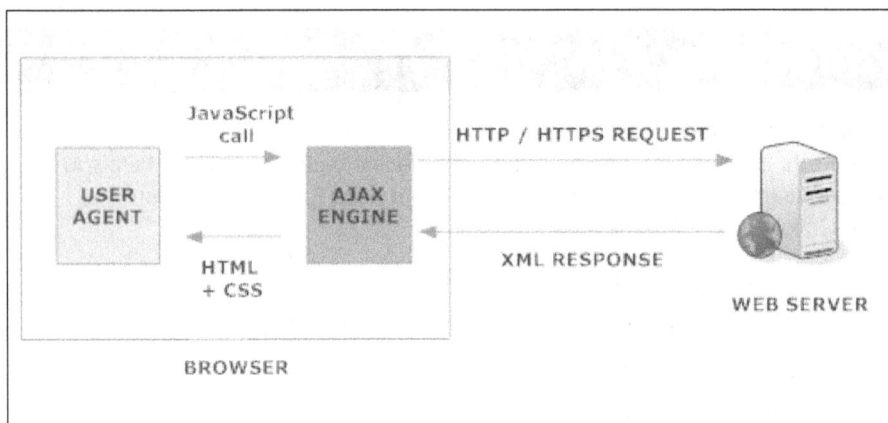

In Ajax-based applications, a JavaScript call is made to the Ajax engine that uses the `XmlHttpRequest` object to send the request asynchronously to the server. As a result, the backend communication becomes transparent and the users' interaction with the application is not interrupted. This enhances the interactivity of the page; thus improving the users' experience. At the same time, the performance and speed of the page is improved.

The jQuery library provides many methods for working with Ajax. In this chapter, we will explore the use of the following methods:

- `$.ajaxSetup(options)`: This method can be used to define default settings for making Ajax calls on the page. The setup is done at one time and all the subsequent Ajax calls on the page are made using these default settings.

- `$.ajax(settings)`: This is a generic low-level function that helps you create any type of Ajax request. There are a number of configuration settings that can be applied using this function such as the type of HTTP request (`GET`/`POST`/`PUT`/`DELETE`), the request URL, parameters to be sent to the server, data type of the response, as well as the callback functions to be executed on the successful/unsuccessful invocation of the Ajax call.

- `$("...").load()`: This is a shortcut method used to load text or HTML content from the server and display it in the matched elements.

- `$.getJSON()`: This method posts an HTTP `GET` request to the server. The data is returned in the JSON format.

> The data type of the response received from the server can be text, HTML, XML, JSON, or JSONP. Under the hood, the shortcut methods use the `$.ajax()` method to post requests to the server.

Setting up Ajax with ASP.NET using jQuery

This recipe demonstrates the use of the `$.ajaxSetup()` function to configure global settings for making Ajax calls on a web page. These settings will be used across multiple Ajax calls. The constructs used in this example are summarized in the following table:

Construct	Type	Description
`$("#identifier")`	jQuery selector	This selects an element based on its ID
`$.ajax()`	jQuery function	This posts an Ajax request to the server with the set options.
`$.ajaxSetup()`	jQuery function	This sets up default values for Ajax requests.
`.append()`	jQuery method	This inserts content at the end of each matched element.

Construct	Type	Description
`click`	jQuery event	This is fired when you click on an element. It corresponds to the JavaScript `click` event.
`.each()`	jQuery method	This iterates over the matched elements and executes a function for each element.
`event. preventDefault()`	jQuery method	This prevents the default action of the event from being triggered.
`.find()`	jQuery method	This finds all elements that match the filter.
`.html()`	jQuery method	This returns the HTML content of the first matched element or sets the HTML content of every matched element.
`.load()`	jQuery method	This loads text or HTML data from the server and displays it in the matched element.
`.on()`	jQuery event binder	This attaches an event handler for one or more events to the matched elements.
`.text()`	jQuery method	This returns the combined text content of each of the matched elements or sets the text content of every matched element.

Getting ready

Follow these steps to setup Ajax with ASP.NET using jQuery:

1. Let's create a web page that triggers Ajax calls to retrieve the HTML and XML data, respectively. On loading, the page will display a `Button` control, as shown in the following screenshot:

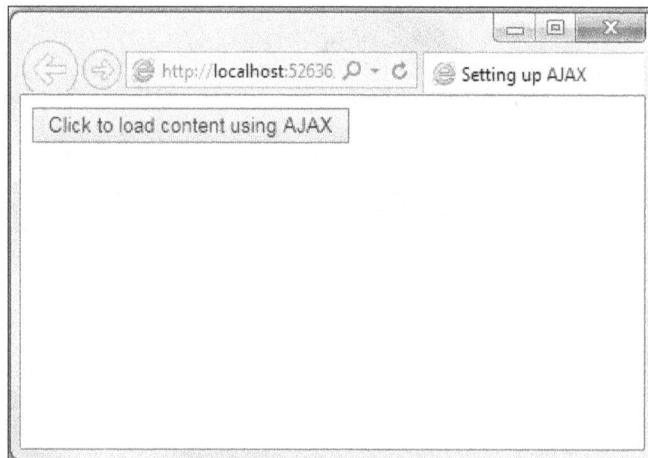

After clicking on the `Button` control, the page will retrieve the contents from the respective sources and display them on the page in the following format:

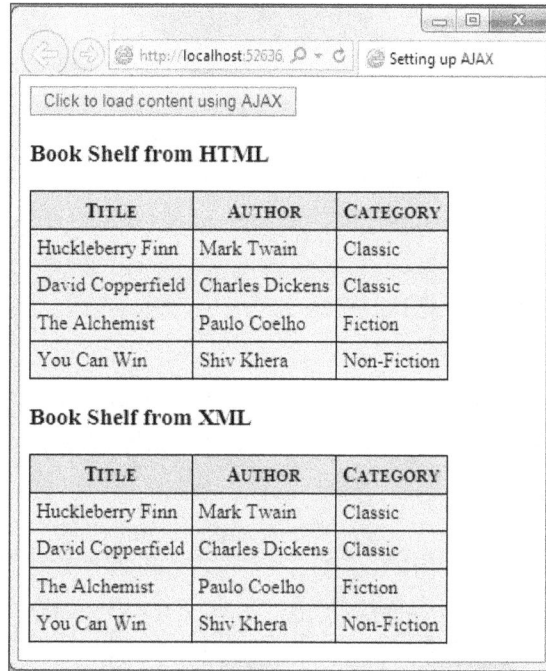

2. To create this page, launch an **ASP.NET Web Application** project in Visual Studio using the **Empty** template and name it `Recipe1` (or any other suitable name).

3. Add the jQuery library to the project in a `Scripts` folder.

4. Add a web form to the project and include the jQuery library in the form.

5. Next, we will create an HTML file containing some test data. To do this, right-click on the project in the **Solution Explorer** tab and go to **Add | New Item**. From the **Installed templates** section in the dialog box, go to **Web | HTML Page**. Name the file, `Sample.html`. Add the following content to this HTML file:

```html
<!DOCTYPE html>
<html>
  <head>
    <title></title>
    <meta charset="utf-8" />
  </head>
  <body>
    <h3>Book Shelf from HTML</h3>
    <table>
      <tr>
```

```
        <th>Title</th><th>Author</th><th>Category</th>
      </tr>
      <tr>
        <td>Huckleberry Finn</td><td>Mark
Twain</td><td>Classic</td>
      </tr>
      <tr>
        <td>David Copperfield</td><td>Charles
Dickens</td><td>Classic</td>
      </tr>
      <tr>
        <td>The Alchemist</td><td>Paulo
Coelho</td><td>Fiction</td>
      </tr>
      <tr>
        <td>You Can Win</td><td>Shiv Khera</td><td>Non-
Fiction</td>
      </tr>
    </table>
  </body>
</html>
```

6. Add an XML file to the project by right-clicking on the project in the **Solution Explorer** tab and navigating to **Add | New Item**. From the dialog box, which is displayed, go to **Data | XML File** from the **Installed templates** section. Name the file `Sample.xml` and include the following content in the file:

```
<?xml version="1.0" encoding="utf-8" ?>
<BookShelf>
  <Book>
    <Title>Huckleberry Finn</Title>
    <Author>Mark Twain</Author>
    <Category>Classic</Category>
  </Book>
  <Book>
    <Title>David Copperfield</Title>
    <Author>Charles Dickens</Author>
    <Category>Classic</Category>
  </Book>
  <Book>
    <Title>The Alchemist</Title>
    <Author>Paulo Coelho</Author>
    <Category>Fiction</Category>
  </Book>
  <Book>
    <Title>You Can Win</Title>
```

```
    <Author>Shiv Khera</Author>
    <Category>Non-Fiction</Category>
  </Book>
</BookShelf>
```

7. Add a `Button` control to the form along with two empty `div` elements: one to display the HTML content and the other to display the XML content. Thus, the markup of the form will be as follows:

```
<asp:Button ID="btnLoad" runat="server" Text="Click to load
content using AJAX" />
<div id="htmlcontent">
</div>
<div id="xmlcontent">
</div>
```

8. To style the content retrieved from the HTML and XML files, add the following styles to the `head` element:

```
<style type="text/css">
table, th, td {
  border: 1px solid black;
  border-collapse: collapse
}
th{
  font-weight:700;
  font-variant:small-caps;
  text-align:center;
  background-color:lightgray;
  padding:5px;
}
td{
  background-color:lavender;
  padding:5px;
}
</style>
```

How to do it...

Include the following jQuery code in a `script` block on the page:

```
script type="text/javascript">
  $(document).ready(function() {
    $.ajaxSetup({
      method: "GET",
      data: {},
```

```
            timeout: 2000,
            cache: false
        });
        $("#<%=btnLoad.ClientID%>").on("click", function(evt) {
          evt.preventDefault();
          $.ajax({
            url: "Sample.html",
            dataType: "html",
            success: function(response) {
              $("#htmlcontent").html("").append(response);
            },
            error: function(jqXHR, textStatus, errorThrown) {
              if (textStatus == "error") {
                alert("An error has occurred: " + jqXHR.status
+ " " + jqXHR.statusText);
              }
            }
          });
        $.ajax({
          url: "Sample.xml",
          dataType: "xml",
          success: function(response) {
            $("#xmlcontent").html("").append("<h3>Book Shelf
from XML</h3>");
            $("#xmlcontent").append("<table>");
            $("#xmlcontent table").append("<tr><th>Title</
th><th>Author</th><th>Category</th></tr>");
            $(response).find("Book").each(function() {
              $("#xmlcontent table").append("<tr><td>" +
$(this).find("Title").text() + "</td><td>" +
$(this).find("Author").text() + "</td><td>" +
$(this).find("Category").text() + "</td></tr>");
            });
          },
          error: function(jqXHR, textStatus, errorThrown) {
            if (textStatus == "error") {
              alert("An error has occurred: " + jqXHR.status
+ " " + jqXHR.statusText);
            }
          }
        });
      });
    });
</script>
```

How it works...

The retrieval of HTML and XML content using Ajax is done as follows:

1. When the page is launched, the `$.ajaxSetup()` function configures the global settings for all Ajax calls on the page:

```
$.ajaxSetup({
  method: "GET",
  data: {},
  timeout: 2000,
  cache: false
});
```

It sets the following properties:

- The type/method of a request is set to HTTP GET
- Empty data is sent to the server
- A timeout of 2000 milliseconds is set so that the call can be terminated if the server does not respond within this timeframe
- The cache is set to false so that the requested content is not cached by the browser

2. When you click on the button on the page, its corresponding `click` event handler is triggered:

```
$("#<%=btnLoad.ClientID%>").on("click", function (evt)
{…});
```

In this event handler, first, prevent the page from posting back due to the button `click` event:

```
evt.preventDefault();
```

Next, initiate an Ajax call to the `Sample.html` page by setting the required options:

```
$.ajax({
  url: "Sample.html",
  dataType: "html",
  success: function (response) {
    $("#htmlcontent").html("").append(response);
  },
  error: function (jqXHR, textStatus, errorThrown) {
    if (textStatus == "error") {
      alert("An error has occurred: " + jqXHR.status + " "
+ jqXHR.statusText);
    }
  }
});
```

The preceding code snippet sets the following options when making the Ajax call to the HTML page:

- ❑ The request URL is set to `Sample.html`.

- ❑ The data type of the expected response from the server is set to `html`.

- ❑ A callback function is defined when the request made to the server is successful. This function clears the contents of the `div` area with the `htmlcontent` ID and displays the data received from the server in the same.

- ❑ A callback function is defined when the request made to the server fails. This callback function has three parameters: `jqXHR` (the `XMLHttpRequest` object), `textStatus` (types of errors, such as `abort`, `parsererror`, `timeout`, `error`, or `null`), and `errorThrown` (an optional exception object). When the `textStatus` parameter is `error`, we display the `status` and the `statusText` values from the `jqXHR` `XMLHttpRequest` object.

3. Next, initiate another Ajax call to the `Sample.xml` file with the required options:

```
$.ajax({
  url: "Sample.xml",
  dataType: "xml",
  success: function(response) {
    $("#xmlcontent").html("").append("<h3>Book Shelf from
XML</h3>");
    $("#xmlcontent").append("<table>");
    $("#xmlcontent table").append("<tr><th>Title</th><th>Author</
th><th>Catego
ry</th></tr>");
    $(response).find("Book").each(function() {
      $("#xmlcontent table").append("<tr><td>" +
$(this).find("Title").text() + "</td><td>" +
$(this).find("Author").text() + "</td><td>" +
$(this).find("Category").text() + "</td></tr>");
    });
  },
  error: function(jqXHR, textStatus, errorThrown) {
    if (textStatus == "error") {
      alert("An error has occurred: " + jqXHR.status + " "
+ jqXHR.statusText);
    }
  }
});
```

In the preceding request the following options are set:

❑ The request URL is `Sample.xml`.

❑ The expected data type of the server response is `xml`.

❑ A callback function is defined when the request made to the server is successful. This callback function clears the `div` element with the `xmlcontent` ID and adds a header, as shown in the following code snippet:

```
$("#xmlcontent").html("").append("<h3>Book Shelf from
XML</h3>");
```

❑ It then adds an empty table element to this `div` element and appends the `table` header:

```
$("#xmlcontent").append("<table>");
$("#xmlcontent
table").append("<tr><th>Title</th><th>Author</th><th>Catego
ry</th></tr>");
```

❑ For each `Book` node in the XML file, it displays the corresponding child nodes: `Title`, `Author`, and `Category`, as follows:

```
$(response).find("Book").each(function () {
  $("#xmlcontent table").append("<tr><td>" +
$(this).find("Title").text() + "</td><td>" +
$(this).find("Author").text() + "</td><td>" +
$(this).find("Category").text() + "</td></tr>");
});
```

❑ A callback function is defined when the request made to the server is unsuccessful. This callback function has three parameters: `jqXHR` (the `XMLHttpRequest` object), `textStatus` (types of errors, such as abort, parsererror, timeout, error, or null), and `errorThrown` (an optional exception object). When the `textStatus` parameter value is `error`, we display the `status` and the `statusText` values from the `XMLHttpRequest` object.

There's more...

To retrieve text or HTML content asynchronously using the `GET` request, jQuery provides a `.load()` shortcut method. Using this function, we can alternatively make the first Ajax call to the `Sample.html` file, as follows:

```
$("#htmlcontent").html("").load("Sample.html",
function (response, status, xhr) {
  if (status == "error") {
    alert("An error has occurred: " + xhr.status + " " +
xhr.statusText);
  }
});
```

Note that a callback function is specified in this function. This is executed when the .load() method is completed. The callback function has parameters, such as response (which contains the resulting content if the call succeeds), status (which contains the status of the call), and xhr (the XMLHttpRequest object).

See also

The *Consuming page methods* recipe

Consuming page methods

Page methods provide a convenient way of invoking server-side code from the client script. They are simply server-side methods that are decorated with the System.Web.Services. WebMethod label. In this recipe, we will use the Northwind database in a page method to retrieve a list of customers from a particular country. The method will be invoked from the client script using jQuery Ajax.

The constructs used in this example are summarized in the following table:

Construct	Type	Description
$("#identifier")	jQuery selector	This selects an element based on its ID.
$("html_tag")	jQuery selector	This selects all elements with the specified HTML tag.
$.ajax()	jQuery function	This posts an Ajax request to the server with the set options.
.append()	jQuery method	This inserts content at the end of each matched element.
click	jQuery event	This is fired when you click on an element. It corresponds to the JavaScript click event.
event. preventDefault()	jQuery method	This prevents the default action of the event from being triggered.
:gt(i)	jQuery selector	This selects matched elements that have an index greater than i. It uses a zero-based index.
.hide()	jQuery method	This hides the matched elements.
:hidden	jQuery selector	This selects hidden elements.
.is()	jQuery method	This returns a Boolean value if the matched element satisfies a given condition.
.on()	jQuery event binder	This attaches an event handler for one or more events to the matched elements.

Construct	Type	Description
`.remove()`	jQuery method	This deletes the matched elements from the DOM.
`.show()`	jQuery method	This displays the matched elements.
`.trim()`	JavaScript function	This removes whitespaces from the beginning and end of a string.
`.val()`	jQuery method	This returns the value of the first matched element or sets the value of every matched element.
`window.location.href`	JavaScript property	This returns the URL of the current page.

Getting ready

Follow these steps to build a web page that exposes page methods:

1. Let's create a web page with a `DropDownList` control consisting of a list of countries, as shown in the following screenshot:

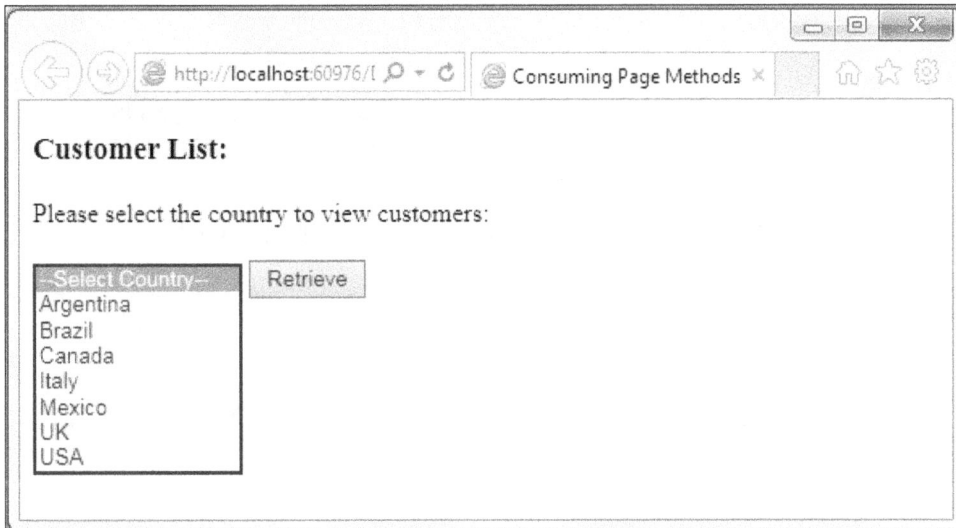

After selecting any country from the dropdown, the page displays the list of customers filtered by the selected country, as shown in the following screenshot :

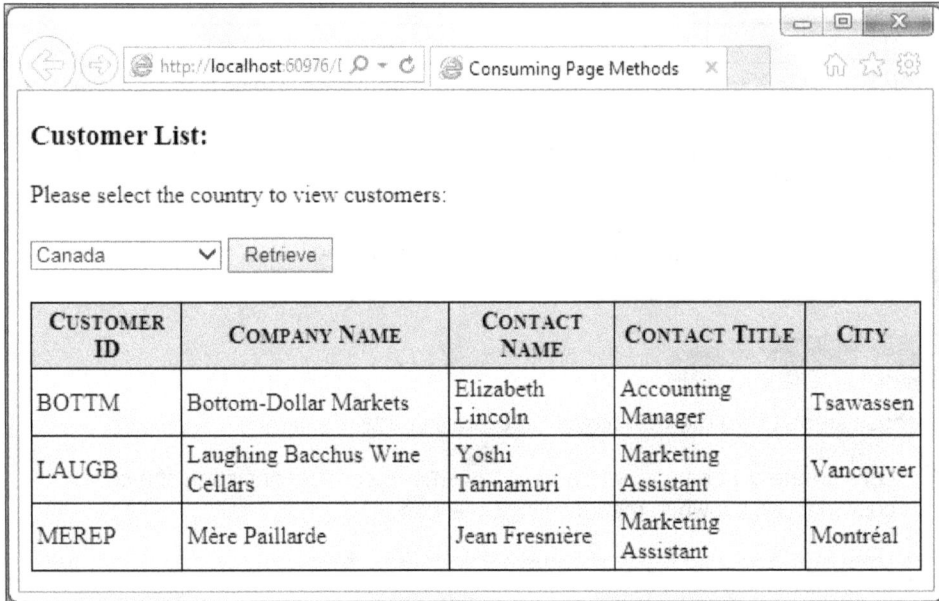

2. To create this application, launch an **ASP.NET Web Application** project in Visual Studio using the **Empty** template and name it `Recipe2` (or any other suitable name).

3. Add the jQuery library to the project in a `Scripts` folder.

4. Add a web form to the project and include the jQuery library in the form.

5. In the **Solution Explorer** tab, right-click on the project and go to **Add | New Item**. From the launched dialog box, select **Data** under the **Installed templates** section on the left-hand panel. Select **ADO.NET Entity Data Model** from the middle panel. Enter a suitable name for the model such as Northwind, and click on the **Add** button:

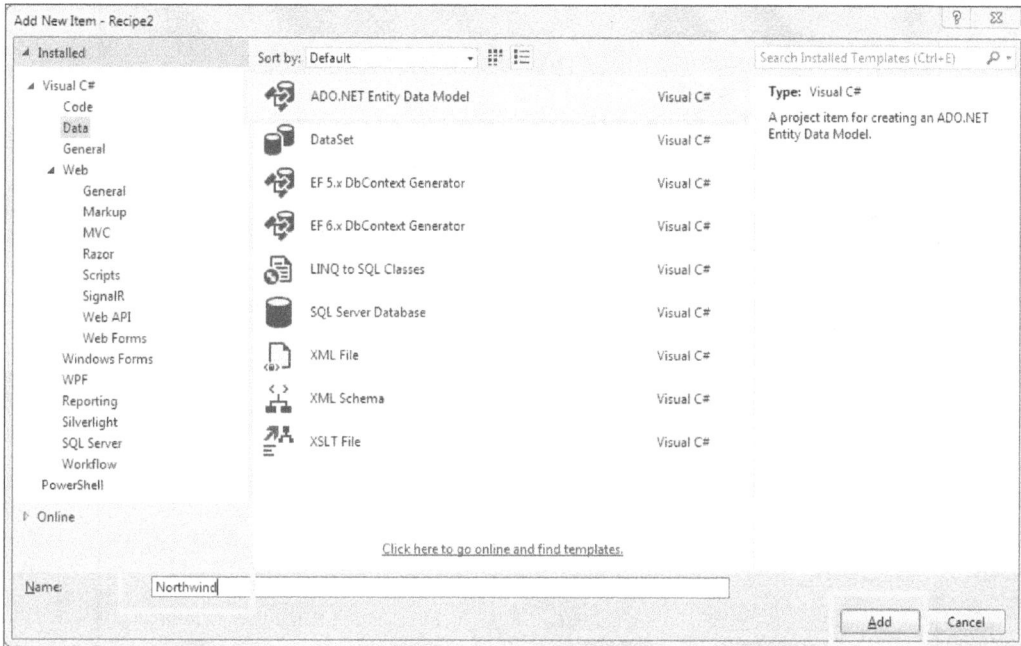

6. This will launch the **Entity Data Model Wizard** dialog box, as shown in the following screenshot. Select **EF Designer from database** and click on the **Next** button:

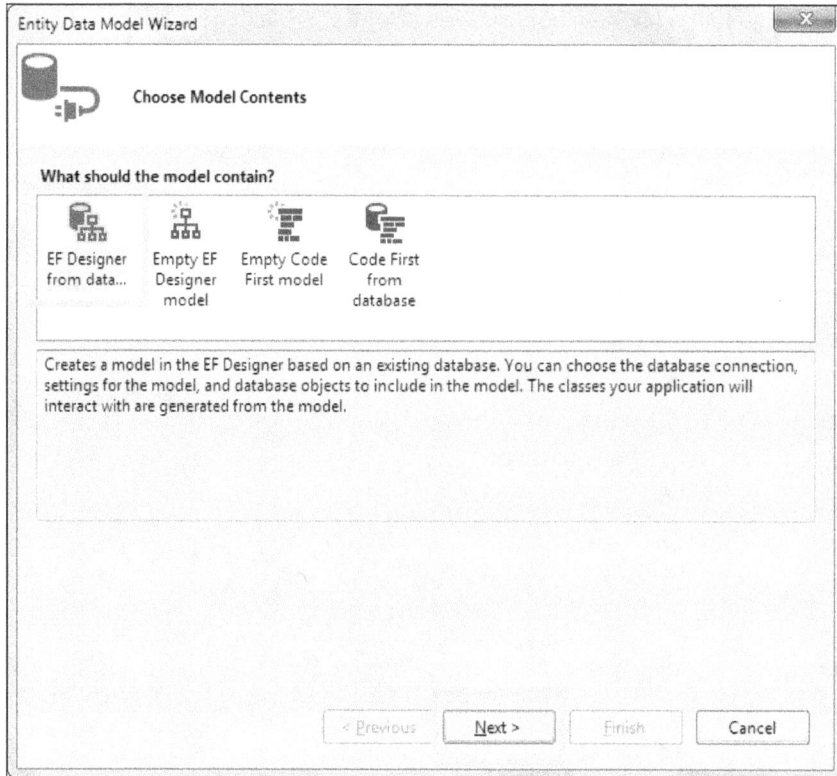

On the next window, add a new connection to the Northwind database. Save this connection in `web.config` as `NorthwindEntities`, and click on **Next**:

Next, check the `Customers` table from the list of table objects, and click on the **Finish** button:

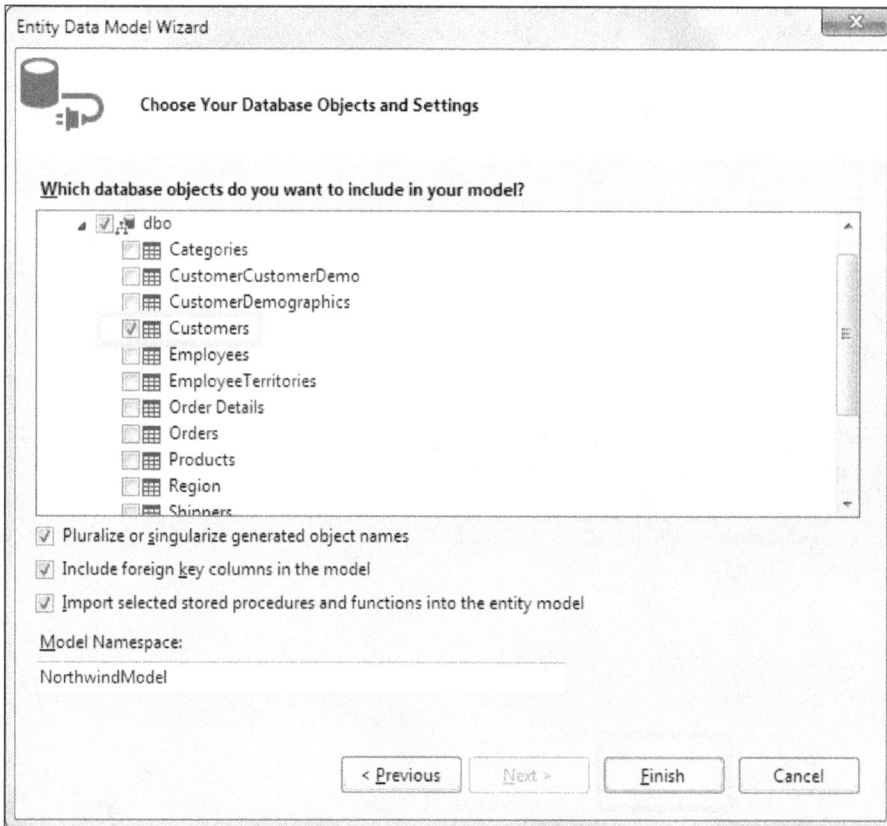

7. In the code-behind file of the web form, that is, `Default.aspx.vb` (VB) or `Default.aspx.cs` (C#), add the following page method.

For VB, the code is as follows:

```
<System.Web.Services.WebMethod>
Public Shared Function GetCustomers(ByVal sCountry As
String) As Customer()
   Dim CustomerList As List(Of Customer) = New List(Of
Customer)()
   Dim db As NorthwindEntities = New NorthwindEntities()
```

```
    Dim Query = From cust In db.Customers
    Where cust.Country = sCountry
    Select cust

    For Each custObj In Query
    Dim CustomerRecord As Customer = New Customer()
    CustomerRecord.CustomerID = custObj.CustomerID
    CustomerRecord.CompanyName = custObj.CompanyName
    CustomerRecord.ContactName = custObj.ContactName
    CustomerRecord.ContactTitle = custObj.ContactTitle
    CustomerRecord.City = custObj.City
    CustomerList.Add(CustomerRecord)
    Next

    Return CustomerList.ToArray
End Function
```

For C#, the code is as follows:

```
[System.Web.Services.WebMethod]
public static Customer[] GetCustomers(string sCountry)
{
  List<Customer> CustomerList = new List<Customer>();
  NorthwindEntities db = new NorthwindEntities();
  var query = from cust in db.Customers
  where cust.Country == sCountry
  select cust;
  foreach (var custObj in query)
  {
    Customer CustomerRecord = new Customer();
    CustomerRecord.CustomerID = custObj.CustomerID;
    CustomerRecord.CompanyName = custObj.CompanyName;
    CustomerRecord.ContactName = custObj.ContactName;
    CustomerRecord.ContactTitle = custObj.ContactTitle;
    CustomerRecord.City = custObj.City;
    CustomerList.Add(CustomerRecord);
  }
  return CustomerList.ToArray();
}
```

8. The preceding `GetCustomers()` page method receives the `country` field as an input parameter. It filters customer records by `country` and returns an array of the `Customer` type.

> Note that the page method is required to have the following configurations:
>
> ▸ The method should be decorated with the `System.Web.Services.WebMethod` label.
> ▸ It should be declared as shared (VB) or static (C#).
> ▸ It takes `sCountry` as an input parameter. This parameter should be sent by the client script through the Ajax call.

9. Add a skeleton table element to the web form to display the list of retrieved customers. Thus, the markup of the form will be as follows:

```
<asp:Label ID="lblSelectCountry" runat="server"
Text="Please select the country to view
customers:"></asp:Label><br /><br />
<asp:DropDownList ID="ddlSelectCountry" runat="server">
  <asp:ListItem Text="--Select Country--"
Value=""></asp:ListItem>
  <asp:ListItem Text="Argentina"
Value="Argentina"></asp:ListItem>
  <asp:ListItem Text="Brazil"
Value="Brazil"></asp:ListItem>
  <asp:ListItem Text="Canada"
Value="Canada"></asp:ListItem>
  <asp:ListItem Text="Italy" Value="Italy"></asp:ListItem>
  <asp:ListItem Text="Mexico"
Value="Mexico"></asp:ListItem>
  <asp:ListItem Text="UK" Value="UK"></asp:ListItem>
  <asp:ListItem Text="USA" Value="USA"></asp:ListItem>
</asp:DropDownList>
<asp:Button ID="btnRetrieve" runat="server" Text="Retrieve"
/>
<br /><br />
<table id="tblResponse">
  <thead>
    <tr>
      <th>Customer ID</th>
      <th>Company Name</th>
      <th>Contact Name</th>
      <th>Contact Title</th>
      <th>City</th>
    </tr>
  </thead>
</table>
```

10. Add the following styles to the head element on the page:

```css
<style type="text/css">
table, th, td {
  border: 1px solid black;
  border-collapse: collapse;
  padding:3px;
}
th{
  font-weight:700;
  font-variant:small-caps;
  text-align:center;
  background-color:lightgray;
}
td{
  background-color:lightyellow;
}
</style>
```

How to do it...

Include the following jQuery code in a `<script>` block:

```javascript
<script type="text/javascript">
  $(document).ready(function() {
    $("#tblResponse").hide();
    $("#<%=btnRetrieve.ClientID%>").on("click", function(evt) {
      evt.preventDefault();
      var sCountry =
$("#<%=ddlSelectCountry.ClientID%>").val().trim();
      if (sCountry != "") {
        var loc = window.location.href;
        $.ajax({
          url: loc + "/GetCustomers",
          method: "POST",
          data: '{ "sCountry": "' + sCountry + '"}',
          dataType: "json",
          contentType: "application/json; charset=utf-8",
          timeout: 5000,
          cache: false,
          success: function(response) {
            $("#tblResponse tr:gt(0)").remove();
            if ($("#tblResponse").is(":hidden"))
              $("#tblResponse").show();
            $.each(response.d,
```

```
        function() {
            $("#tblResponse").append("<tr><td>" +
this['CustomerID'] + "</td><td>" + this['CompanyName'] +
"</td><td>" + this['ContactName'] + "</td><td>" +
this['ContactTitle'] + "</td><td>" + this['City'] + "</td></tr>");
            });
        },
        error: function(jqXHR, textStatus, errorThrown) {
            if (textStatus == "error") {
                alert("An error has occurred: " + jqXHR.status + " "
+ jqXHR.statusText);
            }
        }
    });
    } else
        alert("Please select a country to display the customer
list.");
    });
});
</script>
```

How it works...

Posting an Ajax call to the page method works as follows:

1. When the page is launched, the `table` element that is used to display the list of customers is initially hidden:

   ```
   $("#tblResponse").hide();
   ```

2. An event handler is defined for the `click` function of the button in the form:

   ```
   $("#<%=btnRetrieve.ClientID%>").on("click", function (evt)
   {...});
   ```

   In this event handler, the page is prevented from posting back using the following code:

   ```
   evt.preventDefault();
   ```

   The selected value from the `DropDownList` control, that is, the selected country is retrieved:

   ```
   var sCountry =
   $("#<%=ddlSelectCountry.ClientID%>").val().trim();
   ```

The preceding string is trimmed to remove whitespaces, if any. If the country selected is nonempty, find the URL of the current page using the `window.location.href` JavaScript property:

```
var loc = window.location.href;
```

Now, make an Ajax call to the page method:

```
$.ajax({
  url: loc + "/GetCustomers",
  method: "POST",
  data: '{ "sCountry": "' + sCountry + '"}',
  dataType: "json",
  contentType: "application/json; charset=utf-8",
  timeout: 5000,
  cache: false,
  success: function (response)
  $("#tblResponse tr:gt(0)").remove();
  if ($("#tblResponse").is(":hidden"))
    $("#tblResponse").show();
    $.each(response.d, function () {
      $("#tblResponse").append("<tr><td>" +
this['CustomerID'] + "</td><td>" + this['CompanyName'] +
"</td><td>" + this['ContactName'] + "</td><td>" +
this['ContactTitle'] + "</td><td>" + this['City'] +
"</td></tr>");
    });
  },
  error: function (jqXHR, textStatus, errorThrown) {
    if (textStatus == "error") {
      alert("An error has occurred: " + jqXHR.status + " " +
jqXHR.statusText);
    }
  }
});
```

In the preceding call, the following options are set:

- The request URL is set to the page method, which is accessible at `UrlOfCurrentPage/NameOfPageMethod`.

- The type/method of the request is set to `POST` since we are sending form data to the server.

- The data, that is, the selected country is sent to the server as a JSON formatted string. Remember that the page method has an input parameter, `sCountry`. This is sent as a name/value pair as follows:

```
data: '{ "sCountry": "' + sCountry + '"}',
```

> It is important to note that the sCountry name in the preceding JSON string is the input parameter of the page method.

- The data type of the server response is json.
- The content type of the sent request is set to application/json and the character is set to UTF-8.
- A timeout of 5000 milliseconds is specified after which the request will be terminated if the server fails to respond.
- The cache is set to false so that the content will not be cached by the browser.
- A callback function is defined when the request is successful. In this function, the contents of the display table are emptied by deleting all the rows except the header:

  ```
  $("#tblResponse tr:gt(0)").remove();
  ```

- If the display table is hidden, it is made visible to the user:

  ```
  if ($("#tblResponse").is(":hidden"))
    $("#tblResponse").show();
  ```

- Then, we loop through each element in the returned response, retrieving the CustomerID, CompanyName, ContactName, ContactTitle, and City fields, as follows:

  ```
  $.each(response.d, function () {
    $("#tblResponse").append("<tr><td>" + this['CustomerID']
  + "</td><td>" + this['CompanyName'] + "</td><td>" +
  this['ContactName'] + "</td><td>" + this['ContactTitle'] +
  "</td><td>" + this['City'] + "</td></tr>");
  });
  ```

> Note that in order to access the returned data from the server, we use response.d in the preceding code.

3. A callback function is defined when the request is unsuccessful. If the textStatus parameter is error, then the status and statusText values of the XmlHttpRequest object are displayed.

4. It is also possible that the user may not select any country from the DropDownList control. Hence, the program should display a message when the selected field is empty:

   ```
   alert("Please select a country to display the customer
   list.");
   ```

See also

The *Making AJAX calls to a HTTP handler* recipe

Consuming Web services

jQuery Ajax enables you to consume web services through client code. In this recipe, we will send form data to a web service method. The constructs used in this example are summarized in the following table:

Construct	Type	Description
`$("#identifier")`	jQuery selector	This selects an element based on its ID.
`$("html_tag")`	jQuery selector	This selects all elements with the specified HTML tag.
`$.ajax()`	jQuery function	This posts an Ajax request to the server with the set options.
`.append()`	jQuery method	This inserts content at the end of each matched element.
`click`	jQuery event	This is fired when you click on an element. It corresponds to the JavaScript `click` event.
`event.preventDefault()`	jQuery method	This prevents the default action of the event from being triggered.
`.focus()`	jQuery event binder	This triggers the `focus` event of an element or binds an event handler to the `focus` event.
`:gt(i)`	jQuery selector	This selects matched elements that have an index greater than i. It uses the zero-based index.
`:hidden`	jQuery selector	This selects hidden elements.
`.hide()`	jQuery method	This hides the matched elements.
`.is()`	jQuery method	This returns a Boolean value if the matched element satisfies a given condition.
`.on()`	jQuery event binder	This attaches an event handler for one or more events to the matched elements.
`.remove()`	jQuery method	This deletes the matched elements from the DOM.
`.show()`	jQuery method	This displays the matched elements.
`.text()`	jQuery method	This returns the combined text content of each of the matched elements or sets the text content of every matched element.

Construct	Type	Description
`.trim()`	JavaScript function	This removes whitespaces from the beginning and end of a string.
`.val()`	jQuery method	This returns the value of the first matched element or sets the value of every matched element.

Getting ready

Follow these steps to build a web page that will consume a web service:

1. In this recipe, let's create a form where the user can search for employee records by the first name or last name, as shown in the following screenshot:

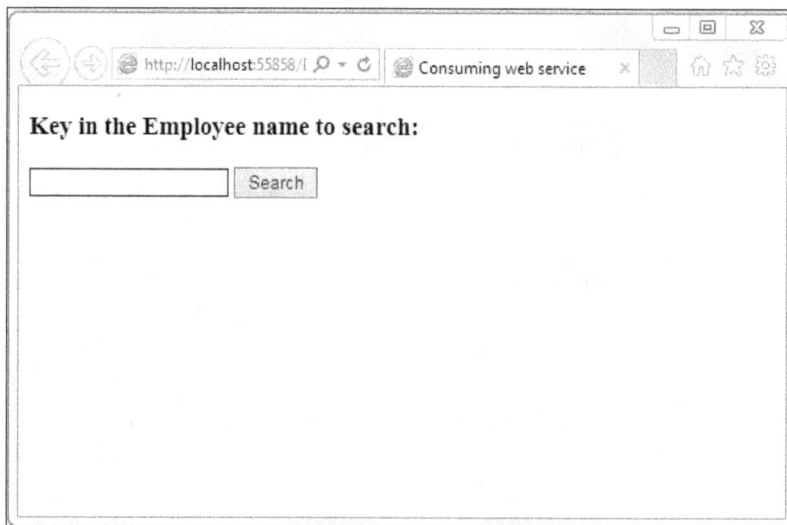

On entering a keyword to be searched, if a match is found, the results are displayed, as shown in the following screenshot:

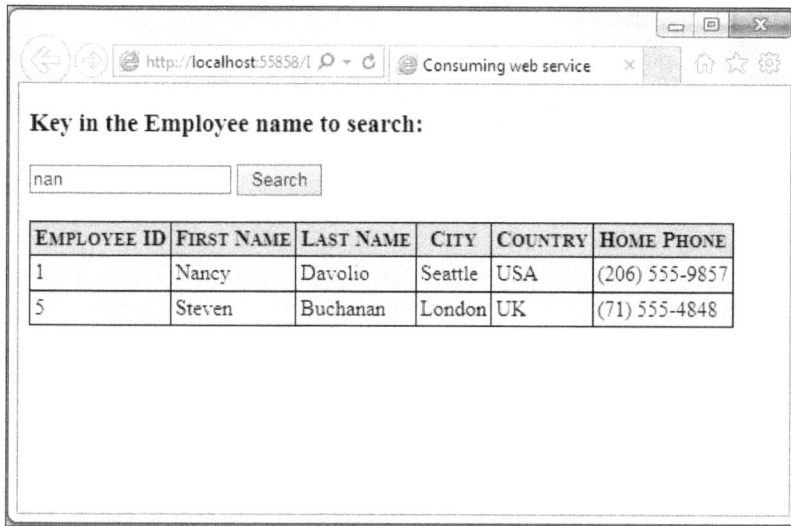

If no match is found, the page simply displays a message, as shown in the following screenshot:

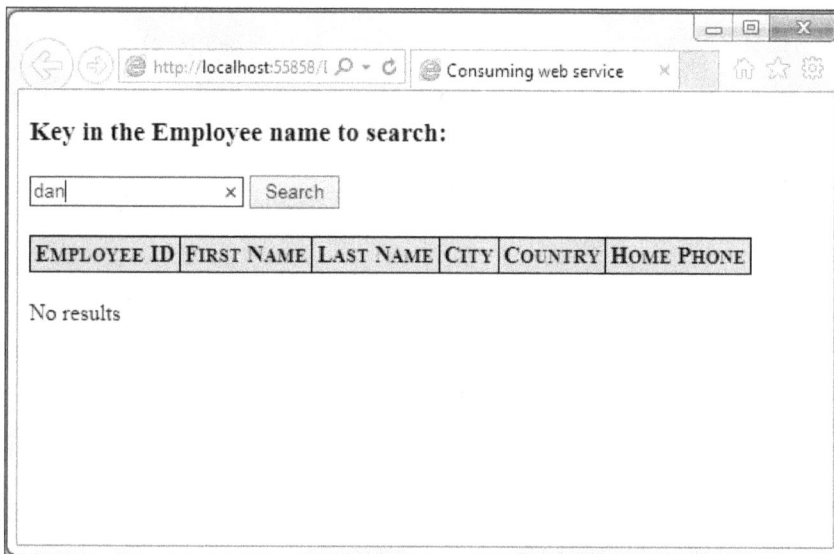

2. To create this application, launch an **ASP.NET Web Application** project in Visual Studio using the **Empty** template and name it `Recipe3` (or any other suitable name).

3. Add the jQuery library to the project in a `Scripts` folder.

4. Add a web form to the project and include the jQuery library in the form.

5. Include the following markup in the form:

```
<h3>Key in the Employee name to search:</h3>
<asp:TextBox ID="txtKeyword" runat="server"></asp:TextBox>
<asp:Button ID="btnSearch" runat="server" Text="Search" />
<br /><br />
<table id="tblResponse">
  <thead>
    <tr>
      <th>Employee ID</th>
      <th>First Name</th>
      <th>Last Name</th>
      <th>City</th>
      <th>Country</th>
      <th>Home Phone</th>
    </tr>
  </thead>
</table>
<br />
<asp:Label ID="lblMessage" runat="server"></asp:Label>
```

Notice that the form has a `Label` control, `lblMessage`. This field will be used to display information/error messages to the user, if any.

6. Style the page elements using the following CSS:

```
<style type="text/css">
  table,
  th,
  td {
    border: 1px solid black;
    border-collapse: collapse;
    padding: 3px;
  }

  th {
    font-weight: 700;
    font-variant: small-caps;
```

```
    text-align: center;
    background-color: lightgray;
  }

  td {
    background-color: lightyellow;
  }
</style>
```

7. Add an `Employee` class to the project by right-clicking on the project and navigating to **Add** | **Class**. Name the class `Employee.vb` (VB) or `Employee.cs` (C#). Add the following properties to the class.

   For VB, the code is as follows:

   ```
   Public Class Employee
       Public Property EmployeeID As String
       Public Property LastName As String
       Public Property FirstName As String
       Public Property City As String
       Public Property Country As String
       Public Property HomePhone As String
   End Class
   ```

   For C#, the code is as follows:

   ```
   public class Employee
   {
       public String EmployeeID { get; set; }
       public String LastName { get; set; }
       public String FirstName { get; set; }
       public String City{ get; set; }
       public String Country { get; set; }
       public String HomePhone { get; set; }
   }
   ```

8. Now, right-click on the project in the **Solution Explorer** tab and go to **Add** | **New Folder**. Name the new folder `Services`.

9.   Right-click on the `Services` folder and go to **Add** | **New Item**. From the launched dialog box, select **Web** from the **Installed** templates on the left-hand side of the screen. From the middle panel, select **Web Service (ASMX)**. Give the service a suitable name, such as `NorthwindService.asmx`, and click on the **Add** button:

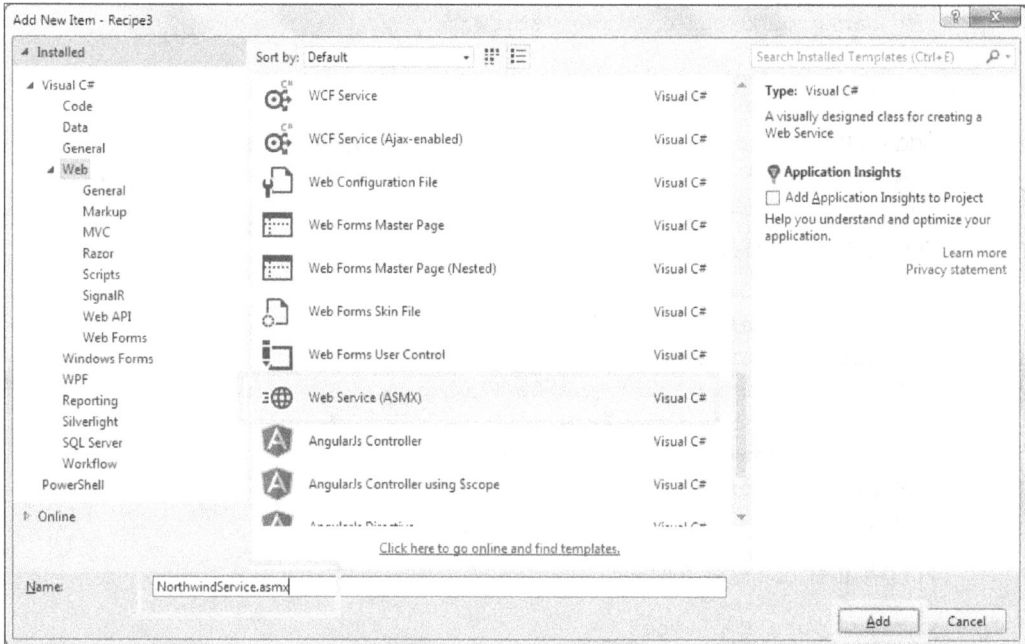

10.   In the code-behind file of `NorthwindService.asmx`, uncomment the following statements at the top of the file to enable the service to be accessed by Ajax:

For VB, the statement is as follows:

```
<System.Web.Script.Services.ScriptService()>
```

For C#, the statement is as follows:

```
[System.Web.Script.Services.ScriptService]
```

11.   Add the following namespace at the top of file. This will enable us to pick the Northwind database connection string from the `web.config` file.

For VB, the code is as follows:

```
Imports System.Web.Configuration
```

For C#, the code is as follows:

```
using System.Web.Configuration;
```

12. Next, add a `GetEmployeeResult()` web method to the code-behind file.

   For VB, the code is as follows:

```vb
<WebMethod()>
Public Function GetEmployeeResult(ByVal sSearch As String)
As Employee()
  Dim employeeList As List(Of Employee) = New List(Of
Employee)()
  Dim strConn As String =
    WebConfigurationManager.ConnectionStrings("
NorthwindConnection").ConnectionString
  Dim con As SqlConnection = New SqlConnection(strConn)
  Dim strSql As String = "SELECT * FROM EMPLOYEES WHERE
    FirstName LIKE '%" + sSearch + "%' or LastName like '%"
    + sSearch + "%'"
  Dim cmd As SqlCommand = New SqlCommand(strSql, con)
  con.Open()
  Dim dr As SqlDataReader = cmd.ExecuteReader()
  While (dr.Read())
    Dim emp As Employee = New Employee()
    emp.EmployeeID = dr("EmployeeID").ToString()
    emp.FirstName = dr("FirstName").ToString()
    emp.LastName = dr("LastName").ToString()
    emp.City = dr("City").ToString()
    emp.Country = dr("Country").ToString()
    emp.HomePhone = dr("HomePhone").ToString()
    employeeList.Add(emp)
  End While
  con.Close()
  Return employeeList.ToArray()
End Function
```

   For C#, the code is as follows:

```csharp
[WebMethod]
public Employee[] GetEmployeeResult(String sSearch)
{
  List<Employee> employeeList = new List<Employee>();
  String strConn =
WebConfigurationManager.ConnectionStrings
["NorthwindConnection"].ConnectionString;
  SqlConnection con = new SqlConnection(strConn);
  String strSql = "SELECT * FROM EMPLOYEES WHERE FirstName
LIKE '%" + sSearch + "%' or LastName like '%" + sSearch +
"%'";
```

```
SqlCommand cmd = new SqlCommand(strSql, con);
con.Open();
SqlDataReader dr = cmd.ExecuteReader();
while (dr.Read())
{
  Employee emp = new Employee();
  emp.EmployeeID = dr["EmployeeID"].ToString();
  emp.FirstName = dr["FirstName"].ToString();
  emp.LastName = dr["LastName"].ToString();
  emp.City = dr["City"].ToString();
  emp.Country = dr["Country"].ToString();
  emp.HomePhone = dr["HomePhone"].ToString();
  employeeList.Add(emp);
}
con.Close();
return employeeList.ToArray();
}
```

The web method defined in the preceding code receives a search keyword from the calling program. It then connects to the Northwind database using ADO.NET and queries the `Employees` table to return records where the `FirstName` or `LastName` column contains the search keyword. The list of records is returned as an array of the `Employee` type.

> Note that the calling program needs to pass the `sSearch` input parameter to the web method.

13. Add the connection string to the Northwind database in the configuration section of the `web.config` file:

```
<connectionStrings>
  <add name="NorthwindConnection"
providerName="System.Data.SqlClient" connectionString="Data
Source=localhost;Initial Catalog=Northwind;Integrated
Security=True;"/>
</connectionStrings>
```

> Note that we are using Windows Authentication for all database driven examples in this book. Hence in the MS SQL Server, it is important to give permission to the Windows account to access the Northwind database.

How to do it...

Include the following jQuery code in a `<script>` block on the page:

```
$(document).ready(function () {
  $("#tblResponse").hide();
  $("#<%=lblMessage.ClientID%>").hide();
  $("#<%=txtKeyword.ClientID%>").focus();
  $("#<%=btnSearch.ClientID%>").on("click", function (evt)
{
    evt.preventDefault();
    $("#<%=lblMessage.ClientID%>").hide();
    var sKeyword =
$("#<%=txtKeyword.ClientID%>").val().trim();
    if (sKeyword != "") {
      $.ajax({
        url:
"/Services/NorthwindService.asmx/GetEmployeeResult",
        type: "POST",
        data: '{ "sSearch": "' + sKeyword + '"}',
        dataType: "json",
        contentType: "application/json; charset=utf-8",
        timeout: 5000,
        cache: false,
        success: function (response) {
          $("#tblResponse tr:gt(0)").remove();
          if ($("#tblResponse").is(":hidden"))
            $("#tblResponse").show();
          if (response.d.length > 0) {
            $.each(response.d, function () {
              ("#tblResponse").append("<tr><td>" +
this['EmployeeID'] + "</td><td>" + this['FirstName'] +
"</td><td>" + this['LastName'] + "</td><td>" + this['City']
+ "</td><td>" + this['Country'] + "</td><td>" +
this['HomePhone'] + "</td></tr>");
            });
          } else $("#<%=lblMessage.ClientID%>").text("No
results").show();
        },
        error: function (jqXHR, textStatus, errorThrown) {
          if (textStatus == "error") {
            alert("An error has occurred: " + jqXHR.status
+ " " + jqXHR.statusText);}
          }
      });
```

```
    }
    else
       alert("Please enter your search keyword");
    });
  });
</script>
```

How it works...

The Ajax call to the web service works as follows:

1. When the page is launched, a text field is displayed to the user to key in the search keywords. The following initializations are done on the page:

    ❑   The result table is hidden, as follows:

    ```
    $("#tblResponse").hide();
    ```

    ❑   The label used to display information/error messages is hidden:

    ```
    $("#<%=lblMessage.ClientID%>").hide();
    ```

    ❑   The cursor is focused on the text field so that the user can key in the required search keywords:

    ```
    $("#<%=txtKeyword.ClientID%>").focus();
    ```

2. An event handler is attached in order to respond to the `click` event of the button on the page:

    ```
    $("#<%=btnSearch.ClientID%>").on("click", function (evt)
    {…});
    ```

    In this event handler, the page is prevented from posting back using the following code:

    ```
    evt.preventDefault();
    ```

    It is possible that the previous query would have displayed information/error messages, so the `lblMessage` control is hidden once again:

    ```
    $("#<%=lblMessage.ClientID%>").hide();
    ```

    Next, the search keyword, entered in the text field, is retrieved. Whitespaces, if any, are trimmed:

    ```
    var sKeyword = $("#<%=txtKeyword.ClientID%>").val().trim();
    ```

If the keyword is not blank, an Ajax call is made to the web service using HTTP POST:

```
if (sKeyword != "") {
  $.ajax({
    url:
"/Services/NorthwindService.asmx/GetEmployeeResult",
    type: "POST",
    data: '{ "sSearch": "' + sKeyword + '"}',
    dataType: "json",
    contentType: "application/json; charset=utf-8",
    timeout: 5000,
    cache: false,
    success: function(response) {
      $("#tblResponse tr:gt(0)").remove();
      if ($("#tblResponse").is(":hidden"))
        $("#tblResponse").show();
      if (response.d.length > 0) {
        $.each(response.d, function() {
          $("#tblResponse").append("<tr><td>" +
          this['EmployeeID'] + "</td><td>" +
this['FirstName'] +
          "</td><td>" + this['LastName'] + "</td><td>" +
this['City'] + "</td><td>" + this['Country'] + "</td><td>"
+ this['HomePhone'] + "</td></tr>");
        });
      } else $("#<%=lblMessage.ClientID%>").text("No
        results ").show();
      },
    error: function(jqXHR, textStatus, errorThrown) {
      if (textStatus == "error") {
        alert("An error has occurred: " + jqXHR.status +
" " + jqXHR.statusText);
      }
    }
  });
}
```

In the preceding Ajax call, the following options are set:

- ❑ The request URL is set to `WebServicePath/WebMethodName`.
- ❑ The type/method of the HTTP request is set to `POST`.
- ❑ The data consists of a JSON formatted string. The searched keyword is sent using a name/value pair. The name is set to `sSearch` and the value is set to the string retrieved from the text field. The JSON formatted string is as follows:

  ```
  '{ "sSearch": "' + sKeyword + '"}'
  ```

- ❑ The expected data type of the response is set to `json`.
- ❑ The content type is set to `application/json` and the character is set to `utf-8`.
- ❑ A timeout of `5000` milliseconds is specified so that the request is terminated if the server fails to respond within this timeframe.
- ❑ The cache is set to `false` so that the response is not cached in the browser.
- ❑ A callback function is specified for the successful completion of the Ajax call. This function, first of all, clears the display table of any previously displayed items:

  ```
  $("#tblResponse tr:gt(0)").remove();
  ```

- ❑ If the table is hidden, it is made visible:

  ```
  if ($("#tblResponse").is(":hidden"))
    $("#tblResponse").show();
  ```

- ❑ Next, it checks whether the response is nonempty. This can be done by checking the length of `response.d`. If the response is nonempty, each item in the response array is displayed:

  ```
  if (response.d.length > 0) {
    $.each(response.d, function () {
      $("#tblResponse").append("<tr><td>" +
  this['EmployeeID'] + "</td><td>" + this['FirstName'] +
  "</td><td>" + this['LastName'] + "</td><td>" + this['City']
  + "</td><td>" + this['Country'] + "</td><td>" +
  this['HomePhone'] + "</td></tr>");
    });
  }
  ```

- ❑ However, if the response is empty, an error is displayed using the `lblMessage` control, as follows:

  ```
  $("#<%=lblMessage.ClientID%>").text("No results").show();
  ```

3. A callback function is specified for an unsuccessful Ajax call. It displays the `status` and `statusText` parameters of `XmlHttpObject` in case of an error.

4. If, however, the search keyword is blank when the user clicks on the button, the following error message is displayed to the user:

```
alert("Please enter your search keyword");
```

See also

The *Consuming WCF services* recipe

Consuming WCF services

Consuming a WCF service is similar to consuming a web service, as discussed in the previous recipe. In this example, we will redo the previous recipe, but this time, using a WCF service. The constructs used in this example are summarized in the following table:

Construct	Type	Description
`$("#identifier")`	jQuery selector	This selects an element based on its ID.
`$("html_tag")`	jQuery selector	This selects all elements with the specified HTML tag.
`$.ajax()`	jQuery function	This posts an Ajax request to the server with the set options.
`.append()`	jQuery method	This inserts content at the end of each matched element.
`click`	jQuery event	This is fired when you click on an element. It corresponds to the JavaScript `click` event.
`event.preventDefault()`	jQuery method	This prevents the default action of the event from being triggered.
`.focus()`	jQuery event binder	This triggers the `focus` event of an element or binds an event handler to the `focus` event.
`:gt(i)`	jQuery selector	This selects matched elements that have an index greater than `i`. It uses the zero-based index.
`:hidden`	jQuery selector	This selects hidden elements.
`.hide()`	jQuery method	This hides the matched elements.
`.is()`	jQuery method	This returns a Boolean value if the matched element satisfies a given condition.
`.on()`	jQuery event binder	This attaches an event handler for one or more events to the matched elements.

Construct	Type	Description
.remove()	jQuery method	This deletes the matched elements from the DOM.
.show()	jQuery method	This displays the matched elements.
.text()	jQuery method	This returns the combined text content of each of the matched elements or sets the text content of every matched element.
.trim()	JavaScript function	This removes whitespaces from the beginning and end of a string.
.val()	jQuery method	This returns the value of the first matched element or sets the value of every matched element.

Getting ready

Follow these steps to build a page that consumes a WCF service:

1. Similar to the previous recipe, the goal here is to search for employee records by the first or last name. When a match is found, the records are displayed, as shown in the following screenshot:

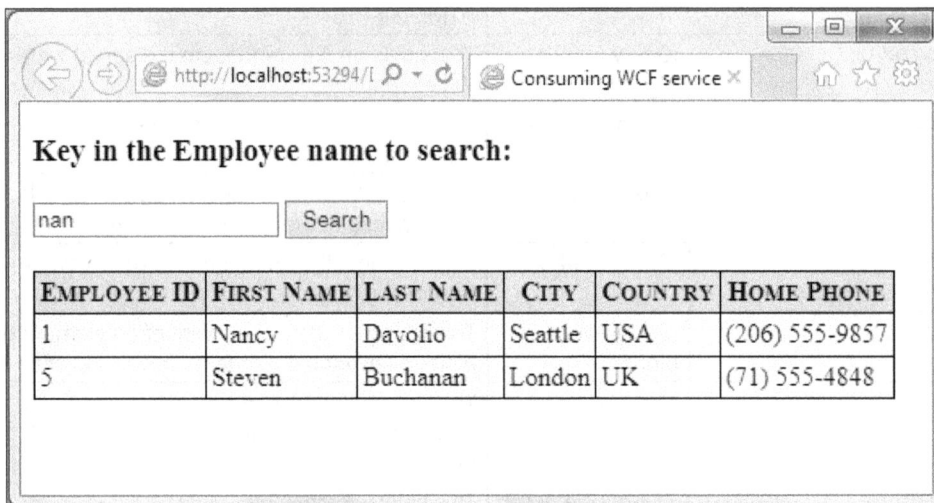

If no match is found, the page displays a corresponding message to the user:

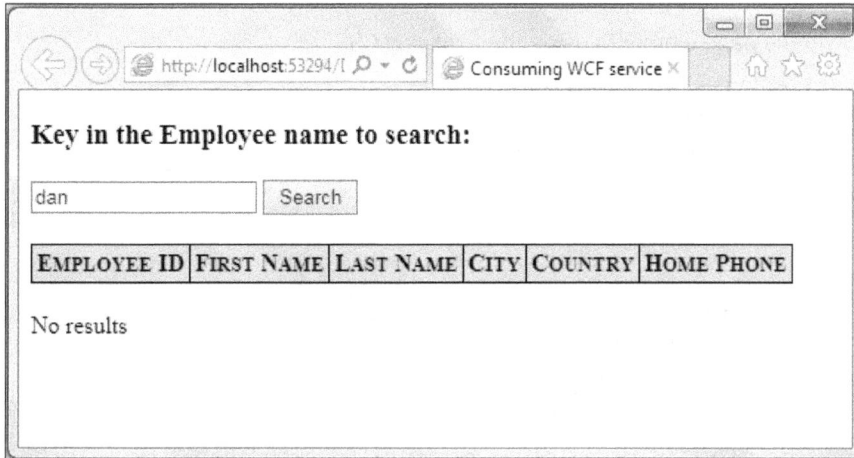

2. To create this application, launch an **ASP.NET Web Application** project in Visual Studio using the **Empty** template and name it `Recipe4` (or any other suitable name).

3. Add the jQuery library to the project in a `Scripts` folder.

4. Add a web form to the project and include the jQuery library in the form.

5. Include the following markup in the form:

```
<h3>Key in the Employee name to search:</h3>
<asp:TextBox ID="txtKeyword" runat="server"></asp:TextBox>
<asp:Button ID="btnSearch" runat="server" Text="Search" />
<br /><br />
<table id="tblResponse">
  <thead>
    <tr>
      <th>Employee ID</th>
      <th>First Name</th>
      <th>Last Name</th>
      <th>City</th>
      <th>Country</th>
      <th>Home Phone</th>
    </tr>
  </thead>
</table>
<br />
<asp:Label ID="lblMessage" runat="server"></asp:Label>
```

Notice that the form has a `Label` control, `lblMessage`. This field will be used to display information/error messages to the user, if any.

6. Style the page elements using the following CSS:

```css
<style type="text/css">
table, th, td {
  border: 1px solid black;
  border-collapse: collapse;
  padding:3px;
}
th{
  font-weight:700;
  font-variant:small-caps;
  text-align:center;
  background-color:lightgray;
}
td{
  background-color:lightyellow;
}
</style>
```

7. Add an `Employee` class to the project by right-clicking on the project and navigating to **Add | Class**. Name the class `Employee.vb` (VB) or `Employee.cs` (C#). Add the following properties to the class.

For VB, the code is as follows:

```vb
Public Class Employee
    Public Property EmployeeID As String
    Public Property LastName As String
    Public Property FirstName As String
    Public Property City As String
    Public Property Country As String
    Public Property HomePhone As String
End Class
```

For C#, the code is as follows:

```csharp
public class Employee
{
    public String EmployeeID { get; set; }
    public String LastName { get; set; }
    public String FirstName { get; set; }
    public String City{ get; set; }
    public String Country { get; set; }
    public String HomePhone { get; set; }
}
```

8. Next, we will add a WCF service to the project. To do this, right-click on the project in the **Solution Explorer** tab, and go to **Add | New Folder**. Name the new folder, `Services`.

9. Right-click on the `Services` folder and go to **Add | New Item**. From the launched dialog box, select **Web** from the **Installed** templates on the left-hand side of the screen. From the middle panel, select **WCF Service (Ajax-enabled)**. Give the service a suitable name such as `NorthwindService.svc`, and click on the **Add** button:

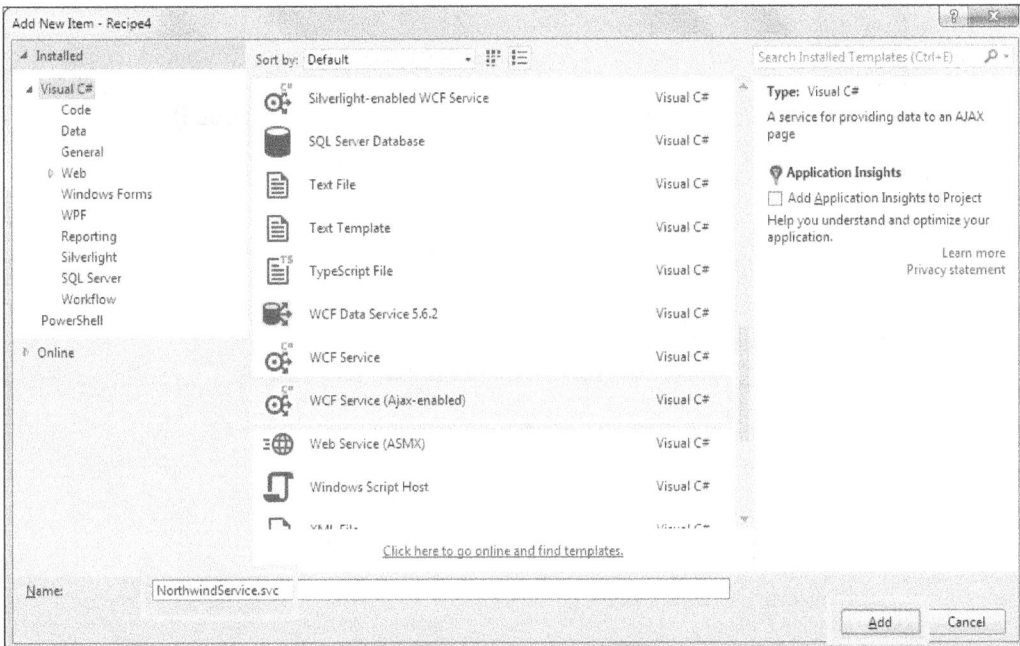

10. In the code-behind file of `NorthwindService.svc`, add the following namespace in order to enable us to retrieve the Northwind database connection string from `web.config`.

For VB, the namespace is as follows:

```
Imports System.Web.Configuration
```

For C#, the namespace is as follows:

```
using System.Web.Configuration;
```

11. Next, add the `GetEmployeeResult()` operation contract to the preceding code-behind file.

For VB, the code is as follows:

```vb
<OperationContract()>
Public Function GetEmployeeResult(ByVal sSearch As String)
As Employee()
  Dim employeeList As List(Of Employee) = New List(Of
Employee)()
  Dim strConn As String =
WebConfigurationManager.ConnectionStrings("NorthwindConnection").
ConnectionString
  Dim con As SqlConnection = New SqlConnection(strConn)
  Dim strSql As String = "SELECT * FROM EMPLOYEES WHERE
FirstName LIKE '%" + sSearch + "%' or LastName like '%" +
sSearch + "%'"
  Dim cmd As SqlCommand = New SqlCommand(strSql, con)
  con.Open()
  Dim dr As SqlDataReader = cmd.ExecuteReader()
  While (dr.Read())
    Dim emp As Employee = New Employee()
    emp.EmployeeID = dr("EmployeeID").ToString()
    emp.FirstName = dr("FirstName").ToString()
    emp.LastName = dr("LastName").ToString()
    emp.City = dr("City").ToString()
    emp.Country = dr("Country").ToString()
    emp.HomePhone = dr("HomePhone").ToString()
    employeeList.Add(emp)
  End While
  con.Close()
  Return employeeList.ToArray()
End Function
```

For C#, the code is as follows:

```csharp
[OperationContract]
public Employee[] GetEmployeeResult(String sSearch)
{
  List<Employee> employeeList = new List<Employee>();
  String strConn =
WebConfigurationManager.ConnectionStrings["NorthwindConnect
ion"].ConnectionString;
  SqlConnection con = new SqlConnection(strConn);
  String strSql = "SELECT * FROM EMPLOYEES WHERE FirstName
LIKE '%" + sSearch + "%' or LastName like '%" + sSearch +
"%'";
```

```
SqlCommand cmd = new SqlCommand(strSql, con);
con.Open();
SqlDataReader dr = cmd.ExecuteReader();
while (dr.Read())
{
    Employee emp = new Employee();
    emp.EmployeeID = dr["EmployeeID"].ToString();
    emp.FirstName = dr["FirstName"].ToString();
    emp.LastName = dr["LastName"].ToString();
    emp.City = dr["City"].ToString();
    emp.Country = dr["Country"].ToString();
    emp.HomePhone = dr["HomePhone"].ToString();
    employeeList.Add(emp);
}
con.Close();
return employeeList.ToArray();
}
```

The operation contract receives a search keyword from the calling program. It then connects to the Northwind database using ADO.NET and queries the `Employees` table to return records where the `FirstName` or `LastName` column contains the search keyword. The list of records is returned as an array of the `Employee` type.

> Note that the calling program needs to pass the `sSearch` input parameter to the WCF operation contract.

12. Add a connection string to the Northwind database in the configuration section of the `web.config` file:

```
<connectionStrings>
    <add name="NorthwindConnection"
providerName="System.Data.SqlClient" connectionString="Data
Source=localhost;Initial Catalog=Northwind;Integrated
Security=True;"/>
</connectionStrings>
```

> Note that we are using Windows Authentication for all database driven examples in this book. Hence in the MS SQL Server, it is important to give permission to the Windows account to access the Northwind database.

How to do it...

Include the following jQuery code in a `<script>` block on the page:

```
<script type="text/javascript">
  $(document).ready(function() {
    $("#tblResponse").hide();
    $("#<%=lblMessage.ClientID%>").hide();
    $("#<%=txtKeyword.ClientID%>").focus();
    $("#<%=btnSearch.ClientID%>").on("click", function(evt) {
      evt.preventDefault();
      $("#<%=lblMessage.ClientID%>").hide();
      var sKeyword = $("#<%=txtKeyword.ClientID%>").val().trim();
      if (sKeyword != "") {
        $.ajax({
          url: "/Services/NorthwindService.svc/GetEmployeeResult",
          type: "POST",
          data: '{ "sSearch": "' + sKeyword + '"}',
          dataType: "json",
          contentType: "application/json; charset=utf-8",
          timeout: 5000,
          cache: false,
          success: function(response) {
            $("#tblResponse tr:gt(0)").remove();
            if ($("#tblResponse").is(":hidden"))
              $("#tblResponse").show();
            if (response.d.length > 0) {
              $.each(response.d, function() {
                $("#tblResponse").append("<tr><td>" +
this['EmployeeID'] + "</td><td>" + this['FirstName'] + "</td><td>"
+ this['LastName'] + "</td><td>" + this['City'] + "</td><td>" +
this['Country'] + "</td><td>" + this['HomePhone'] + "</td></tr>");
              });
            } else
              $("#<%=lblMessage.ClientID%>").text("No results").
show();
          },
          error: function(jqXHR, textStatus, errorThrown) {
            if (textStatus == "error") {
              alert("An error has occurred: " + jqXHR.status + " "
+ jqXHR.statusText);
            }
          }
        });
      } else
```

```
          alert("Please enter your search keyword");
     });
   });
</script>
```

How it works...

The Ajax call to the WCF service works as follows:

1. When the page is launched, a text field is displayed to the user for keying in the search keyword. The following initializations are done on the page:

    ❏   The result table is initially hidden using the following:

    ```
    $("#tblResponse").hide();
    ```

    ❏   The Label field for displaying information / error messages is also hidden:

    ```
    $("#<%=lblMessage.ClientID%>").hide();
    ```

    ❏   The cursor is focused on the text field so that the user can key in the required keywords:

    ```
    $("#<%=txtKeyword.ClientID%>").focus();
    ```

2. An event handler is defined to respond to the `click` event of the button on the page:

    ```
    $("#<%=btnSearch.ClientID%>").on("click", function (evt) {…});
    ```

    In this event handler, the page is prevented from posting back using the following:

    ```
    evt.preventDefault();
    ```

    It is possible that the previous query would have displayed information/error messages, so the `lblMessage` control is hidden once again:

    ```
    $("#<%=lblMessage.ClientID%>").hide();
    ```

3. Next, the keyword entered in the text field is retrieved. Whitespaces, if any, are trimmed:

    ```
    var sKeyword = $("#<%=txtKeyword.ClientID%>").val().trim();
    ```

    If the keyword is not blank, an Ajax call is made to the Web service:

    ```
    if (sKeyword != "") {
      $.ajax({
        url:
    "/Services/NorthwindService.svc/GetEmployeeResult",
        type: "POST",
        data: '{ "sSearch": "' + sKeyword + '"}',
        dataType: "json",
        contentType: "application/json; charset=utf-8",
    ```

```
        timeout: 5000,
        cache: false,
        success: function(response) {
          $("#tblResponse tr:gt(0)").remove();
          if ($("#tblResponse").is(":hidden"))
            $("#tblResponse").show();
          if (response.d.length > 0) {
            $.each(response.d,
              function() {
                $("#tblResponse").append("<tr><td>" +
this['EmployeeID'] + "</td><td>" + this['FirstName'] +
"</td><td>" + this['LastName'] + "</td><td>" + this['City']
+ "</td><td>" + this['Country'] + "</td><td>" +
this['HomePhone'] + "</td></tr>");
              });
          } else $("#<%=lblMessage.ClientID%>").text("No
results").show();
        },
        error: function(jqXHR, textStatus, errorThrown) {
          if (textStatus == "error") {
            alert("An error has occurred: " + jqXHR.status + "
" + jqXHR.statusText);
          }
        }
    });
}
```

In the preceding Ajax call, the following options are set:

- ❏ The request URL is set to WCFPath/OperationContract.

- ❏ The type/method of the HTTP request is set to POST.

- ❏ The data consists of a JSON formatted string. The search keyword is sent as a name/value pair. The name is set to sSearch and the value is set to the string retrieved from the text field, as follows:

  ```
  '{ "sSearch": "' + sKeyword + '"}'
  ```

- ❏ The expected data type of the response is set to json.

- ❏ The content type is set to application/json and the character is set to utf-8.

- ❏ A timeout of 5000 milliseconds is specified so that the request is terminated if the server fails to respond within this timeframe.

- ❏ The cache is set to false so that the response is not cached in the browser.

- ❏ A callback function is specified for the successful completion of the Ajax call. This function, first of all, clears the display table:

  ```
  $("#tblResponse tr:gt(0)").remove();
  ```

If the table is hidden, it is made visible.

```
if ($("#tblResponse").is(":hidden"))
  $("#tblResponse").show();
```

4. Next, it checks whether the response is nonempty. This can be done by checking the length of `response.d`. If the response is nonempty, each item in the response array is displayed:

```
if (response.d.length > 0) {
  $.each(response.d, function () {
    $("#tblResponse").append("<tr><td>" +
this['EmployeeID'] + "</td><td>" + this['FirstName'] +
"</td><td>" + this['LastName'] + "</td><td>" + this['City']
+ "</td><td>" + this['Country'] + "</td><td>" +
this['HomePhone'] + "</td></tr>");
  });
}
```

However, if the response is empty, an error is displayed using the `lblMessage` control:

```
$("#<%=lblMessage.ClientID%>").text("No results").show();
```

5. A callback function is specified for an unsuccessful Ajax call. It displays the `status` and `statusText` parameters of `XmlHttpObject` in case of an error.

6. If, however, the search keyword is blank when the user clicks on the `Button` control, the following error message is displayed to the user:

```
alert("Please enter your search keyword");
```

See also

The *Consuming Web services* recipe

Retrieving data from a Web API

A **Web API** (**Web Application Programming Interface**) is a HTTP API that is created using the .NET framework. It uses the HTTP protocol to return data. Since HTTP is available universally across a wide range of platforms, these APIs can be used on Web and mobile platforms and across various devices.

In this example, we will use jQuery Ajax to post a request to a Web API. The constructs used in this example are summarized in the following table:

Construct	Type	Description
`$("#identifier")`	jQuery selector	This selects an element based on its ID.
`$("html_tag")`	jQuery selector	This selects all elements with the specified HTML tag.
`$.getJSON()`	jQuery function	This loads the JSON data from the server using the HTTP GET request.
`.append()`	jQuery method	This inserts content at the end of each matched element.
`click`	jQuery event	This is fired when you click on an element. It corresponds to the JavaScript `click` event.
`event.preventDefault()`	jQuery method	This prevents the default action of the event from being triggered.
`.focus()`	jQuery event binder	This triggers the `focus` event of an element or binds an event handler to the `focus` event.
`:gt(i)`	jQuery selector	This selects matched elements that have an index greater than i. It uses a zero-based index.
`.hide()`	jQuery method	This hides the matched elements.
`:hidden`	jQuery selector	This selects hidden elements.
`.is()`	jQuery method	This returns a Boolean value if the matched element satisfies a given condition.
`.on()`	jQuery event binder	This attaches an event handler for one or more events to the matched elements.
`.remove()`	jQuery method	This deletes the matched elements from the DOM.
`.show()`	jQuery method	This displays the matched elements.
`.text()`	jQuery method	This returns the combined text content of each of the matched elements or sets the text content of every matched element.
`.trim()`	JavaScript function	This removes whitespaces from the beginning and end of a string.
`.val()`	jQuery method	This returns the value of the first matched element or sets the value of every matched element.

Getting ready

Follow these steps to build a page that will load data from a Web API:

1. Let's create a web page that allows you to search for customer records from the Northwind database using either `Customer ID` or `Customer Name`. When a match is found, the results are returned, as shown in the following screenshot:

Key in the Customer ID or Name to search:

QUE	Search

CUSTOMER ID	COMPANY NAME	CONTACT NAME	PHONE	COUNTRY
ANTON	Antonio Moreno Taqueria	Antonio Moreno	(5) 555-3932	Mexico
QUEDE	Que Delícia	Bernardo Batista	(21) 555-4252	Brazil
QUEEN	Queen Cozinha	Lúcia Carvalho	(11) 555-1189	Brazil

If no match is found, a message is displayed, as shown in the following screenshot:

Key in the Customer ID or Name to search:

stev	Search

CUSTOMER ID	COMPANY NAME	CONTACT NAME	PHONE	COUNTRY

No results

2. To create this application, launch an **ASP.NET Web Application** project in Visual Studio using the **Empty** template and name it `Recipe5` (or any other suitable name).

> Note that we are using the **Empty** template in this recipe. If **Web API** is chosen from the available templates, the API is created using ASP.NET MVC.

3. Add the jQuery library to the project in a `Scripts` folder.

4. Add a web form to the project and include the jQuery library in the form. In the `head` element, add the following styles:

```
<style type="text/css">
table, th, td {
   border: 1px solid black;
   border-collapse: collapse;
   padding:3px;
}
th{
   font-weight:700;
   font-variant:small-caps;
   text-align:center;
   background-color:lightgray;
}
td{
   background-color:lightyellow;
}
</style>
```

5. Add a **Model** folder by right-clicking on the project in the **Solution Explorer** tab and navigating to **Add | New Folder**. Next, right-click on the **Model** folder and go to **Add | Class**. Name the class `Customer.vb` (VB) or `Customer.cs` (C#). Add the following properties to this file.

For VB, the code is as follows:

```
Public Class Customer
   Public Property CustomerID As String
   Public Property CompanyName As String
   Public Property ContactName As String
   Public Property Phone As String
   Public Property Country As String
End Class
```

For C#, add the following code:

```
public class Customer
{
```

```
    public String CustomerID { get; set;}
    public String CompanyName { get; set; }
    public String ContactName { get; set; }
    public String Country { get; set; }
    public String Phone { get; set; }
}
```

6. Add a **Controllers** folder by right-clicking on the project and navigating to **Add** | **New Folder**. Next, right-click on the **Controllers** folder and go to **Add** | **Controller**. Select **Web API 2 Controller – Empty** from the list of available templates, as shown in the following screenshot, and click on the **Add** button:

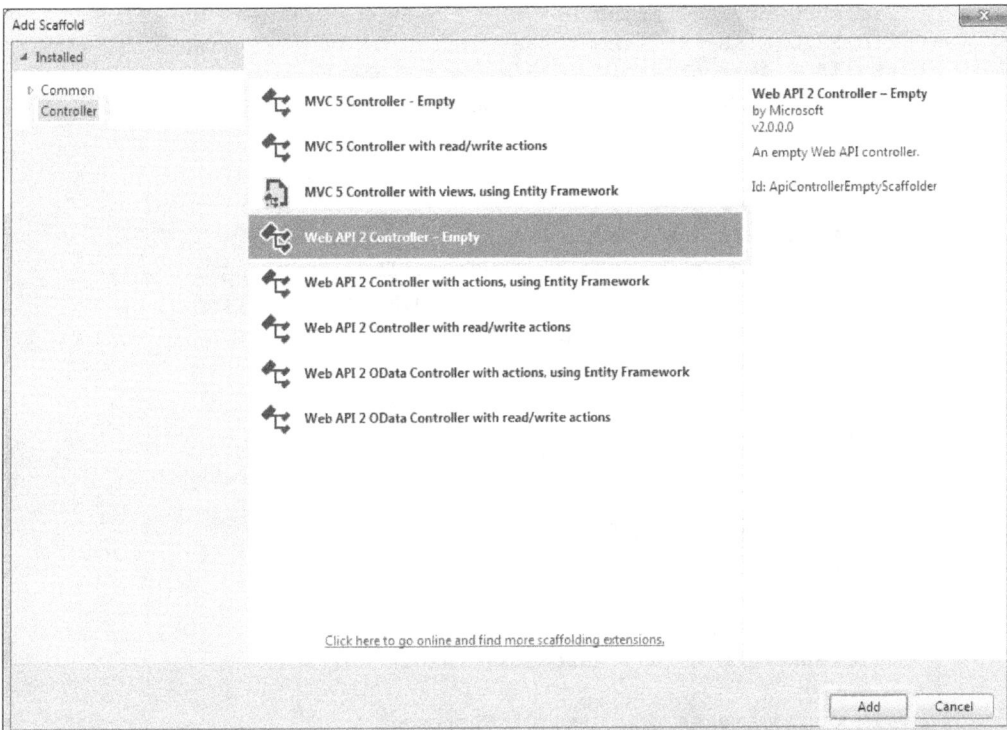

In the next dialog box, enter a suitable name for the controller. We have named the controller, **CustomerController**:

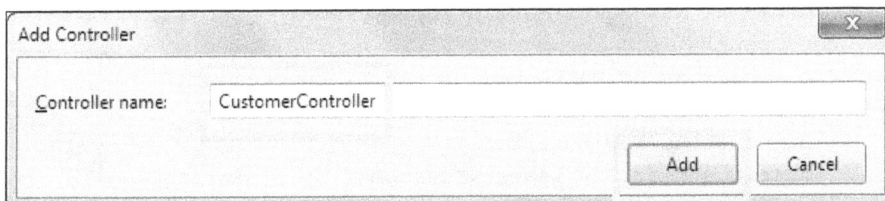

7. Open the code-behind file of `CustomerController`, that is, `CustomerController.vb` (VB) or `CustomerController.cs` (C#) and add the following methods.

For VB, the code is as follows:

```vb
' GET api/<controller>/keyword
Public Function GetCustomers(ByVal searchKeyword As String)
As IEnumerable(Of Customer)
  Dim customers As New List(Of Customer)
  Dim con As New
SqlConnection(WebConfigurationManager.ConnectionStrings
("NorthwindConnection").ConnectionString)
  Dim strQuery As String = "SELECT * FROM CUSTOMERS WHERE
CUSTOMERID LIKE '%" + searchKeyword + "%' OR COMPANYNAME
LIKE '%" + searchKeyword + "%'"
  Dim cmd As New SqlCommand(strQuery, con)
  con.Open()
  Dim reader As SqlDataReader = cmd.ExecuteReader()
  While (reader.Read())
    Dim cust As New Customer()
    cust.CustomerID = reader("CustomerID").ToString()
    cust.CompanyName = reader("CompanyName").ToString()
    cust.ContactName = reader("ContactName").ToString()
    cust.Country = reader("Country").ToString()
    cust.Phone = reader("Phone").ToString()
    customers.Add(cust)
  End While
  con.Close()
  Return customers
End Function


' GET api/<controller>
Public Function GetAllCustomers() As IEnumerable(Of
Customer)
  Dim customers As New List(Of Customer)
  Dim con As New
SqlConnection(WebConfigurationManager.ConnectionStrings
("NorthwindConnection").ConnectionString)
  Dim strQuery As String = "SELECT * FROM CUSTOMERS"
  Dim cmd As New SqlCommand(strQuery, con)
  con.Open()
  Dim reader As SqlDataReader = cmd.ExecuteReader()
  While (reader.Read())
    Dim cust As New Customer()
    cust.CustomerID = reader("CustomerID").ToString()
```

```
    cust.CompanyName = reader("CompanyName").ToString()
    cust.ContactName = reader("ContactName").ToString()
    cust.Country = reader("Country").ToString()
    cust.Phone = reader("Phone").ToString()
    customers.Add(cust)
  End While
  con.Close()
  Return customers
End Function
```

For C#, the code is as follows:

```csharp
public IEnumerable<Customer> GetCustomers(String
searchKeyword)
{
  List<Customer> customers = new List<Customer>();
  SqlConnection con = new
SqlConnection(WebConfigurationManager.ConnectionStrings
["NorthwindConnection"].ConnectionString);
  String strQuery = "SELECT * FROM CUSTOMERS WHERE
CUSTOMERID LIKE '%" + searchKeyword + "%' OR COMPANYNAME
LIKE '%" + searchKeyword + "%'" ;
  SqlCommand cmd = new SqlCommand(strQuery, con);
  con.Open();
  SqlDataReader reader = cmd.ExecuteReader();
  while (reader.Read())
  {
    Customer cust = new Customer();
    cust.CustomerID = reader["CustomerID"].ToString();
    cust.CompanyName = reader["CompanyName"].ToString();
    cust.ContactName = reader["ContactName"].ToString();
    cust.Country = reader["Country"].ToString();
    cust.Phone = reader["Phone"].ToString();
    customers.Add(cust);
  }
  con.Close();
  return customers;
}
public IEnumerable<Customer> GetAllCustomers()
{
  List<Customer> customers = new List<Customer>();
  SqlConnection con = new
SqlConnection(WebConfigurationManager.ConnectionStrings
["NorthwindConnection"].ConnectionString);
  String strQuery = "SELECT * FROM CUSTOMERS";
  SqlCommand cmd = new SqlCommand(strQuery, con);
```

```
con.Open();
SqlDataReader reader = cmd.ExecuteReader();
while (reader.Read())
{
    Customer cust = new Customer();
    cust.CustomerID = reader["CustomerID"].ToString();
    cust.CompanyName = reader["CompanyName"].ToString();
    cust.ContactName = reader["ContactName"].ToString();
    cust.Country = reader["Country"].ToString();
    cust.Phone = reader["Phone"].ToString();
    customers.Add(cust);
}
con.Close();
return customers;
}
```

We have defined two GET methods in the Web API. The GetCustomers() method takes in a searchKeyword string parameter and returns the list of all the customers from the Customer table of the Northwind database, where the CustomerID or CustomerName column contains this keyword. The second GetAllCustomers() method takes no parameters and returns the entire set of records from the Customer table.

Also, add the following namespaces at the top of the file.

For VB, the namespace is as follows:

```
Imports System.Web.Http
Imports System.Data.SqlClient
Imports System.Web.Configuration
```

For C#, the namespace is as follows:

```
using System.Web.Http;
using System.Data.SqlClient;
using System.Web.Configuration;
```

8. To connect to the Northwind database, add the following connection string to the configuration section of web.config:

```
<connectionStrings>
    <add name="NorthwindConnection"
providerName="System.Data.SqlClient" connectionString="Data
Source=localhost;Initial Catalog=Northwind;Integrated
Security=True;"/>
</connectionStrings>
```

> Remember to give permission to the Windows account to the Northwind database.

9. Add the routing information to the Web API in the `Application_Start` procedure in `Global.asax`.

For VB, the code is as follows:

```
Sub Application_Start(ByVal sender As Object, ByVal e As
EventArgs)
   RouteTable.Routes.MapHttpRoute("CustomerApi",
"api/{controller}/{searchKeyword}",
   defaults:=New With {.searchKeyword =
System.Web.Http.RouteParameter.Optional})
End Sub
```

For C#, the code is as follows:

```
protected void Application_Start(object sender, EventArgs e)
{
  RouteTable.Routes.MapHttpRoute(
    name: "CustomerApi",
    routeTemplate: "api/{controller}/{searchKeyword}",
    defaults: new { searchKeyword = RouteParameter.Optional
}
  );
}
```

This exposes the methods of the Web API at `api/controller/keyword`.

> If the `RouteTable.Routes.MapHttpRoute` method is not recognized, add a reference to the `System.Web.Http` and `System.Web.Http.WebHost` assemblies by right-clicking on the project in the **Solution Explorer** tab and navigating to **Add | Reference**.

How to do it...

Add the following jQuery code to a `<script>` block on the page:

```
<script type="text/javascript">
  $(document).ready(function() {
    $("#tblResponse").hide();
    $("#<%=lblMessage.ClientID%>").hide();
    $("#<%=txtKeyword.ClientID%>").focus();
```

```
$("#<%=btnSearch.ClientID%>").on("click", function(evt) {
    evt.preventDefault();
    $("#<%=lblMessage.ClientID%>").hide();
    var sKeyword = $("#<%=txtKeyword.ClientID%>").val().trim();
    var uri = ((sKeyword == "") ? "api/customer" :
"api/customer/" + sKeyword);
    $.getJSON(uri).done(function(data) {
        $("#tblResponse tr:gt(0)").remove();
        if ($("#tblResponse").is(":hidden"))
          $("#tblResponse").show();
        if (data.length > 0) {
          $.each(data, function(key, val) {
              $("#tblResponse").append("<tr><td>" + val.CustomerID +
"</td><td>" + val.CompanyName + "</td><td>" + val.ContactName +
"</td><td>" + val.Phone + "</td><td>" + val.Country +
"</td></tr>");
          });
        } else
          $("#<%=lblMessage.ClientID%>").text("No
results").show();
    }).fail(function(jqXHR, textStatus, errorThrown) {
        alert("An error has occurred: " + textStatus + " " +
errorThrown);
    });
  });
});
</script>
```

How it works...

The Ajax call to the Web API is made through the following steps:

1. When the page is loaded, the result table is hidden from the user:

   ```
   $("#tblResponse").hide();
   ```

2. The `label` control, used to display information/error messages to the user, is also hidden initially:

   ```
   $("#<%=lblMessage.ClientID%>").hide();
   ```

3. Next, the cursor is focused on the search keyword text field:

   ```
   $("#<%=txtKeyword.ClientID%>").focus();
   ```

4. The page will call the Web API when you click on the Search button. Hence, we write an event handler for the `click` event of this button:

```
$("#<%=btnSearch.ClientID%>").on("click", function (evt)
{...});
```

In this event handler, the page is prevented from posting back, as follows:

```
evt.preventDefault();
```

Next, the label used to display information/error messages is hidden:

```
$("#<%=lblMessage.ClientID%>").hide();
```

The search keyword is retrieved from the text field on the form. It is trimmed to remove whitespaces, if any:

```
var sKeyword = $("#<%=txtKeyword.ClientID%>").val().trim();
```

The Web API provides two `GET` methods: one with a parameter, that is, the `GetCustomers()` method and the other without a parameter, that is, the `GetAllCustomers()` method. The `GetCustomers()` method can be accessed at `api/customer/searchKeyword`, whereas the `GetAllCustomers()` method can be accessed at `api/customer`.

Hence, depending on whether the keyword is provided or not, we set the two respective URIs, as follows:

```
var uri = ((sKeyword == "") ? "api/customer" :
"api/customer/" + sKeyword);
```

5. Now, we make the Ajax call to the Web API by sending a request to the URI set in the preceding code using the `$.getJSON()` method:

```
$.getJSON(uri)
```

The return object provides the `.done()` and `.fail()` callback methods for successful and unsuccessful requests, respectively:

```
.done(function (data){...})
.fail(function (jqXHR, textStatus, errorThrown) {...});
```

6. The preceding `.done()` callback method clears the result table by deleting all the rows except the header row:

```
$("#tblResponse tr:gt(0)").remove();
```

If the result table is not visible, it is shown to the user:

```
if ($("#tblResponse").is(":hidden"))
  $("#tblResponse").show();
```

Next, we check the length of the data object returned from the Web API. If the object is not empty, we print each record, as follows:

```
if (data.length > 0){
  $.each(data, function (key, val) {
    $("#tblResponse").append("<tr><td>" + val.CustomerID +
"</td><td>" + val.CompanyName + "</td><td>" + val.ContactName +
"</td><td>" + val.Phone + "</td><td>" + val.Country +
"</td></tr>");
  });
}
```

If the object is empty, simply display an information message to the user:

```
$("#<%=lblMessage.ClientID%>").text("No results").show();
```

7. In the `.fail()` callback method of `$.getJSON()`, display the `status` and `statusText` parameters of the `jqXHR` object, as follows:

```
if (textStatus == "error") {
  alert("An error has occurred: " + jqXHR.status + " " +
jqXHR.statusText);
}
```

See also

The *Consuming page methods* recipe

Making Ajax calls to a controller action

Ajax calls can also be made to a `Controller` action in ASP.NET MVC applications. In this example, let's post a request to the controller action from a View. The constructs used in this example are summarized in the following table:

Construct	Type	Description
`$("#identifier")`	jQuery selector	This selects an element based on its ID.
`$.ajax()`	jQuery function	This posts an Ajax request to the server with the set options.
`change`	jQuery event	This is fired when the value of an element changes. It corresponds to the JavaScript `change` event.
`.on()`	jQuery event binder	This attaches an event handler for one or more events to the matched elements.

Construct	Type	Description
.text()	jQuery method	This returns the combined text content of each of the matched elements or sets the text content of every matched element.
.trim()	JavaScript function	This removes whitespaces from the beginning and end of a string.
.val()	jQuery method	This returns the value of the first matched element or sets the value of every matched element.

Getting ready

Follow these steps to create a MVC application that will use Ajax to post a request to the controller action:

1. Let's create a web page in ASP.NET MVC that returns the weather of a particular city. When the page is loaded, it displays a drop-down menu with a list of cities, as shown in the following screenshot:

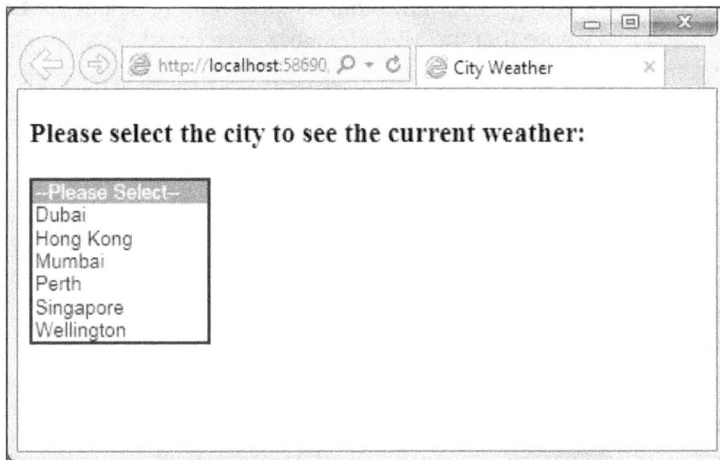

When a particular city is selected from the drop-down menu, the weather information is retrieved from the `Controller` action and displayed on the page, as shown in the following screenshot:

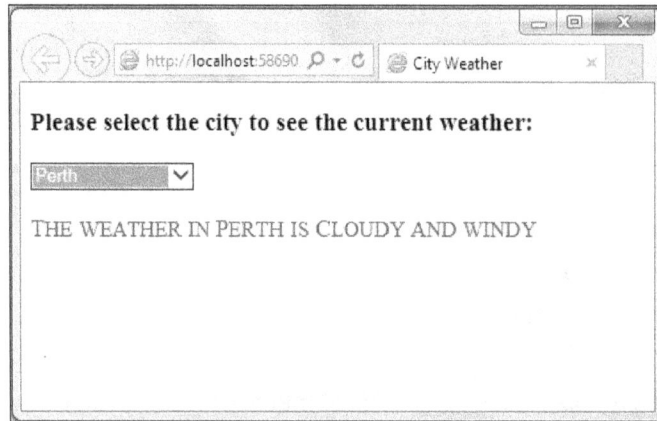

2. To create this application, launch an **ASP.NET Web Application** project in Visual Studio and name it `Recipe6` (or any other suitable name). Select the **Empty** template and make sure that the MVC checkbox is selected, as shown in the following screenshot:

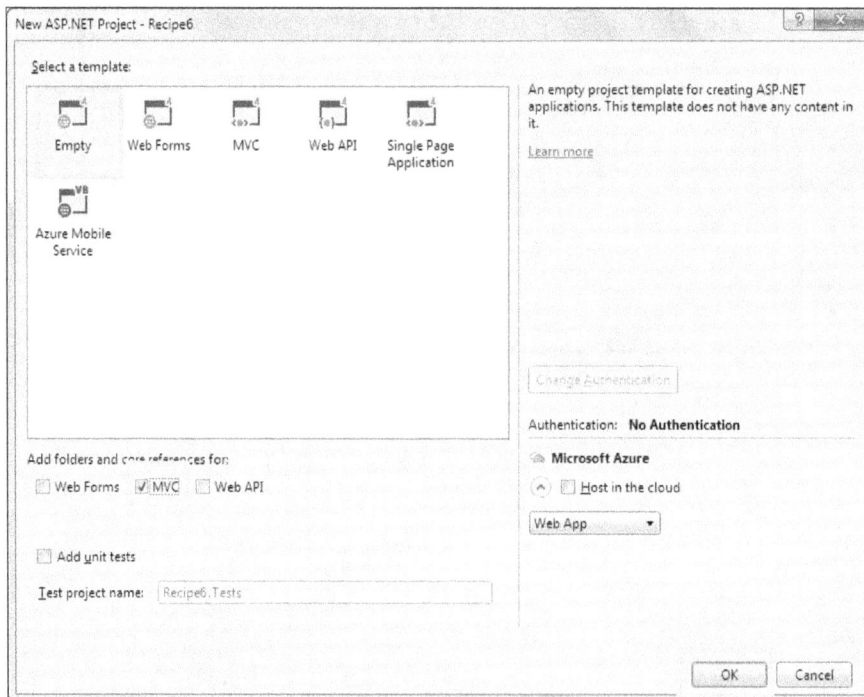

3. Click on the **OK** button to proceed.

4. Add the jQuery library to the project in a `Scripts` folder.

5. In the **Solution Explorer** tab, right-click on the `Controllers` folder and go to **Add | Controller**. From the **Add Scaffold** dialog box that is launched, choose **MVC5 Controller – Empty**, and click on the **Add** button:

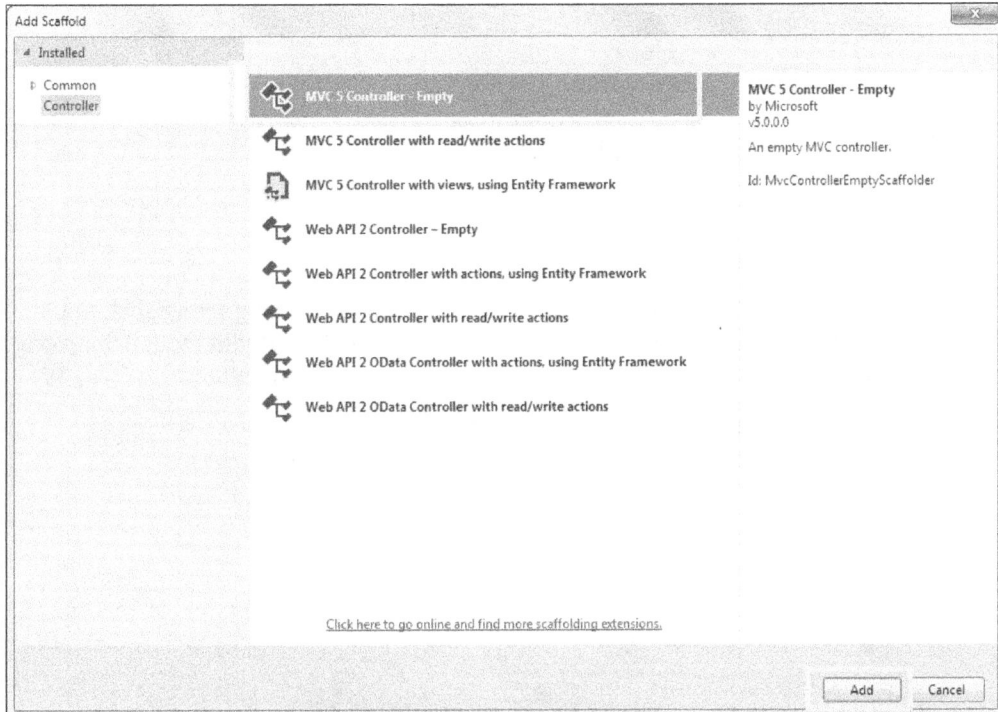

Name the controller `HomeController` in the following dialog box, and click on the **Add** button:

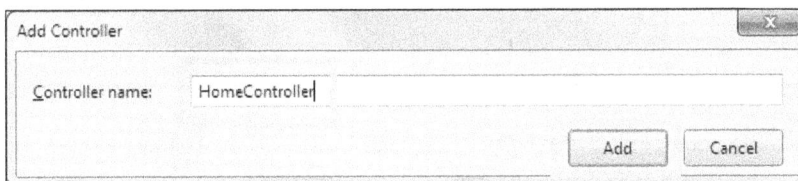

6. In the code-behind file of `HomeController`, you will notice that, by default, an `ActionResult` method called `Index` is defined. Right-click on the `Index` method, and click on the **Add View...** menu option, as shown in the following screenshot:

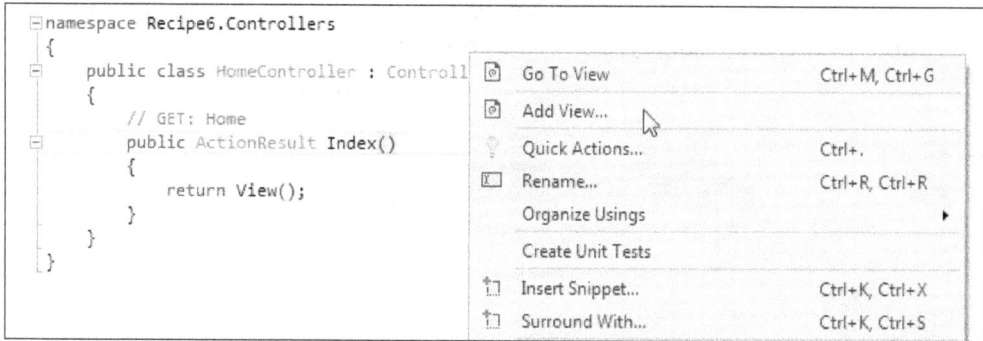

```
namespace Recipe6.Controllers
{
    public class HomeController : Controll    ⌐  Go To View              Ctrl+M, Ctrl+G
    {
        // GET: Home                          ⌐  Add View...
        public ActionResult Index()
        {                                     ⯑  Quick Actions...        Ctrl+.
            return View();
        }                                     ☐  Rename...               Ctrl+R, Ctrl+R
    }
}                                                Organize Usings                      ▶

                                                 Create Unit Tests

                                              ↰  Insert Snippet...       Ctrl+K, Ctrl+X
                                              ↰  Surround With...         Ctrl+K, Ctrl+S
```

This will launch the **Add View** window, as shown in the following screenshot. Enter `Index` for the **View name** text field and select the **Empty (without model)** template. Uncheck the **Use a layout page** option, and click on the **Add** button:

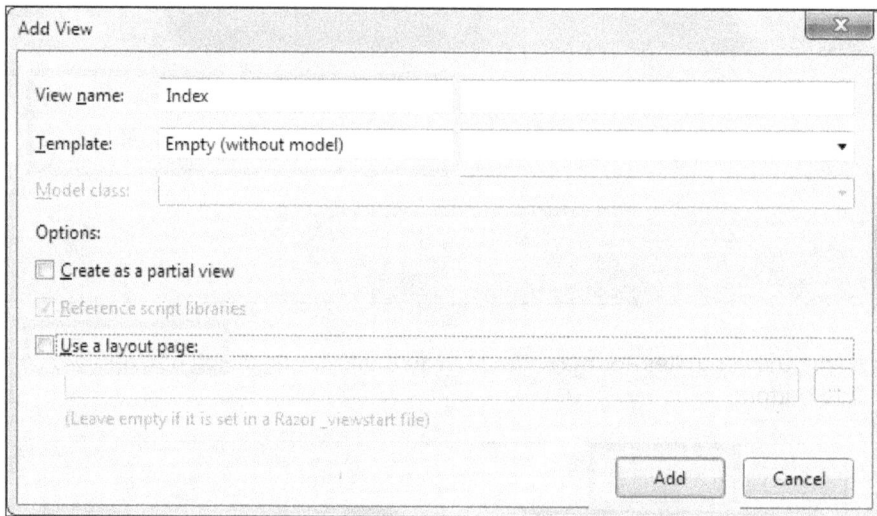

```
Add View                                                              ☒

    View name:      Index

    Template:       Empty (without model)                              ▼

    Model class:                                                       ▾

    Options:
    ☐ Create as a partial view
    ☑ Reference script libraries
    ☐ Use a layout page:
                                                                  [...]
       (Leave empty if it is set in a Razor _viewstart file)

                                          Add            Cancel
```

7. Open the code-behind file of the `Index` view and add the following markup:

```html
<!DOCTYPE html>
<html>
  <head>
    <meta name="viewport" content="width=device-width" />
    <title>City Weather</title>
    <script src="~/Scripts/jquery-2.1.4.js"></script>
```

```
<style type="text/css">
  #divResult {
  font-variant: small-caps;
  color: blue;
  font-size: large;
  }
</style>
</head>
<body>
  <form id="form1">
    <div>
      <h3>Please select the city to see the current
weather:</h3>
      <select id="ddlCities">
        <option value="">--Please Select--</option>
        <option value="Dubai">Dubai</option>
        <option value="Hong Kong">Hong Kong</option>
        <option value="Mumbai">Mumbai</option>
        <option value="Perth">Perth</option>
        <option value="Singapore">Singapore</option>
        <option value="Wellington">Wellington</option>
      </select>
    </div>
    <br />
    <div id="divResult"></div>
  </form>
</body>
</html>
```

8. Add a GetCityWeather() method to the code-behind file of HomeController to return the weather of a particular city. This method will take in one parameter, that is, the city name, and return a string containing the weather information.

For VB, the code is as follows:

```
Public Function GetCityWeather(ByVal sCity As String) As
String
  Dim sWeather As String = String.Empty
  Select Case sCity
    Case "Dubai"
      sWeather = "Hot and sunny"
    Case "Hong Kong"
      sWeather = "Sunny"
    Case "Mumbai"
      sWeather = "Partially sunny"
    Case "Perth"
```

```
        sWeather = "Cloudy and windy"
      Case "Singapore"
        sWeather = "Hot and cloudy"
      Case "Wellington"
        sWeather = "Mostly cloudy"
      Case Else
        sWeather = "No weather information found"
    End Select
    Return sWeather
End Function
```

For C#, the code is as follows:

```
public string GetCityWeather(string sCity)
{
    string sWeather = String.Empty;
    switch (sCity)
    {
      case "Dubai": sWeather = "Hot and sunny";
        break;
      case "Hong Kong": sWeather = "Sunny";
        break;
      case "Mumbai": sWeather = "Partially sunny";
        break;
      case "Perth": sWeather = "Cloudy and windy";
        break;
      case "Singapore": sWeather = "Hot and cloudy";
        break;
      case "Wellington": sWeather = "Mostly cloudy";
        break;
      default: sWeather = "No weather information found";
        break;
    }
    return sWeather;
}
```

> Note that the controller action accepts a `sCity` input parameter of the string type. This parameter should be provided by the client script in the Ajax request.

How to do it...

Add the following jQuery code to a `<script>` block on the View:

```
<script type="text/javascript">
  $(document).ready(function() {
    $("#ddlCities").on("change", function() {
      $("#divResult").text("");
      var sCity = $(this).val().trim();
      if (sCity != "") {
        $.ajax({
          url: "/Home/GetCityWeather",
          type: "POST",
          data: '{ "sCity": "' + sCity + '"}',
          dataType: "text",
          contentType: "application/json; charset=utf-8",
          timeout: 5000,
          cache: false,
          success: function(response) {
            $("#divResult").text("The weather in " + sCity
  + " is " + response);
          },
          error: function(jqXHR, textStatus, errorThrown) {
            if (textStatus == "error") {
              alert("An error has occurred: " +
  jqXHR.status + " " + jqXHR.statusText);
            }
          }
        });
      }
    });
  });
</script>
```

How it works...

The posting of Ajax request to the controller action works as follows:

1. The `div` element `divResult` is used to display the weather information that is retrieved asynchronously from the controller action.

2. The Ajax request is posted when the selected item in the dropdown changes. Hence, an event handler is written to respond to the `change` event of the dropdown, as follows:

    ```
    $("#ddlCities").on("change", function () {…});
    ```

In the preceding event handler, the contents of the div element are cleared initially:

```
$("#divResult").text("");
```

The name of the selected city is retrieved. Whitespaces, if any, are trimmed:

```
var sCity = $(this).val().trim();
```

If the city name is not blank, an Ajax request is posted to the controller action, as follows:

```
if (sCity != "") {
  $.ajax({
    url: "/Home/GetCityWeather",
    type: "POST",
    data: '{ "sCity": "' + sCity + '"}',
    dataType: "text",
    contentType: "application/json; charset=utf-8",
    timeout: 5000,
    cache: false,
    success: function (response) {
      $("#divResult").text("The weather in " + sCity + " is
" + response);
    },
    error: function (jqXHR, textStatus, errorThrown) {
      if (textStatus == "error") {
        alert("An error has occurred: " + jqXHR.status + "
" + jqXHR.statusText);
      }
    }
  });
}
```

In the preceding Ajax call, the following options are set:

- The request URL is set to Controller/Action.
- The type/method of the HTTP request is set to POST.
- The data consists of a JSON formatted string. The selected city is sent as a name / value pair using sCity as the name and the selected value from the dropdown as its value, as follows:

  ```
  '{ "sCity": "' + sCity + '"}'
  ```

- The expected data type of the response is set to text since the weather information sent by the controller action is in a string format.
- The content type is set to application/json and the character is set to utf-8.

- ❑ A timeout of `5000` milliseconds is specified so that the request is terminated if the server fails to respond within this timeframe.

- ❑ The cache is set to `false` so that the response is not cached in the browser.

- ❑ A callback function is specified for the successful completion of the Ajax call. This function simply displays the response text in the `div` area, as follows:

```
function (response) {
  $("#divResult").text("The weather in " + sCity + " is " +
  response);
}
```

- ❑ A callback function is specified for an unsuccessful Ajax call. It displays the `status` and `statusText` parameters of `XmlHttpObject` in case of an error:

```
function (jqXHR, textStatus, errorThrown) {
  if (textStatus == "error") {
    alert("An error has occurred: " + jqXHR.status + " " +
  jqXHR.statusText);
  }
}
```

See also

The *Retrieving data from a Web API* recipe

Making Ajax calls to a HTTP handler

A HTTP handler is a process that is executed when a request is made for a particular resource. For example, ASP.NET provides a page handler to process `*.aspx` files. Another example of an inbuilt handler is the web service handler used to process `*.asmx` files.

In this recipe, let's write a generic HTTP handler that will return custom data to the calling script. The constructs used in this example are summarized in the following table:

Construct	Type	Description
`$("#identifier")`	jQuery selector	This selects an element based on its ID
`$.ajax()`	jQuery function	This posts an Ajax request to the server with the set options
`$.map()`	jQuery function	This transforms an array or object into another array
`.autocomplete()`	jQuery UI method	This attaches the autocomplete widget to the required element

Follow these steps to build a page that will make Ajax calls to a HTTP handler:

1. Let's create a web page that provides an autocomplete text field. The values in the autocomplete are filtered dynamically using the characters entered in the text field, as shown in the following screenshot:

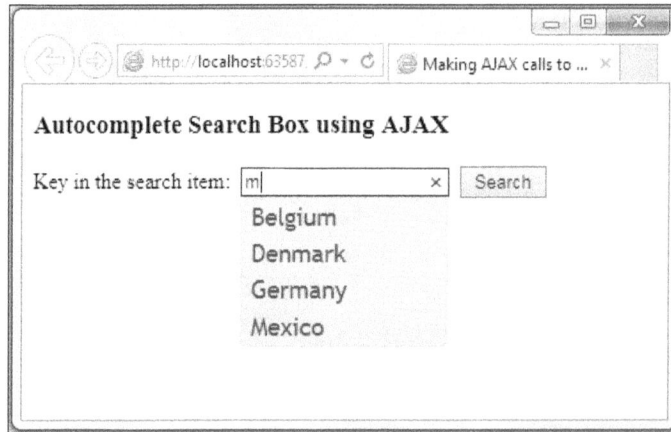

   Note that autocomplete consists of a list of countries retrieved from the `Country` column of the `Customers` table in the Northwind database.

2. To create this application, launch an **ASP.NET Web Application** project in Visual Studio using the **Empty** template and name it `Recipe7` (or any other suitable name).

3. Next, we will add a **LINQ to SQL class** to access data from the `Customers` table of the Northwind database. To do this, right-click on the project in **Solution Explorer** and go to **Add | New Item**. From the launched dialog box, select **Data** from the **Installed** templates from the left-hand side panel and **LINQ to SQL classes** from the middle panel. Name the item `Northwind.dbml`, and click on the **Add** button:

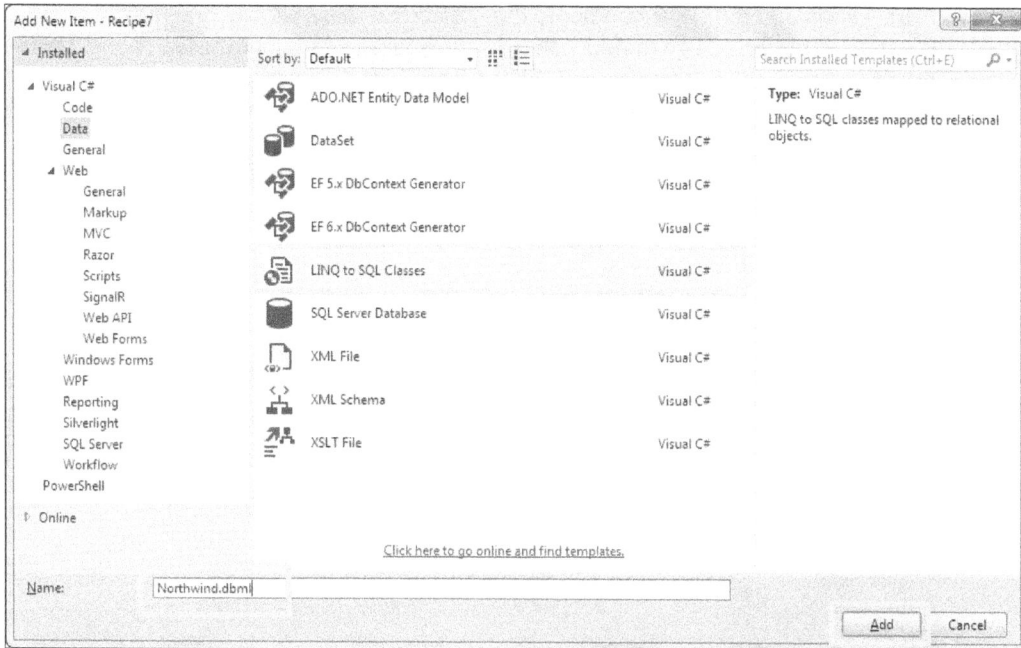

4. Connect to the Northwind database in **Server Explorer** and drag and drop the Customers table on Northwind.dbml, as shown in the following screenshot:

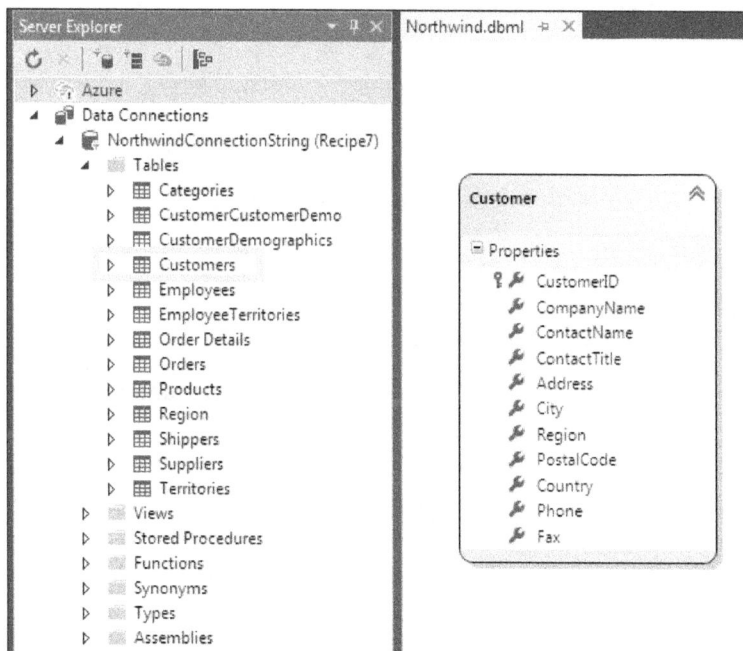

5. Next, we will add the HTTP handler to the project. So, right-click on the project in **Solution Explorer** and go to **Add | New Item**. From the dialog box, click on the **Web** tab from the **Installed** templates in the left-hand side panel and **Generic Handler** in the middle panel. Enter the name `SearchKeys.ashx` and click on the **Add** button:

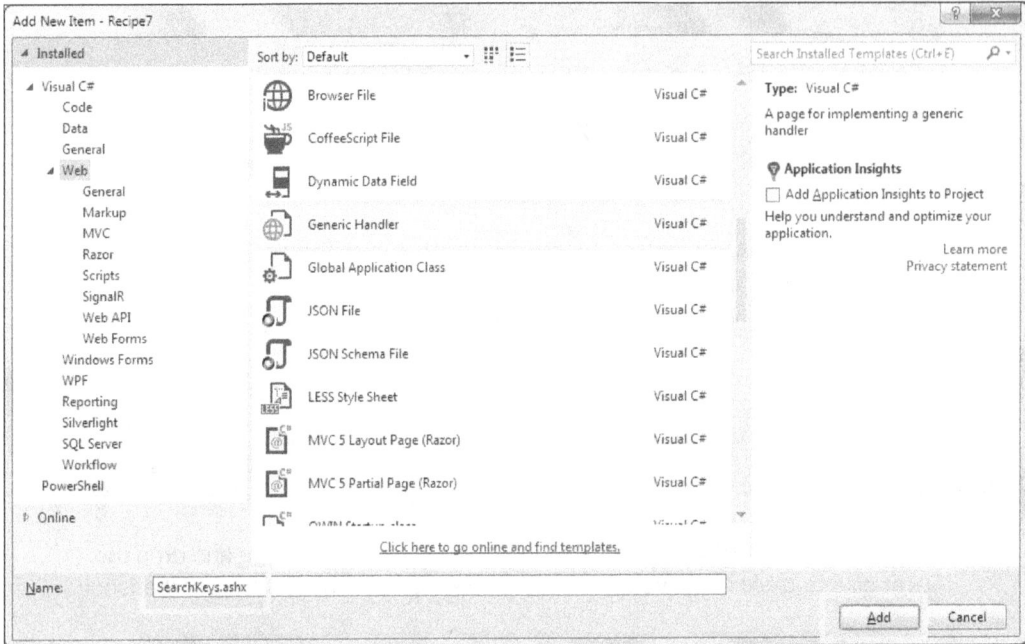

6. In the code-behind file of the HTTP handler, add the following namespaces on the top.

   For VB, the namespace is as follows:

   ```
   Imports System.Data.Linq.SqlClient
   Imports System.Web.Script.Serialization
   ```

   For C#, the namespace is as follows:

   ```
   using System.Data.Linq.SqlClient;
   using System.Web.Script.Serialization;
   ```

7. Update the `SearchKeys` class to include a `ProcessRequest` method, as follows.

   For VB, the code is as follows:

   ```
   Public Class SearchKeys
   Implements System.Web.IHttpHandler


   Sub ProcessRequest(ByVal context As HttpContext) Implements
   IHttpHandler.ProcessRequest
   ```

```
   Dim strSearchText As String =
context.Request.QueryString("sSearchText").Trim()
   Dim db As NorthwindDataContext = New
NorthwindDataContext()
   Dim countryList As List(Of String) = (From cust In
db.Customers
   Where SqlMethods.Like(cust.Country, "%" + strSearchText +
"%")
   Select cust.Country).Distinct().ToList()
   Dim serializer As JavaScriptSerializer = New
JavaScriptSerializer()
   Dim jsonString As String =
serializer.Serialize(countryList)
   context.Response.Write(jsonString)
End Sub

ReadOnly Property IsReusable() As Boolean Implements
IHttpHandler.IsReusable
   Get
      Return False
   End Get
End Property
End Class
```

For C#, the code is as follows:

```csharp
public class SearchKeys : IHttpHandler
{
   public void ProcessRequest(HttpContext context)
   {
      string strSearchText = context.Request.
QueryString["sSearchText"].Trim();
      NorthwindDataContext db = new NorthwindDataContext();
      List<string> countryList = (from cust in db.Customers
      where SqlMethods.Like(cust.Country, "%" + strSearchText + "%")
      select cust.Country).Distinct().ToList();
      JavaScriptSerializer serializer = new JavaScriptSerializer();
      string jsonString = serializer.Serialize(countryList);
      context.Response.Write(jsonString);
   }

   public bool IsReusable
   {
      get
```

```
        {
          return false;
        }
      }
    }
```

> The HTTP handler created in the preceding code implements the
> `IHttpHander` interface. This interface requires the handler to implement
> the `IsReusable` property and `ProcessRequest` method. When the
> handler is invoked, the `ProcessRequest` method is called. Hence,
> this method contains the code to generate the necessary output. The
> `IsReusable` property indicates that the `IHttpHandlerFactory` (that
> is, the object that calls the hander) can put the handler in a pool and reuse it
> from the pool to improve the performance. If this property is set to `false`, a
> new handler is created each time the handler is invoked.

The `ProcessRequest` method takes a single argument of the `HttpContext` type.
The search term is extracted from this argument using `Request.QueryString`.

> Note that the client script needs to pass the search keyword to the handler as
> a query string parameter with the `sSearchText` name.

The list of countries from the `Customers` table is filtered using the search keyword.
The list is then serialized into a JSON string using the `Serialize` method of the
`JavaScriptSerializer` class.

8. Next, we will add the jQuery UI autocomplete widget to the project. To download
    this package using NuGet, from the menu at the top of the Visual Studio IDE, go
    to **Project | Manage NuGet Packages**. In the NuGet window, search for **jQuery UI
    autocomplete**, as shown in the following screenshot. Click on the **Install** button to
    install the package and its dependencies:

NuGet: Recipe7 ⊹ ✕

NuGet Package Manager: Recipe7

Package source: api.nuget.org ▾   Filter: All ▾   ☑ Include prerelease

jquery ui autocomplete   ✕ ▾   ⚙

---

jQuery **jQuery.UI.Widgets.Autocomplete**
Part of jQuery UI Widgets. Creates an autocomplete widget.

jQuery **jQuery.UI.Combined**
The full jQuery UI library as a single combined file. Includes the base theme.

jQuery
jQuery is a new kind of JavaScript Library.
   jQuery is a fast and concise JavaScript Library th...

Each package is licensed to you by its owner. Microsoft is not responsible for, nor does it grant any licenses to, third-party packages.

☐ Do not show this again

jQuery **jQuery.UI.Widgets.Autocomplete**

Action: **Version:**

Install   ▾   Latest stable 1.8.9   ▾

[Install]

Options
☑ Show preview window

Dependency behavior: Lowest   ▾

File conflict action: Prompt   ▾

Learn about Options

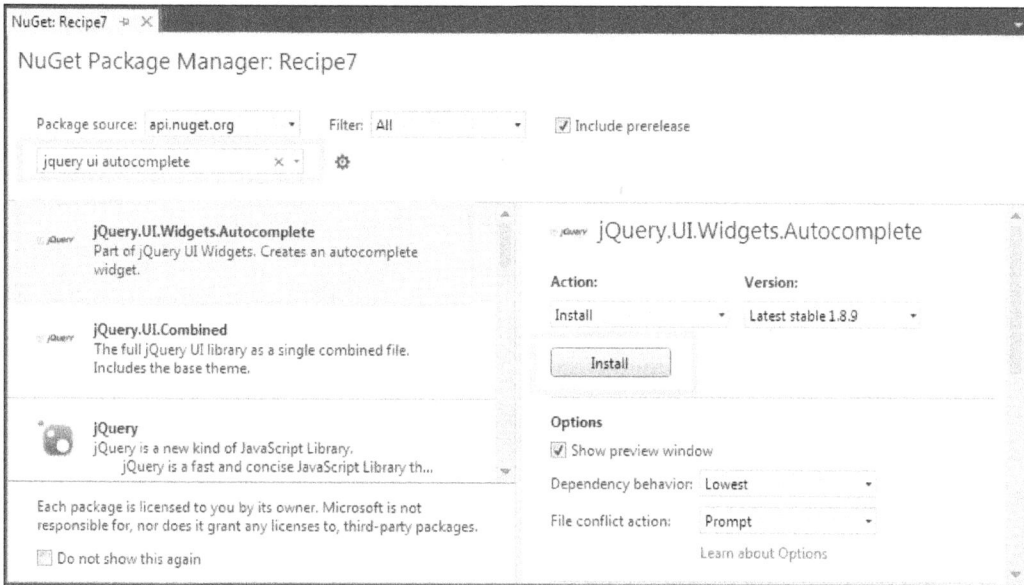

Notice that after the installation is completed, a `Scripts` folder is created with a list of files, as shown in the following screenshot:

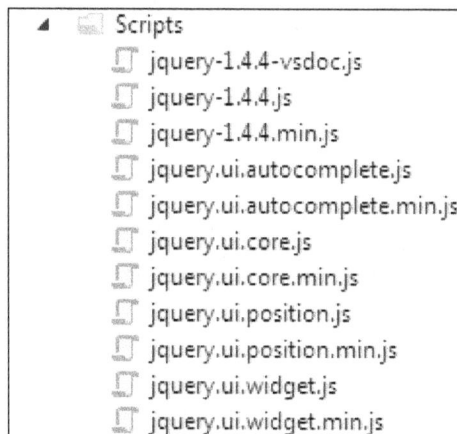

▲ 📁 Scripts
   🗋 jquery-1.4.4-vsdoc.js
   🗋 jquery-1.4.4.js
   🗋 jquery-1.4.4.min.js
   🗋 jquery.ui.autocomplete.js
   🗋 jquery.ui.autocomplete.min.js
   🗋 jquery.ui.core.js
   🗋 jquery.ui.core.min.js
   🗋 jquery.ui.position.js
   🗋 jquery.ui.position.min.js
   🗋 jquery.ui.widget.js
   🗋 jquery.ui.widget.min.js

Retain the downloaded version of jQuery to ensure compatibility with the jQuery UI files.

9. Add a web form to the project and include the downloaded scripts in the head section:

```
<script src="Scripts/jquery-1.4.4.js"></script>
<script src="Scripts/jquery.ui.core.js"></script>
<script src="Scripts/jquery.ui.position.js"></script>
<script src="Scripts/jquery.ui.widget.js"></script>
<script src="Scripts/jquery.ui.autocomplete.js"></script>
```

10. Add the following markup to the form:

```
<div>
  <h3>Autocomplete Search Box using AJAX</h3>
  <asp:Label ID="lblSearchText" runat="server" Text="Key in
the search item:"></asp:Label> 
  <asp:TextBox ID="txtSearchText"
runat="server"></asp:TextBox> 
  <asp:Button ID="btnSearch" runat="server" Text="Search"
/>
</div>
```

11. Include the jQuery UI style sheet in the form in the head section. This style sheet can be downloaded from `https://jqueryui.com`:

```
<link href="Styles/jquery-ui.css" rel="stylesheet" />
```

How to do it...

Add the following jQuery code to a `<script>` block on the page:

```
<script type="text/javascript">
  $(document).ready(function() {
    $("#<%=txtSearchText.ClientID%>").autocomplete({
      source: function(request, response) {
        $.ajax({
          url: "SearchKeys.ashx?sSearchText=" + request.term,
          type: "POST",
          dataType: "json",
          contentType: "application/json; charset=utf-8",
          timeout: 5000,
          cache: false,
          success: function(data) {
            response($.map(data, function(item) {
              return {
                value: item
              }
            }));
```

```
                },
                error: function(jqXHR, textStatus, errorThrown) {
                    if (textStatus == "error") {
                        alert("An error has occurred: " + jqXHR.status + " "
+ jqXHR.statusText);
                    }
                }
            });
        },
        minLength: 1
    });
});
</script>
```

How it works...

The posting of the Ajax request to the HTTP handler works as follows:

1. The jQuery UI autocomplete widget can be added to any field that takes in an input. In this example, the widget is added to the search text field, as follows:

   ```
   $("#<%=txtSearchText.ClientID%>").autocomplete({…});
   ```

2. The `autocomplete()` method provides a `source` option that can be set to an array, string, or function. In this case, we set the `source` to a function with two arguments, namely, a `request` object and a `response` callback.

   The request object has a `term` property that holds the text currently typed in the field by the user. An Ajax request is then posted to the HTTP handler using the `term` property as a query string parameter. This query string parameter is called `sSearchText` and is retrieved in the `ProcessRequest` method of the HTTP handler:

   ```
   source:
   function(request,response){
     $.ajax({
       url: "SearchKeys.ashx?sSearchText=" + request.term,
       type: "POST",
       dataType: "json",
       contentType: "application/json; charset=utf-8",
       timeout: 5000,
       cache: false,
       success: function (data) {
         response($.map(data, function (item)
         {
           return { value: item }
         }));
   ```

```
    },
    error: function (jqXHR, textStatus, errorThrown)
    {
       if (textStatus == "error") {
          alert("An error has occurred: " + jqXHR.status + "
" + jqXHR.statusText);
       }
    }
   });
 },
```

In the preceding Ajax call, the following options are set:

❑ The request URL is set to `URLOfHTTPHandler?QueryStringParam=Req`
`uest.term`.

❑ The type/method of the HTTP request is set to `POST`.

❑ The expected data type of the response is set to `json`.

❑ The content type is set to `application/json` and the character is set to
`utf-8`.

❑ A timeout of `5000` milliseconds is specified so that the request is terminated
if the server fails to respond within this timeframe.

❑ The cache is set to `false` so that the response is not cached in the browser.

❑ A callback function is specified for the successful completion of the Ajax call.
This function sets the argument of the response callback to the data to be
suggested to the user using the `$.map()` function, as follows:

```
function (data) {
   response($.map(data, function (item) {
      return { value: item }
   }));
},
```

❑ A callback function is specified for an unsuccessful Ajax call. It displays
the `status` and `statusText` parameters of `XmlHttpObject` in case
of an error:

```
function (jqXHR, textStatus, errorThrown) {
   if (textStatus == "error") {
      alert("An error has occurred: " + jqXHR.status + " " +
jqXHR.statusText);
   }
}
```

3. The autocomplete widget also provides the `minLength` option to set the number of characters the user needs to type in before the search is triggered. In this example, we will set the `minLength` option to `1` character, as follows:

```
minLength: 1
```

See also

The *Making Ajax calls to a controller action* recipe

8

Creating and Using jQuery Plugins

This chapter teaches you how to create and use plugins. The recipes discussed in this chapter are as follows:

- ▸ Creating and using a simple plugin
- ▸ Using the $ alias in the plugin
- ▸ Calling methods on DOM elements
- ▸ Providing default values
- ▸ Providing method chaining
- ▸ Adding actions to plugins
- ▸ Using the form validation plugin
- ▸ Downloading plugins using the NPM

Introduction

jQuery enables developers to build on top of the features of the core library by creating plugins. A plugin is basically an extension of the core library. It is a JavaScript file that is included on web pages along with the jQuery library. It usually provides a set of configurable items that developers can use to customize according to the requirements of their applications.

A wide variety of useful plugins are written and available for use. They cover many aspects of development, such as animations, graphics, forms, UI, and responsiveness. To maintain all plugins in a centralized location, a plugin repository was launched at `http://plugins.jquery.com` in 2013. However, this site now offers a read-only access to plugins and new releases can be made to the **NPM** (**Node Package Manager**). Plugins can be downloaded and used from the NPM.

In this chapter, let's get started with creating our own plugins. We will also download and use a popular jQuery plugin for validation of forms.

Creating and using a simple plugin

In this example, we will write a simple plugin to familiarize you with the process of creating and using plugins. The programming constructs used in this example are summarized as follows:

Construct	Type	Description
`.append()`	jQuery method	This inserts content at the end of each matched element
`jQuery`	jQuery function	This refers to the jQuery function
`jQuery("html_tag")`	jQuery selector	This selects all elements with the specified HTML tag

Getting ready

Follow these steps to create a simple jQuery plugin:

1. Launch a new **ASP.NET Web Application** project in Visual Studio using the **Empty** template and name it `TestApplication` (or any other suitable name).

2. Create a `Scripts` folder in the project. Add the jQuery library files to this folder.

3. Add a JavaScript file to the project by right clicking on the **Scripts** folder in the **Solution Explorer** tab and navigating to **Add | JavaScript File**. Name the file `jquery.sample.js`. This is our plugin file to which we will add the custom functions to extend the jQuery library.

> It is a good practice to name the plugin `jquery.{pluginname}.js`.

4. Add a new web form to the project and name it `Sample.aspx`. This form will be used to call the functions from the plugin.

5. Open the `Sample.aspx` page in the **Source** mode and drag and drop the jQuery library and plugin files to generate the following code in the head element:

```
<script src="Scripts/jquery-2.1.4.js"></script>
<script src="Scripts/jquery.sample.js"></script>
```

How to do it...

Use the $ alias in the plugin as follows:

1. Open the plugin file and add a `sampleMethod1()` function to the `jQuery` namespace, as shown in the following code snippet:

```
jQuery.sampleMethod1 = function(){
   jQuery("body").append("Inside the sample 1 method");
};
```

2. Next, call the function defined earlier by adding the following code to the `Sample.aspx` web form:

```
<script type="text/javascript">
$(document).ready(function () {
   $.sampleMethod1();
});
</script>
```

How it works...

On running the page in the browser, the plugin function displays the following text in the body of the page:

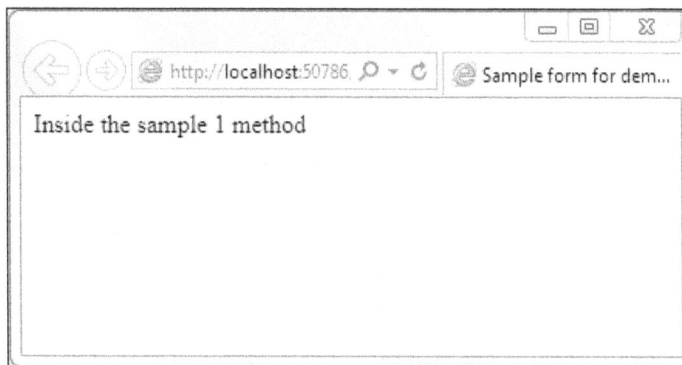

Since the function is defined in the `jQuery` namespace, it can be directly called on the $ object.

> The jQuery library defines many utility functions as global functions in the `jQuery` namespace. Some examples of these utility functions are `$.map()`, `$.each()`, and `$.ajax()`.

See also

The *Using the $ alias in the plugin* recipe

Using the $ alias in the plugin

In this example, let's modify the function defined in the plugin in the previous recipe to use the $ alias instead of the full `jQuery` name. The use of the $ shortcut enhances the readability of the code, but its availability is not always guaranteed. It is possible that other libraries in a project also use $. The use of the `$.noConflict()` method releases the control of $ by jQuery to other libraries.

The constructs used in this example are summarized as follows:

Construct	Type	Description
$	jQuery function	This refers to the jQuery function. $ is an alias for jQuery.
$("html_tag")	jQuery selector	This selects all elements with the specified HTML tag.
.append()	jQuery method	This inserts content at the end of each matched element.
jQuery	jQuery function	This refers to the jQuery function.

Getting ready

Let's see the requirements for using the $ alias in the jQuery plugin:

1. We will reuse the web form (`Sample.aspx`) and the plugin (`jquery.sample.js`) created in the previous recipe.

2. The plugin will be updated to include a wrapping function that takes $ as a parameter. The `jQuery` object will be passed as an argument to this function, as shown in the following code snippet:

   ```
   (function($){}) (jQuery);
   ```

   The passing of the `jQuery` object as an argument enables the use of the $ shortcut within this wrapping function.

How to do it...

Follow these steps to add a method to the plugin:

1. Replace the code in the `jquery.sample.js` file with the following code:

```
(function($) {
    $.sampleMethod2 = function() {
        $("body").append("Inside the sample 2 method");
    };
})(jQuery);
```

2. Change the method name in the `Sample.aspx` web form to use the one defined earlier:

```
<script type="text/javascript">
$(document).ready(function () {
    $.sampleMethod2();
});
</script>
```

How it works...

Run the page in the browser. The output is similar to the one in the previous recipe, that is, the required text is appended to the body of the page, as shown in the following screenshot:

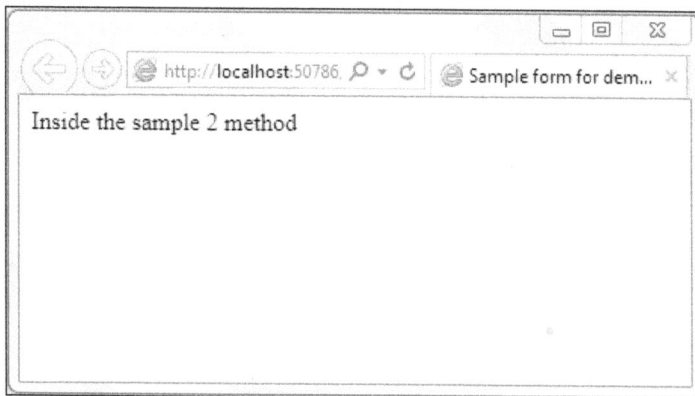

Since the method is defined in the `jQuery` namespace, it can be called directly on the `$` shortcut.

There's more

It is possible to define more than one function in a plugin. To add more functions, simply append them to the original plugin file inside the wrapping function. To demonstrate this, update the `jquery.sample.js` file with the following code:

```
(function ($) {
  $.sampleMethod1 = function () {
    $("body").append("Inside the sample 1 method<br/><br/>");
  };
  $.sampleMethod2 = function () {
    $("body").append("Inside the sample 2 method<br/><br/>");
  };
}) (jQuery);
```

To execute these functions from the web form, call them independently, as shown in the following code snippet:

```
<script type="text/javascript">
$(document).ready(function () {
  $.sampleMethod1();
  $.sampleMethod2();
});
</script>
```

On running the page, we find that both the functions are executed, as shown in the following screenshot:

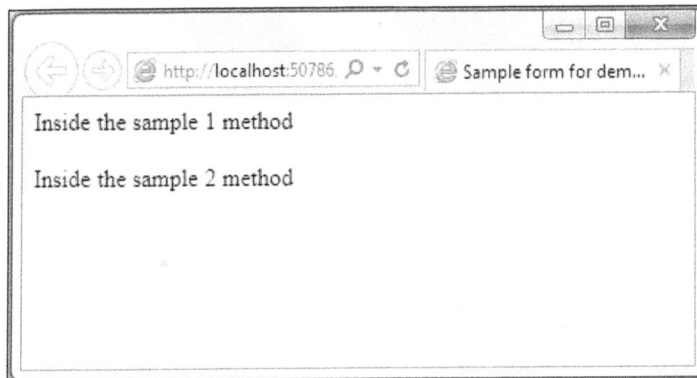

See also

The *Creating and using a simple plugin* recipe

Calling methods on DOM elements

In the previous recipe, the plugin is called on the $ shortcut. In this recipe, we will create a plugin that can be called directly on the DOM elements. This is possible by extending the jQuery.prototype, that is, the jQuery.fn object.

> Every object in JavaScript is derived from Object and inherits properties and methods from Object.prototype. When a property or method is attached to the prototype, all instances of the object reflect that property or method.

The constructs used in this example are summarized as follows:

Construct	Type	Description
$	jQuery function	This refers to the jQuery function. $ is an alias for jQuery.
$("#identifier")	jQuery selector	This selects an element based on its ID.
$("html_tag")	jQuery selector	This selects all elements with the specified HTML tag.
$(this)	jQuery object	This refers to the current jQuery object.
.css()	jQuery method	This gets the style property for the first matched element or sets the style property for every matched element.
.each()	jQuery method	This iterates over the matched elements and executes a function for each element.
.hasClass()	jQuery method	This returns true if the specified CSS class is attached to an element.
jQuery	jQuery function	This refers to the jQuery function.
setInterval(function, delay)	JavaScript function	This executes a function repeatedly after the specified delay in milliseconds.

Getting ready

Follow these steps to create a plugin that will provide methods on DOM elements:

1. Let's create a plugin that animates the text content of an element by switching its colors at regular intervals. For example, consider the following text on the page. At specific intervals, the color of the text will change to the colors in a rainbow (that is, violet, indigo, blue, green, yellow, orange, and red) one by one in a cyclic manner.

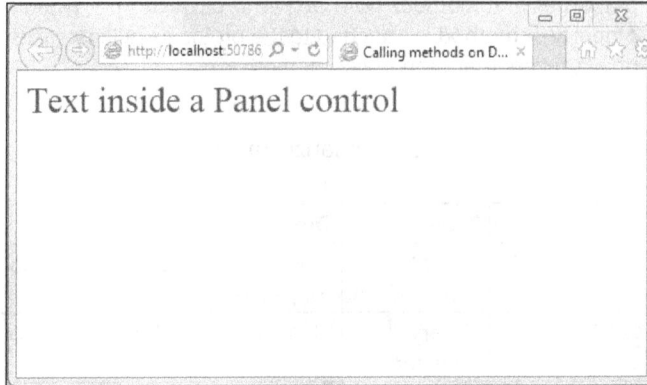

2. Use the **TestApplication** project created earlier, and add a new web form called `Rainbow-1.0.aspx`.

3. In the **Scripts** folder, add a new plugin by right-clicking on the folder in the **Solution Explorer** tab and navigating to **Add | JavaScript File**, name the plugin `jquery.rainbow-1.0.js`.

4. Include both the jQuery library and plugin in the web form by dragging and dropping from the **Solution Explorer** tab to generate the following code:

```
<script src="Scripts/jquery-2.1.4.js"></script>
<script src="Scripts/jquery.rainbow-1.0.js"></script>
```

5. To style the text content on the page, add the following CSS class to the `head` element:

```
<style type="text/css">
.sampleText{
  font-family:'Times New Roman', Times, serif;
  font-size:30px;
}
</style>
```

6. Drag and drop a **Panel** control on the form. Add the CSS class defined earlier to the `Panel`. Also, add some random text to generate the following markup:

```
<asp:Panel ID="pnlTest" CssClass="sampleText"
runat="server" >
Text inside a Panel control
</asp:Panel>
```

How to do it...

Follow these steps to add a method to the plugin:

1. In the plugin file, add a method named `rainbow()`, as shown in the following code:

```
(function($) {
  $.fn.rainbow = function() {
    var $ele = this;
    var colors = ["violet", "indigo", "blue", "green", "yellow",
      "orange", "red"
    ];
    var interval = 1000;
    var cnt = 0;
    setInterval(function() {
      if (cnt >= colors.length)
        cnt = 0;
      $ele.css("color", colors[cnt]);
      cnt++;
    }, interval);
  };
})(jQuery);
```

2. In the `Rainbow-1.0.aspx` web form, call the plugin method on the `Panel` control, as follows:

```
<script type="text/javascript">
$(document).ready(function () {
  $("#<%=pnlTest.ClientID%>").rainbow();
});
</script>
```

How it works...

The plugin works as follows:

1. In the plugin, we have created a `rainbow()` method in the `$.fn` object:

   ```
   (function ($) {
   $.fn.rainbow = function () {… };

   })(jQuery);
   ```

   > $.fn is an alias for $.prototype, that is, the jQuery prototype.

2. In this method, the current DOM element can be accessed using the `this` keyword:

   ```
   var $ele = this;
   ```

3. Next, we define an array of `colors` to iterate over the DOM element:

   ```
   var colors = ["violet", "indigo", "blue", "green",
   "yellow", "orange", "red"];
   ```

4. The `interval` of switching the text color is set to `1000` milliseconds using a variable, which is defined as follows:

   ```
   var interval = 1000;
   ```

5. A counter variable is initialized to zero. This variable will keep track of the color that is currently being displayed from the `colors` array:

   ```
   var cnt = 0;
   ```

6. We use the JavaScript `setInterval()` function to repeatedly refresh the color every `1000` milliseconds:

   ```
   setInterval(function () {…}, interval);
   ```

   In this function, we check whether the counter has exceeded the length of the array. If yes, then the counter is reset to zero. This is to ensure that the `colors` are applied to the text in a cyclic manner; that is, the first color is repeated after reaching the last color from the array:

   ```
   if (cnt >= colors.length)
      cnt = 0;
   ```

   The CSS property, `color`, is updated to the next color from the array:

   ```
   $ele.css("color", colors[cnt]);
   ```

The counter is incremented by one to get the next color from the array for the subsequent iteration:

```
cnt++;
```

There's more...

So far, we have defined a basic plugin method. However, it is incomplete, and there are many possibilities for improvement. To demonstrate one possible enhancement, add another `Panel` to the form and add some random text to it, as follows:

```
<asp:Panel ID="pnlTest" CssClass="sampleText" runat="server">
  Text inside a Panel control
</asp:Panel>
<br /><br />
<asp:Panel ID="pnlTestNew" runat="server">Text inside a new Panel
control
</asp:Panel>
```

Note that the CSS class `sampleText` is not applied to the new `Panel` control.

Let's say within the plugin method, we want to selectively apply the animation to only those elements that have the CSS class `sampleText` applied to them. So, we will update the method to include this condition, as follows:

```
(function($) {
  $.fn.rainbow = function() {
    var $ele = this;
    if ($ele.hasClass("sampleText")) {
      var colours = ["violet", "indigo", "blue", "green",
        "yellow", "orange", "red"
      ];
      var interval = 1000;
      var cnt = 0;
      setInterval(function() {
        if (cnt >= colours.length)
          cnt = 0;
        $ele.css("color", colours[cnt]);
        cnt++;
      }, interval);
    }
  };
})(jQuery);
```

Now, run the page once again by calling the plugin method on both the `Panel` controls by using the HTML selector. Note that this selector matches multiple elements:

```
$("div").rainbow();
```

The output is shown in the following screenshot. Note that instead of the animation being applied to the first `Panel` only, it is incorrectly applied to both the `Panel` controls:

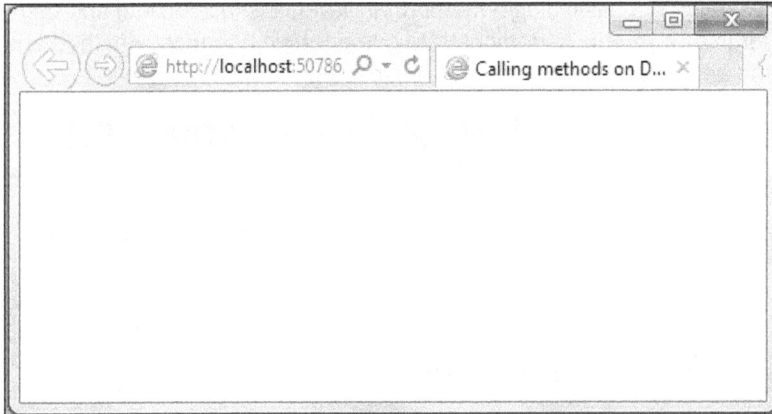

This is because of including the `.hasClass("sampleText")` condition, which returns the result of the check on the first matched element on the DOM.

To ensure that the plugin method is applied correctly to all elements, it is advisable to enclose the method within `.each()`. Thus, modify the preceding code to the following code:

```
(function($) {
  $.fn.rainbow = function() {
    this.each(function() {
      var $ele = $(this);
      if ($ele.hasClass("sampleText")) {
        var cnt = 0;
        var colours = ["violet", "indigo", "blue", "green",
          "yellow", "orange", "red"
        ];
        var interval = 1000;
        setInterval(function() {
          if (cnt >= colours.length)
            cnt = 0;
          $ele.css("color", colours[cnt]);
          cnt++;
```

```
        }, interval);
      }
    });
  };
}) (jQuery);
```

As a result, the animation will be applied to the element with the CSS class `sampleText`, that is, the first `Panel` control, as shown in the following screenshot:

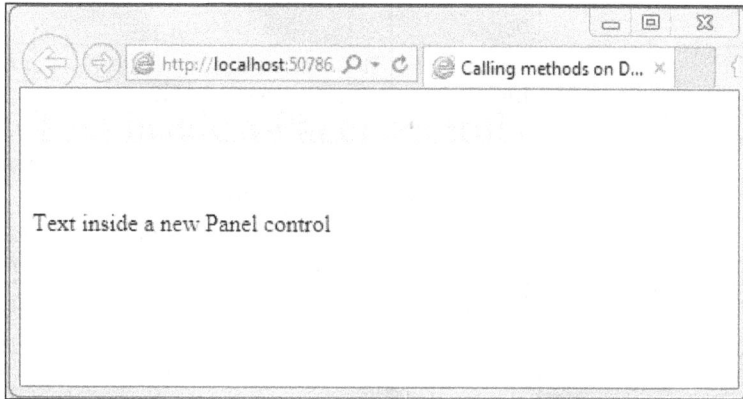

See also

The *Providing default values* recipe

Providing default values

It is a good practice to provide configurable items in plugin methods to enable developers to customize according to the requirements of their application. The use of an `options` object enables us to achieve this. A default set of options can also be provided so that developers can selectively override the configurations that they want.

In this example, let's build the plugin created in the previous recipe to provide the options object as well as provide a map of default values.

The constructs used in this example are summarized as follows:

Construct	Type	Description
`$`	jQuery function	This refers to the jQuery function. $ is an alias for jQuery.
`$("#identifier")`	jQuery selector	This selects an element based on its ID.
`$(this)`	jQuery object	This refers to the current jQuery object.
`$.extend()`	jQuery function	This merges the contents of two or more objects into the first object.
`.css()`	jQuery method	This gets the style property for the first matched element or sets the style property for every matched element.
`.each()`	jQuery method	This iterates over the matched elements and executes a function for each element.
`.hasClass()`	jQuery method	This returns true if the specified CSS class is attached to an element.
`jQuery`	jQuery function	This refers to the jQuery function.
`setInterval(function, delay)`	JavaScript function	This executes a function repeatedly after the specified delay in milliseconds.

Getting ready

Follow these steps to create a web form for calling the plugin method with default values:

1. To keep the code separate from the previous recipe, let's create another web form named `Rainbow-1.1.aspx` in the **TestApplication** project.

2. Add another plugin by right-clicking on the **Scripts** folder in the **Solution Explorer** tab and navigating to **Add | JavaScript File**. name the `jquery.rainbow-1.1.js` file.

3. Open `Rainbow-1.1.aspx` in the **Source** mode and drag and drop the jQuery library and the plugin on the page in the `head` element to generate the following code:

```
<script src="Scripts/jquery-2.1.4.js"></script>
<script src="Scripts/jquery.rainbow-1.1.js"></script>
```

4. To style the text on the page, add the following CSS class:

```
<style type="text/css">
.sampleText{
  font-family:'Times New Roman', Times, serif;
  font-size:30px;
}
</style>
```

5. Drag and drop a **Panel** control on the web form. Add the preceding CSS class and some random text to it:

```
<asp:Panel ID="pnlTest" runat="server"
CssClass="sampleText">
  Text inside a Panel control
</asp:Panel>
```

How to do it...

Add the following code to the plugin file:

```
(function($) {
  $.fn.rainbow = function(opts) {
    var defaults = {
      colors: ["violet", "indigo", "blue", "green", "yellow",
"orange", "red"],
      interval: 1000
    };
    var options = $.extend(defaults, opts);
    this.each(function() {
      var $ele = $(this);
      var cnt = 0;
      setInterval(function() {
        if (cnt >= options.colors.length)
          cnt = 0;
        $ele.css("color", options.colors[cnt]);
        cnt++;
      }, options.interval);
    });
  };
}) (jQuery);
```

Call the plugin from the web form by adding the following code. Note that we have provided an array of `colors` as well as an interval in milliseconds to override the default configuration:

```
<script type="text/javascript">
$(document).ready(function () {
  $("#<%=pnlTest.ClientID%>").rainbow({
    colours: ["red", "blue", "green"],
    interval: 2000
  });
});
</script>
```

How it works...

The plugin method works as follows:

1. The `rainbow()` plugin method is updated so that it takes a map named `opts` as a parameter:

   ```
   (function($) {
       $.fn.rainbow = function(opts) {…}
     };
   })(jQuery)
   ```

2. A default map is provided to cater for scenarios when none or some of the configurable values are provided. As shown in the following code snippet, this plugin has two configurable items, that is, an array of `colors` and the `interval` of switching of colors:

   ```
   var defaults = {
     colors: ["blue", "green", "yellow", "orange", "red"],
     interval:1000
   };
   ```

3. Next, merge the `defaults` and `opts` maps using the jquery `$.extend()` function, as follows:

   ```
   var options = $.extend(defaults, opts);
   ```

   Here, the `defaults` object is modified, and any property that it shares with the `opts` object is overwritten. New properties are added to the `defaults` object. If the `defaults` object is blank, the target object returned will be the same as the `opts` object.

4. Next, for each calling element, execute a function, as follows:

```
this.each(function () {…}
```

Within the preceding function, first of all, get the current element:

```
var $ele = $(this);
```

Set a counter to zero. This counter will keep track of the color currently being used:

```
var cnt = 0;
```

Use the `setInterval()` function to execute a function at the `interval` specified in the `options` object in step 3. If no `interval` is provided by the calling element, it will use the default `interval`. Note that the `colors` are also read from the `options` object. If no `colors` are provided from the calling page, the default `colors` are used:

```
setInterval(function() {
  if (cnt >= options.colors.length)
    cnt = 0;
  $ele.css("color", options.colors[cnt]);
  cnt++;
}, options.interval);
```

There's more...

The plugin method can be called in multiple ways. Since the parameters are optional, the user may choose to pass none or some of them selectively, as shown in the following code:

```
$("#<%=pnlTest.ClientID%>").rainbow();
```

OR

```
$("#<%=pnlTest.ClientID%>").rainbow({
  colours: ["red", "blue", "green"]
});
```

OR

```
$("#<%=pnlTest.ClientID%>").rainbow({
  interval:1000
});
```

See also

The *Providing method chaining* recipe

Providing method chaining

Chaining more than one method is a very useful feature when programming in jQuery. Chaining is possible since most jQuery methods return an object allowing the calling of other methods on the returned object. Since the child methods are executed in the returned object instead of the entire DOM, the code runs faster. This allows you to write code, which is not only shorter but also faster.

The plugin that we have worked with so far does not support chaining. In this example, let's modify the plugin to include this feature.

The programming constructs used in this example are summarized as follows:

Construct	Type	Description
`$`	jQuery function	This refers to the jQuery function. `$` is an alias for jQuery.
`$("#identifier")`	jQuery selector	This selects an element based on its `ID`.
`$(this)`	jQuery object	This refers to the current jQuery object.
`$.extend()`	jQuery function	This merges the contents of two or more objects into the first object.
`.addClass()`	jQuery method	This adds the specified CSS class to each matched element.
`.css()`	jQuery method	This gets the style property for the first matched element or sets the style property for every matched element.
`.each()`	jQuery method	This iterates over the matched elements and executes a function for each element.
`.find()`	jQuery method	This finds all elements that match the filter.
`.hasClass()`	jQuery method	This returns true if the specified CSS class is attached to an element.
`jQuery`	jQuery function	This refers to the jQuery function.
`setInterval(function, delay)`	JavaScript function	This executes a function repeatedly after the specified delay in milliseconds.

Getting ready

Follow these steps to create a web page that will use the modified plugin:

1. In the `TestApplication` project created earlier, add a new web form named `Rainbow-1.2.aspx`.

2. Add a new plugin file by right-clicking on the **Scripts** folder in the **Solution Explorer** tab and navigating to **Add | JavaScript File**. name the file `jquery.rainbow-1.2.js`.

3. Include the jQuery library and the plugin in the form by dragging and dropping the files on the form to generate the following markup:

```
<script src="Scripts/jquery-2.1.4.js"></script>
<script src="Scripts/jquery.rainbow-1.2.js"></script>
```

4. Go to **Toolbox | Standard** and add the `Panel` and `Table` controls to the form. Add some random content to the controls to generate the following markup:

```
<asp:Panel ID="pnlTest" runat="server"
CssClass="sampleText">
  Text inside a Panel control
</asp:Panel>
<br /><br />
<asp:Table ID="tblTest" runat="server">
  <asp:TableHeaderRow>
    <asp:TableHeaderCell>Title</asp:TableHeaderCell>
    <asp:TableHeaderCell>Author</asp:TableHeaderCell>
    <asp:TableHeaderCell>Category</asp:TableHeaderCell>
  </asp:TableHeaderRow>
  <asp:TableRow>
    <asp:TableCell>The Alchemist</asp:TableCell>
    <asp:TableCell>Paulo Coelho</asp:TableCell>
    <asp:TableCell>Fiction</asp:TableCell>
  </asp:TableRow>
  <asp:TableRow>
    <asp:TableCell>You Can Win</asp:TableCell>
    <asp:TableCell>Shiv Khera</asp:TableCell>
    <asp:TableCell>Non-Fiction</asp:TableCell>
  </asp:TableRow>
</asp:Table>
```

5. To style the text in the `Panel` control, add the following CSS class:

```css
.sampleText{
  font-family:'Times New Roman', Times, serif;
  font-size:30px;
}
```

6. To style the `Table` control, add the following CSS style to the table elements:

```css
table, th, td {
  border: 1px solid black;
  border-collapse: collapse;
  padding:5px;
}
```

7. To style the table header, include the following style. It will be added to the table header through the chained code later:

```css
.headerStyle{
  font-weight:700;
  font-variant:small-caps;
  text-align:center;
  background-color:lightgray;
  padding:5px;
}
```

How to do it...

Update the plugin as follows:

1. In the `jquery.rainbow-1.2.js` plugin file, add the following code:

```javascript
(function($) {
  $.fn.rainbow = function(opts) {
    var defaults = {
      colors: ["violet", "indigo", "blue", "green",
"yellow", "orange", "red"],
      interval: 1000
    };
    var options = $.extend(defaults, opts);
    return this.each(function() {
      var $ele = $(this);
      var cnt = 0;
      setInterval(function() {
        if (cnt >= options.colors.length)
          cnt = 0;
        $ele.css("color", options.colors[cnt]);
```

```
        cnt++;
      }, options.interval);
    });
  };
})(jQuery);
```

2. Call the plugin method on the `Panel` and `Table` controls in the `Rainbow-1.2.aspx` web form. Add chained methods to the plugin method to test whether chaining is working as required:

```
<script type="text/javascript">
$(document).ready(function() {
  $("#<%=pnlTest.ClientID%>").rainbow({
    interval: 2000
  }).css("backgroundColor", "lightyellow");
    $("#<%=tblTest.ClientID%>").rainbow().find("th").addClass("
headerStyle");
});
</script>
```

How it works...

The chaining works as follows:

1. For chaining to work, the plugin method needs to return a `jQuery` object to the calling code. This is possible by updating the plugin to add the `return` keyword, as follows:

   ```
   return this.each(function () {…});
   ```

2. Now, when the `rainbow()` method is called on the `Panel` control, we can chain the `.css()` method to change the background color in the following statement:

   ```
   $("#<%=pnlTest.ClientID%>").rainbow({interval:2000}).css("b
   ackgroundColor","lightyellow");
   ```

3. Similarly, when the `rainbow()` method is called on the `Table` control, we can chain the `.find()` method to only filter the table header, that is, `th` rows, and add the CSS class `headerStyle` to it, as we did in the following statement:

   ```
   $("#<%=tblTest.ClientID%>").rainbow().find("th").addClass("
   headerStyle");
   ```

Thus, the color transitions and style updates are applied to both the controls on the form, as shown in the following screenshot:

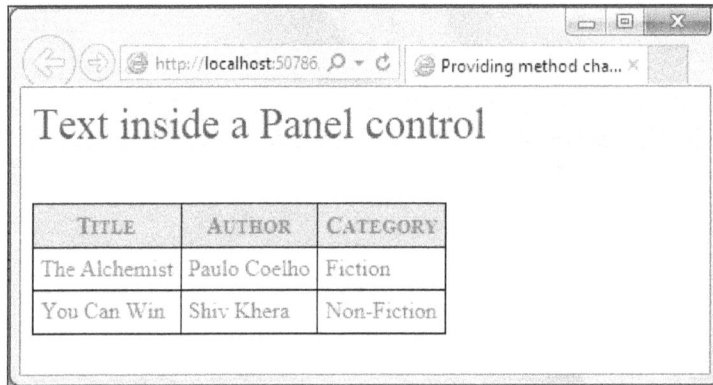

See also

The *Providing default values* recipe

Adding actions to plugins

In this example, let's create a plugin that can perform more than one action by taking in the desired action as an argument. The programming constructs used in this example are summarized as follows:

Construct	Type	Description
`$("#identifier")`	jQuery selector	This selects an element based on its ID
`$(this)`	jQuery object	This refers to the current jQuery object
`$.extend()`	jQuery function	This merges the contents of two or more objects into the first object
`.animate()`	jQuery method	This performs a custom animation on the specified CSS properties
`.css()`	jQuery method	This gets the style property for the first matched element or sets the style property for every matched element
`.each()`	jQuery method	This iterates over the matched elements and executes a function for each element
`setInterval(function, delay)`	JavaScript function	This executes a function repeatedly after the specified delay in milliseconds

Getting ready

Follow these steps to create a web form for calling different actions on a plugin method:

1. In this recipe, let's create a plugin that can perform different types of effects on text content. We will focus on three effects: blink, color transition, and pulsation, as shown in the following screenshot:

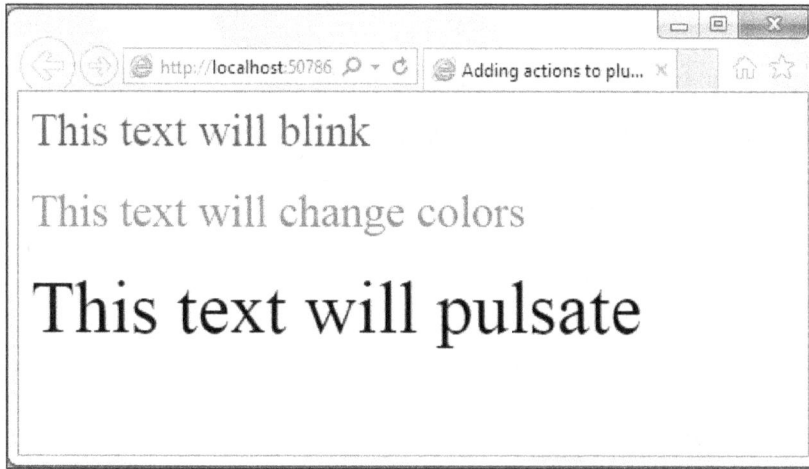

2. To get started, in the `TestApplication` project, create a new web form named `TextEffects.aspx`.

3. Add a new plugin file to the **Scripts** folder by right-clicking on the **Solution Explorer** tab and navigating to **Add** | **JavaScript File**. name the file `jquery.texteffects.js`.

4. Include the jQuery library and the plugin in the form:

```
<script src="Scripts/jquery-2.1.4.js"></script>
<script src="Scripts/jquery.texteffects.js"></script>
```

5. Drag and drop three `Label` controls from the **ToolBox**. The markup is shown as follows:

```
<asp:Label ID="lblTest1" runat="server" Text="This text
will blink"></asp:Label><br /><br />
<asp:Label ID="lblTest2" runat="server" Text="This text
will change colours"></asp:Label><br /><br />
<asp:Label ID="lblTest3" runat="server" Text="This text
will pulsate"></asp:Label>
```

6. At runtime, the `Label` controls are rendered as `span` elements. So, to style the `Label` controls, add the following style to the page:

```css
span{
  font-family:'Times New Roman', Times, serif;
  font-size:30px;
}
```

How to do it...

Update the plugin and the web form as shown below:

1. To the plugin file, add the following code:

```javascript
(function ($) {
  $.fn.texteffects = function(action, opts) {
    if (action == "blink") {
      var defaults = {
        interval: 1000
      };
      var options = $.extend(defaults, opts);
      var halfInterval = options.interval / 2;
      return this.each(function() {
        var $ele = $(this);
        setInterval(function() {
          $ele.animate({
            opacity: 0
          }, halfInterval).animate({
            opacity: 1
          }, halfInterval);
        }, options.interval);
      });
    } else if (action == "pulsate") {
      var defaults = {
        minSize: "20",
        maxSize: "40",
        interval: 2000
      };
      var options = $.extend(defaults, opts);
      var halfInterval = options.interval / 2;
      return this.each(function() {
        var $ele = $(this);
        setInterval(function() {
```

```
            $ele.animate({
                fontSize: options.maxSize + "px"
            }, halfInterval).animate({
                fontSize: options.minSize + "px"
            }, halfInterval);
        }, options.interval);
    });
  } else if (action == "rainbow") {
    var defaults = {
        colors: ["violet", "indigo", "blue", "green",
"yellow", "orange", "red"],
        interval: 1000
    };
    var options = $.extend(defaults, opts);
    return this.each(function() {
        var $ele = $(this);
        var cnt = 0;
        setInterval(function() {
            if (cnt >= options.colors.length)
                cnt = 0;
            $ele.css("color", options.colors[cnt]);
            cnt++;
        }, options.interval);
    });
  }
 };
}) (jQuery);
```

2. In the `TextEffects.aspx` web form, call the `blink` action on the first `Label` control:

```
$("#<%=lblTest1.ClientID%>").texteffects("blink");
```

3. Call the `rainbow` action on the second `Label` control:

```
$("#<%=lblTest2.ClientID%>").texteffects("rainbow", {
interval: 2000 });
```

4. Call the `pulsate` action on the third `Label` control:

```
$("#<%=lblTest3.ClientID%>").texteffects("pulsate",{
maxSize: 50, minSize: 30, interval: 3000 });
```

How it works...

The calling of different actions on the plugin method works as follows:

1. The plugin method takes in two parameters: the desired `action` and the options map.

2. Three actions have been defined in this plugin: `blink`, `rainbow`, and `pulsate`. Using the `action` argument passed to the method, the respective action can be called, as shown in the following code snippet:

```
(function($) {
  $.fn.texteffects = function(action, opts) {
    if (action == "blink") {
      //DEFINE BLINK ACTION HERE
    } else if (action == "pulsate") {
      //DEFINE PULSATE ACTION HERE
    } else if (action == "rainbow") {
      //DEFINE COLOUR TRANSITIONS HERE
    }
  };
})(jQuery);
```

3. Within the `blink` action, the default value for the blinking `interval` is set using a map:

```
var defaults = {
  interval: 1000
};
```

The default values are merged with the options passed by the developer from the calling page:

```
var options = $.extend(defaults, opts);
```

Within the specified interval, the text will fade out and fade in. So, a half interval is defined in which the opacity of the text will be animated to zero. In the remaining half interval, the opacity of the text will be animated back to unity:

```
var halfInterval = options.interval / 2;
```

To enable chaining, we use the `return` keyword to return a jQuery object to the calling code, as follows:

```
return this.each(function () {
  var $ele = $(this);
  setInterval(function () {
    $ele.animate({ opacity: 0 }, halfInterval).animate({
opacity: 1 }, halfInterval);
  }, options.interval);
});
```

The `setInterval()` JavaScript function is used to repeat the process at the specified interval that is read from `options.interval`. Two consecutive animations are chained to the element, as follows:

```
$ele.animate({ opacity: 0 }, halfInterval).animate({
opacity: 1 }, halfInterval);
```

The duration of each animation is set to `halfInterval`.

4. Within the pulsate action, the default values for the minimum and maximum font size and the `interval` of repetition are set using a map, as follows:

```
var defaults = {
   minSize: "20",
   maxSize: "40",
   interval: 2000
};
```

The default values are merged with the `options` provided by the developer from the calling page:

```
var options = $.extend(defaults, opts);
```

A half interval is defined. During the first half interval, the font size is animated so that it increases to the maximum size. During the second half interval, the font size is animated so that it reduces to the minimum defined size:

```
var halfInterval = options.interval / 2;
```

Next, we use the `return` keyword to return a jQuery object to the calling code, as follows:

```
return this.each(function () {
   var $ele = $(this);
   setInterval(function () {
      $ele.animate({ fontSize: options.maxSize + "px" },
halfInterval).animate({ fontSize: options.minSize + "px" },
halfInterval);
   }, options.interval);
});
```

Repetition of the animation is possible by the use of the `setInterval()` JavaScript function. The process is repeated at the duration specified by `options.interval`. Two consecutive animations are chained to the element, as follows:

```
$ele.animate({ fontSize: options.maxSize + "px" },
halfInterval).animate({ fontSize: options.minSize + "px" },
halfInterval);
```

The duration of each animation is set to `halfInterval`.

5. Within the `rainbow` action, we will update the color of the text at regular intervals. The `colors` are read from an array. The default list of `colors` and the `interval` of the `color` switch is defined in the following map:

```
var defaults = {
   colors: ["violet", "indigo", "blue", "green", "yellow",
"orange", "red"],
   interval: 1000
};
```

The default values are merged with the actual `options` provided by the developer from the calling page:

```
var options = $.extend(defaults, opts);
```

To enable chaining, we use the `return` keyword and return a jQuery object to the calling page, as shown in the following code:

```
return this.each(function () {
   var $ele = $(this);
   var cnt = 0;
   setInterval(function () {
      if (cnt >= options.colors.length)
         cnt = 0;
      $ele.css("color", options.colors[cnt]);
      cnt++;
   }, options.interval);
});
```

The `setInterval()` JavaScript function is used to switch the colors at the duration specified by `options.interval`. The CSS property, `color`, of the element is updated and set to the current color from the array, as follows:

```
$ele.css("color", options.colors[cnt]);
```

If we reach the end of the array, the colors are looped, and we can start once again with the first color in the array:

```
if (cnt >= options.colors.length)
   cnt = 0;
```

Before we begin with the next iteration, the counter is incremented to retrieve the next `color` from the array.

See also

The *Using the form validation plugin* recipe

Using the form validation plugin

Plugins written by other developers can be searched and downloaded from the central plugin repository at `https://plugins.jquery.com`. On searching for the `validation` keyword, we come across the jQuery validation plugin written in 2006 by *Jörn Zaefferer*, a member of the core jQuery team. The official site of the plugin is at `http://jqueryvalidation.org`.

In this example, let's download and use this plugin in our application. The programming constructs used in this example are summarized as follows:

Construct	Type	Description
`$("#identifier")`	jQuery selector	This selects an element based on its ID.
`$("html_tag")`	jQuery selector	This selects all elements with the specified HTML tag.
`click`	jQuery event	This is fired when you click on an element. It corresponds to the JavaScript `click` event.
`.closest()`	jQuery method	For each matched element, this returns the first element that matches the selector by traversing up the DOM tree.
`event.preventDefault()`	jQuery method	This prevents the default action of the event from being triggered.
`.hide()`	jQuery method	This hides the matched elements.
`.html()`	jQuery method	This returns the HTML content of the first matched element or sets the HTML content of every matched element.
`.insertAfter()`	jQuery method	This inserts the element after the target.
`.on()`	jQuery event binder	This attaches an event handler for one or more events to the matched elements.
`.prop(propertyName)` or `.prop(propertyName, value)`	jQuery method	This returns the value of the specified property for the first matched element or sets the value of the specified property for all matched elements.
`.resetForm()`	Validation plugin method	This resets validations for a form.
`.show()`	jQuery method	This displays the matched elements.
`.siblings()`	jQuery method	This retrieves the siblings of the matched elements.

Construct	Type	Description
`.val()`	jQuery method	This returns the value of the first matched element or sets the value of every matched element.
`.validate()`	Validation plugin method	This validates a form and returns a validator object.

Getting ready

To use the validation plugin on a web form, follow these steps:

1. The first step is to download the validation plugin, which can be obtained in many ways. It can be downloaded from the official website at `http://jqueryvalidation.org`. It is also available from package managers, such as Bower or NuGet. Alternatively, it can be referenced from CDN.

> To download it using Bower, refer to the *Downloading plugins using NPM* recipe.

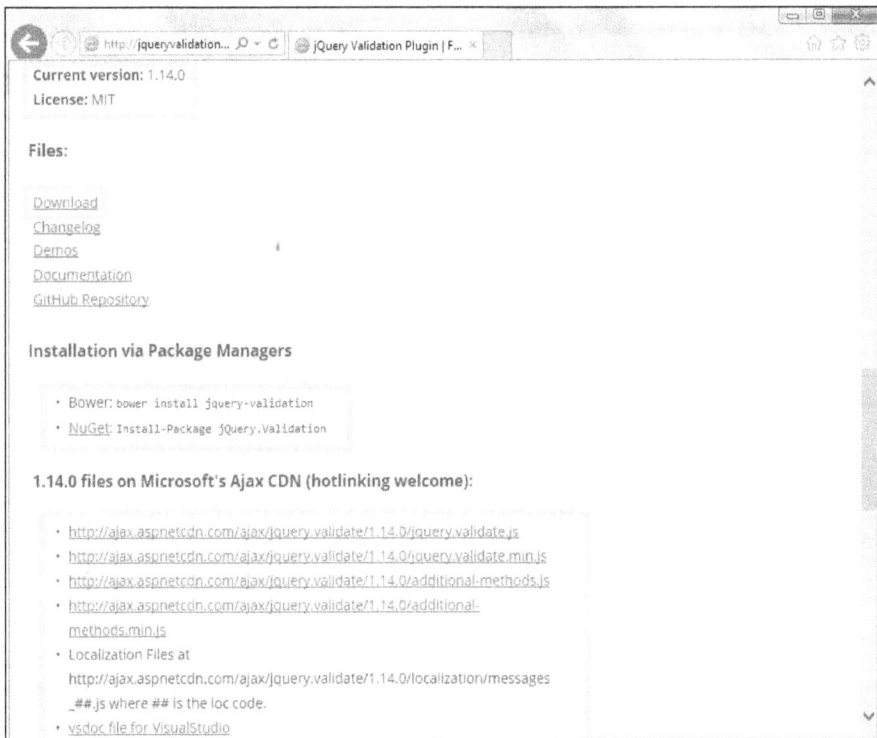

2. In the **TestApplication** project, let's download the plugin from NuGet. To launch NuGet, in the **File** menu, go to **Tools | NuGet Package Manager | Manage NuGet Packages for Solution**. In the NuGet screen, as shown in the following screenshot, search for `jquery validation`. Select **jQuery.Validation**, and click on the **Install** button:

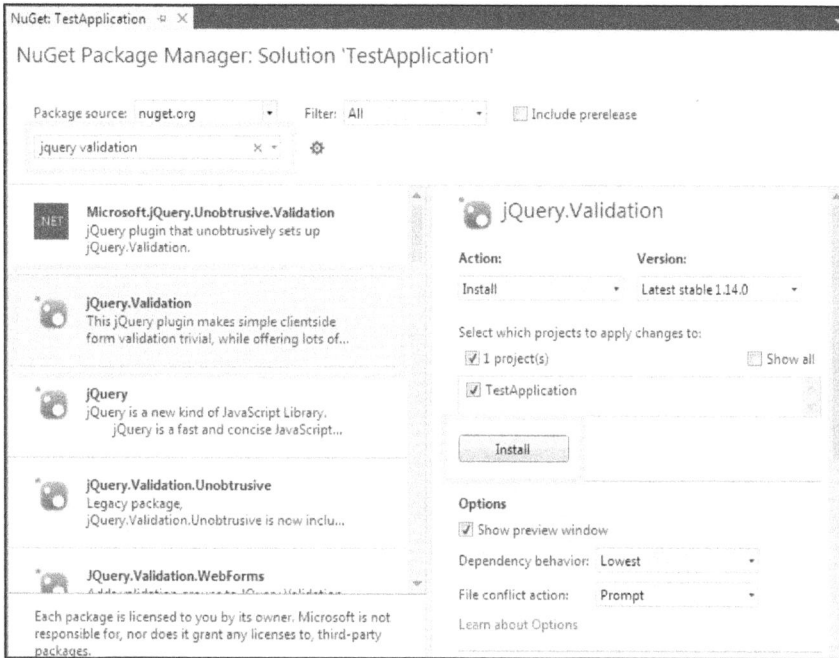

When the installation completes, you will notice that the following files are added to the **Scripts** folder:

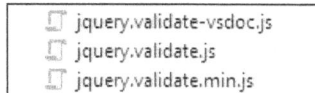

3. Add a new web form to the project and name it `FormValidation.aspx`. Include the jQuery library and validation plugin in the form, as follows:

```
<script src="Scripts/jquery-2.1.4.js"></script>
<script src="Scripts/jquery.validate.js"></script>
```

4. Create a registration form that accepts different types of data, such as the text, e-mail, password, and so on, as shown in the following screenshot:

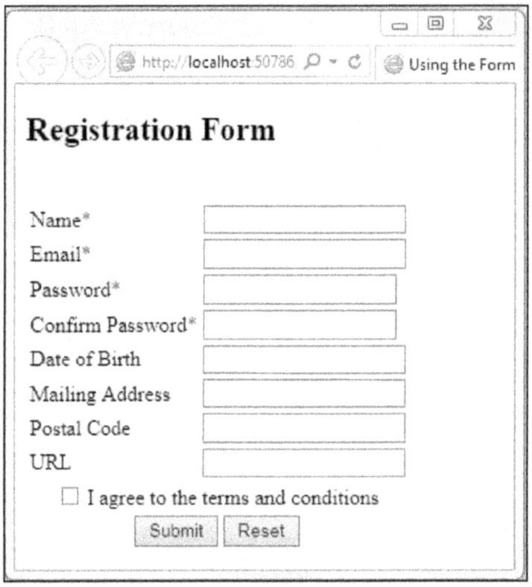

Use the following markup to create the form:

```
<form id="frmRegistration" runat="server">
  <h2>Registration Form</h2>
  <div id="summary"></div>
  <br />
  <table>
    <tr>
      <td>
        <asp:Label ID="lblName" runat="server"
Text="Name"></asp:Label><span class="mandatory">*</span></td>
      <td>
        <asp:TextBox ID="txtName" runat="server"></asp:TextBox>
      </td>
    </tr>
    <tr>
      <td>
        <asp:Label ID="lblEmail" runat="server"
Text="Email"></asp:Label><span class="mandatory">*</span></td>
      <td>
        <asp:TextBox ID="txtEmail" runat="server"></asp:TextBox>
      </td>
    </tr>
    <tr>
      <td>
```

```
        <asp:Label ID="lblPassword" runat="server"
Text="Password"></asp:Label><span class="mandatory">*</span></td>
      <td>
          <asp:TextBox ID="txtPassword" runat="server"
TextMode="Password"></asp:TextBox>
      </td>
    </tr>
    <tr>
      <td>
          <asp:Label ID="lblConfirmPassword" runat="server"
Text="Confirm Password"></asp:Label><span class="mandatory">*</
span></td>
      <td>
          <asp:TextBox ID="txtConfirmPassword" runat="server"
TextMode="Password"></asp:TextBox>
      </td>
    </tr>
    <tr>
      <td>
          <asp:Label ID="lblDOB" runat="server" Text="Date of
Birth"></asp:Label>
      </td>
      <td>
          <asp:TextBox ID="txtDOB"
runat="server"></asp:TextBox>
      </td>
    </tr>
    <tr>
      <td>
          <asp:Label ID="lblMailAddr" runat="server"
Text="Mailing Address"></asp:Label>
      </td>
      <td>
          <asp:TextBox ID="txtMailAddr"
runat="server"></asp:TextBox>
      </td>
    </tr>
    <tr>
      <td>
          <asp:Label ID="lblPostal" runat="server"
Text="Postal Code"></asp:Label>
      </td>
      <td>
          <asp:TextBox ID="txtPostal"
runat="server"></asp:TextBox>
```

```
              </td>
           </tr>
           <tr>
              <td>
                 <asp:Label ID="lblUrl" runat="server"
   Text="URL"></asp:Label>
              </td>
              <td>
                 <asp:TextBox ID="txtUrl"
   runat="server"></asp:TextBox>
              </td>
           </tr>
           <tr>
              <td colspan="2" class="center">
                 <asp:CheckBox ID="chkAgree" runat="server" />
                 <asp:Label ID="lblAgree" runat="server" Text="I
   agree to the terms and conditions"></asp:Label>
              </td>
           </tr>
           <tr>
              <td colspan="2" class="center">
                 <asp:Button ID="btnSubmit" runat="server"
   Text="Submit" />
                 <asp:Button ID="btnReset" runat="server"
   Text="Reset" />
              </td>
           </tr>
        </table>
   </form>
```

5. Add the following styles to the form:

```
.mandatory{
   color:red;
}
.center{
   text-align:center;
}
```

6. After validating the form, the validation plugin generates error messages in label elements with the CSS class, `error`. To customize the style of the error messages, we can add our own styles, as follows:

```
label.error {
   color: red;
   padding-left:5px;
}
```

7. The form provides a `div` element on the top to display the total number of invalid elements. Let's add the following style to this element:

```css
#summary{
  text-align:center;
  border:solid;
  border-width:1px;
  background-color:lavender;
  width:400px;
  height:20px;
}
```

How to do it...

Add the following jQuery code to a `<script>` block on the form:

```javascript
<script type="text/javascript">
$(document).ready(function() {
  $("#summary").hide();
  $("#<%=btnSubmit.ClientID%>").on("click", function() {
    var validator = $("#frmRegistration").validate({
      rules: {
        <%=txtName.ClientID%>: "required",
        <%=txtEmail.ClientID%>: {
          required: true,
          email: true
        },
        <%=txtPassword.ClientID%>: {
          required: true,
          minlength: 8
        },
        <%=txtConfirmPassword.ClientID%>: {
          required: true,
          minlength: 8,
          equalTo: "#<%=txtPassword.ClientID%>"
        },
        <%=txtDOB.ClientID%>: {
          date: true
        },
        <%=txtMailAddr.ClientID%>: {
          maxlength: 200
        },
        <%=txtPostal.ClientID%>: {
          digits: true
        },
```

```
                 <%=txtUrl.ClientID%>: {
                   url: true
                 },
                 <%=chkAgree.ClientID%>: "required"
             },
         messages: {
             <%=txtName.ClientID%>: "Please enter your Name",
             <%=txtEmail.ClientID%>: {
                 required: "Please enter your Email",
                 email: "Please enter a valid Email address"
             },
             <%=txtPassword.ClientID%>: {
                 required: "Please enter your Password",
                 minlength: "Password should be at least 8 characters
     long"
             },
             <%=txtConfirmPassword.ClientID%>: {
                 required: "Please confirm your Password",
                 minlength: "Password should be at least 8 characters
     long",
                 equalTo: "Your entered passwords do not match"
             },
             <%=txtDOB.ClientID%>: "Enter a valid date",
             <%=txtMailAddr.ClientID%>: "Your address exceeds 200
     characters",
             <%=txtPostal.ClientID%>: "Please enter only digits",
             <%=txtUrl.ClientID%>: "Please enter a valid Url",
             <%=chkAgree.ClientID%>: "Please accept the terms and
     conditions to proceed"
             },
         errorPlacement: function(error, element) {
             if (element.prop("id") == "<%=chkAgree.ClientID%>") error.
     insertAfter(element.siblings("#<%=lblAgree.ClientID%>"));
             else
                 error.insertAfter(element);
             },
         invalidHandler: function() {
             $("#summary").html("Please correct the " +
     validator.numberOfInvalids() + " invalid field(s) on the
     form.").show();
             }
         });
     });
```

```
$("#<%=btnReset.ClientID%>").on("click", function(evt) {
    evt.preventDefault();
    $("#summary").hide();
    $("input[type=text]").val("");
    $("input[type=password]").val("");
    $("input[type=checkbox]").prop("checked", false);
    $("#frmRegistration").validate().resetForm();
});
});
</script>
```

How it works...

The validation plugin works as described below:

1. On running the page in the browser, if the **Submit** button is clicked without entering any data into the fields, we will see that the following error messages are displayed for invalid fields along with a summary on the top:

2. When data is entered in the form, you will notice that the error messages will get updated to give you more specific details about the invalid fields, as shown in the following screenshot:

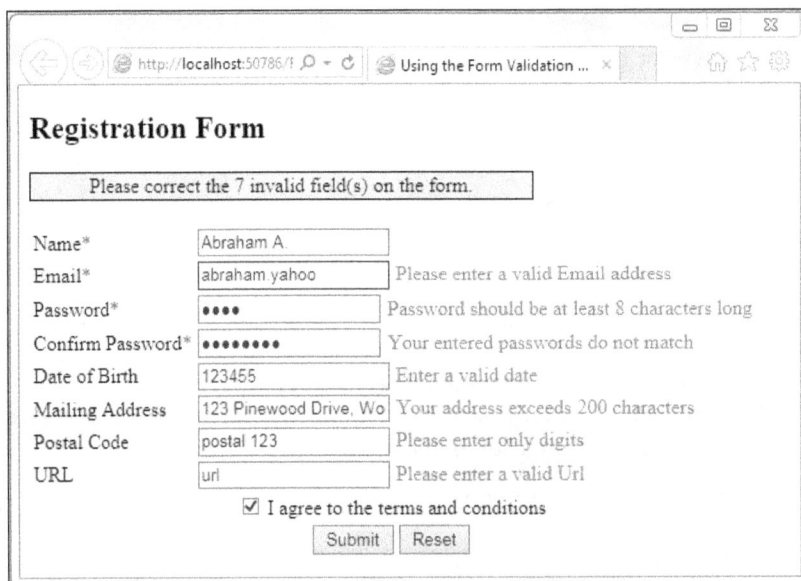

When you click on the **Reset** button, it clears all fields and error messages.

3. To validate the fields, we call the `validate()` method on the form when you click on the **Submit** button:

```
$("#<%=btnSubmit.ClientID%>").on("click", function () {
var validator = $("#frmRegistration").validate({…});
```

The `validate()` method takes a number of options. We will make use of the following options:

- **rules**: This consists of key/value pairs that are used to validate the controls on the form.

- **messages**: This consists of key/value pairs that are used to define custom error messages.

- **errorPlacement**: This executes a function that is used to customize the placement of error messages. The first argument of the function is the `error` label, which is provided as a `jQuery` object, and the second argument is the `invalid` element, which is provided as a `jQuery` object.

- **invalidHandler**: This executes a `callback` function when the form is marked as invalid.

These preceding options are applied to the `validate()` method in the following manner:

```
var validator = $("#frmRegistration").validate({
  rules: {
  },
  messages: {
  },
  errorPlacement: function(error, element) {
  },
  invalidHandler: function() {
  }
});
```

4. The rules option takes in the following name/value pairs to list the validation rules:

   ❑ The **Name** field is mandatory:

   ```
   <%=txtName.ClientID%>: "required",
   ```

   ❑ The **Email** field is mandatory and should have a valid `email`:

   ```
   <%=txtEmail.ClientID%>: { required: true, email: true },
   ```

   ❑ The **Password** field is mandatory and the length of the entered password should be at least 8 characters:

   ```
   <%=txtPassword.ClientID%>: { required: true, minlength: 8 }
   ```

   ❑ The **Confirm Password** field is also mandatory and the length of the entered password should be at least 8 characters. More importantly, the data entered should match the `Password` field:

   ```
   <%=txtConfirmPassword.ClientID%>: { required: true,
   minlength: 8 , equalTo: "#<%=txtPassword.ClientID%>"},
   ```

   ❑ The **Date of Birth** field should have a valid `date`:

   ```
   <%=txtDOB.ClientID%>: { date: true },
   ```

   ❑ The maximum length of text entered in the **Mailing Address** field is 200 characters:

   ```
   <%=txtMailAddr.ClientID%>: { maxlength: 200 },
   ```

   ❑ The **Postal Code** field should have only digits:

   ```
   <%=txtPostal.ClientID%>: { digits: true },
   ```

   ❑ The **URL** field should have a valid URL:

   ```
   <%=txtUrl.ClientID%>: { url: true },
   ```

❑ The terms and conditions should be agreed upon, that is, the checkbox is required to be checked:

```
<%=chkAgree.ClientID%>:"required"
```

5. For the preceding rules, define the corresponding error messages. These error messages will override the default error messages provided by the validation plugin:

❑ The **Name** field:

```
<%=txtName.ClientID%>: "Please enter your Name",
```

❑ The **Email** field:

```
<%=txtEmail.ClientID%>: {required: "Please enter your Email",
email: "Please enter a valid Email address"},
```

❑ The **Password** field:

```
<%=txtPassword.ClientID%>: {required: "Please enter
your Password",
minlength:"Password should be at least 8 characters long"},
```

❑ The **Confirm Password** field:

```
<%=txtConfirmPassword.ClientID%>: {required: "Please confirm
your Password", minlength:"Password should be at least 8
characters long", equalTo: "Your entered passwords do not
match"
},
```

❑ The **Date of Birth** field:

```
<%=txtDOB.ClientID%>: "Enter a valid date",
```

❑ The **Mailing Address** field:

```
<%=txtMailAddr.ClientID%>: "Your address exceeds 200
characters",
```

❑ The **Postal Code** field:

```
<%=txtPostal.ClientID%>: "Please enter only digits",
```

❑ The **URL** field:

```
<%=txtUrl.ClientID%>: "Please enter a valid Url",
```

❑ The terms and conditions checkbox:

```
<%=chkAgree.ClientID%>:"Please accept the terms and
conditions to proceed"
```

6. Each of the preceding error messages are displayed next to the respective invalid element. To override this default placement, we can attach a function to the `errorPlacement` option. Let's do this for the checkbox since we want to display the error message after the label **I agree to the terms and conditions** instead of next to the checkbox element. This can be done as follows:

```
errorPlacement: function(error, element){
if (element.prop("id") == "<%=chkAgree.ClientID%>")
    error.insertAfter(element.siblings("#<%=lblAgree.ClientID%>"));
else
    error.insertAfter(element);
},
```

Thus, if the element is `chkAgree`, the `error` label is inserted after the `lblAgree` element.

7. Lastly, execute a callback function when the form is marked as invalid. This callback function will display the total number of invalid fields on the form:

```
invalidHandler: function () {
  $("#summary").html("Please correct the " +
validator.numberOfInvalids() + " invalid field(s) on the
form.").show();
}
```

The preceding error message is displayed in the `summary` div at the top of the form.

8. When you click on the **Reset** button, first of all the posting of the form is prevented:

```
evt.preventDefault();
```

The div used to display the validation `summary` is hidden:

```
$("#summary").hide();
```

Next, all the form fields are emptied/reset:

```
$("input[type=text]").val("");
$("input[type=password]").val("");
$("input[type=checkbox]").prop("checked",false);
```

The `resetForm()` method is called on the validator object returned by the `validate()` method so that all the validations are reset:

```
$("#frmRegistration").validate().resetForm();
```

There's more...

Let's say we have a group of controls that we would like to validate together. For example, a **Phone** field can be used to enter a **Hand Phone**, **Work Phone**, or **Home Phone**, as shown in the following diagram:

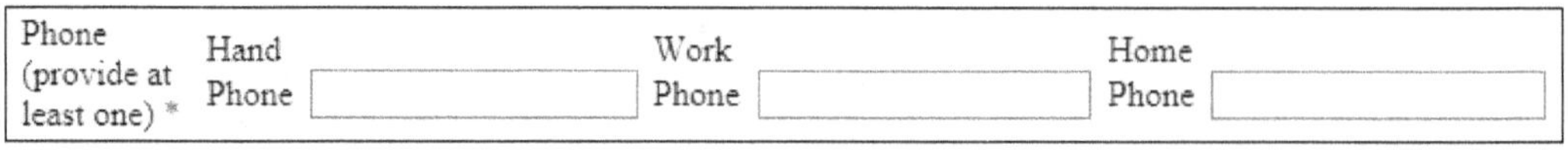

Phone (provide at least one) *	Hand Phone		Work Phone		Home Phone	

If we need to validate these three fields in such a way that at least one phone number is entered, use the `require_from_group` method provided by the validation plugin. This method is available in the `additional-methods.js` file that is available in the distribution and can be downloaded from `http://jqueryvalidation.org`.

To validate the Phone field, follow these steps:

1. Download the `additional-methods.js` file from `http://jqueryvalidation.org` and include it in the `Scripts` folder in the project. Include this file in the form:

   ```
   <script src="Scripts/additional-methods.js"></script>
   ```

2. Add the markup for the Phone fields on the form:

   ```
   <tr>
     <td>
       <asp:Label ID="lblPhone" runat="server" Text="Phone
   (provide at least one)"></asp:Label><span
   class="mandatory">*</span></td>
     <td>
       <table>
         <tr>
           <td>
             <asp:Label ID="lblHandphone" runat="server"
   Text="Hand Phone"></asp:Label> 
             <asp:TextBox ID="txtHandphone"
   CssClass="phonegroup" runat="server"></asp:TextBox>
           </td>
           <td>
             <asp:Label ID="lblWorkphone" runat="server"
   Text="Work Phone"></asp:Label> 
             <asp:TextBox ID="txtWorkphone"
   CssClass="phonegroup" runat="server"></asp:TextBox>
           </td>
           <td>
   ```

```
            <asp:Label ID="lblHomephone" runat="server"
Text="Home Phone"></asp:Label> 
            <asp:TextBox ID="txtHomephone"
CssClass="phonegroup" runat="server"></asp:TextBox>
        </td>
      </tr>
    </table>
  </td>
</tr>
```

3. Note that the TextBox controls in the group are assigned the same CSS class, phonegroup.

4. In the validate() method, add the following rules:

```
<%=txtHandphone.ClientID%>: {require_from_group: [1,
".phonegroup"], phoneUS: true},
<%=txtWorkphone.ClientID%>: {require_from_group:[1,
".phonegroup"], phoneUS: true},
<%=txtHomephone.ClientID%>:
{require_from_group:[1,".phonegroup"], phoneUS: true},
```

The require_from_group method requires the following two options:

  ❏ **Option 1**: Number of fields that are required to be filled in a group

  ❏ **Option 2**: CSS selector for the group

It also indicates that the fields are phone fields by setting phoneUs to true.

5. Add the corresponding error messages:

```
<%=txtHandphone.ClientID%>: {phoneUS: "Please enter a
correct phone number"},
<%=txtWorkphone.ClientID%>: {phoneUS: "Please enter a
correct phone number"},
<%=txtHomephone.ClientID%>:{phoneUS: "Please enter a
correct phone number"},
```

6. To display a common message for all the three controls, we use the groups option of the validate() method:

```
groups: {
phoneFields: "<%=String.Concat(txtHandphone.ClientID, "
")%><%=String.Concat(txtWorkphone.ClientID, "
")%><%=txtHomephone.ClientID%>"
},
```

In the preceding code snippet, we have assigned an arbitrary name, that is, `phoneFields` to the group. The value assigned to the field is a space-separated list of controls in the group. At runtime, `phoneFields` will be evaluated to the following string:

```
phoneFields: "txtHandphone txtWorkphone txtHomephone"
```

7. The `errorPlacement` option is also updated in order to display the error for this group at a suitable location. Here, the `error` label is attached to the parent container table:

```
errorPlacement: function(error, element) {
    if ((element.prop("id") == "<%=txtHandphone.ClientID%>") ||
    (element.prop("id") == "<%=txtWorkphone.ClientID%>") || (element.
prop("id") == "<%=txtHomephone.ClientID%>"))
        error.insertAfter(element.closest("table"));
    else if (element.prop("id") == "<%=chkAgree.ClientID%>")
        error.insertAfter(element.siblings("#<%=lblAgree.
ClientID%>"));
    else
        error.insertAfter(element);
}
```

8. Thus, on validation, a common error message is displayed for the three controls:

Phone (provide at least one) *	Hand Phone		Work Phone		Home Phone	
Please fill at least 1 of these fields.						

9. On entering incorrect data into any of the phone fields, the error message will change to the following:

Phone (provide at least one) *	Hand Phone		Work Phone	3df45	Home Phone	
Please enter a correct phone number						

See also

The *Downloading plugins using the NPM* recipe

Downloading plugins using the NPM

Since the jQuery plugin repository is now in read-only mode, it is recommended that you use **NPM** (**Node Package Manager**) to manage plugins. In this recipe, we will download the jQuery validation plugin using NPM and Bower.

> Bower is a browser package manager. It is optimized to manage frontend packages. However, to use Bower, you need to install **Node.js** and **NPM**. Some bower packages also require **Git** to be installed.

Getting ready

Bower can be set up as follows:

1. The first step is to install Node.js and NPM on your machine. Node.js is available at `https://nodejs.org`. On the home page, click on the Download link to download the required version:

2. After completing the installation, test it using the following commands in a terminal window (for example, cmd on a Windows machine):

```
node -v

npm -v
```

3. Next, download the installer for Git from `http://git-scm.com`. Run and complete the installation.

4. Next, install Bower as a global node module. To do this, open the terminal window and enter the following command:

```
npm install -g bower
```

How to do it...

Now that we have all the required software installed, you can install the jQuery validation plugin using Bower by entering the following command in the terminal window:

```
bower install jquery-validation
```

The terminal window will display the following installation messages:

```
Administrator: C:\Windows\System32\cmd.exe

D:\Demo>bower install jquery-validation
bower not-cached      git://github.com/jzaefferer/jquery-validation.git#*
bower resolve         git://github.com/jzaefferer/jquery-validation.git#*
bower download        https://github.com/jzaefferer/jquery-validation/archive/1.14
.0.tar.gz
bower extract         jquery-validation#* archive.tar.gz
bower resolved        git://github.com/jzaefferer/jquery-validation.git#1.14.0
bower cached          git://github.com/jquery/jquery.git#2.1.4
bower validate        2.1.4 against git://github.com/jquery/jquery.git#>= 1.7.2
bower install         jquery-validation#1.14.0
bower install         jquery#2.1.4

jquery-validation#1.14.0 bower_components\jquery-validation
└── jquery#2.1.4

jquery#2.1.4 bower_components\jquery

D:\Demo>
```

How it works...

1. Bower creates a `bower_components` folder on the machine and downloads the plugin and its dependencies, that is, the jQuery library, in this folder.

2. After going to the `jquery-validation` folder, we can see the downloaded files:

```
    build
    dist
    src
    .bower
    bower
    changelog.md
    CONTRIBUTING.md
    Gruntfile
    LICENSE.md
    package
    README.md
    validation.jquery
```

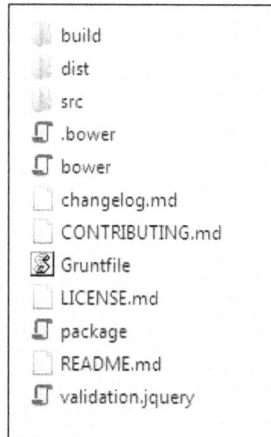

3. The validation plugin files can be found in the distribution folder, that is, `bower_components/jquery-validation/dist`, as shown in the following screenshot:

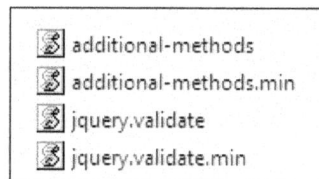

```
    additional-methods
    additional-methods.min
    jquery.validate
    jquery.validate.min
```

See also

The *Using the form validation plugin* recipe

Index

Symbols

5 star rating control
creating 309-315
$ alias
used, in plugin 406-408

A

actions
adding, to plugins 424-430
AdRotator control
alt text, animating of 234-242
Ajax
about 325
defining 326, 327
setting up with ASP.NET,
jQuery used 327-336
using 187
Ajax calls
making, to controller action 382-390
making, to HTTP handler 391-400
alt text
animating, of AdRotator control 234-242
anonymous function 53
Application Programming
Interface (API) 4, 180
ASP.NET controls
defining 50
selecting 70
ASP.NET Master Page
jQuery, adding 22-26
ASP.NET MVC
Hello World, displaying with jQuery 43-45
jQuery, bundling 34-42
jQuery, loading with CDN 42, 43

ASP.NET web project
jQuery, adding with script block 10-17
jQuery, adding with ScriptManager
control 17-22
Asynchronous JavaScript and XML. *See* **Ajax**

C

CDN
about 5
CDNJS CDN 7
Google CDN 6
jQuery's CDN 6
jsDelivr CDN 7
list 5
Microsoft CDN 6
used, for loading jQuery in
ASP.NET MVC 42, 43
using, for new releases 7
working 7
CDNJS CDN
URLs 7
constructs
defining 54, 63, 69
used, for adding items 215
used, for AdRotator control 234
used, for building photo gallery 296
used, for consuming page methods 336
used, for consuming WCF services 361, 362
used, for consuming Web services 349
used, for controller action 382
used, for creating 5 star rating control 309
used, for creating image scroller 281
used, for detaching events 172, 173
used, for event delegation
and event bubbling 145

used, for event handlers 151
used, for event trigger 158, 159
used, for filter 205, 206
used, for form events 138
used, for HTTP handler 391
used, for keyboard events 133
used, for Menu control 223
used, for mouse events 128
used, for namespacing 167
used, for parent and child controls 188
used, for plugin 404-406
used, for previewing image uploads 316
used, for retrieving data from Web API 372
used, for setting up Ajax with
    ASP.NET 327, 328
used, for sibling controls 198
used, for z-index CSS property 290
used, for zooming images
    on mouseover 274, 275
used, in GridView control 259
used, in Panel control 250, 254
used, in TreeView control 243, 244
Content Delivery Network. *See* **CDN**
control
disabling, on web form 102-109
enabling, on web form 102-109
selecting, by attribute 83-88
selecting, CSS class used 63-68
selecting, HTML tag used 69-83
selecting, ID used 54-62
value, displaying 54-62
controller action
Ajax calls, making to 382-390
CSS class
used, for selecting control 63-68

D

data
passing, with events 167-172
retrieving, from Web API 371-382
default values
providing 415-419
default web application template
jQuery reference, adding 28-32
development/debug mode
application, running 22

digital clock
creating, via animating
    Label control 229-233
Document Object Model (DOM) 179
DOM elements
adding 180-187
methods, calling on 409-415
removing 180-187

E

edge servers 7
element
selecting, by its position in DOM 88-101
event
binding 125
detaching 172-177
running only once 151-158
triggering, programmatically 158-166
event bubbling 126
event delegation
about 126
used, for attaching events to
    future controls 145-150
event handler 125
event namespacing
using 167-172

F

filter
used, for refining selection 205-214
form events
responding to 138-144
form validation plugin
using 431-446

G

Git
about 447
URL 448
Google CDN
URLs 6
GridView control
displaying, with explode effect 259-268
hiding, with explode effect 259-268

H

Hello World
  displaying, in ASP.NET MVC with
     jQuery 43-45
  displaying, in web project with jQuery 32-34
HTML tag
  used, for selecting control 69-83
HTTP handler
  Ajax calls, making to 391-400

I

ImageMap control
  used, for building photo gallery 296-304
images
  animating, in TreeView control 243-250
  spotlight effect, creating on 270-274
  used, for creating effects in
     Menu control 304-309
  zooming, on mouseover 274-280
image scroller
  creating 281-289
image uploads
  previewing, in MVC 316-323
items
  adding, to controls at runtime 215-220

J

JavaScript Object Notation (JSON) format 167
jQuery
  about 2, 221, 269, 403
  adding, programmatically to web form 27, 28
  adding, to ASP.NET Master Page 22-26
  adding, to ASP.NET web project with script
     block 10-17
  adding, to ASP.NET web project with
     ScriptManager control 17-22
  animations, stopping 223
  bundling, in ASP.NET MVC 34-42
  CDN 5
  custom effects 222
  disadvantages 2
  downloading 2-5
  downloading, NuGet Package
     Manager used 8-10

  elements, displaying 221
  elements, fading 222
  elements, hiding 221
  elements, sliding 222
  URL 1
  used, for displaying Hello World in
     ASP.NET MVC 43, 45
  used, for displaying Hello World in
     web project 32, 33
  used, for setting up Ajax with
     ASP.NET 327-336
  using 270
jQuery, ASP.NET MVC
  loading, CDN used 42, 43
jQuery code
  debugging, in Visual Studio 45-48
jQuery event binders
  defining 127
jQuery events
  URL 126
jQuery library
  compressed format 4
  methods, defining 327
  uncompressed format 4
jQuery reference
  adding, in default web application
     template 28-32
jQuery selectors
  attribute selectors 52
  basic selectors 51
  defining 51
  form selectors 52
  hierarchy selectors 51
  position filters 53
  URL 53
jQuery UI
  URL 248
jQuery UI style sheet
  URL 398
jQuery validation plugin
  references 444
  URL 431

K

keyboard events
  responding to 133-137

L

Label control
  animating, for creating digital clock 229-233

M

Menu control
  animating 223-229
  effects creating, images used 304-308
method chaining
  providing 420-423
methods
  calling, on DOM elements 409-415
Microsoft CDN
  URLs 6
minified version 4
Model View Controller (MVC)
  about 34
  image uploads, previewing 316-323
mouse events
  responding to 128-132
MVC applications
  selectors, using 110-122

N

node
  defining 237
Node.js
  about 447
  URL 447
Northwind database
  about 72
  installing 71
  URL 72
NPM (Node Package Manager)
  about 404, 447
  used, for downloading plugins 447-449
NuGet Package Manager
  used, for downloading jQuery 8-10

P

page methods
  consuming 336-348
Panel control
  scrolling text, creating 250-253

  used, for creating vertical accordion
    menu 254-258
parent and child controls
  accessing 188-198
photo gallery
  building, ImageMap control used 296-304
  building, z-index property used 290-295
plugin
  $ alias, using 406-408
  actions, adding to 424-430
  creating 404, 405
  downloading, NPM used 447-449
  using 404, 405
plugin repository
  URL 404
position, in DOM
  selecting 88-101
programming constructs
  defining 180, 181
  used, in form validation plugin 431
  used, in method chaining 420
  using 424

S

sample databases
  URL 153
script block
  used, for adding jQuery to ASP.NET
    web project 10-17
ScriptManager control
  used, for adding jQuery to ASP.NET
    web project 17-22
ScriptResourceDefinition object
  CdnDebugPath property 21
  CdnPath property 21
  CdnSupportsSecureConnection property 21
  DebugPath property 21
  LoadSuccessExpression property 21
  Path property 21
scrolling text
  creating, in Panel control 250-253
selection
  refining, filter used 205-214
selectors
  using, in MVC applications 110-122

sibling controls
  accessing 198-205
spotlight effect
  creating, on images 270-274

T

TreeView control
  images, animating 243-250

V

validate() method
  options 440
vertical accordion menu
  creating, Panel controls used 254-258
Visual Studio
  jQuery code, debugging 45-48

W

WCF services
  consuming 361-371
Web API
  about 371
  data, retrieving from 371-382

web form
  controls, disabling 102-109
  controls, enabling 102-109
  jQuery, adding programmatically 27, 28
web page 49
web project
  Hello World, displaying with jQuery 32-34
Web services
  consuming 349-360
wiring 125

X

XmlHttpRequest object 325

Z

z-index property
  used, for building photo gallery 290-295

Thank you for buying
ASP.NET jQuery Cookbook,
Second Edition

About Packt Publishing

Packt, pronounced 'packed', published its first book, *Mastering phpMyAdmin for Effective MySQL Management*, in April 2004, and subsequently continued to specialize in publishing highly focused books on specific technologies and solutions.

Our books and publications share the experiences of your fellow IT professionals in adapting and customizing today's systems, applications, and frameworks. Our solution-based books give you the knowledge and power to customize the software and technologies you're using to get the job done. Packt books are more specific and less general than the IT books you have seen in the past. Our unique business model allows us to bring you more focused information, giving you more of what you need to know, and less of what you don't.

Packt is a modern yet unique publishing company that focuses on producing quality, cutting-edge books for communities of developers, administrators, and newbies alike. For more information, please visit our website at www.packtpub.com.

Writing for Packt

We welcome all inquiries from people who are interested in authoring. Book proposals should be sent to author@packtpub.com. If your book idea is still at an early stage and you would like to discuss it first before writing a formal book proposal, then please contact us; one of our commissioning editors will get in touch with you.

We're not just looking for published authors; if you have strong technical skills but no writing experience, our experienced editors can help you develop a writing career, or simply get some additional reward for your expertise.

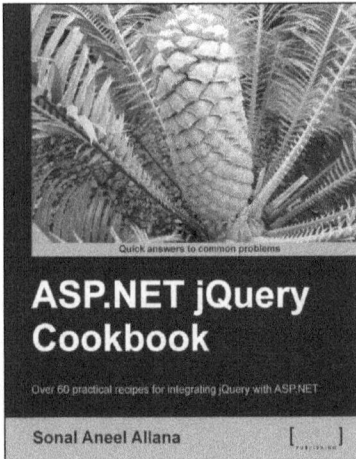

ASP.NET jQuery Cookbook

ISBN: 978-1-84969-046-1   Paperback: 308 pages

Over 60 practical recipes for integrating jQuery
with ASP.NET

1. Tips and tricks for interfacing the jQuery library
   with ASP.NET controls.

2. Boost ASP.NET applications with the power
   of jQuery.

3. Use a problem-solution based approach with
   hands-on examples for ASP.NET developers.

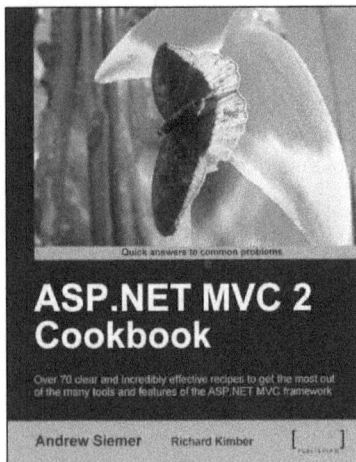

ASP.NET MVC 2 Cookbook

ISBN: 978-1-84969-030-0   Paperback: 332 pages

Over 70 clear and incredibly effective recipes to get the
most out of the many tools and features of the ASP.NET
MVC framework

1. Solutions to the most common problems
   encountered with ASP.NET MVC development.

2. Build and maintain large applications with ease
   using ASP.NET MVC.

3. Recipes to enhance the look, feel, and user
   experience of your web applications.

4. Expand your MVC toolbox with an introduction to
   lots of open source tools.

Please check **www.PacktPub.com** for information on our titles

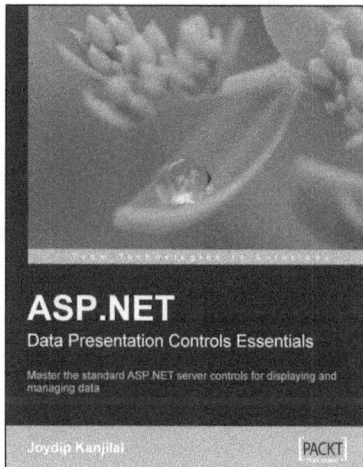

www.ingramcontent.com/pod-product-compliance
Lightning Source LLC
Chambersburg PA
CBHW080127220326
41598CB00032B/4983